DRINK IN THE EIGHTEENTH AND NINETEENTH CENTURIES

Perspectives in Economic and Social History

Series Editors: Andrew August
                   Jari Eloranta

Titles in this Series

1 Migrants and Urban Change: Newcomers to Antwerp, 1760–1860
Anne Winter

2 Female Entrepreneurs in Nineteenth-Century Russia
Galina Ulianova

3 Barriers to Competition: The Evolution of the Debate
Ana Rosado Cubero

4 Rural Unwed Mothers: An American Experience, 1870–1950
Mazie Hough

5 English Catholics and the Education of the Poor, 1847–1902
Eric G. Tenbus

6 The World of Carolus Clusius: Natural History in the Making, 1550–1610
Florike Egmond

7 The Determinants of Entrepreneurship: Leadership, Culture, Institutions
José L. García-Ruiz and Pier Angelo Toninelli (eds)

8 London Clerical Workers, 1880–1914: Development of the Labour Market
Michael Heller

9 The Decline of Jute: Managing Industrial Change
Jim Tomlinson, Carlo Morelli and Valerie Wright

10 Mining and the State in Brazilian Development
Gail D. Triner

11 Global Trade and Commercial Networks: Eighteenth-Century Diamond
Merchants
Tijl Vanneste

12 The Clothing Trade in Provincial England, 1800–1850
Alison Toplis

13 Sex in Japan's Globalization, 1870–1930: Prostitutes, Emigration and
Nation Building
Bill Mihalopoulos

14 Financing India's Imperial Railways, 1875–1914
Stuart Sweeney

15 Energy, Trade and Finance in Asia: A Political and Economic Analysis
Justin Dargin and Tai Wei Lim

16 Violence and Racism in Football: Politics and Cultural Conflict in British
Society, 1968–1998
Brett Bebber

17 The Economies of Latin America: New Cliometric Data
César Yáñez and Albert Carreras (eds)

18 Meat, Commerce and the City: The London Food Market, 1800–1855
Robyn S. Metcalfe

19 Merchant Colonies in the Early Modern Period
Victor N. Zakharov, Gelina Harlaftis and Olga Katsiardi-Hering (eds)

20 Markets and Growth in Early Modern Europe
Victoria N. Bateman

21 Welfare and Old Age in Europe and North America: The Development
of Social Insurance
Bernard Harris (ed.)

22 Female Economic Strategies in the Modern World
Beatrice Moring (ed.)

23 Crime and Community in Reformation Scotland: Negotiating Power
in a Burgh Society
J. R. D. Falconer

24 Policing Prostitution, 1856–1886: Deviance, Surveillance and Morality
Catherine Lee

25 Narratives of Drunkenness: Belgium, 1830–1914
An Vleugels

26 Respectability and the London Poor, 1780–1870: The Value of Virtue
Lynn MacKay

27 Residential Institutions in Britain, 1725–1970: Inmates and Environments
Jane Hamlett, Lesley Hoskins and Rebecca Preston (eds)

28 Conflict, Commerce and Franco-Scottish Relations, 1560–1713
Siobhan Talbott

Forthcoming Titles

Merchants and Profit in the Age of Commerce, 1680–1830
Pierre Gervais, Yannick Lemarchand and Dominique Margairaz (eds)

Jewish Immigrants in London, 1880–1939
Susan L. Tananbaum

A Global Conceptual History of Asia, 1860–1940
Hagen Schulz-Forberg (ed.)

Commercial Networks and European Cities, 1400–1800
Andrea Caracausi and Christof Jeggle (eds)

Consuls and the Institutions of Global Capitalism, 1783–1914
Ferry de Goey

Insanity and the Lunatic Asylum in the Nineteenth Century
Thomas Knowles and Serena Trowbridge (eds)

Philanthropy and the Funding of the Church of England, 1856–1914
Sarah Flew

Franco Modigliani and Keynesian Economics
Antonella Rancan

DRINK IN THE EIGHTEENTH AND NINETEENTH CENTURIES

EDITED BY

Susanne Schmid and Barbara Schmidt-Haberkamp

LONDON AND NEW YORK

First published 2014 by Pickering & Chatto (Publishers) Limited

Published 2016 by Routledge
2 Park Square, Milton Park, Abingdon, Oxfordshire OX14 4RN
711 Third Avenue, New York, NY 10017, USA

First issued in paperback 2015

Routledge is an imprint of the Taylor & Francis Group, an informa business

© Taylor & Francis 2014
© Susanne Schmid and Barbara Schmidt-Haberkamp 2014

To the best of the Publisher's knowledge every effort has been made to contact
relevant copyright holders and to clear any relevant copyright issues.
Any omissions that come to their attention will be remedied in future editions.

All rights reserved, including those of translation into foreign languages. No part
of this book may be reprinted or reproduced or utilised in any form or by any
electronic, mechanical, or other means, now known or hereafter invented, including
photocopying and recording, or in any information storage or retrieval system,
without permission in writing from the publishers.

Notice:
Product or corporate names may be trademarks or registered trademarks, and
are used only for identification and explanation without intent to infringe.

BRITISH LIBRARY CATALOGUING IN PUBLICATION DATA

Drink in the eighteenth and nineteenth centuries. – (Perspectives in economic
and social history)
1. Drinking behaviour – Great Britain – History – 18th century. 2. Drinking
behaviour – Great Britain – History – 19th century. 3. Drinking behaviour
– North America – History – 18th century. 4. Drinking behaviour – North
America – History – 19th century.
I. Series II. Schmid, Susanne, editor of compilation. III. Schmidt-Haberkamp,
Barbara, editor of compilation.
394.1'2'0941-dc23

ISBN-13: 978-1-138-66301-5 (pbk)
ISBN-13: 978-1-8489-3436-8 (hbk)

Typeset by Pickering & Chatto (Publishers) Limited

CONTENTS

Acknowledgements	ix
List of Contributors	xi
List of Figures and Tables	xv

Introduction – *Susanne Schmid and Barbara Schmidt-Haberkamp*   1

Part I: Ritual and Material Culture

  1 Politics by Design: Consumption, Identity and Allegiance
    – Karen Harvey   11

  2 Drinks, Domesticity and the Forging of an American Identity in
    Susan Warner's *The Wide, Wide World* (1850) *– Caroline Rosenthal*   23

Part II: Institutions and Social Class

  3 *Café* or Coffeehouse? Transnational Histories of Coffee and
    Sociability *– Brian Cowan*   35

  4 Claret at a Premium: Ned Ward, the True Tory Defender of
    Fine Wines? *– Fritz-Wilhelm Neumann*   47

  5 Eighteenth-Century Travellers and the Country Inn
    – Susanne Schmid   59

  6 Drinking, Fighting and Working-Class Sociability in
    Nineteenth-Century Britain *– John Carter Wood*   71

Part III: Temperance and the Misery of Alcohol

  7 Romantic Radicalism and the Temperance Movement
    – Rolf Lessenich   81

  8 The Myth of 'Misery Alcoholism' in Early Industrial England:
    The Example of Manchester *– Gunther Hirschfelder*   91

Part IV: Intoxication and Therapy

  9 Alcohol, Sympathy and Ideology in George Gissing's *The Nether
    World* (1889) and *The Odd Women* (1893) *– Anja Müller-Wood*   103

  10 Legends of Infernal Drinkers: Representations of Alcohol in
    Thomas Hardy and Nineteenth-Century British Fiction
    – Norbert Lennartz   115

  11 The Spirit of Medicine: The Use of Alcohol in Nineteenth-Century
    Medical Practice *– Jonathan Reinarz and Rebecca Wynter*   127

viii *Drink in the Eighteenth and Nineteenth Centuries*

Part V: Case Studies: Rum, Cocoa and Magical Potions
    12 'Been to Barbados': Rum(bullion), Race, the *Gaspée* and the
        American Revolution – *Eva-Sabine Zehelein*   141
    13 A Beverage for the Masses: The Democratization of Cocoa in
        Nineteenth-Century American Fiction – *Monika Elbert*   151
    14 The Power of the Potion: From Gothic Horror to Health Drink, or,
        How the Elixir became a Commodity – *Elmar Schenkel*   167

Notes   181
Index   225

ACKNOWLEDGEMENTS

A cup of tea, a glass of wine, a bottle of rum; or, an afternoon in a café, a dinner for eight, a beach party – drinking, like scholarship, can be a solitary or a communal activity. We spent a lot of time at our desks; yet without the help of many others, this book would not have been possible.

From 5 to 7 November 2010, we brought our contributors together in the hospitable rooms of the *Universitätsclub* at the Rheinische Friedrich Wilhelms-Universität Bonn in order to discuss our contributions and debate methodologies. First and foremost, our thanks go to the German Research Foundation (DFG) and to the University of Bonn for their generous funding of this conference. We also want to thank the DFG for sponsoring the panel 'Luxury Goods and Exotic Tastes in the Eighteenth Century' at the ASECS conference in Montreal in 2006, which proved to be the origin of this project.

Moreover, Susanne Schmid would like to thank the DFG and the German Academic Exchange Service (DAAD) for financing further trips to ASECS conferences in Portland and Albuquerque, and the Humboldt Foundation for sponsoring several research stays at Princeton that enabled her to collect material on and do research into sociability.

We received a lot of support from individuals and want to express our thanks to Claudia Brodsky, Jochen Ecke, Inge Erhardt, Edmunda Ferreira, Miriam Gertzen, Carolin Hoffmann, Mathilde Hüskes, Verena Jain-Warden, Shipra Kren, Sabine Schmidt, Frauke Schröder, Sandra Schwab, Elisa Valerie Thieme, Gunda Windmüller and John Carter Wood.

We would also like to thank the Victoria and Albert Museum for the permission to reproduce an example of John Cartwright's poem and drawings in 'Original Drawing Book no. 1', Hartley, Green & Co, Victoria and Albert Museum: E.576-1941. © Victoria and Albert Museum, London.

LIST OF CONTRIBUTORS

Brian Cowan teaches British and European history at McGill University in Montreal, Canada, where he holds the Canada Research Chair in Early Modern British History. His research focuses on various aspects of early modern sociability, food history and media cultures. His major publications include *The State Trial of Doctor Henry Sacheverell* (2012) and *The Social Life of Coffee* (2005), which was awarded the Wallace K. Ferguson Prize by the Canadian Historical Association. He also co-edits the *Journal of British Studies* with Elizabeth Elbourne for the North American Conference on British Studies.

Monika Elbert is Professor of English and University Distinguished Scholar at Montclair State University, NJ, USA. She is editor of the *Nathaniel Hawthorne Review* and has published widely on nineteenth-century American literature and on Gothic fiction. Among her recent publications are several essays on Hawthorne, a co-edited collection, *Transnational Gothic: Literary and Social Exchanges in the Long Nineteenth Century* (2013), which includes her essay on New England Gothic women writers and Catholicism, and a co-edited collection, *Culinary Aesthetics and Practices in Nineteenth-Century American Literature* (2009), which contains her essay on Hawthorne's food preferences and national loyalties in old and New England.

Karen Harvey is Reader in Cultural History in the Department of History at the University of Sheffield, England. Her main areas of research are gender, material culture and sexuality in eighteenth-century Britain. Her publications include *Reading Sex in the Eighteenth Century: Bodies and Gender in English Erotic Culture* (2004) and *The Little Republic: Masculinity and Domestic Authority in Eighteenth-Century Britain* (2012) as well as the collection *History and Material Culture* (2009).

Gunther Hirschfelder is Professor of Comparative European Ethnology at the University of Regensburg, Germany. His main research areas are transformations of traditional food cultures in postmodern societies, European identities and rituals in transition. Publications include studies on alcohol consumption in the early industrial age (*Alkoholkonsum am Beginn des Industriezeitalters*,

– xi –

2 vols, 2003–4), the history of European food culture (*Europäische Esskultur. Geschichte der Ernährung von der Steinzeit bis heute*, 2001) and on Cologne's trade relations in the late Middle Ages (*Die Kölner Handelsbeziehungen im Spätmittelalter*, 1994). He has also edited several collections of essays, for example on future nutrition (2011) and on the virtualization of work (2004).

Norbert Lennartz is Professor of English Literature at the University of Vechta, Germany. His teaching and research range from Shakespeare to Romanticism, from the Victorian Age to the early twentieth century. Among his major publications are a book-length study on the deconstruction of eroticism in seventeenth-century poetry (*'My Unwasht Muse': (De-)Konstruktionen der Erotik in der englischen Literatur*, 2009), a collection of essays on representations of food (*The Pleasures and Horrors of Eating: The Cultural History of Eating in Anglophone Literature*, 2010, co-edited with Marion Gymnich) and another collection on new directions in Dickens criticism (*Dickens's Signs, Readers' Designs*, 2012, with Francesca Orestano).

Rolf Lessenich is Emeritus Professor of English Literature in the Department of English, American and Celtic Studies at the University of Bonn, Germany. His main areas of comparative research include the European Baroque, the long eighteenth century (1660–1800), Romanticism, the Victorians and the Classical Tradition. Among his numerous book and essay publications are *Elements of Pulpit Oratory 1660–1800* (1972), *Aspects of English Preromanticism* (1989) and *Neoclassical Satire and the Romantic School 1780-1830* (2012).

Anja Müller-Wood is Professor of English Literature and Culture at Johannes Gutenberg University Mainz, Germany. In research and teaching she specializes in early modern, twentieth-century and contemporary British literature and culture. Among her publications are *Angela Carter: Identity Constructed/Deconstructed* (1997) and *The Theatre of Civilized Excess: New Perspectives on Jacobean Tragedy* (2007) as well as numerous journal articles and book chapters. Her more recent interests centre on literature, cognitive sciences and evolutionary psychology. She is the co-coordinator and supervisor of the Mainz Graduate Research Group Literary Linguistics and co-editor of the Open Access *International Journal of Literary Linguistics*, for which she edited a special issue, *Language and Dialogue* (2013).

Fritz-Wilhelm Neumann has recently retired from the Chair of English Literature at Erfurt University, Germany. Apart from having taught extensively and widely, his principal areas of research have been English literature and culture at the beginning of the eighteenth century and computing in the humanities (with a focus on using the SNOBOL/ SPITBOL languages of programming). He was founder and editor-in-chief of *Erfurt Electronic Studies in English* (EESE), currently succeeded by JESELL (*Jena Electronic Studies in English Language and Literature*). His most recent publication is a book on Ned Ward and London around 1700 (2012).

Jonathan Reinarz is Reader and Director at the History of Medicine Unit, University of Birmingham, England. His PhD thesis dealt with the social history of British brewing, a subject on which he has published extensively. His recent publications include *Permeable Walls: Institutional Visiting in Historical Perspective* (with Graham Mooney, 2009), *Healthcare in Birmingham: The Birmingham Teaching Hospitals, 1779–1939* (2009), a special issue of the *Journal for Eighteenth-Century Studies*, *The Senses and the Enlightenment* (with Leonard Schwarz, 2012), a history of smell (2013) and an edited collection on the medical history of skin (with Kevin Siena, 2013).

Caroline Rosenthal is Professor of American Literature at the Friedrich-Schiller-University in Jena, Germany. Her main areas of research are Comparative North American Studies, contemporary city fiction, American Romanticism, Gender Studies as well as questions of ideology and canon formation. Her books include *Narrative Deconstructions of Gender in Works by Audrey Thomas, Daphne Marlatt, and Louise Erdrich* (2003), *New York and Toronto Novels after Postmodernism: Explorations of the Urban* (2011) as well as the co-edited essay collections *Space and Gender: Spaces of Difference in Canadian Women's Writing* (with Doris Eibl, 2009) and *Fake Identity? The Impostor Narrative in American Culture* (with Stefanie Schäfer, 2014).

Elmar Schenkel is Professor of English Literature at the University of Leipzig, Germany, where he also directs the General Studies Programme. His research interests include the interactions between literature, science and religion as well as travel writing and children's literature. He has taught at Russian, German and American universities and has published biographies of H. G. Wells and Joseph Conrad, books on eccentric scientists (*Die elektrische Himmelsleiter*, 2005), on alchemy and literature (*Die Elixiere der Schrift*, 2005) and on bicycles and literature (*Cyclomanie*, 2008). He also writes travel books, essays and stories and is a reviewer for the *Frankfurter Allgemeine Zeitung*.

Susanne Schmid is Guest Professor in the Department of English and Linguistics at Johannes Gutenberg University Mainz, Germany. Her main areas of research include the eighteenth century, Romanticism, the nineteenth century, book studies, the history of sociability and of beverages, film studies and contemporary culture. Her most important publications are *Shelley's German Afterlives, 1814–2000* (2007), *The Reception of P. B. Shelley in Europe* (co-edited with Michael Rossington, 2008) and *British Literary Salons of the Late Eighteenth and Early Nineteenth Centuries* (2013).

Barbara Schmidt-Haberkamp is Professor of English in the Department of English, American and Celtic Studies at the University of Bonn, Germany. Her main areas of specialization are eighteenth-century British literature and culture and postcolonial studies. Her publications include a study on the work of the Third Earl of Shaftesbury (*Die Kunst der Kritik*, 2000). She has co-edited a book on cultural transfer in eighteenth-century Europe (*Europäischer Kulturtransfer im 18. Jahrhundert*, 2003) and edited a collection of essays, *Europa und die Türkei im 18. Jahrhundert/Europe and Turkey in the Eighteenth Century* (2011).

John Carter Wood is a research fellow at the Leibniz Institute of European History in Mainz, Germany. Alongside established specializations on crime, violence and policing in modern Britain, he is currently researching British Christian responses to the European crises of the 1930s and 1940s. His publications include *Violence and Crime in Nineteenth-Century England: The Shadow of Our Refinement* (2004), *The Most Remarkable Woman in England: Poison, Celebrity and the Trials of Beatrice Pace* (2012) and the article '"The Third Degree": Press Reporting, Crime Fiction and Police Powers in 1920s Britain' (*Twentieth Century British History*, 2010).

Rebecca Wynter is an honorary research fellow in history, a teaching associate in the History of Medicine Unit (University of Birmingham, England) and a postdoctoral fellow at Woodbrooke Quaker Study Centre, Birmingham. Her PhD thesis dealt with *Material Culture and Control in Staffordshire County Gaol and Lunatic Asylum, c. 1793–1866* (University of Birmingham, 2007). Her current research centres on material culture, nineteenth-century curative institutions, mental deficiency and epileptic colonies, and the Friends' Ambulance Unit, 1914–19. Her publications include '"Good in All Respects": Appearance and Dress at Staffordshire County Lunatic Asylum, 1818–54' (*History of Psychiatry*, 2011) and '"Horrible Dens of Deception": An Asylum and its Discontents, c. 1815–1860', in *Insanity and the Lunatic Asylum in the Nineteenth Century*, edited by Thomas Knowles and Serena Trowbridge (forthcoming).

Eva-Sabine Zehelein is currently Professor of American Studies at the University of Regensburg, Germany. Her major fields of interest are contemporary North American literature and popular culture as well as the interface between the life sciences and the arts. Her major publications are '*Space as Symbol*': John Updikes '*Country of Ideas*' in den Rabbit-Romanen (2003) and *Science: Dramatic: Science Plays in America and Great Britain, 1990–2007* (2008).

LIST OF FIGURES AND TABLES

Figure 1.1: An example of John Cartwright's poem and drawings in
'Original Drawing Book no. 1', Hartley, Green & Co. 15

Figure 13.1: Advertisement, Baker's Vanilla Chocolate and Breakfast
Cocoa, *Century Magazine* (1885) 158

Figure 13.2: Advertisement, Walter Baker Chocolate Drink Cocoa,
Dorcester, MA, 'La Belle Chocolatière', original print ad (1906) 160

Table 11.1: Alcohol consumption in the General Hospital, Birmingham,
1865–7 and 1881–4 137

INTRODUCTION

Susanne Schmid and Barbara Schmidt-Haberkamp

His [the farmer's] honest Friends, at thirsty hour of Dusk,
Come uninvited; he with bounteous Hand
Imparts his smoking Vintage, sweet Reward
Of his own Industry; the well fraught Bowl
Circles incessant.

John Philips, *Cyder* (1708)[1]

John Philips's *Cyder: A Poem in Two Books* (1708) teaches the reader in great detail not only how to produce superior cider but also how to enjoy this 'home-brew' in an atmosphere of rural conviviality. His two-part georgic, 1,465 lines long, ranges from a description of the rural year's cycle to digressions about British history. *Cyder*, published one year after the Act of Union (1707), is more than a recipe in rhyme about a fermented drink made from apples: it constitutes a symbolic celebration of a united England and Scotland – thus drinking cider, and writing about it, become national statements.[2]

Cider, rum, wine, beer, coffee, tea, cocoa, even water, are all forms of liquid refreshment and nourishment, and their consumption signals individual preferences; yet they are also emblems of lifestyles, of political affiliations, even of religious creeds. Eighteenth- and nineteenth-century drink was coded in terms of nationality, class and gender. If, in the early eighteenth century, cider came to be seen as English, rural and masculine, chocolate, on the other hand, occasionally mentioned in contemporary debates around luxury, was regarded as an aphrodisiac, as urban and later as a comforting drink particularly suited to female needs. Especially in the Victorian Age, tea and the tea ceremony became the centre of a domesticity for which women were considered to be responsible.[3] In the American War of Independence, tea, like other goods imported from Britain, was no longer acceptable for patriotic Americans, who resorted to herbal infusions or to tea from Holland instead.

The topics of food and drink have always been popular, among readers and writers, among *literati* and particularly among scholars of various disciplines. Indeed, a large body of research testifies to a continuous interest in these topics. If, at the one end of the spectrum, we find studies offering a broad survey such as

– 1 –

C. Anne Wilson's *Food and Drink in Britain* (1975) and Andrew Barr's *Drink: A Social History of America* (1999), which both cover a wide range of beverages and, in the case of Wilson, also a wide time span, at the other end of the spectrum, we encounter shorter publications, which concentrate on only one drink or one type of institution in a locally and temporally restricted context: Arthur Jones's *Royston: Inns and Public Houses* (1990), published by the Local Historical Society, a thirty-two-page booklet with a detailed history of local inns, is one such example. A glimpse at the British Library's online catalogue shows dozens of publications of this type, which often provide the information that feeds into the longer books.[4] In between are scholarly studies which focus on one drink, one century, one institution.

In recent years, a veritable deluge of sources has become available through universally accessible databases like *Early English Books Online*, *Eighteenth Century Collections Online*, *Early American Imprints* and others, which allow the consideration of popular and ephemeral texts like broadsheets, sermons, newspaper articles, satirical poems and travelogues, thus facilitating research into artefacts, consumer items, spaces of drink as well as rituals. Scholars no longer have to travel to research libraries to access sources like the above-quoted poem in the original, which can now be read anywhere: at one's desk, on a garden bench or in the local pub, even in bed. Furthermore, annotated editions making use of archival material and forgotten printed matter like Thomas Brennan's four-volume *Public Drinking in the Early Modern World* (2011) or Markman Ellis's *Tea and the Tea-Table in Eighteenth-Century England* (2010) have also been immensely helpful to anyone conducting research on hitherto neglected areas of everyday consumer history.[5]

If some older studies like Wilson's, which spans centuries, are 'grand récits' of food and drink culture, more recent research, like Brian Cowan's *Social Life of Coffee* (2005) or Monika Elbert and Marie Drews's volume *Culinary Aesthetics and Practices in Nineteenth-Century American Literature* (2009),[6] aims at an analysis of individual drinks, social practices and institutions. This latter 'case study' approach with a focus on one drink or institution and a shorter time span promises more precise results. As there seems to be surprisingly little exchange between academics working on individual aspects related to drink, we felt it was about time to bring a convivial group of scholars together for an exchange of ideas about select alcoholic and non-alcoholic beverages such as beer, wine, tea, coffee, cocoa, gin and magical potions, about institutions and discursive milieus like the urban tavern, the coffeehouse, the country inn and the domestic tea ceremony, about key mediator figures like Ned Ward, about drinking vessels and inn signs, about fictional and non-fictional texts, visual material and cultural practices in the English-speaking world as well as methodologies of examining drink cultures. Drink needs to be dealt with as an interdisciplinary topic, from fields as varied as English and American studies, history, the history of medicine and ethnology. Presented here are fourteen unique case studies, all based on original material, which centre on representations of and practices connected with drink cultures in eighteenth- and nineteenth-century Britain and North America.

The temporal focus of this volume, the 'long' eighteenth and nineteenth centuries, makes sense for several reasons. Even though drink culture has evolved steadily, there are some caesuras or decades in which changes are particularly prominent, starting with the late seventeenth century. In his *Social History of Drinks*, John Burnett argues that the history of drink in Britain has witnessed 'two great periods of transformation when the adoption of new drinks acquired revolutionary scale', naming the period from the mid-seventeenth to the mid-eighteenth centuries and the decades from the 1960s onwards.[7] The late seventeenth century was a time when several new, or, as the satirical pamphlet *The Women's Petition Against Coffee* (1674) states, 'new-fangled'[8] drinks became widely available, among them coffee, tea and chocolate, but also alcoholic drinks such as gin. As a result of British imperial expansion, colonial production and global trading, these new and exotic commodities from the far reaches of the British Empire entered everyday British life, their easier distribution being facilitated by substantial improvements in transport and by urban growth.[9] These modish consumer items manifested themselves in new licensing laws and new drinking venues, but also in a large body of texts and in material objects like coffee cups or tea pots. With the cargoes of tea, for example, travelled the Chinese porcelain ware used to brew and serve tea, which in turn inspired the local British pottery industry to imitate such products and later manufacturers to provide the appropriate furniture for the domestic tea ceremony. In the *Review of the State of the British Nation* of 8 January 1713, Daniel Defoe commented on the beneficial effects of the new drinks on the local economy:

> It is impossible that *Coffee*, *Tea*, and *Chocolate* can be so advanc'd in their Consumption, without an eminent Encrease of those Trades that attend them; whence we see the most noble Shops in the City taken up with the valuable Utensils of the Tea-Table. The *China* warehouses are little Marts within themselves ... and the Eminent Corner Houses in the chief Streets of *London*, are chosen out by the Town Tinkers to furnish us with Tea-Kettles, and Chocolate Pots.[10]

Medical tracts investigated the physical and psychological effects as well as the therapeutic uses of the new drinks, while satires issued warnings against the supposedly negative or even fatal effects of some drinks. Thus, in the already mentioned *Women's Petition Against Coffee*, the women argue that coffee renders their husbands impotent. The drinking venues, the first coffeehouses and other public drinking places, were deemed dangerous because they seemed to invite unrestrained conversation as well as a social 'levelling': 'you may see a silly *Fop*, and a worshipful *Justice*, a griping *Rook*, and a grave *Citizen*, a worthy *Lawyer*, and an errant *Pickpocket*, a Reverend *Nonconformist*, and a Canting *Mountebank*; all blended together; to compose an *Oglio* of Impertinence'.[11] This social chaos soon gave way to increasing social stratification as London drinking places become more differentiated in the course of the eighteenth century; the nineteenth century saw a further differentiation of such spaces along the lines of social class and profession as well as gender.

Any analysis of drink in the eighteenth and nineteenth centuries is connected to the debate around the Habermasian public sphere. Jürgen Habermas's famous study *The Structural Transformation of the Public Sphere* (1962) situates the emergence of an urban public sphere in the eighteenth century. This public sphere was connected to a sociability that often occurred in spaces where drink was available. The London coffeehouse is a prime example of a centre of communication, where commercial, political and private interests were negotiated. Its lower-class and rural counterparts, the alehouse, the tavern and the country inn, likewise fostered sociability, albeit one that was closer to the tenets of the local squirearchy and the church. These institutions were instrumental to the forging of the public sphere. To contemporaries, they were also spaces of amusement, play and relaxation, which went hand in hand with drink, often with alcoholic beverages. Habermas's study, which has enjoyed cult status in Germany, claims that institutions such as the coffeehouse were places of reasonable discourse.[12] However, public drinking spaces in the long eighteenth century also hosted violent arguments, prostitution, the abuse of alcohol and debates far removed from reasonable exchange, as many texts and images, among them Ned Ward's graphic descriptions of London's taverns or William Hogarth's satirical prints, show. In the Quaker pub episode in Ward's *London Spy* (1698–9), the visitors to the tavern deliberately order a different measure of drink to emphasize how different they are from the Quakers, commenting: 'We ... soon discovered our religion by our drinking'.[13] Steven Earnshaw concludes his discussion of this scene by stating: 'Thus the religious/political symbolism of drinking emerges in the unlikeliest of places'.[14] The contributions to this volume emphasize the significance of institutions like the London tavern, the country inn, domestic spaces for the tea ceremony; they analyse the interplay between institution, space and social practice and demonstrate that the concept of the public sphere can and should be expanded to include 'unruly' and 'unreasonable' practices, which are essential for the formation of the public sphere, too.

A large body of texts testifies to such ongoing debates. Taverns, coffeehouses and cafés were chosen as settings for literary texts: Henry Fielding's novel *Joseph Andrews* (1742) revolves around various encounters in country inns. Medical writing, which has always flourished the moment a new drink enters the scene, dealt with the properties of beverages, like Richard Bradley's *The Virtue and Use of Coffee, With Regard to the Plague and Other Infectuous Distempers* (1721).[15] 'Doctors had appropriated coffee, as they did everywhere else, at least for the purposes of dissertation', Maguelonne Toussaint-Samat writes in her *History of Food*; 'Pocock, Sloane and Radcliffe declared it a panacea for all ills, a remedy for consumption, ophthalmic catarrh, dropsy, gout, scurvy and smallpox – although taken mixed with milk it might give you leprosy'.[16] The wild speculations of earlier medical texts eventually gave way to more scientific argument, as in Thomas Trotter's *Essay, Medical, Philosophical, and Chemical, on Drunkenness and Its Effects on the Human Body* (1804).[17] Sermons, tracts and graphic material warned against the abuse of alcohol. Famous examples are Hogarth's prints *Gin Lane* and *Beer Street* (1751), the first marking out oppression by the ruling classes as a contributing factor in the gin craze, while the second, depicting the benefits of being nourished by native beer, can be read as a celebration of Englishness. James Gillray's famous caricature 'Anti-Saccharites or John Bull and his Family Leaving off the Use of Sugar' (1792) admonishes the British in the face of slavery that they ought to take their tea without sugar. Nineteenth-century novels like Susan Warner's *Wide, Wide World* (1850)[18] again refer to tea to negotiate social identity, in this case through picturing the domestic tea ceremony. Thomas Hardy's and George Gissing's novels also participate in current debates through their graphic depictions of the miseries of alcoholism.

Drinks are not only commodities that can be analysed with respect to the economic and social processes of their production, distribution and consumption, but they are also embedded in social and cultural practices that signify individual and collective identities – not only in the sense that they are indicative of the cultural parameters of a given time and region, but also in the sense that through repeated performance of cultural rituals, they function to sustain and create these cultural parameters. In historical perspective, the cultural significations of individual drinks are not stable over time, but subject to constant change and adaptation. Representations of alcohol consumption, for example, change from eighteenth-century images of conviviality to an iconography of secular hell and gloom in nineteenth-century British fiction. The temperance movement of the early nineteenth century brought about significant changes in the evaluation of and associations connected with drinks such as wine, beer and gin. Wine had always been a central symbol in the Christian religion and its rites, yet a controversy led to attempts on the side of teetotallers to substitute biblical references with 'non-alcoholic forms', as Burnett points out.[19] The temperance movement, which, in its demand for abstention from alcohol, followed in the footsteps of some eighteenth-century Dissenters, also influenced the medical use of this substance and thus one of the oldest therapeutic traditions in Western medicine.

The focus of our volume on the eighteenth and nineteenth centuries and on a variety of drinks serves to bring the shifting patterns in drinking behaviour and the changing codifications of individual drinks as well as of the places in which they were consumed into sharper relief. While the contributions to this volume are united by their regional focus on drinks in Britain and North America and by their temporal focus on the eighteenth and nineteenth centuries, they are marked by a diversity of interests and methodologies. As the rigid compartmentalization of research by subject has become outdated in recent years, we opted for an interdisciplinary and multidisciplinary approach to the practices and representations connected to drink. Although our contributors come from a number of disciplines (English literature, American literature, cultural studies, anthropology, history, history of medicine) and work with different source materials, their essays generally 'speak with each other' and thus participate in communication across academic disciplines. If one focus of this volume lies on representations of drink in literature, this is owing to the fact that firstly, cultural practices of the past are accessible to us only through their representations, in whatever form, and secondly, fictional texts constitute such representations of cultural practices. Thirdly, fiction, especially novels, shows how social norms are conceptualized by staging them; fiction is thus performative. Fourthly, works of fiction are frequently self-reflexive. Thus, fiction holds an important position in this volume, yet it can only function as a valid source if it stands alongside a variety of visual as well as textual material, the basis for our histories of drinks and drinking patterns in eighteenth- and nineteenth-century Britain and North America.

Overview

The volume is organized in five thematic clusters to illustrate the diverse uses and shifting significations of drinks and drinking in the eighteenth and nineteenth centuries. Part I, 'Ritual and Material Culture', examines how both objects and rituals associated with the female domestic sphere become expressive of not only personal, but also political and national identities, thus disrupting the traditional identification of separate and gendered spheres. In 'Politics by Design: Consumption, Identity and Allegiance', Karen Harvey addresses the material politics of drinking and presents a reading of objects as articulate political texts. Harvey argues that not only the choice of venues, but also the choice and design of drinking vessels expressed political allegiance. Her case study, John Cartwright's design for a set of punch bowls in the 1780s, demonstrates the ways in which drinking vessels and their designs created factional, national and gendered identities. Caroline Rosenthal's 'Drinks, Domesticity and the Forging of an American Identity in Susan Warner's *The Wide, Wide World*' investigates the significance of the tea ceremony in an American sentimental novel of the mid-nineteenth century, where preparing and serving tea is a central task of women in the domestic sphere and an activity that is imbued with spiritual and religious significance. The tea ceremony emphasizes inwardness and is part of a domestic ideology that not only separates women from the public sphere but gives them a certain autonomy and limited power over a realm of their own.

Part II, 'Institutions and Social Class', concentrates on the coffeehouse, the tavern and the country inn as venues for the consumption of drinks in conjunction with issues of social class. Brian Cowan's contribution, '*Café* or Coffeehouse? Transnational Histories of Coffee and Sociability', addresses the possibility of writing a transnational and comparative history of the drink and the institution, particularly in a European context. Moreover, he shows that histories of the coffeehouse have the tendency to take the pattern of a rise-and-fall narrative. Rather than search for reasons for this institution's supposed decline, Cowan argues, one ought to consider post-eighteenth-century coffeehouses as being subject to constant change. In 'Claret at a Premium: Ned Ward, the True Tory Defender of Fine Wines?', Fritz-Wilhelm Neumann probes into the work of the London journalist and tavern owner Ned Ward, whose *London Spy* (1698–9) and whose poetry offer unique insights into a variety of drinking venues and into the drinking habits of his contemporaries. This case study deals with red wine, namely French claret, and pays special attention to the logistics behind conspicuous consumption and the vicissitudes of disrupted supplies; at the same time, it offers a semiotic analysis of the struggles Ward's narrators experience with their representation of the changing metropolis and the middle classes' self-fashioning.

Critically engaging with both Jürgen Habermas's *Structural Transformation of the Public Sphere* and recent theories of space, Susanne Schmid in her contribution on 'Eighteenth-Century Travellers and the Country Inn' investigates the British rural inn as an example of the rural public sphere in which concepts of modernity as opposed to backwardness were negotiated and as a space that was under control of the Anglican Church and the local squirearchy. The country inn, sometimes imbued with associations of a mythical Englishness, looms large as a setting in eighteenth-century novels, especially in picaresque novels; her case studies combine visual material, such as inns signs and William Hogarth's print *The Stage Coach* (1747), and novels and travel writing by Henry Fielding, Tobias Smollett and Sir Walter Scott. John Carter Wood's contribution, 'Drinking, Fighting and Working-Class Sociability in Nineteenth-Century Britain', examines male fighting, which was often public and alcohol-related, at a time when the tolerance for drunken violence was declining. His sources, Old Bailey Proceedings and witness depositions from the south-eastern circuit of the 'assizes', lead him to distinguish between different types of fights, for example those arising from disputes and so-called 'amicable contests'.

Part III, 'Temperance and the Misery of Alcohol', continues to explore shifting attitudes towards the consumption of alcohol in eighteenth- and nineteenth-century Britain. In 'Romantic Radicalism and the Temperance Movement', Rolf

Lessenich focuses on the multi-layered nature of public debates about alcoholic drinks in eighteenth- and early nineteenth-century Britain. Drawing on both medical and literary discourse, he argues that nineteenth-century temperance and teetotalling campaigns were a legacy of eighteenth-century religious Dissent, which fostered Radical Whiggism. Radicals, especially Radical psychiatrists and hygienists, advocated total abstinence from, for example, wine for the maintenance and recovery of mental health, not least because they associated it with the sinful and debilitating luxuries of colonial exploitation and slavery. Gunther Hirschfelder's essay, 'The Myth of "Misery Alcoholism" in Early Industrial England: The Example of Manchester', counters the cliché that factory workers in nineteenth-century industrial Manchester consumed alcohol merely to drown their misery. Drawing on sources from archives in the Manchester area, Hirschfelder shows that the 'misery' thesis is an incomplete explanation and needs to be differentiated according to occupational groups. Both male and female factory workers drank alcohol systematically to cope with their working and living conditions, but in some cases also strategically in order to demonstrate their new social status. That the cliché of 'misery alcoholism' is still perpetuated may be due to the fact that working people's alcohol consumption was viewed in more negative terms than alcohol consumption among the middle classes.

The essays in the fourth cluster, 'Intoxication and Therapy', juxtapose representations of alcoholism in nineteenth-century British fiction and an exploration of the medical use of alcohol for therapeutic purposes. Anja Müller-Wood's 'Alcohol, Sympathy and Ideology in George Gissing's *The Nether World* and *The Odd Women*' investigates how Gissing's representations of alcohol are entangled in his intricate plots and how they contribute to steering the reader's reaction. Gissing not only pointed at the problem of alcoholism and the despair it created but used alcohol as a device to orchestrate his plots, harnessing reader sympathies through emotional stimuli and cliff hangers. If, as Gissing maintains, alcohol is systemic in the real world, it is also part of the 'systems' of his novels. His functional aesthetics of alcohol defies the reader's wish to establish distance to and moral superiority over the characters. Norbert Lennartz's essay, 'Legends of Infernal Drinkers: Representations of Alcohol in Thomas Hardy and Nineteenth-Century British Fiction', continues with another late-nineteenth-century author who denounced alcohol in *Jude the Obscure* and others of his novels. Lennartz shows that the representation of alcohol consumption in these texts is not only worlds apart from the glorifications of alcohol in French *fin-de-siècle* texts. It is also part of a movement that replaced the heritage of eighteenth-century conviviality with an iconography of secular hell and gloomy degeneration, in which alcohol became the devil's paramount instrument. A more varied view of the properties of alcohol emerges in Jonathan Reinarz and Rebecca Wynter's contribution, 'The Spirit of Medicine: The Use of Alcohol in Nineteenth-Century

Medical Practice', which deals with the benefits of alcohol from the perspective of medical historians. Focusing on Birmingham, they trace the decline of the medicinal use of alcohol in the nineteenth century. The demise of alcohol therapy, they argue, was linked to doubts about its efficacy, the development of new pharmaceutical products as well as the dissemination of new medical paradigms.

The final cluster, 'Case Studies: Rum, Cocoa and Magical Potions', explores the shifting properties and significations of individual beverages: rum, cocoa and, central to human imagination for centuries, magical potions. In '"Been to Barbados": Rum(bullion), Race, the *Gaspée* and the American Revolution', Eva-Sabine Zehelein analyses the political and economic role of sugar and rum in a transatlantic framework by investigating issues of trade and race, pointing out that not only tea but also rum ought to be considered when looking at the events (and drinks) leading up to the American Revolution. Rum, produced from sugar grown in the Caribbean, became a sign of British attempts to dominate the American colonies economically. The torching of the British customs vessel *Gaspée* in Providence Harbor in 1772, committed by citizens of Rhode Island as an act of open resistance against British policies, has sometimes been considered as the first act of violence leading to or triggering the American War of Independence. Yet another beverage that deserves to be mentioned in connection with the American Revolution is cocoa, which was also consumed as an alternative to British tea. Monika Elbert's contribution, 'A Beverage for the Masses: The Democratization of Cocoa in Nineteenth-Century American Fiction', traces the fates of a popular drink, which at first was a status symbol for the wealthy, then became a signifier for aspirations of upward social mobility and eventually a commodity widely available to the American consumer, regardless of class. Elbert shows how references to cocoa in fiction, for example by Frank Norris, Kate Chopin and Edith Wharton, serve to question traditional assumptions about gender roles. Finally, whoever considered the fictional world of magical potions a world apart from that of global trade and conspicuous consumption will learn from Elmar Schenkel's essay how easily alchemical practices and archaic memories revived in late nineteenth-century British fiction fitted into the new world of commerce. In 'The Power of the Potion: From Gothic Horror to Health Drink, or, How the Elixir Became a Commodity', Schenkel shows how the advent of modern science was accompanied by a revival of archaic memories and a nostalgic return to ancient magic, witnessed by Victorian and Edwardian writers like Lewis Carroll, Edward Bulwer-Lytton, Christina Rossetti and H. G. Wells. Schenkel explores the functions of magical potions in literature with a view to modern chemistry and anti-modern alchemy as well as the traditionally close relationship between magic and commerce.

1 POLITICS BY DESIGN: CONSUMPTION, IDENTITY AND ALLEGIANCE

Karen Harvey

In eighteenth-century studies, the history of consumption and material culture is indivisible from the study of the home and women, such that the objects brought into focus are invariably drawn from a feminized domestic interior. The outcome, as Frank Trentmann has put it, 'is the dominance of the "soft," decorative, and visible'.[1] The material culture of certain drinks has been prominent in this field. The arrival in eighteenth-century houses of new hot drinks – tea, coffee and chocolate – and the objects necessary for their consumption were arguably the kernel of a new set of social practices centred on non-commercial domestic sociability orchestrated by leisured women. This was to revolutionize the culture of the house, providing the tools which would kick-start the emergence of a culture of domesticity.[2] Indeed, the eighteenth-century house was the engine of the intensification in consumer demand, the seat of the 'industrious revolution' and, ultimately, a driver of the industrial revolution.[3] What of alcoholic drinks, however? This chapter focusses on one man's designs for a set of punch bowls. While developing some of the themes in work on eighteenth-century material culture, I will make two particular interventions. First, this chapter is concerned with *men's* – indeed, one man's – engagement with material culture. Arguably, women have historically been more visible in representations (particularly critiques) of consumption.[4] Historians have also argued that women's consumption was more regular, visible, mundane and repetitive than men's.[5] Yet there is ample evidence that men were engaged in the new material world of goods, particularly if consumption is expanded to include non-decorative items and objects not typically included in the raft of 'new' 'consumer' goods.[6] Second, this chapter foregrounds the apparently 'hard' topics of *public politics* rather than domesticity and the associated themes of comfort, taste and style. Eschewing the gendered distinctions of 'hard' and 'soft', though, this discussion will explore how these issues connect. In this case study, I hope to show that style, status and family were inseparable from politics.

Putting objects in a political context is not new. A history of consumption that emphasizes commodities in particular tends to foreground the issues of power attendant on economic processes. Matthew Johnson's important argument for the commodification of material culture over the seventeenth and eighteenth centuries does not concern simply how consumed objects were increasingly those that had been traded in a market. Instead, commodification constituted a changing political context in which emerged 'a new order or set of discursive rules governing consumption of material goods', rules informed by secular notions such as fashion and taste, rules which '"de-spiritualized" the material world'.[7] Yet in general, the increasing social significance of codes of fashion and taste has tended to empty out public politics from the history of consumption. In explaining the momentous changes in the British material world during the eighteenth century, a focus on new social constructions of personal desires has dominated until recently. Neil McKendrick, John Brewer and J. H. Plumb established the importance of a commercialized culture of marketing and advertising that encouraged consumers to want what others had: emulation-driven demand.[8] Colin Campbell posits 'modern, autonomous, imaginative hedonism' as the generator of the consumer revolution. This drove people to repeatedly buy new items in order to fulfil fantasies of pleasure engendered by a 'romantic' culture that sanctioned self-seeking desires and that were embraced fully by the late-eighteenth-century 'general cultural movement' of 'Romanticism'.[9] These are extremely important arguments, yet they do not always account well for the consciously-shared motives of groups of consumers, nor even for those of some individuals engaged in acquiring new goods.

Objects are articulate, political texts, and consumption has been shaped as much by this as by emulation or fantasies of self-expression and self-realization. This is a familiar notion for those working on modern material culture. The anthropologist Daniel Miller made a passionate plea in 1995 for consumers to rise as a new political class, to ensure 'a progressive role for consumption' and become 'the vanguard of history'.[10] Some notable historical studies have established this political force of communities of consumers. Perhaps most familiar are the late eighteenth- and early nineteenth-century boycotts dominated by women, with historical accounts emphasizing the moral motivations of these feminine actions.[11] T. H. Breen provides a more thoroughgoing argument for the political role played by consumption in the past. Breen demonstrates how the eighteenth-century American public were mobilized as a political community precisely through their consciousness and shared experience of an identity as consumers. A crucial component of this was 'the invention of choice': as Breen puts it, 'the invitation to make choices from among competing brands, colors, and textures – decisions of great significance to the individual – held within itself the potential for a new kind of collective politics'.[12] This culture of consumer politics was not limited to women or to moral issues, but consisted of a broad activism driven by demands for democracy and national sovereignty. Martin Daunton and Matthew Hilton have helpfully laid out two components of this relationship between material culture and politics.[13] First, the 'politics of material culture' pertains to how consumption as a practice has been politicized. In this essay, though, my primary concern is with the second element, the 'material culture of politics': how consumer politics has articulated wider political identities of gender, race, ethnicity or nation, and additionally how objects have expressed notions of personal, political and national identities. Consumption of particular types of alcoholic drinks in certain spaces was a politicized act, for example. The articulacy of these occasions depended on the nature of the space, the form of ritual and the variety of beverage. But the type of object also mattered: everyday drinking vessels expressed political identities.[14] In developing this second strand in particular, this chapter will analyse a set of designs for punch bowls to show how this form of consumption expressed and helped create factional, national and gendered identities. Objects operated not simply as symbols but as active texts able to communicate complex political positions.

For much of the early eighteenth century and before, punch bowls were regarded as objects of rough male sociability and contrasted with the tea wares of refined feminine domesticity. Domestic drinking ceremonies had transformed around mid-century to accommodate both these earlier traditions of male homosociability *and* feminine domesticity.[15] The celebrations of rowdy male sociability, or merriment within bounds, were replaced by a more restrained gathering. It is into this context that we must place the designs for a set of three punch bowls dating from November and December 1783. The designs were included in letters to the Leeds factory of Hartley, Green & Co., preserved in the manufacturer's pattern book. Hartley, Green & Co. were a manufactory renowned for creamware.[16] Traditionally, punch bowls had been made from a range of different materials, including glass, pewter and silver. From the middle of the eighteenth century, though, most punch bowls – like other objects for the domestic table – were made in ceramic.[17] Creamware was particularly significant in the development of British ceramics. Home-grown ceramics had only been able to imitate the paleness and delicacy of imported Eastern porcelain by covering brown earthenware with glazes and enamel. Developed by Josiah Wedgwood in mid-century, creamware offered a robust stone-ware with a light-coloured body and a fine glaze. It rapidly became exemplary of British design innovation and simple but refined tastes. Indeed, Wedgwood branded his creamwares 'with British liberty and a British political discourse on classical Greek and Roman virtue and citizenship', ceramic objects that embodied, as he put it, the 'Elegance and simplicity of the Ancients'.[18] Elite customers often ordered bespoke ceramic items; indeed, punch bowls were often decorated with names, personal mottoes or company insignias. Yet these letters are distinctive in the close attention that the client gave to the details of the objects.

The letters were written by John Cartwright (1740–1824), born into a landed family and later to become a naval officer, militia Major and political reformer. These are a remarkable set of letters because they provide rare access into the detailed process of design made by an individual consumer. Furthermore, because this set of manuscript designs belonged to a prolific writer of the late eighteenth century, we can situate the designs alongside these other works. By drawing on his published books, I will argue that the design of these vessels was as expressive about politics as Cartwright's canonical 'political' writings. In furthermore drawing upon his other letters and personal documents, I will show how Cartwright's bowls were part of a wider personal material world through which he expressed his own political beliefs to himself, his family and his nation.

Exercised by the fraught relations between Britain and the American colonies, John Cartwright wrote over eighty works between 1774 and 1824, advocating universal manhood suffrage in 1776 and providing direct inspiration for the Chartist demands for extension of the franchise.[19] His keen interest in the American colonies would have exposed Cartwright to the political articulacy of consumption, and he supported many of the interventions that the Americans wrought to the liberal tradition. While these views provide important background to the punch bowl designs, it is also important to consider the events taking place in Cartwright's domestic and political life around the time he wrote the letters. By the beginning of the 1780s, the Cartwright family was not as wealthy as it had once been. Cartwright married Anne Dashwood in 1780 and in the following year he bought the family's Nottinghamshire estate at auction and spent the subsequent eleven years restoring it to economic viability. He wrote very little in that period and Hemmings suggests that the estate took him away from political activity.[20] As we shall see, Cartwright certainly felt under financial pressure during this period, particularly in respect of his older brother's loss of fortune. Nevertheless, he did publish several works during this period – including *Give us Our Rights* (1782), *Internal Evidence* (1784) and *A Declaration of the Rights of Englishmen* (1784) – all urgent in tone.[21] As in the case of his other books, Cartwright's aim was to rouse people to action for the cause of reform.[22] This period was a tense time for reformers. Following William Pitt's resignation as Prime Minister, Charles James Fox and Lord North created a coalition cabinet in April 1783. Pitt introduced a bill for parliamentary reform in May, though this was heavily defeated. Political uncertainty culminated in George III inviting Pitt to form a cabinet in mid-December, yet this new ministry struggled for support within the Commons into the new year of 1784. Thus, as Cartwright sat down at his desk to design a set of three punch bowls, the outlook for political reform remained uncertain (see Figure 1.1).[23]

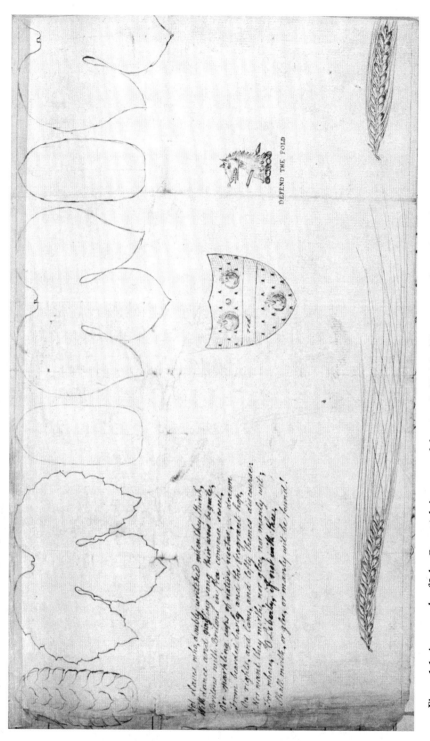

Figure 1.1: An example of John Cartwright's poem and drawings in 'Original Drawing Book no. 1'; Hartley, Green & Co, Victoria and Albert Museum, E.576-1941. Reproduced with kind permission of the Victoria and Albert Museum, London.

Cartwright's designs were clear and intricate. The close attention to detail, the deeply personal design and the various changes provide a somewhat accentuated example of the power of choice, the factor underlined by Breen as critical to the new politics of material culture in mid-century America. The designs had several different written and visual components. With just one exception, the images were all drawn by Cartwright on his letters. They included the arms and the crest of the Cartwright family, the former replete with three red fireballs issuing flames on the arms and the crest featuring a wolf's head pierced through the neck with a spear.[24] These self-evident markers of family were flanked by indications of another component of lineage: land. Cartwright provided several carefully observed drawings of a branch of a hop plant – 'my coarse sketch' – as well as a detail of a leaf from the plant.[25] Significantly, these designs were based on Cartwright's first-hand experience of handling the plant, a fact that he drew attention to in the first extant letter. For example, he explained in a lengthy discussion how he had struggled to describe the correct shade of green: 'As they vary in colour according to seasons, a middle green may answer very well; rather inclining to dark than the contrary'.[26] Hops might seem a peculiar choice for a punch vessel, as punch was made from imported spirits, not from fermented beer, but as a native plant they accorded well with dominant associations of hearty British manliness. As such, they mitigated for the exotic and foreign connotations of punch.[27] They were also part of a well-established tradition of delftware bowls illustrated with rustic scenes, including designs of hops or fruit, or of farming or husbandry.[28] This was compounded by what would have been the most striking image on the bowls, and yet the only one missing from the letters: the central image of hop-picking comprising 'an elegant group of dancing peasants from a copper plate, taken from a picture of Claude Lorraine'.[29] Providing a fascinating glimpse of domestic relations between John and Anne, Cartwright admitted in one letter that he could not send the plate itself, as 'Mrs. C is from home with the key of the drawer where it is kept'.[30] Cartwright was to sell the family estate some years later, ending his years in 1824 in much less comfortable circumstances in the London street now renamed in his honour as Cartwright Gardens. In 1783, however, he was very much the gentleman landowner and political reformer, writing letters at home in Marnham.

Indeed, Cartwright's connection to the land and its expression of lineage is evident in many of his family letters. In late 1777, for example, he negotiated the purchase of the Willersley estate for his brother-in-law, Thomas Hallet Hodges; he did so because, as he told Hodges, 'I can secure you what we want on much easier terms than if it should be known that it is for you'.[31] But Cartwright did more than play the role of broker. His letter to Hodges offers to become tenant on the estate, and proceeds to make suggestions as to the alterations Hodges may wish Cartwright to enact on his behalf: enclosure, planting, ploughing or laying out 'in the most ornamental manner'. In this way, Cartwright would 'have the convenience of a farm that would just provide housekeeping in the cabin' he would inhabit.[32] The letter demonstrates his understanding of and inclination for husbandry and estate management, both echoed in another letter to Hodges advising him on how best to store acorns and other tree seeds before planting (spread them thinly in the drawing room, turning every day, for a week before planting).[33] He would also have the pleasure of 'seeing this *darling child of mine* rise in beauty & elegance superior to every rival within the watry wall of Great Britain'.[34] The much-loved niece to whom he refers here was to write the first biography of Cartwright's soon after his death. Cartwright's investment in English soil was thus personal, familial and material as well as political.

Cartwright's designs presented a coherent vision. This is best illustrated by aligning the two components that would have been on opposite sides of the bowls' exterior. The rural utopia of Lorraine on the one side would have been reinforced by a text on the other side, a poem written by Cartwright himself:

> Not slaves, who doubly wretched when they think,
> With dance and gingling [*sic*] song their woes beguile,
> Britons with Britons in free converse sweet,
> O'er sparkling cups of native nectar, drawn
> From bearded barley and the fragrant hop,
> On rights, and laws, and lofty themes discourse:
> Nor want they mirth, nor glee, nor manly wit;
> For where, O Liberty, if not with thee,
> Shall mirth, or glee, or manly wit be found![35]

Just as he adjusted the illustrations for the bowls, so Cartwright sent Hartley, Green & Co. a revised version:

> Not slaves, who, doubly wretched when they think,
> With dissipating arts and childish din
> And silly pageantries their woes beguile,
> Britons, more blest, in social converse sweet,
> O'er sparkling cups of native nectar, drawn
> From bearded barley and the fragrant hop,
> On rights, and laws, and lofty themes discourse:
> Nor want they song, nor dance, nor frolic mirth;
> For where, O Liberty, if not with thee,
> Should song, or dance, or frolic mirth be found![36]

The poem articulated Cartwright's political views clearly. The opening reference to slaves echoes his passionate writings on the evils of the slave trade, but is particularly significant given Cartwright's repeated assertion that the political system made slavery the condition of the majority of Britons. Written around the same time as the letters, *A Declaration of the Rights of Englishmen* ([*c.*1784]) declared that those unable to vote 'are absolutely *enslaved* to those who *have* votes, and to their *Representative*'; those unable to vote were the majority, 'enslaved to a *small number*.[37] This had been a major theme in Cartwright's writing since his first major work, *Take Your Choice!* (1776), and clearly endured in later works and in his designs. Notably for Cartwright, alcohol did not cause drunkenness, but cups of nectar enabled freedom from enslavement. As an inscription for the bowls stated, 'With gratitude, receive; with temperance, enjoy'.[38]

For Cartwright, slavery represented a perversion of native British culture grounded in an ancient constitution which safe-guarded liberty. The loss of these Anglo-Saxon liberties was urgently expressed in his early work, *Take Your Choice!* The description of 'native nectar' and the established growth of barley and hops on British soil in the poem suggested the rootedness of ancient law. This aspect of the designs also reflected Cartwright's recently acquired rural estate, including the substantial hop grounds located a short distance north of that estate, which had been in the family since 1731 and which Cartwright acquired in 1784.[39] The 'sweet' and 'lofty' conversation of Britons in the poem echoes the simple style of writing that Cartwright adopted in *Take Your Choice!*: 'a plainer and indeed a coarser language is necessary for the unrefined, though sensible, bulk of the people', he explained.[40] Indeed, the simple pleasures of native drink and honest mirth in the poem perhaps serve as the refuge from the 'alehouses, those hotbeds of idleness and vice' as well as the 'gaming and adultery, amongst the higher ranks of the people' he abhorred in *Take Your Choice!*[41]

Late-eighteenth-century British culture romanticized the rural poor, and Cartwright's criticisms of the political elite were invariably accompanied by a celebration of the labouring class. Indeed, it is tempting to see the 'elegant group of dancing peasants' in the Lorraine illustration as a visual representation of those rural manual labourers who have no property in land but do possess dignity and value: 'It is certain that every man who labours with his hands, has a *property* which is of importance to the state'.[42] The appellation 'peasant' was crucial for Cartwright:

> The poorest peasant of our state, I have shewn to be an important member of it; and that he hath as high a title to liberty as the most illustrious nobleman. I have shewn likewise that, in justice, the voice of the peasant goes as far as that of the richest commoner towards the nomination of a member of parliament. The name of a peasant will consequently, be of as much value in a petition to the throne, or any public act of the commons in their social capacity, as that of any freeholder or borough voter whatever. It will be the signature of a freeman.[43]

For Cartwright, Lorraine's 'dancing peasants' depicted the utopia of a reformed Britain.

Indeed, despite the allusion to slavery, the tone of Cartwright's poem is light and celebratory. The first version repeats the phrase 'mirth, or glee, or manly wit' to describe the tone of this celebration. In the final version, though, this was replaced by 'song, or dance, or frolic mirth'. The excision was highly significant in the context of what we might call the aesthetics of corruption and reform articulated in

Cartwright's published works. Cartwright's understanding of 'glee' and 'wit' are particularly important to the resonance of the poem. First, 'glee' was incompatible with virtue. *Take Your Choice!* had included a vision of what would happen if a bill was presented for the reform of the House of Commons: 'The *jocular* Lord *North*, after once more diverting himself and his play-fellows with this "popular squib", gives the usual signal, and, it is no no no'd out of the house in an instant, and honour'd at its exit with a horse laugh'.[44] Here, the self-congratulatory and gleeful North is despicable, corrupt and antithetical to the honest conduct of the English peasant. Cartwright's insistence on avoiding frivolity and silliness in the poem, and in particular his excision of 'manly wit' in his revised version, deploys a second opposition, that between a 'wit' and a 'reformer'. Its preface dating from 17 July 1784 and thus likely to have been written as the bowls were designed, *Internal Evidence* (1784) was a response to Soame Jenyns's *Thoughts on a Parliamentary Reform* (1784).[45] Undertaking an extended criticism of Jenyns, Cartwright rests his case on the juxtaposition between a genuine political reformer and a 'wit':

> The reformer, in laying down his system, thinks it absolutely necessary to build it on the foundations of justice; to fortify it at every point with simplicity, convenience, sound policy, and happy effects; and to defend it with the batteries of honesty and truth; the wit, who professes to demolish this system, makes proclamation of his intent by sound of trumpet, and marches forth in gallant array; but so far from approaching near enough to shake a foundation, or silence a single gun, he is content to shew himself before the outworks, which, to speak in phrase military, he *insults* by some ridiculous bravado, and opens his rattling but harmless batteries of ludicrous description, humorous caricature, witty declamation, and frothy argument.[46]

The political reformer is effective, but the wit is impotent. The personal corruption displayed by Cartwright's adversary is all the more reprehensible in the case of a well-read scholar such as Jenyns, for example, than in the case of the 'illiterate poor' or 'necessitous wretch'.[47] Poverty was never a vice and simplicity always a virtue for Cartwright, whereas embellishment and showiness often disguised abuses of power. 'Song, or dance, or frolic mirth' were antithetical to corrupt slavish frivolity and were instead simple and pure pleasures arising honestly from liberty and 'lofty themes'.

Cartwright's poem is a distillation of some of the principal themes of his political writings. One theme that is missing from his notes for the punch bowls, however, is Christian faith; Cartwright's vision of British liberty was thoroughly confessional: 'the all-wise creator hath likewise made men by nature equal, as well as free'.[48] Notwithstanding, the designs are unmistakeable Cartwright: a utopian and celebratory vision to balance the dystopian call to action in his political writings, in which he warned of the dangers of long parliaments and unchecked corruption: 'adieu to the British constitution! adieu to British liberty for ever!', he grieved in *Internal Evidence*.[49] The object articulates the vision of a reformed Britain in a familiar register and with qualities suitable for an object used in merry sociable occasions, yet it is nevertheless a profoundly political text.

Despite the undeniably strong cultural association of women and china in the eighteenth century, arguably the typical ceramic consumer was a man.[50] Contemporary producers recognized the importance of appealing to male consumers.[51] Certain ceramic objects, such as the smoking pipe, had strong associations with men. Significantly, Carole Shammas has recognized the extent to which clay smoking pipes, widely represented as an indispensable male accessory, provided a boost to the production of domestic ceramic goods.[52] Prominent men established themselves as fashion leaders in ceramic ware. Perhaps it was significant for John Cartwright, an admirer of America, that George Washington was an avid collector of ceramics as of many other kinds of objects. In fact, Washington helped draw American taste away from the purely English, buying ceramics directly from China and France. In this influential family, it was George Washington – 'a careful household manager' – who did the ordering of ceramics.[53] Notably, though Washington was known as a rational man of probity, one contemporary remarked that 'the only Luxury he indulges himself in is a few Glasses of Punch after Supper'.[54] Cartwright was also a man for whom consumption of china expressed political views, as well as reflecting the extent to which such views were rooted in domestic life and personal and familial material culture. Having just bought their father's estate after it had been squandered away by his elder brother George, Cartwright was certainly preoccupied with family matters, including his and his brother's financial situation, as he designed these bowls. Discussing a debt that George owed to Joseph Banks, Cartwright explained to Banks that he was unable to pay the debt himself because 'certain undertakings' had required funds.[55] Reflecting back upon the autumn of 1783, he later explained that he could not pay the debt 'without extreme inconvenience'. 'As a younger brother', he continued, 'I have no estate, but what my father gave me on my marriage about three and a half years ago, besides what little I have since purchased'.[56] In his bowl Cartwright blended politics and domestic life, linking family and lineage with liberty and nation. The design of this object was one way in which Cartwright was able to simultaneously remain politically active while also primarily acting as manager of the family estate.

The design expressed the political and the domestic, yet the bowls were also decorative objects manufactured in the context of eighteenth-century taste and fashion. In the eighteenth century, questions of taste were moral questions, and in the changing descriptions of his designs we can observe Cartwright's burden of making the correct – the tasteful – decisions. Rather than a barbaric folk art outside the domain of refined politeness, these objects manifest a peculiarly British masculine, reforming taste that was a continuation – or resurgence – of a vibrant native culture of drinking, song and husbandry.[57] This chimed with the resurgence of older styles of masculinity as politeness waned at the end of the eighteenth century.[58] Styles of masculinity had a political resonance, then.

Cartwright's turning back to older styles of decoration helped articulate his backward-looking glance to the ancient rights of free-born Englishmen.

It should come as no surprise that men cared about the design of drinking vessels. There was a close relationship between men and their material things in the eighteenth century: men spent large amounts on their material possessions (more on clothes, for example, than their wives[59]), and we know that men liked to drink. Men endowed particular objects with special meaning, as John Cartwright's will demonstrates. Historians using women's wills have shown not only that proportionately more women bequest goods, but that they left certain objects to particular individuals and described these objects in some detail.[60] Yet Cartwright's will shows a similar practice. The document is brief, with only five instructions, the first three concerning the bequests to his wife and niece. The fourth is a most distinctive wish:

> To my Country, anxiously desiring her welfare, I leave a fervent wish for such necessary, deep and salutary reforms in her institutions, as would not only restore her lost freedom, but purify from the odiousness and debasement of unfaithfulness and corruption all her public departments.

Almost a page follows, the lengthiest direction of the will.[61] The Memorandum to the will provides important additional detail. Cartwright requested that his wife leave small tokens to family members. These include: 'the silver buttons (of my own device) that I once wore as a Militia Officer', his 'original silver-hilted militia sword having on its blade this motto – Pro Legibus et Libertate', and medals 'on each of which is inscribed the genuine Polity of our country, that I caused to be struck' and that he later describes as 'bronze medal[s] of Englands Antient Polity or, (as I hold it to be to this day) her genuine constitution'.[62] John Cartwright had clearly shaped some of his personal material world to express his strongly-held political views. These bequests were for the male members of the family. Aside from his wife (who received the remainder of his possessions) and his niece (his executrix, who left drawings and several bound volumes from which to craft a biography), the other seven women mentioned by name were left a different kind of object: white silk tokens with Cartwright's name wrought in black letters. Unlike Cartwright's careful choice of objects for the male relations – he matched some of them to their occupations – the women's tokens were, as Cartwright put it, 'similar' and 'the same'. Unfortunately, the will does not mention Cartwright's punch bowls, or any other drinking vessels. Yet it does demonstrate that Cartwright's few cherished objects were of considerable value in a network of homosocial kin, and it exposes his practice of using the design process for these manly objects to express his political views. Cartwright's three punch bowls from Hartley, Green & Co. were part of this highly gendered material culture that straddled the familial and political.

By the early nineteenth century, dining, drinking and toasting were part of a popular politics that had become distinct from the culture of the ruling elites.[63] James Epstein argues that this was a distinctively radical *plebeian* or working-class set of rituals, involving dining and drinking in particular, and that it played an important role in 'the emerging political and class solidarities of the early nineteenth century'.[64] This culture incorporated 'an internationalist allegiance rooted in the Enlightenment impulses of the American and French Revolutions, and a nationalist claim to the inheritance of free-born Englishmen', and commemorated notable radicals present and past, the latter group including John Cartwright.[65] Epstein examines symbolic expression through social practice. Yet objects themselves are expressive. Close attention to Cartwright's punch bowl designs suggests an earlier and distinctive radical culture of the 1780s, one that incorporated allusions to ancient British rights and the honesty of manual labour yet was crafted by landed 'gentleman reformers' such as Cartwright. In mid-century, the license of men to get drunk expressed their cultural and political authority, and broad groups of men cohered around fraternity through ritual acts of drinking.[66] Cartwright took a vessel that had connotations of urban middling and merry sociability, male license and the exotic reaches of the globe, and domesticated this into a more serious, restrained and self-consciously British style. Through the material culture of politics – acting as a man, an estate manager, the heir of the Cartwright family crest, a political campaigner and a consumer – he articulated a reformed political community that, rhetorically at least, dissolved traditional divisions and united people across boundaries of class.

2 DRINKS, DOMESTICITY AND THE FORGING OF AN AMERICAN IDENTITY IN SUSAN WARNER'S *THE WIDE, WIDE WORLD* (1850)

Caroline Rosenthal

Introduction

Drinks and drinking not only sustain and nourish the body but, as a social practice, represent the symbolic orders of a particular culture in a specific historical setting. Drinks 'signify', as Roland Barthes put it with respect to food, because they obtain a symbolic value which moves well beyond their function as substance.[1] Drinking practices enforce social structures and serve as symbolic acts in which gender, class, ethnic, regional or national identities are constituted. A 'geography of drinks', David Grigg claims, reveals a society's intra- and international political agendas.[2] Drinks signify the value systems of a culture as well as the rituals necessary for constituting distinctive cultural identities; they often highlight competing ideologies. Literary texts in particular allow us to reconstruct the significance of drinking practices of earlier periods.

The following essay will investigate the meaning and function of drinks in Susan Warner's sentimental novel *The Wide, Wide World*.[3] An analysis of the representation of tea, coffee and wine shows that Warner's text cannot merely be read as sentimental or domestic fiction but that it contributed to defining 'Americanness', an undertaking of fundamental importance for the period of the American Renaissance, in which Warner's novel was written. By looking at various representations of drinks in *The Wide, Wide World*, this chapter seeks to illustrate how Warner transfers the rhetoric and values of the domestic sphere into the arena of international politics and thus partakes in defining Americanness and in promoting American democracy. After a consideration of the novel's history of reception and canonization, this essay will investigate scenes relating to tea, coffee and wine to show how each drinking practice is used to define American values as opposed to European drinking practices and values. Thus, Warner's *Wide, Wide World* will be shown to be indicative of major changes in the understanding of American national identity.

– 23 –

Canon Formation, the Sentimental Novel and the Idea of America

The term 'American Renaissance' for the period of American Romanticism (1837–65) was established in 1941 with the publication of F. O. Matthiessen's book *The American Renaissance: Art and Expression in the Age of Whitman and Emerson*.[4] Matthiessen called the period American Renaissance because he saw it as 'America's way of producing a renaissance, by coming to its first maturity and affirming its rightful heritage in the whole expanse of art and culture'.[5] At a time when Fascism pervaded Europe and other parts of the world, Matthiessen sought to define and promote a liberal humanist subject as well as American democracy, which he saw represented in the texts of select American Romanticists like Ralph Waldo Emerson, Nathaniel Hawthorne, Herman Melville, Walt Whitman or Henry David Thoreau. Matthiessen picked these authors as representative of the period because of 'their devotion to the possibilities of democracy'.[6] Authors whose texts did not display this devotion to (American) democracy were excluded from Matthiessen's selection, and as his book became the founding text for the discipline of American Studies, from the literary canon at large. The first generation of American Studies following Matthiessen was the 'Myth and Symbol School', called so because it was interested in recurring images, patterns and themes in American literature that would testify to America's national and cultural distinctiveness. The period of the American Renaissance was defined in retrospect in the 1940s and 1950s, at a time when a canon of genuinely American literature first took shape. Such a canon, among other things, wanted to stress that the United States was the oldest democracy of modern times and embodied values like liberty, self-reliance and independence, values which, in the eyes of 1950s critics, were palpable in the aforementioned male authors' texts but not in women writers' sentimental novels, which had been highly popular among contemporaries.

Among these were Maria S. Cummins's *The Lamplighter* (1854), E. D. E. N. Southworth's *The Hidden Hand* (1859) or Susan Warner's *The Wide, Wide World* (1850), which appeared in fourteen editions in less than two years, sold more than half a million copies in the United States and was very popular in England, too. All these sentimental novels sold extremely well in their time but none of them became key texts of what was later called the period of the American Renaissance.[7] Until the 1980s, sentimental novels were excluded from the canon because instead of dealing with political questions and with the public arena, they were concerned with spirituality and set in the private sphere of the home.[8] Written exclusively by women, sentimental novels were systematically forgotten because they propagated values that seemed diametrically opposed to what critics wanted to see represented in American literature: an emancipated, progressive subject, enhancing democracy at home and beyond. The plot line of the sentimental novel is often described as that of a *Bildungsroman* in reverse because a core element in sentimental novels is not to develop but to extinguish the heroine's personality and to teach her to sublimate her desires and emotions, in fact, to utterly submit them to divine and patriarchal authority.[9] Feminist critics since the 1980s have reread this sublimation as an act of resistance and have considered sentimental novels as alternative versions of subject formation and of understanding American democracy.

Sentimental novels were denigrated as shallow mass-produced literature by male critics – Hawthorne was enraged by the 'damned mob of scribbling women'[10] – and twentieth-century criticism labelled them as escapist. Henry Nash Smith, for instance, dismissed sentimental fiction as banal because, in his view, it shunned reality and was incapable of investigating the complex and darker aspects of the human psyche.[11] Since the 1980s, critics have counteracted the claim that sentimental fiction is escapist and unrealistic by showing that what we today see as melodramatic and exaggerated emotions or as irrelevant religious questions fundamentally touched upon the reality of people's lives, especially women's lives, in the nineteenth century. In her book *Sensational Designs* (1985), Jane Tompkins argues that the spiritual examination of one's soul was no trivial matter but an epistemological question of major importance in antebellum America.[12] Drawing on methods of New Historicism, Tompkins places the sentimental novel in the context of nineteenth-century religious Tract Societies. These societies, which published 'thirty-seven million tracts at a time when the entire population of the country was only eleven million', saw their prime purpose in providing members of the community with spiritual guidance.[13] Among their principal publications were didactic tales illustrating fundamental Christian virtues like obedience, faith and sobriety. These virtues were considered to be preserved best in the domestic sphere, which became the spatial equivalent to the spiritual closet of the heart so that a central message of many tracts was: 'Go from your closet to your work and from your work return again to the closet'.[14] This dual 'closet' of the heart and home is the realm in which the sentimental novel takes place. Tompkins here rebuts Smith's academic scorn for sentimental novels in a two-fold way: She argues that the genre was anything but escapist because it dealt with individuals' real predicaments and furthermore points out that by addressing the tension between the individual's wish for freedom and the need of submitting to divine authority, sentimental novels explored complex aspects of the human psyche. What Tompkins's argument essentially shows is that the exclusion of the sentimental novel from the literary canon in the 1940s and 1950s occurred not only because it supposedly lacked aesthetic merit but also because it did not fit the rhetoric and ideological parameters of the time for defining Americanness. One could also argue that the rediscovery and subsequent inclusion of Warner's novel in many syllabi and reading lists since the 1990s owes much to Tompkins's institutional power and the authority of her reading of Warner's text.[15]

The novel's historical context and reception history form the basis of the following analysis, which considers the symbolic value of drinks and drinking

26 *Drink in the Eighteenth and Nineteenth Centuries*

and aims to show that *The Wide, Wide World* not only deals with the closet of the heart but participates in major political discourses of its time. Although Warner's novel lacks the dense symbolic imagery used by contemporary male writers such as Hawthorne or Melville, it nevertheless resembles them in displaying a devotion to democracy that made a specifically American domesticity the spearhead of a bigger nationalistic project. In Warner's novel, the domestic inner sphere reaches out into the world by propagating American values, thus developing its very own national impetus.

The Tea Ceremony and the Domestic Sphere

The Wide, Wide World opens with a tea ceremony, which simultaneously illustrates the close bond between mother and daughter and also represents Warner's understanding of sentimentality and domesticity. This is no happy scene because the heroine, Ellen Montgomery, is preparing her mother's tea for the last time. They are facing a separation as Ellen's father is taking her sickly mother to Europe while sending Ellen to his sister in the countryside. Ellen and her mother know that they will probably never meet again because of Mrs Montgomery's poor health. The little girl is heartbroken and her mother tries to teach her that she must control her passions and trust in divine providence instead of quarrelling with fate. While Mrs Montgomery is represented as spiritually mature, Ellen's 'passions were by nature very strong, and by education very imperfectly controlled; and time, "that rider that breaks youth", had not yet tried his hands upon her' (p. 11). The separation from her mother is merely one of many ordeals and hardships Ellen has to endure in her maturation process, in which she learns to master her emotions by realizing that while worldly things and hardships are ephemeral, God's love and glory is eternal. Her submission to divine will and authority becomes her sanctuary, an escape route from a world and fate she has no say in and a stabilizing factor of her identity. 'The closet of the heart' turns into the primary arena of human action, while the outside world is superseded by another, a truer world, the wide, wide world of spiritual examination.[16]

Before Ellen lights the fire to make tea and toast, the room is described as 'dark and cheerless'. Ellen feels 'stiff and chilly' (p. 10) but is revived by her daily routine of preparing her mother's tea: 'To make her mother's tea was Ellen's regular business. She treated it as a very grave affair, and loved it as one of the pleasantest in the course of the day' (p. 12). Tea-making is not only a quotidian routine in this scene but acquires symbolic value as it forges an intimate bond between mother and daughter; it comes to stand for love and devotion but also perseverance in making the home a closet of the heart, a sphere invested with care, as the detailed description of Ellen's activities in tea-making show:

> She used in the first place to make sure that the kettle really boiled; then she carefully poured some water into the teapot and rinsed it, both to make it clean and to make it hot; then she knew exactly how much tea to put into the tiny little tea-pot, which was just big enough to hold two cups of tea, and having poured a very little boiling water to it, she used to set it by the side of the fire ... She knew, and was very careful to put in, just the quantity of milk and sugar that her mother liked; and then she used to carry the tea and toast on a little tray to her mother's side. (p. 12)

Ellen indeed treats tea-making as a 'grave affair'; it is quotidian, but not trivial at all. The above-quoted passages convey how much skill, both emotional and practical, is involved in getting the tea right. The kettle must 'really' have boiled, one must know 'exactly' how much tea to put in and the pot is 'just' big enough to hold two cups of tea – another reminder of the intimacy that is forged between mother and daughter in this daily ritual. Besides these skills, the most important ingredient in the tea ceremony is Ellen's heart-felt attention to her daily chores:

> All this Ellen did with the zeal that love gives, and though the same thing was to be gone over every night of the year, she was never wearied. It was real pleasure; she had the greatest satisfaction in seeing that the little her mother could eat was prepared for her in the nicest possible manner; she knew her hands made it taste better; her mother often said so. (p. 13)

The tea ceremony invests the domestic sphere with love, care and spirituality as mother and daughter read the twenty-third psalm, 'The Lord is My Shepherd', together. Warner is careful to establish this because later, in the coffee-drinking scenes, we will encounter a domestic sphere that is far more efficient and practical but lacks true devotion and spirituality. Aunt Fortune, her father's sister, whom Ellen is going to live with, was born in America and embodies American pragmatism in her household chores. In Aunt Fortune's house, coffee is served, and while the aunt is lacking in religiousness, she teaches Ellen vigour, strength and pragmatism. As H. Hoeller has noticed, in the above-quoted scene describing the preparation of tea, everything is diminutive: 'the little tea-pot', 'a very little boiling water', 'a little tray', and there is only 'little' Ellen's mother can eat (p. 13).[17] The atmosphere is one of great attention but also of feebleness, sickness and powerlessness.

Ellen's mother had been born in Scotland, emigrated to America and still retains strong emotional bonds to her motherland. In *The Wide, Wide World* the preparation of tea can be seen as a performative act,[18] one in which a gendered domestic sphere is constituted. Furthermore, tea drinking marks the Montgomerys as members of the white middle class and as belonging to the regional culture of New England. Tea drinking was introduced to the colonies via British immigrants in the seventeenth century, but after the American Revolution in the eighteenth century and the ban on British products, tea was regarded as an unpatriotic beverage for Americans. As Grigg delineates, however, the bonds of the east coast with England were very strong so that when tea was finally imported by American ships in the nineteenth century, it became quite fashionable again among the middle class in the New England states.[19] In *The Wide, Wide World* tea drinking can be read as drawing a parallel between 'the mother' and 'the mother country England', from which Ellen emancipates herself in the course of the plot. In the logic of the sentimental novel, Ellen must lose her mother to find God; similarly, she has to grow apart from her mother's roots and find pragmatism and temperance; she must acquire discipline and faith.

Country Coffee and American Common Sense

Soon after the tea scene, Ellen is sent to Aunt Fortune Emerson, who turns out to be an efficient and practical yet stern and unsympathetic woman: 'The ruling passion of this lady was thrift, her next, good housewifery' (p. 338). The figure of Aunt Fortune serves two important functions: in her relentless demands and in her unfairness, she is one of the trials Ellen has to master on her way to happiness; and secondly, Aunt Fortune is an example of a woman who rules the domestic sphere in practical terms but does not affect it spiritually. While she perfectly organizes and industriously manages the home, she does not make it into a 'closet of the heart' by inspiring it religiously. Aunt Fortune not only teaches Ellen the proper skills of housewifery but is elemental for Ellen's process of Americanization, which is time and again expressed via coffee drinking. When Ellen comes downstairs to her aunt's kitchen the first morning after her arrival, this is what she sees:

> Before a good fire stood Miss Fortune, holding the end of a very long iron handle by which she was kept in communication with a flat vessel sitting on the fire, in which Ellen soon discovered all this noisy and odorous cooking was going on. A tall tin coffee-pot stood on some coals in the corner of the fireplace. (p. 103)

Not only does the aunt drink coffee instead of tea but, unlike the little tea pot at Ellen's mother's house, the coffee-pot here is tall, signifying sturdiness instead of feebleness.[20] Miss Fortune belongs to a lower stratum of the middle class than the other people Ellen encounters in the course of the novel, which may partly account for her coffee drinking. But the country coffee brewed and consumed at Aunt Fortune's house also transports homely values and a down-to-earth pragmatic and wholesome attitude, which is inextricably connected to her Americanness. When Ellen has her first breakfast at her aunt's house, she reflects that 'never was coffee so good as this country coffee; nor any thing so excellent as the brown bread and butter, both as sweet as bread and butter could be; neither was any cookery so entirely satisfactory as Miss Fortune's fried pork and potatoes' (p. 106). What we find expressed in representations of tea versus coffee is an opposition of classes and regions, of city and country, but also of different ethnic, cultural and national affiliations. Aunt Fortune thinks little of Mrs Montgomery's practical life skills and common sense and connects that to her national background at one point by saying about her brother: 'I wish Morgan could have had the gumption to marry in his own country; but he must go running after a Scotch woman! A Yankee would have brought up his child to be worth something. Give me Yankees!' (p. 158). As Hoeller observes, Warner contrasts Mrs Montgomery's 'European sophistication with the homegrown "republican simplicity" of Aunt Fortune Emerson and her rigorous food production'.[21] While Aunt Fortune cannot spiritually and religiously guide Ellen, she certainly introduces her to American foodways, which do not leave Ellen unaffected.

Critics have read food in *The Wide, Wide World* as a gift of Christian charity or an enactment of the Christian sacrament of communion.[22] These interpretations focus on the fact that on her way to becoming a perfect Christian woman, Ellen often shares and gives away food rather than eating it herself. However, Ellen wholeheartedly enjoys American country foods in many scenes. As historian and anthropologist Sydney Mintz has claimed, the United States did not develop a distinct national cuisine but ways of 'eating American', regional foodways and more than that, a style of eating and home-cooking that makes the best of available foods.[23] As Monica Elbert and Marie Drews put it, authors in nineteenth-century America 'were also proclaiming a culinary declaration of independence, articulating national ideologies of consumption unique to the nation's plentitude'.[24] Landscape and the multitude of species in the flora and fauna of America were important elements in constructing American identity and American exceptionalism in the nineteenth century. Warner's contemporary, the transcendentalist Henry David Thoreau, dwelled on the abundance and variety of things growing on American soil in his nature essays. The multitude of berries alone proved the nation's superiority to the old world, so that for Thoreau, to go 'a-huckleberrying' turned into an activity of fundamental philosophical and epistemological importance.[25] *The Wide, Wide World* draws on this topos of affluence, too, when Aunt Fortune, who has a great harvest of apples and an abundance of pork waiting to be turned into sausages, invites her neighbours to a bee and a subsequent feast. That the invitation is not issued out of hospitality is shown by her refusal to serve tea. As she tells the man working for her when planning the bee: 'But I won't have 'em to tea, mind you. I'll rather throw apples and all into the fire at once' (p. 229). The bee is held to avoid wasting food and not as a social event. Aunt Fortune is the embodiment of the frugal American housewife, whom Lydia Maria Child praised in her bestselling cookbook of the same title, published in 1829.[26] Child wanted to set herself off from British cooking and instil pride in Americans and their unique dealings with food. In *The Wide, Wide World*, Aunt Fortune often turns alleged waste into delicious dishes.

Because of her often callous ways and crude manners, Ellen cannot relate to her aunt emotionally, but she is nonetheless thoroughly Americanized by her cooking. Ellen ingests American values associated with how to harvest, preserve and prepare foods. Her aunt's cooking is very physical, sensual and corporeal – the noises, the strength needed and the odours of cooking are described in great detail – and in this respect, her aunt's household poses another opposition to Mrs Montgomery's.[27] While it is true that Aunt Fortune cannot inspire, guide or educate Ellen spiritually because the older woman lacks any religious demeanour, she is responsible for her niece's health, which makes Ellen very much an American girl of her time. Often Ellen's process of maturation, in which she severs her close bonds to her mother, is only interpreted as a sign that Ellen learns to submit to divine authority and to trust in God's love. Ellen also outgrows her close attachment to her mother's background and comes to love the landscape and customs of her own native land.

In a moment of deep despair over her aunt's bossiness and slighting remarks, Ellen meets her neighbour Alice Humphrey, who becomes her motherly friend, surrogate sister and role model in religious matters as well as in womanhood. Alice introduces Ellen to her brother John Humphrey, who from then on educates Ellen with adamant love and discipline, and of course it is John whom Ellen marries at the end of the novel when she has matured into the perfect woman. The Humphreys, who become Ellen's 'true' family, lead a life of Christian virtue that values spiritual depth and shuns worldly matters and material success. In a highly symbolic scene in which Alice again gives Ellen spiritual advice and acts as her mentor and guardian, she prepares tea for Ellen. Although she belongs to the upper middle class, Alice Humphrey insists on making the cakes which accompany the tea herself and sends the servant away. When tea and cakes are ready, the women sit down, and Alice goes through Ellen's list of spiritual troubles. Tea is frequently associated with female bonding, intimacy and spiritual virtues, whereas coffee at Aunt Fortune's house appears as physically nurturing. When Ellen, for example, comes downstairs to her aunt's kitchen after having spent some time on the sickbed, her aunt addresses her saying: 'make haste and ... drink a cup of coffee; you're as blue as skim milk' (p. 228). While in the novel tea invigorates theological investigation and the soul, coffee supports the body. The aunt's refusal to serve tea before the bee not only emphasizes that she does not care about social conventions but epitomizes her lack of spirituality and religiousness.

Wine Drinking, Colonialism and American Democracy

While tea and coffee drinking in Warner's novel signify different attitudes, mentalities and affiliations within the nation, wine-drinking practices point to national differences. Once Ellen has grown into a spiritually mature person and, moreover,

Drinks, Domesticity and the Forging of an American Identity 31

is under the influence of American rural values, Warner makes her heroine prove those values on an international level. After the deaths of her mother and her friend Alice, Ellen is sent to Scotland to live with her mother's relatives, who have decided to adopt her. The family in Scotland not only lovingly receives Ellen but takes complete possession of her, demanding that she forget being an American. When her grandmother Lindsay embraces Ellen for the first time, she says, 'I will never let you go' (p. 502), and her uncle adds: 'Forget that you were American, Ellen ... you belong to me; your name is not Montgomery any more, – it is Lindsay; – and I will not have you call me "uncle" – I am your father; – you are my own little daughter, and must do precisely what I tell you' (p. 510). Ellen is immersed in a completely different set of values against which she has to position herself personally and spiritually as well as nationally. In that Ellen is faced with a fundamental conflict: she has grown to accept and internalize patriarchal authority without questioning. 'Though we *must* sorrow, we must not rebel' (p. 12), her mother tells Ellen upon their parting – and that sentence is programmatic for the sentimental novel.[28] On the other hand, the plot in Scotland is the final stage in Ellen's process towards becoming a good Christian and serves to test her convictions and spiritual steadfastness before she can return home to marry John Humphrey. Without a guardian she now has to prove that she will find the right path by trusting her internalized religious values. Ellen accepts her new life in Scotland without complaint; she does, however, draw a firm line at intrusions into her religious sphere and defends her national identity. Ellen grows not only into a good Christian but into a good American in the course of the novel. The new world, as the scenes in Scotland illustrate, may be lacking in tradition but proves superior in spirituality and in its devotion to democracy, to draw on Matthiessen's phrase.

Ellen is rarely granted a mind of her own, as this would run counter to the sentimental novel's goal of the heroine's submission to divine guidance, but when it comes to defending American democratic ideals, she is surprisingly outspoken. At one point Ellen, arguing politics with Mr Lindsay, states her predilection for the Scots because they 'never would be conquered by the English' and because 'they would be free'. Ellen's uncle, half angry and half amused by her 'taste for freedom', asks his niece, 'pray, are all the American children as strong republicans as yourself?', to which Ellen replies: 'I don't know, sir; I hope so' (p. 515). True to the project of America and the spirit of her time, Warner fuses religion and politics and propagates the idea of American exceptionalism and Manifest Destiny. Although Ellen declares that she likes the Scots' fight for freedom, she carefully sets this off from the American quest. When Mr Lindsay praises the Scot Robert the Bruce for heroically defeating the English, Ellen declares that she likes George Washington better because Bruce 'did what he did for *himself*, – Washington didn't' (p. 515). George Washington appears as an altruistic, morally and politically sovereign saint, and the American nation as the 'new nation of men' that Ralph Waldo Emerson conjured up in his 'American Scholar'.[29] Unlike her usual self that entirely defers to male authority and wisdom, Ellen is standing her ground in this argument on democracy with her new father.[30]

Immediately after this political argument on freedom, Mr Lindsay pours Ellen a glass of sweet wine. And, 'that glass of wine looked to Ellen like an enemy marching up to attack her' (p. 517). Ellen is shocked because Alice and John had taught her never to touch alcohol. The war imagery graphically conveys that Ellen has to brace herself against the invasion of the old world into the new. As Amy Kaplan cogently phrased it, Ellen's 'journey to live with her Scottish relatives can be seen as a feminized reenactment of the American Revolution against the British empire'.[31] When Ellen at first politely and then more adamantly refuses to taste the wine, Mr Lindsay orders her to drink it. She has a sip but he insists, 'You are to drink it all, Ellen'. Immediately afterwards, Mr Lindsay draws Ellen close and insists on her calling him father: 'Never let me hear you call me any thing else, Ellen. You are mine own now – my own child – my own little daughter' (p. 518). The novel's many father–daughter relationships have erotic underpinnings and even an incestuous subtext. Warner also frequently draws parallels between women's position in the family and colonial issues. The wine-drinking scene confers America's former close bonds to its motherland England onto the relationship between Mr Lindsay and Ellen. Drinking practices demarcate different cultural identities and states of mind. For Mr Lindsay, wine drinking belongs to the sophisticated education he plans for Ellen. It is hence reminiscent of colonial encounters because what is good, civilized and sophisticated is determined by Mr Lindsay and not by the little American savage he wants to reform. Mr Lindsay claims Ellen, as the repetition of the possessive pronoun highlights. The Lindsays want Ellen to relinquish her identity also by forbidding her to keep her praying hour in the morning, which John had taught her to value, and they force spirits on her that she detests. For Ellen, a taboo is broken when she consumes the wine, and her identity is forcefully infringed. The violence involved in this is made tangible when after drinking the wine Ellen is 'trembling from head to foot' (p. 519). The temperance movement was a major part of American society and of American domesticity in nineteenth-century America, and what Ellen tries to defend in not drinking the wine is her loyalty both to John and to her country. Ellen's attitude is emphasized by the political argument about the moral and democratic superiority of the American cause for freedom right before the wine-drinking scene. Wine drinking in the novel is associated with extravagance and the degraded moral values of an old order while America is shown to be a rising empire on the right side of history and ethics. In the end, Mr Lindsay grudgingly gives up his beloved new daughter and lets her return to America because John Humphrey visits him and asks for Ellen's hand. And as John Humphrey is impeccable in character and morals, this demand cannot be refused.

Conclusion

The representations of three different drinks in *The Wide, Wide World* mark important steps in the heroine's development but also signify intra- as well as international differences in lifestyles and belief systems. Tea is associated with intimacy and spirituality. Initially it is the intimacy between mother and daughter that later broadens into experiencing the 'closet of the heart' in general. Ellen outgrows the close bond to her mother and learns to accept the spiritual guidance, first of other good Christian people – and these lessons are very often accompanied by tea as well – and then of God himself by internalizing Christian rules and principles. Coffee, in contrast, signifies the corporeal. It stands for the physical, sturdy, healthy and enduring – and it is inextricably connected with America. The consumption of coffee in the space of the home comes to stand for an American country way of life. Wine, the third drink, is closely connected to the notion of colonial control by the British Empire and by American libertarian impulses. Contrary to what one might expect, there are no depictions of tea-drinking scenes in the part of the plot taking place in Scotland. The wine-drinking scene is carefully crafted and portrays Ellen as exporting her domestic values.

In 'Manifest Domesticity', Kaplan argues that in women's fiction in nineteenth-century America, 'domestic' acquires a double meaning, referring to both the household and to politics. What Ellen does in Scotland is precisely to argue domestic politics in that double sense of the word. When confronted with the Other or with an outsider, the nation turns into a domestic space, Kaplan claims, and 'if domesticity plays a key role in imagining the nation as home, then women, positioned at the center of the home, play a major role in defining the contours of the nation and its shifting borders with the foreign'.[32] Understanding the domestic as referring to both the private and the nation challenges the notion of separate gender spheres, of the public male sphere of politics and the private female sphere of domesticity. Such an ideology, Kaplan maintains, neglects that the rhetoric of the home and the domestic was not only inward-looking and private but was a political tool in defining the American nation in nineteenth-century America. The wine-drinking scene analysed above and the political argument going along with it illustrate that Warner's sentimental or domestic novel did partake in the patriotic devotion of its time. This and other sentimental novels such as *The Hidden Hand* differ vastly in their aesthetic means and notions of the subject from texts written by male authors like Hawthorne, Emerson, Thoreau or Melville, but they cannot simply be dismissed because they are concerned with spirituality and the private sphere only. The private sphere in nineteenth-century America certainly turned into an arena for negotiating spirituality but also for defining distinctly American domestic values, which were often represented by food and drinking practices.

3 *CAFÉ* OR COFFEEHOUSE? TRANSNATIONAL HISTORIES OF COFFEE AND SOCIABILITY

Brian Cowan

In a 2005 essay for the *New York Review of Books*, the late historian Tony Judt offered a telling comparison between American coffee and Italian espresso. He asked his readers:

> Consider a mug of American coffee. It is found everywhere. It can be made by any-one. It is cheap – and refills are free. Being largely without flavor it can be diluted to taste. What it lacks in allure it makes up in size. It is the most democratic method ever devised for introducing caffeine into human beings. Now take a cup of Italian espresso. It requires expensive equipment. Price-to-volume ratio is outrageous, sug-gesting indifference to the consumer and ignorance of the market. The aesthetic satisfaction accessory to the beverage far outweighs its metabolic impact. It is not a drink; it is an artifact.[1]

The article was significantly titled 'Europe vs. America'. Judt used this simple comparison between American and Italian coffee culture as a means of intro-ducing his real theme: the deep divergences and tensions between European and American attitudes towards culture, economy and politics in an age of globaliza-tion. Although he may not have known it when he wrote these words, Judt was following an established tradition of critical writing about coffee and nationality.

Almost since its discovery in the late fifteenth- and sixteenth-century Otto-man world, coffee has been central to consumption routines and to practices of sociability in the societies to which it has been introduced. Not long after the spread of coffee to the rest of Europe and later to the rest of the world, the various ways in which coffee drinking has been received in different contexts have been understood as indicative of important national and cultural differences. The rise of coffee drinking throughout the world may indeed be one of the great com-mercial successes of the modern age – it looks likely to outlast its most vigorous competitor, namely tobacco, as the drug of choice for modern consumers – but its popularity has not been due to its uniform acceptance in a standard form.

It is striking how often these various forms of coffee preparation and con-sumption have been associated with national or cultural differences. Apart from Italian espresso and its numerous variants, there is Turkish coffee (which is often also tellingly associated with other ethnic groups from the former Ottoman empire such as the Greeks or Armenians), the French *cafetière* or 'French press'. The American coffee brand Starbucks has been indelibly associated with contemporary American culture.[2] The English coffeehouse has been understood to have been a very different social space than the French café or the German and Austrian *Kaffeehaus*: the forms of sociability that predominated in each have often been understood to be characteristic of the broader national culture and have often been directly associated with the larger national narrative of each culture. Thus, the English coffeehouse has been part of the story of the long English revolution of the seventeenth century, the French café as part of the origins and consequences of revolutionary republicanism and working-class formation in the eighteenth and nineteenth centuries, and the glory days of the *fin-de-siècle* cafés of Berlin and Vienna are thought to have come to an end with the Nazi accession in 1933 and the Austrian *Anschluss* of 1938.[3] How and why has national identity been associated with coffee drinking since its introduction to non-Ottoman Europe in the mid-seventeenth century?

This essay addresses the problems and promises inherent in the prospect of writing a transnational and comparative history of coffee drinking and coffeehouse sociability, particularly in a European context. After many years of neglect, transnational, comparative and even (perhaps especially) global histories are currently fashionable.[4] The global history of food has also emerged in recent years as an important new field of study.[5] But it is also exceptionally difficult to do global history well: one must master not only the different source materials from different countries or regions, but also the different (and often contrasting) historiographies of those areas. Although it may seem easy enough to identify the various forms which coffee drinking and coffeehouses took and then to compare them, in practice this often means working with different kinds of source materials that are not easily comparable. England, for example, has nothing like the guild records or police reports that must form the core of any complete social history of the French café; and yet few other European cultures had a print and news culture as developed as that in early modern England. A history of the French café must necessarily rely on the archival records of the French state, whereas a history of the English coffeehouse must depend upon the rich and varied reports of coffeehouse society found in the papers and pamphlets produced by the English press. These different kinds of sources will lead to rather different kinds of national histories of coffeehouses, and they are not easily comparable.

Yet alongside the national and comparative history of the coffeehouse, there has also paradoxically developed a cosmopolitan, and consciously international, aspect to the history of European coffeehouses from their very inception, and this has also influenced the history of the coffeehouse. Although Jürgen Habermas used only evidence from English coffeehouses in his celebrated account of their role in the making of the 'bourgeois public sphere', his argument lent itself to inspire further investigations of the ways in which other European cafés and coffeehouses might have also played a role in the making of that public sphere.[6] The coffeehouses of early modern Europe were clearly important institutions in the development of an international culture of 'enlightenment', and they have been studied as an integral part of that cosmopolitan culture.[7]

How then do we reconcile these two rather different perspectives on the history of the coffeehouse? Was each coffeehouse indelibly associated with the different national character of the country in which it was located? Or was there something like an international, cosmopolitan coffeehouse culture that remained more or less constant throughout the European world, and perhaps even beyond? Of course, these need not be seen as entirely opposite propositions, and I will make such a case here. The various different coffeehouses that emerged in the wake of the late medieval Ottoman discovery of coffee in different national contexts often did bear their own distinctive properties, and these different properties could not help but be shaped by the particular legal, cultural and economic contexts of the different states in which they developed. But at the same time, they also maintained a certain family resemblance to one another. The English coffeehouse was clearly related to the French café or the Germanic *Kaffeehaus* and as such they can be understood as individual parts of a broader, transnational and indeed global history of the discovery and rapid diffusion of coffee and the revolution in sociability that this brought about.[8]

We also need to address the important question of chronology and the periodization of coffeehouse histories. Many histories of the coffeehouse or the café end with a story of decline, but there has been little agreement as to when this supposed decline of the golden age of the coffeehouse began. And, of course, the moment of decline varies significantly according to the national or cultural tradition of coffeehouse being considered. The end of classical coffeehouse culture has been variously dated to early nineteenth-century England, to the Nazi German ascendancy in central Europe and to the post-war 'Americanization' throughout Western Europe.[9] With so many possible moments marking the beginning of the end for the coffeehouse, it would appear that the institution has been in continual decline for the last two hundred years. And yet we still drink coffee, and there are probably more commercial establishments selling coffee to the public today than there have been in the past. The narrative of decline is not a particularly helpful way to construct a useful narrative for the history of any national coffeehouse tradition, nor is it conducive to developing a useful paradigm for understanding the comparative or transnational histories of the coffeehouse. It is perhaps better to imagine the history of the coffeehouse in terms of constant change and adaptation, rather than as a dramatic 'rise and fall' narrative, and I will outline here a series of potentially instructive moments of transformation in the long-term history of the coffeehouse over the last four hundred years.

The Cosmopolitan Coffeehouse

From the moment of its introduction to Western Europe in the seventeenth century, the coffeehouse had an air of otherness and of cosmopolitanism about it. In *The Social Life of Coffee* (2005), I argued that it was precisely this exotic cosmopolitanism that gave the early coffeehouse such an appeal in certain social circles. While the exotic strangeness of the new coffeehouses was not welcomed by all, it was certainly not denied or covered up by their proponents and proprietors. When it was still new to Western Europe, the coffeehouse revelled in its reputation for cosmopolitan sociability, and for this reason it remained quite distinct from more traditional spaces for alcoholic sociability such as taverns, inns and alehouses. Its cosmopolitanism may have also enhanced the association with news culture and intellectual debate that characterized the reputation of the early coffeehouses, especially in England and the Netherlands.

This seems not to have been the case in the Ottoman world, and the Ottoman coffeehouse seems to have remained integrated into the local social worlds of the far-flung empire. Although it was controversial in the Ottoman world as well, it seems that the terms of debate about the propriety of the coffeehouse were somewhat different than in the rest of Europe, with the possible exception of perennial concerns among all sovereigns that coffeehouse sociability could provide a focus for discontent with the regime and hence a centre of sedition.[10] Coffeehouses quickly became integrated into the urban life of early modern Ottoman cities such as Istanbul, Cairo and Aleppo, and they often provided a space for sociability similar to that found in elite households.[11] As the first culture to discover and assimilate coffee into its consumption routines, and the first society to invent a new social space called the coffeehouse, or *kahvehane* in Turkish, the Ottomans did not see coffee as exotic, foreign or strange.

By contrast, the seventeenth-century European coffeehouse revelled in its strangeness and in its aping of the appearance and the customs of the Turkish coffeehouses. One reason was that many of the first proprietors of these coffeehouses had direct experience with the Ottoman world. The London coffeehouse, probably established in 1652 by Pasqua Rosee, who had been born into the ethnic Greek community of Ragusa, Sicily, and later entered into the service of an English Levant merchant named Daniel Edwards in the Ottoman city of Smyrna, is the best documented candidate for the first café in Christian Europe.[12] Rosee's coffeehouse was a success and his establishment was quickly imitated by others in London and elsewhere in England. Coffeehouses were founded in Amsterdam in the Dutch Republic no later than the 1660s. In 1666, another ethnic Greek entrepreneur residing in Amsterdam took out a loan to finance his venture to found what was perhaps the first Dutch *koffiehuis*.[13] The French traveller Jean de la Roque claimed that the Levantine merchants of

Marseille had encouraged the establishment of a café there by 1670. If true, this would have been the first French café, preceding the founding of the first Parisian café by one year in 1671, when an Armenian named Pascal began to sell coffee publicly at the Foire St Germain. It would be an Italian, one Francesco Procopio dei Coltelli, however, who would establish Paris's most famous and longest lasting café, the Procope at the St Germain fair.[14]

While coffee had been consumed privately in Venice by members of the Turkish merchant community residing there as early as 1575 and was later sold by apothecaries there for medicinal purposes, the city of Venice would not see its own public coffeehouse established until 1683, several decades after the institution had begun to flourish in north-western Europe.[15] The coffeehouse would spread through the Germanic lands of central Europe somewhat later than it did in Western Europe, but its popularity was irrepressible. A coffeehouse was opened in Hamburg in 1671, while Vienna's first coffeehouse was founded in 1685 by an Armenian, Johannes Diodato, in the wake of the defeat of Turkish armies at the outskirts of the city. Regensburg and Nuremberg in 1686, Frankfurt am Main in 1689 and Leipzig in 1694 all followed suit with their own coffeehouses. Berlin was perhaps one of the last of the major German cities to found a coffeehouse; it had to wait until 1721, perhaps because of opposition from the Hohenzollern crown.[16]

In most of these early coffeehouses, the Ottoman Turkish influence was clear. The earliest cafés were established by entrepreneurs who had lived in and had extensive experience with the cafés of the Mediterranean Ottoman world: many were of Greek, Italian, Armenian, Jewish or Turkish ethnicity.[17] Some early cafés, such as the Procope, had waiters in 'Turkish' garb and served sorbets, another new Turkish food.[18] The 1664 English play *Knavery in All Trades* scoffed at the new English coffeehouses and featured a Turkish character named Mahoone, who runs a coffeehouse.[19] Many early cafés took on the name of 'The Turk's Head' or the sign of the sultan as a means of advertising their new and exotic wares. The Turkish origins of the European café were no secret in the seventeenth century; they were indeed a vital part of the appeal of this new institution.

The first patrons of the early coffeehouses in Western Europe were attracted to the otherness and the exoticism of the new public houses. Although the ways in which the early coffeehouses were established and regulated often conformed to the local customs and laws regarding more traditional public houses, they presented themselves to the general public as something new and different. The cosmopolitan consumption routines of coffee drinking and smoking tobacco were also associated with an air of intellectual adventurousness and excitement that was quite different from the rough and tumble social world of the alehouse or the tavern.[20] In England, the new coffeehouses were often compared favourably to private academies of learning, and some people referred to them, both favourably and satirically, as comparable to universities.[21] This is hardly surprising as their earliest patrons and promoters were themselves participants in the international cosmopolitan social world of the virtuosi, and these virtuosi imported many of their mores and habits into the commercial world of the early coffeehouse and thus set a template for future coffeehouse sociability.

Perhaps because the cosmopolitan template for coffeehouse sociability had been set by these virtuosi at its inception in seventeenth-century England, the coffeehouses that spread throughout the rest of the European world tended to follow suit. London coffeehouses had become so numerous by the end of the seventeenth century that they became substantially differentiated from one another in order to serve and cater to different clienteles, and particularly to the various different ethnic or linguistic groups living in the cities of early modern Europe.[22] The British Coffeehouse, the Edinburgh Coffeehouse and the Caledonian Coffeehouse, all catered to Scottish residents in eighteenth-century London. The Paris Coffeehouse in London also served a similar service for continental expatriates living in the city. Although the proprietor was French and French was the common language spoken at the coffeehouse, most of his clientele were Germans.[23] During his visit to London in 1710, Zacharias Conrad von Uffenbach (1683–1734) made the Paris Coffeehouse his social centre, and he met and befriended there several Silesian virtuosi and an Italian antiquarian from Lucca. Uffenbach concluded that at the Paris Coffeehouse,

> there is very good company to be found there, especially Germans, who are charmed to be able to converse for once in a way. For one is forced to act the deaf and dumb man on account of the desperately hard language and, above all, of the pronunciation, of which every foreigner complains, even if he imagines he is far advanced in the language and can read everything.[24]

English coffeehouses specializing in Latin conversation were established in the Restoration era, and they continued to flourish well into the eighteenth century. William Hogarth's father established one in the early years of the eighteenth century, although the venture was hardly a success.[25] Other coffeehouses offered instruction in learning how to speak French, Latin or Italian.[26] The polyglot coffeehouse was probably even more common on the continent. John Strang remarked upon the coffeehouses of 1830s Vienna that 'the Turke, the Greek, the Armenian, the Jew, and the Gentile, are constantly to be seen amusing themselves, and realising, in respect to the variety of tongues spoken, no imperfect idea of Babel'.[27] As a key and novel aspect of metropolitan sociability, the idea of the early modern coffeehouse established an air of cosmopolitanism that would make its social scene distinctive.

Another common aspect of early coffeehouse culture was its association with newspapers and print culture. The early English coffeehouses in particular became a prime site for consuming the news of the day, sometimes as oral gossip, but also in printed or manuscript newspapers or political pamphlets. This connection between coffeehouses and news culture has remained strong more or less until the present-day rise of the internet café, but it was particularly important at a time when the newspaper and the news industry were also nascent institutions.

Although the English coffeehouses may have been precocious in this regard, they were hardly unique and the theme has endured into the modern age. In the early eighteenth century, John Macky could observe of London coffeehouses that 'in all the coffee-houses you have not only the foreign prints, but several English ones with the foreign occurrences, besides papers of morality and party-disputes.'[28] By the middle of the century, certain London coffeehouses served as libraries and were well stocked with books and pamphlets as well as newspapers.[29] By the nineteenth century, if not earlier, this practice was taken up on the continent as well. The cafés of Paris and the coffeehouses of central Europe were also stocked with newspapers, pamphlets and books. Some were so well equipped that they functioned as libraries as well as public drinking houses. In late imperial Berlin, the Café Bauer offered over 600 different newspapers and magazines for its patrons. In the mid-nineteenth century, the French historian of Parisian cafés Marc Constantin noted that 'we are always obliged to remember that the creation of political newspapers itself dates from the age of the establishment of the public cafés.'[30]

We find a curious continuity between the ways in which the earliest English coffeehouses were described by their champions and the idealized descriptions of the modernist café or coffeehouse in continental Europe. In 1888, the ardent French modernist Émile Goudeau described the public life of the French café in ways that would have been very familiar to the English readers of Addison and Steele over a century and a half beforehand:

> It is necessary to descend into the crowd, to intermingle with the passers-by, to live, like the Greeks and Latins, in the agora and the forum. Under the rainy skies of Paris, the agora and the forum is the café, you see, for the neighbourhood politicians, the humble cornershop wine merchant. The cafés are the places of reunion, where, between two games of cards or dominoes, there take place long dissertations – sometimes confused, hélas! – on politics, military strategy, the law and medicine. What is more, these establishments have replaced the Academy, in whose famous gardens, philosophers walked back and forth, declaiming their inductions and deductions.[31]

One is immediately reminded of Joseph Addison's famous declaration in the *Spectator* no. 10 (12 March 1711):

> It was said of *Socrates*, that he brought Philosophy down from Heaven, to inhabit among Men; and I shall be ambitious to have it said of me, that I have brought Philosophy out of Closets and Libraries, Schools and Colleges, to dwell in Clubs and Assemblies, at Tea-tables, and in Coffee-Houses.[32]

This cosmopolitan and philosophical coffeehouse ideal has had enormous staying power. The Austrian intellectual Stefan Zweig's mid-twentieth-century reminiscences of the pre-war Viennese coffeehouse bears a striking resemblance to the French observations of Constantin a century earlier and to the copious English commentary on their own coffeehouses in the seventeenth and eighteenth centuries. For this reason, it bears citing at length:

> As a matter of fact, [the Viennese café] is a sort of democratic club to which admission costs the small price of a cup of coffee. Upon payment of this mite every guest can sit for hours on end, discuss, write, play cards, receive his mail, and, above all, can go through an unlimited number of newspapers and magazines. In the better-class Viennese cafés all the Viennese newspapers were available, and not the Viennese alone, but also those of the entire German Reich, the French, English, Italian, and American papers, and in addition all the important literary and art magazines of the world ... And so we knew everything that took place in the world at first hand, we learned about every book that was published, and every production no matter where it occurred; and we compared the notices in every newspaper. Perhaps nothing has contributed as much to the intellectual mobility and the international orientation of the Austrian as that he could keep abreast of all world events in the café, and at the same time discuss them in the circle of his friends.[33]

What strikes one most about this passage is how much it echoes previous commentators on the social and cultural importance of the coffeehouse. Similar sentiments on the edifying cosmopolitanism of English coffeehouse culture had been voiced by the English virtuoso John Houghton in the 1690s. He opined that

> *Coffee-houses* make all sorts of people sociable, the rich and the poor meet together, as also do the learned and unlearned ... For here an inquisitive man, that aims at good learning, may get more in an evening than he shall by Books in a month: he may find out such *coffee-houses*, where men frequent, who are studious in such matters as his enquiry tends to, and he may in short space gain the pith and marrow of the others reading and studies. I have heard a worthy friend of mine ... who was of good learning ... say, that he did think, that *coffee-houses* had improved useful knowledge, as much as [the universities] have, and spake in no way of slight to them neither.[34]

One could just as easily cite the influential early eighteenth-century essays of Addison and Steele on their ideal of 'polite' coffeehouse society. Steele's Mr Spectator promoted the coffeehouse as a place where 'men who have business or good sense in their faces' visit 'either to transact affairs or enjoy conversation', while consistently criticizing what he thought were improper or impolite uses of the coffeehouse.[35]

There is an as yet unwritten intellectual history of the idea (and the ideal) of the coffeehouse that would cover the articulation and development of this cosmopolitan coffeehouse culture from its mid-seventeenth inception until the twentieth century. This would be a history that would run roughly from the age of Addison and Steele to that of Habermas. As a very late Enlightenment intellectual, who has based much of his famous notion of a bourgeois public sphere on his understanding of the works of English writers such as Addison and Steele, Habermas is indeed a fitting culmination for the history of the cosmopolitan coffeehouse ideal.[36] Given the striking commonalities between the descriptions of these coffeehouse ideals in various places and over the course of many centuries, it seems likely that the original English coffeehouse ideal was imitated and adapted to local contexts as it made its way across space and time.

The National Coffeehouse

There is another history that should be written as well, however, and this one is rather different and indeed would be much more difficult to research. This is the history of the ways in which each local or national context created its own distinctive coffeehouse tradition. In rough terms, this would be the history that could explain why Italy developed the espresso machine and why the United States took to the coffee mug. How, in other words, did distinctive national cultures affect the further development of their own coffeehouses?

This history of differentiation follows from the development and continued articulation of a growing sense of national distinctiveness, particularly amongst the emergent nation states of Europe during the long eighteenth century. By the middle of the eighteenth century, coffeehouses had become common throughout Europe and the European colonial world. Many historians have argued that the long eighteenth century saw a burgeoning sense of national identity and even nationalist politics, particularly in Britain, France and later, Germany.[37] And it seems to have been in the later eighteenth century when national differences between coffeehouse cultures became most apparent. Contemporaries begin to remark on these differences with greater frequency and detail in the later eighteenth century than they did during the seventeenth century.

Historians such as Steve Pincus have argued that there were substantial differences between the earliest English coffeehouses of the seventeenth century and those on the continent, notably the first French cafés in Paris.[38] It is likely that there were far more coffeehouses in London than in Paris at the beginning of the eighteenth century. London's coffeehouse society would always remain as distinctive as the place of London itself in the European urban hierarchy. London has been by far the largest and most diverse city in all of Europe (excepting for a brief period, Constantinople) from the late seventeenth century until the present day.[39] For this reason, it is difficult to compare the London coffeehouses with those of other European cities, as London was large enough to support a much wider variety of coffeehouses than could most other European cities. By the early eighteenth century, Paris was the second largest city in Europe, but it could only support one third as many coffeehouses as London. This proportion likely remained constant throughout the rest of the century, even as the absolute number of coffeehouses in both cities continued to rise substantially.[40] London had at least several hundred if not more than a thousand coffeehouses by 1700, whereas Paris had possibly 280 to 380 cafés by the 1720s. The contrast with the central European coffeehouses was even more pronounced. By 1737, Vienna's coffeehouse population had also grown substantially, and the city hosted perhaps thirty-seven cafés, but London had at least fifteen times that many coffeehouses.[41]

The varying commercial cultures of the different cities of Europe can account for many of the differences between the coffeehouses of those cities. London was almost unique in early modern Europe not only in size, but also in the way in which it served as both a court city and centre of government (especially after Parliament continued meeting regularly after 1689) like Vienna or Rome, and also as a major commercial centre and trading entrepôt like cities such as Hamburg or Amsterdam. Constantinople in its heyday combined these courtly and commercial functions as well, and as the first European city to host coffeehouses, it too was replete with coffeehouses, perhaps even as many as in London: there may have been as many as 2,500 coffeehouses in Constantinople by the early nineteenth century.[42] But the Islamic religious and legal traditions of the city meant that its coffeehouses would have a very different character. In Italy, some of the most renowned coffeehouses seem to have operated primarily under princely or aristocratic patronage, rather than as purely commercial institutions.[43] More research may indeed reveal that this was common elsewhere in Europe as well.

Other differences between coffeehouses in various countries could result from the various forms of regulation, both official and unofficial, in different contexts. English coffeehouses tended to be regulated at the local level, through local licensing authorities. A few furtive attempts to suppress or regulate them by royal fiat during the Restoration era fell flat.[44] Studies of public houses in central Europe have revealed a patchwork of different forms of licensing which varied according to local tradition and legal authorities.[45] French coffeehouses were more carefully policed and regulated by the monarchical state, although more research in this area is still needed. They also regulated themselves through forming a guild of *limondiers* in 1676.[46] No such coffeehouse-keepers' guild ever emerged in England, or the rest of Britain. Further research on the existence or absence of proprietors' guilds in other European national contexts is needed, but it appears that the French case was exceptional in this regard.

Commentators on the differences in national characters throughout Europe began to see these differences reflected in the various coffeehouse sociabilities found throughout Europe. In the early nineteenth century, John Strang thought that Berliners were 'certainly a more domestic race than the citizens of [Paris]', but that 'they nevertheless spend much more time in [coffeehouses] than we do in Britain'.[47] Whether this was really true or not is certainly debatable; far too little is known about the social life of the Romantic coffeehouse in Britain or indeed elsewhere in Europe.

In the course of the great culture wars between eighteenth-century France and Britain, a commonplace stereotype arose of the voluble but flighty French cafés as opposed to the solemn, silent and serious air of the English coffeehouse. Johann Wilhelm von Archenholz's comments in 1785 are typical of this belief. He claimed that an English coffeehouse

> has no resemblance to a French or German one. You neither see billiards nor back-gammon tables; you do not even hear the least noise; every body speaks in a low tone, for fear of disturbing the company. They frequent them principally to read the papers, a task that is absolutely necessary in that country.[48]

Remarks upon the quiet and solitary character of late eighteenth-century English coffeehouses are common, and there do not seem to have been similar such descriptions of continental coffeehouses.[49] One need not agree entirely with Paul Langford's conclusion that 'by continental standards English coffee houses were always dull places and not sociable at all', to note that rather general stereotypes of national character found their expression in the ways in which the coffeehouses of the Romantic age were described.[50] In the descriptions of the Romantic era coffeehouses of England, one may find the origins of the stereotypically 'stiff upper-lipped' Englishman, a character type that would predominate discussions of national character in the Victorian era.

As concepts of national difference became more clearly articulated within the general culture, it should not be surprising to find that differences between the coffeehouse cultures of the various European nations were also observed with greater acuity. The challenge for the historian of this process is, as ever, to sort through the representations and match them as best as possible to an understanding of lived social experience.

National characteristics never seem so clear as when they are juxtaposed to those of others, so one particularly promising place to investigate the ways in which coffeehouses became associated with national cultures is the coffeehouse world of the European colonies. The far-flung British Empire was replete with coffeehouses in both its American and its Asian colonies. Boston had its first coffeehouse by at least 1686, when the English bookseller Benjamin Harris established the London Coffee House.[51] By the early eighteenth century, New York City and Philadelphia also had developed a flourishing coffeehouse society in colonial British North America.[52] After the conquest of French Canada during the Seven Years' War, Québec City and Montréal would also see the establishment of English-styled coffeehouses; while these cities had seen the development of public drinking establishments such as *auberges* and *cabarets*, their later eighteenth-century coffeehouses were a British import.[53] This was also the case for the new Indian colonial cities of British Calcutta and Bombay; although coffee itself had been consumed in South Asia long before it was introduced to England, it took the establishment of a British colonial presence there to introduce the coffeehouse to Indian society. The first coffeehouses in British India appear to have sprung up in Calcutta in the 1780s in direct imitation of the famed London coffeehouses of the day.[54]

In these creole coffeehouses of the eighteenth-century British Empire, a conscious effort seems to have been made to emulate the coffeehouses of metropolitan London. Many of them even took the name 'London Coffeehouse' as a sign of just what they were trying to imitate.[55] Interestingly, the most prominent coffeehouse of late nineteenth-century Budapest was known as the New York Coffeehouse (1894), evidence perhaps that the ideal of the British coffeehouse also had influence in the rapidly developing coffeehouse culture of Eastern Europe, as well as within the formal empire. The opulent coffeehouse building itself, it must be said, hardly resembled the modest British coffeehouses, and it was designed instead to imitate the grand palaces of the Italian Renaissance. However, the name of the coffeehouse, the 'New York', shows that by the late nineteenth century, the United States could rival Great Britain as an example of wealth, power and cosmopolitanism to the rest of the world.[56]

Not enough is yet known about the coffeehouses and cafés of the other European empires to be sure whether they also had their own creole imitators in other parts of the world as well, but it seems safe to conclude that the British model remained dominant outside Europe through much of the nineteenth century, much like the formal and informal British Empire itself. What is puzzling, then, is why the continental cafés of Paris and Vienna should have captured the imagination of modernist culture in the later nineteenth and early twentieth century. For it is clear that they did precisely this: at the very moment when the ideal of the coffeehouse was receding in the anglophone imagination, it was emerging in the self-conception of continental European culture, particularly in francophone and germanophone Europe.[57] The narratives of decline that have dominated the history of the European coffeehouse have strangely left the nineteenth-century story of the mutation of the coffeehouse, in both its cosmopolitan and its nationalist forms, incomplete.

While the coffeehouse now figures prominently in histories of Europe's 'long eighteenth century', it still remains obscure for the equally important 'long nineteenth century', and it is here, I will suggest in conclusion, where future historians have much yet to discover about the changing character of the coffeehouse in the modern age. The age of decline may well turn out to be an age of transformation, but forms and character of that transformation remain to be discovered.

4 CLARET AT A PREMIUM: NED WARD, THE TRUE TORY DEFENDER OF FINE WINES?

Fritz-Wilhelm Neumann

I.

'I have no apology to offer for Ned Ward'.[1] Howard Troyer's disclaimer of warranty, made in 1946, responds to the continuing climate of Victorian criticism prevailing in the first half of the twentieth century. In making this statement, Troyer, the author of a book-length study on Ward, bowed to respectable academic forefathers like Walter Besant, who dismissed Ward's style of writing as 'unsavoury':

> The coarseness prevalent in the eighteenth century, the gross indecencies and ribaldry of its songs, of the daily and common talk, makes itself felt in the whole of its literature ... when we consult the unsavoury books of Ned Ward and Tom Brown; when we read how the ladies spoke freely of things ... there is nothing left but to confess that of all the centuries which have sinned in this respect – they all have sinned, including our own – the eighteenth century is the worst.[2]

Due to the cultural turn in the humanities, a turn away from moral commitment, aesthetic contemplation or deconstruction, the writings of Ward should by now have become acceptable to researchers. Still, even promoters of this paradigm shift may raise objections in the face of inconsistencies and discrepancies in this new field of research,[3] and acknowledged Pope and Swift experts might feel unease about seeing 'Grubstreeters' like Ward[4] appear alongside the greatest minds of the period. Ward criticism opens up new perspectives and adds complexity, yet it may cause concern among scholars who see themselves confronted with new insights into metropolitan life, especially its unsavoury sides, and who have to accept the existence of a modern capitalism released from all constraint. Socio-historical studies abound with references to Ned Ward, and especially historians of London life have continuously made use of his writings as a comprehensive and invaluable source of evidence.[5] Take, for example, the three-volume *Dictionary of Sexual Language and Imagery in Shakespearean and Stuart Literature* by Gordon Williams (1994), which draws upon Ward's writings like no other work of intellectual or social history. Despite his controversial status, for the purpose of this essay on early eighteenth-century consumer culture, Ned Ward is acknowledged as an authoritative reporter on how to drink beer and wine and how to enjoy decent food in London around 1700. If some episodes in his much-quoted *London Spy* (1698–9) let English eating and drinking habits appear as ludicrous, others, especially those relating to his self-advertising as a host and tavern owner, draw a more positive image.[6] This essay addresses the problem of how to analyse the basic gratification of human needs as a complicated process of symbolization. In focusing on Ward, one can demonstrate the necessity of a semiotic approach to culture, which supersedes traditional categories like aesthetic perfection and intellectual complexity. The reader of Ward has to come to terms with the disturbing perception of everyday life under the pressure from the metropolis.

Ward's writings were both different from those of his contemporaries and they were popular with readers. It is his complex use of language in particular that attracted comment from his contemporaries and later critics. Jonathan Swift, who, as an advisor to the Prime Minister, reacted to the book market but rarely acknowledged individual names, later mentioned his acquaintance with Ward:[7]

> Thus furnished, they [the young men from the universities] come up to Town, reckon all their Errors for Accomplishments, borrow the newest Sett of Phrases, and if they take a Pen into their Hands, all the odd Words they have picked up in a Coffee-House, or a Gaming Ordinary, are produced as Flowers of Style; and the Orthography refined to the utmost. To this we owe those monstrous Productions, which under the Names of *Trips, Spies, Amusements*, and other conceited Appellations, have over-run us for some Years past.[8]

Ward's prose reflects the state of the English language towards the end of the seventeenth century.[9] Intellectuals like Dryden and Swift felt the crisis that had ensued from the expansion of the English language during the century and that was fuelled by satirists like Ward, who often peered into the bottomless pit of social and cultural change. Ward did not conform to the Royal Society's principles of rational usage, nor did he strive for a language consisting of 'those happy combinations of words which distinguish poetry from prose'.[10] In *The London Spy*, Ward's style vacillates between rare words requiring an eminently educated reader and extreme slang, that of Billingsgate and of the boatmen on the Thames. The language awareness of his prose corresponds to the complexity of the post-revolution era in general.[11] Thus Ward created a clash of cultures even at the linguistic level.

Semiotically speaking, the sign system of *The London Spy* reflects what Roland Posner has termed the coming into disuse of conventional codes. While the hold on reality is usually ensured by a limited code in proper, functioning conditions,[12] this is different in moments of transition. In the tension between the 'official' culture and its counterculture, the Wardian narrators wreak havoc on the established code not just because of their poor taste but because they feel the spreading of a jungle-like counterculture in the metropolis. The satirist has two options: either to censure deviation from the cultural norm, or, if he thinks there is none, to lash out at the failure of order and reason in general. The Wardian narrator hits upon a new marker of class distinction: the display of spending power. One typical reaction is sheer nostalgia channelled into drinking: Ward's protagonist finds in the maze of the city a few havens for merrymaking and heroic drinking in the 'good old Tory' manner that is intertwined with a sense of community. Systemic pressures normally produce a high degree of conformity and consistency of various code levels and code sub-systems, among which literature may be a minor one. In times of change as around 1700, the individual is likely to be disturbed by the failing of cognitive as well as emotional assumptions about the goodness of the world. Codes fail with the individual's loosening hold on reality.[13]

Ward's presumed countercultural programme consisted of four main components: misogyny (marginal in our context), anti-aesthetics, character writing and a fascination with commodities. Firstly, with regard to aesthetics, Ward's bad reputation was not undeserved. His key slogan, 'a fart for Virgil and his elegance',[14] referred not only to the education he violently opposed in the opening passage of *The London Spy*, but also to John Dryden's prize-winning translation of Virgil, published in 1697. Ward obviously aimed at the wholesale rejection of the taste shared by the educated readership of the day ready to pay considerable sums for the elegant revival of the Ancients in calf-bound tomes. To Ward, heroic elegance was outdated, while scurrilous parody made popular reading matter. Secondly, Ward sketched out a sophisticated taxonomy for the new urban character types representing in their majority the rising Dissenting class. As a model, he adopted a technique of character writing successfully practised in Samuel Butler's *Hudibras* (complete edn 1684).[15] Thus, he bore accurate witness to social change in the metropolis. Lastly, the Wardian reporters focus on the middle class, depict their habits of conspicuous consumption and self-fashioning as well as the presentation of new commodities – food and drink included – on the metropolitan stage. Ward's protagonists walked through London and, like the flâneurs of a later age, took in the rush of city life.[16]

In the abstract terms of semiotics, Ward created a sign system built on the debris of conventional language to come to terms with the changing and, in his view, culturally decaying metropolis, which resulted in a turmoil of oblique paraphrase and metonymy. By burlesquing heroic or educated discourse as dysfunctional for rendering the urban environment, by creating new taxonomies to grasp the variety of London life and by referring to the unwritten code of conduct for the display of spending power, Ward created a new image of the metropolis.

'To expose the vanities and vices of the town as they should, by any accident, occur to my knowledge'[17] proved a mission beyond the limits of experience, a yet unmet epistemological challenge. In many literary texts, the codes of politeness and sensibility that emerge among the middle classes merely serve to tone down the ever increasing pressures from capitalism, commercialization and consumerism.

Ward had started his best-selling career with the satirical travelogue *The Trip to Jamaica* (1698) and *The London Spy*. The latter was an important pioneer work on the market of periodicals and could even substitute a tourist guide book.[18] Both works established him as a popular writer, for Ward hit the nerve of the nation with his topics: London, the Empire and, interestingly, marriage. Travelogues reflected the expansion of economic interest, as did the rise of domestic tourism. If *The London Spy* concentrates on the capital, Ward's literary travels also extended to Bath, Cambridge, Charlton, Islington and Kent. Finally, his treatment of marriage and bachelordom centred upon the economic foundations of family life. Whatever the variegations of his style, Ward could not fail with his reading public. He saw an astonishing number of collected and miscellaneous editions and re-editions of *The London Spy* between 1705 and 1718, and even many of his pieces on marriage, such as *Female Policy Detected* (1695) and *Nuptial Dialogues and Debates* (1710), continued to be reprinted throughout the century. Thus, Ward, one of a few best-selling Grubstreeters, took care of his reputation and succeeded in accumulating a small stock of capital. When he felt the tide turn, he abandoned his political commitment and invested into the 'catering business', an enterprise conforming to the ever growing economy, and turned publican and tavern owner.[19] Ward's age, the years approximately between 1695 and 1725, saw, in historiographical terms, the climb of the Whigs to supremacy. In terms of social history, this was the age of the rise of the Dissenting middle classes of London, and in terms of political history, the age which saw the transition to the era of Sir Robert Walpole at the helm of the nation, and likewise the transition to an efficient system of political corruption. This was the dawn of the age of 'possessive individualism',[20] which reached an early apogee of collective greed in the first great stock-exchange crash after an unheard-of wave of speculation.

II.

The acceptance of alcohol consumption just below the inebriation level, likewise exuberant drinking habits, varies from culture to culture and from period to period. Today, the media and the advertisement industry in particular influence our perception of how much alcohol consumption is right or wrong. In early eighteenth-century England 'hard drinking was barely even a vice'.[21] The Societies for the Reformation of Manners, for example, had included excessive drinking only at the bottom of their agenda. Drinks and drinking venues in early eighteenth-century England were manifold. Drinking has several functions: it gratifies the basic human needs for company and ritual, and since it is deeply embedded in communication, it is intensely signifying. Spending power, metropolitan lifestyle and the infrastructure of sociability, comprising for example, alehouses, taverns, coffeehouses, clubs and ordinaries, were all connected with drink; they were part of an economy that changed the character of London and its communication.[22] Coffeehouses had at first marketed the new commodities supplied by overseas merchants. That they spread over London as places of communication at the centre of the economy is a visible expression of the city's dynamism. In terms of drink culture, gin was another issue in those years. Following the estimate by Drummond and Wilbraham, 'the consumption of real gin, that is spirit on which duty had been paid and which was probably more or less drinkable, rose from half a million gallons in 1700 to more than five million gallons in 1735, when the authorities began to take steps to check the evil.'[23] That the authorities reacted only with hesitation to the mass pauperization caused by the abuse of cheap liquor was a political problem aggravated by the distillers' and brewers' lobbyism.[24] To reformers like John Gonson it made sense to suppress alcoholism, but hard drinking was socially accepted, and not only among the ruling classes.[25]

Another frequently mentioned drink with which Ward was also concerned was 'noble claret', the prestigious red from Bordeaux.[26] The French Wars eventually led to the distinction between 'claret' and 'port', in the same way that they had led to a polarization between Whigs and Tories. When Bordeaux wines became less available due to the embargo policy against France, claret rose to a commodity of even higher distinction.[27] Thus, the prestige of French culture lived on unhampered by war,[28] for claret had already reached the status of being 'naturaliz'd' in England, as Richard Ames put it in one of his poems.[29] In his survey of the wine trade, A. D. Francis even called Ward 'a leading defender of claret'.[30] In the early 1690s, numerous ballads and broadsheets took up the issue of prohibition and the launching of Portuguese instead of French wines, of which Richard Ames's *The Search after Claret* and *A Farewell to Wine* complain.[31] The question, however, is, what exactly did Ward defend?

Among the educated classes, claret had already been established as the beverage of distinction as, for example, Richard Steele's description of 'a worthy old Batchelour, who sets in for his Dose of Claret every Night at such an Hour'[32] shows. Even in Addison and Steele's *Spectator*, the position of claret remained, with a few exceptions, undisputed. A closer look into the semantic field of fine wines during the period reveals that the connotations of claret were sometimes blurred. As a result of the Anglo-Portuguese (Methuen) Treaty concluded in 1703, French wines were so exorbitantly taxed that the British felt forced to become a nation of port drinkers.

The political situation was mirrored by the semantic shift around claret. In *Spectator* no. 43 (19 April 1711), Steele ridicules provincial club life in Oxford. Since port is not yet socially accepted, it is specified as 'good Solid Edifying'.[33] The letter was signed by 'Abraham Froth', whose name links him to beer or, worse, adulterated wines. Froth was unable to understand the meaning of foreign policy and the 1703 treaty, and he turns his preference for port into a pompous act of Whiggish patriotism delivered at George's Coffeehouse:[34]

> Verily, Mr. *Spectator*, we are much offended at the Act for Importing *French* Wines: A Bottle or two of good Solid Edifying Port, at Honest *George's*, made a Night Cheerful, and threw off Reserve. But this plaguy *French* Claret, will not only cost us more Money, but do us less good: Had we been aware of it, before it had gone too far, I must tell you, we would have petitioned to be heard upon that Subject. But let that pass.[35]

During the Anglo-French War in particular, the consumer's life had been encumbered by numberless cases of wine fraud. Steele's ridicule of Abraham Froth of the Oxford club alludes to a petition to Parliament against the deteriorating quality of wine, to which Ward referred in his poem on 'Quack Vintners', subtitled 'A Satyr Against Bad Wine. With Directions where to have Good' (1710).[36] In this poem, he attacked the common practice of adulterating wines, as he also did in *British Wonders* (1717), where he simply enumerated what the prosperous British drinkers were longing for: brandy from Nantes, white Burgundy and red Bordeaux, 'Mountain' from Malaga and, lastly, port.

> And to the great reproach of *France*,
> Damn'd *English* Spirits vouch'd for *Nantz*:
> Besides rare Wines of e'ery Sort,
> *White, Claret, Mountain, Port,*
> Tho' none of 't e'er had cross'd the Seas,
> Or from the Grape deriv'd its lees,
> But made at Home, 'twixt Chip and Dash,
> Of Sugar, Sloes, and Grocer's Trash,
> Or *Cyder* dy'd with Cochineal,
> If Fame their Secrets can reveal.[37]

The joke, presumably a popular one, is that adulteration was so common that many vintners must have abstained from drinking their own concoctions, as Ward also remarked in *The Humours of a Coffee-House* (1707), his only venture into play-writing, which, however, never saw the stage. The following passage, a good example of Posner's 'cultural garbage' principle, shows Ward's linguistic games and his anti-art of metaphorical distortion, likewise his strategy of overloading the text with personal associations. Compare the elegant chiasm in the opening of Pope's 'Windsor Forest' ('Where order in variety we see, / And where, tho' all things differ, all agree')[38] with Ward's 'destroy'd in twice the time by Physicians Advice, and Apothecaries Physick'. Ward's irreverence for the stylistic elegance of Dryden and Pope is immediately obvious:

Truck. You may observe, go to what Tavern you will, Vintners don't care of late to Trust their own Bodies with their own Wine. But if you ask 'em to sit down, they will make twenty excuses to avoid Drinking, rather than keep you Company.

Snarl. A P— take 'em for a parcel of Brewing Canary-Birds; there's one of the greatest Pleasures of Life lost for fear of being Poison'd by 'em. I have been a *Claret* Bibber so long, that I can no more give my Vessel true Lading with Malt Guzzle, than you can Freight a Ship with Dry Spunges. Muddy Ale is fit for nothing but for a Man to Ballast himself withal; and keep him from turning Keel uppermost.

Scan-all. That's the Truth on't, they have dealt very barbarously by Mankind a great while. And I dare Swear, ever since the happy Revolution, they have Kill'd more People Yearly with their Adulterated Wines, than ever were destroy'd in twice the time by Physicians Advice, and Apothecaries Physick.[39]

The shortage of genuine claret not only increased the longing for it but ensured that its rank remained undisputed. Ward's poem 'The Wine Bibber' (1709) celebrates a drinker's vision of an ocean of alcohol, replacing the Atlantic by the 'clarety Main'. The 'Wine Bibber' longs to drown or 'to swim around the World in a Sea of good Wine', or, when dead, to find heaven at the bottom of this sea.[40]

Upstart alcoholics, however, would pay no attention to the divide between Bordeaux and port. From Ward's point of view, the members of the Dissent, who had consumed cheap ale in the not so distant past, were now encroaching upon the realm of the claret-drinkers. At Southwark market, the elite of the Quaker merchant class is represented by a family butcher, who proudly wears the marks of the excessive consumption of red wines even when worshipping and preaching in his meeting house. He is guided by the 'Light' which can only have risen from regular inebriation, be it on claret or on port:

His Cheeks and Nose are of a true
Refulgent Bacchanalian hue,
So dy'd with Claret, that, in short,
His Face sweat nothing else but Port.
His Principles are Het'rodox,
As taught by Naylor and by Fox;
And when he's well inspir'd by Claret,
Like them can babble by the Spirit,
And at the Meeting prate and say,
As much dull stuff, Poz roz, as they;[41]
Yet notwithstanding that, the Light
Within him shines so very bright.[42]

The Quakers appear as drunks who believe themselves to be inspired. Here, the speaker articulates a trauma produced by his perception of the Quakers' economic superiority. Ward goes on to describe the butcher's overburdened stall. His text provides a semiotic disruption, which expresses a state of consciousness hardly able to come to terms with the change in English society, although the Quaker's mock-artistic effort, the display in his poulterer's curiosity shop, is presented in a humorous way. The Quaker's sermonizing appears as bizarre as the layout of his stall:

> Next to his Preaching and his Guzz'ling,
> He's famous for the Art of Puzz'ling,
> For on his Stall sometimes is laid
> A Turkey with a Goose's Head,
> And oft he stitches, to our wonder,
> A Turkey-Cock's-Comb to a Gander.
> Thus puzzles Fools with monstrous Fowls,
> By joining Woodcocks Bills to Owls,
> And making Partridges and Plover
> Change Heads and Wings with one another.[43]

This passage allegorically presents a grotesque and carnivalesque violation of God's creation.

The spending power of the London Quakers enabled them to climb a step or two on the social ladder, and claret thus became an object with the power of marking social identity. The Quaker elite could afford expensive French wines and indulged in quality drinking while disregarding restrictions that could have been brought forward on religious grounds. However, to share commodities with members of the Dissent causes unease to Ward's narrator, as becomes apparent in the Quaker pub episode in *The London Spy*. Despite prohibitive regulations, premium claret is guaranteed in Amminadib, the Quakers' tavern. Although the Quakers drink from very small glasses containing just one gill (0.1 l), they are served continuously so that the Lord will be unable to notice their sinful behaviour until the alcohol achieves its effect. Without the least regard to the customs of the place, the narrator emphasizes that he is different, immediately orders a quart (that is, two pints, the Tories' true measure). The Wardian narrator's visit to the Quaker tavern shows how a Tory can react heroically and pompously in the face of such hypocrisy; he starts a drinking bout that culminates in a hymn on the pleasures of life, in which he hurls the principle of *joie de vivre* at the Quakers:

> Why should Christians be restrained
> From the brisk enlivening juice,
> Heaven only has ordained
> (Through love to man) for human use?
> Should not claret be denied

To the Turks, they'd wiser grow;
Lay their Alkoran aside
And soon believe as Christians do.

Chorus

For wine and religion, like music and wine,
As they're good in themselves, do to goodness incline,
And make both the spirit and flesh so divine
That our faces and graces both equally shine.
Then still let the bumper round Christendom pass,
For Paradise lost may be found in a glass.[44]

The confrontation ends with the appearance of the tavern owner, a dwarf under a giant Quaker's hat, who unceremoniously ushers the visitors out.

In Ward's opinion, wine and women were incompatible, as is evidenced by a number of his drinking songs, which disrupt the traditional images of paradise and romantic love.[45] Venereal disease was one reason why the post-Restoration age channelled and repressed desire in a most atrocious way. While Hogarth indirectly points at this mechanism by referring to quicksilver therapy, Ward is often more outspoken. His sense of alienation, rooted in his origin as the second son of a land-owning family and in his Tory set of beliefs, must have been pervasive, and the experience of the incompatible disguised as comic relief shaped his language. To him, religious fervour and the capitalist's greed appeared to be one and the same; furthermore, under the rules of early capitalism, love had to remain unrequited, so that the rational Tory's true existence could only be found in drinking rituals that revived a merry past.

Wine and sex, however, were compatible. Masquerades were a popular part of English culture throughout the century, and claret became eponymous with the feasting of the 'Quality' together with the less respectable classes. In *Amorous Bugbears: or, The Humours of a Masquerade* (1725), visiting a masked ball at the King's Theatre in the Haymarket, the Wardian flâneur, under the mask of a friar, is going to physically accost the ladies (the majority of them being prostitutes) after downing a few glasses of red wine in order to throw off his inhibitions. Interestingly, the narrator emphasizes the origin of the red wine – of course, it is French claret:

Raised by *French* Claret to this airy degree of Fondness, I now began to be very impertinent with the Fair-Sex ... and deported myself among 'em with so much freedom and familiarity, as if I had been a weekly Customer to a Buttock-Ball, and had by that means arriv'd to such a pitch of Confidence as might enable me to attack the most accomplish'd Curtesan, from the Kept-Mistress, to the *Drury*-Brimstone, notwithstanding they had disguis'd themselves in sober Weeds, and very aukwardly dissembl'd, as they walk'd about, the modest Ayre of Quality.[46]

56 *Drink in the Eighteenth and Nineteenth Centuries*

Finally, in Ward's poems, the distinctive divide between the established and the upstart, social panoramas and drinking habits are intertwined. 'The Contending Candidates: or, The Broom-Staff Battles, Dirty Skirmishes, and other Comical Humours of the Late Southwark Election' (1724) describes a powerful suburban pageant of the four Farnham candidates for the London elections, who are in their majority Dissenters and thus necessarily the butt of satire. The Lord Mayor's processions, funded by the leading guilds, were among the highlights of city life and attracted large crowds. Throughout history, London's processions were unique opportunities for representing society in its entirety: the governing moral principles were represented by allegorical statues on floats, while the population stood on balconies, at the windows or along the streets.[47] The following satirical presentation of yet another procession in *A Journey to H***** (1700) shows a parade of 'Hogwash' drinkers, consumers of poor-quality beer or ale, formerly the proletariat and now the rising middle class. In terms of literary history, this is Ward's tribute to Quevedo's hellish crowd:

> Behind th'Squire a swanking Troop
> Of Vict'lers, came in order up,
> Whose dropsick Guts, b'ing over tallow'd
> With fattening Hogwash they had swallow'd,
> Projected, as they sat a Straddle,
> Full half a Yard beyond the Saddle ...
>
> Their great fat Arses hanging o'er
> Behind, as did their Guts before,
> Some nodding as they rode, some winking,
> O'ercome with Lethargies by Drinking[48]

Again, the lines reflect the ongoing conflict of new culture versus old culture. However, Ward the satirist did not fall into black depression. In a late poem, *The Delights of the Bottle* (1720), he hailed the acknowledged masters of the new age as the torch-bearers of civilization by ignoring their well-known political leanings. These were members of the famous Kit-Cat Club: Joseph Addison and the painter Godfrey Kneller.

> Yet first, my Muse shall let you see
> What Vintners are, or ought to be,
> Those Demy Gods, from whose rich Cellars
> Arise, *Popes, Addisons* and *Knellers,*
> And ev'ry Worthy that can claim
> A place in the Records of Fame;
> For all that's excellent or fine,
> Derive their Origin from Wine,
> And should each Vintner shut his Door,
> Love, Wit and Arts would be no more,
> But all the Land become at once,
> A dirty Hive of stupid Drones.[49]

These leading minds warranted a nostalgic *joie de vivre* as the only remedy against the Dissent or the virtuous society that was ironically, or menacingly, imagined by Mandeville in the *Fable of the Bees*.[50] In the last four lines of this quotation, Ward has adapted Mandeville's idea of society. What kind of human community will arise if art and intellectual beauty disappear? In the dirty hive of raw capitalism and hypocrisy, a class of mindless money-grabbers will take over. Throwing overboard the Tory–Whig divide, Ward, for a moment, envisions a new reality, made up of genuine claret and undiluted humankind, of culture and counterculture.

Conclusion

In his classic contribution to cultural studies, *The Country and the City* (1973), Raymond Williams discusses the problems caused by the shifting appearance of the city in the period under discussion here: 'Men accustomed to seeing their immediate environment through received intellectual and literary forms had by the eighteenth century to notice another dramatic alteration of landscape: the rapidly expanding and changing city'.[51] Following Williams, we ought to adopt the historian's view in order to overcome what he calls the persistent 'commonplaces of middle-class observation'.[52] It is precisely this focus that has until recently led to the scholarly neglect of Ned Ward and his work. The contexts of drinking culture under the dynamics of early capitalism were equally likely to be disregarded in a branch of learning, literary studies, that focused on ethics, aesthetic contemplation and the educational value of literature. The process of social evolution, however, has many undercurrents that deserve our attention. Aesthetically indifferent yet rich in detail and emotion, if biased in many directions, Ward's semiotic carnival records an almost palpable experience of change. As we read Ward, Clifford Geertz's words are worth keeping in mind: 'The besetting sin of interpretive approaches to anything – literature, dreams, symptoms, culture – is that they tend to resist, or to be permitted to resist, conceptual articulation and thus to escape systematic modes of assessment'.[53] The true gain of a cultural studies approach is an increase in complexity that requires us to appreciate the divergent undercurrents of social evolution and that shows that any aesthetic achievement is deeply rooted in the evolution of society, the laws of the market and the commodities of the age.

5 EIGHTEENTH-CENTURY TRAVELLERS AND THE COUNTRY INN

Susanne Schmid

A man who travels with a family of five persons, must lay his account with a number of mortifications; and some of these I have already happily overcome. Though I was well acquainted with the road to Dover, and made allowances accordingly, I could not help being chagrined at the bad accommodation and impudent imposition to which I was exposed. These I found the more disagreeable, as we were detained a day extraordinary on the road, in consequence of my wife's being indisposed.

I need not tell you this is the worst road in England, with respect to the conveniences of travelling, and must certainly impress foreigners with an unfavourable opinion of the nation in general. The chambers are in general cold and comfortless, the beds paultry, the cookery execrable, the wine poison, the attendance bad, the publicans insolent, and the bills extortion; there is not a drop of tolerable malt liquor to be had from London to Dover.

Tobias Smollett, *Travels Through France and Italy* (1766)[1]

Thus complained the 'traveller-novelist'[2] Tobias Smollett, a self-appointed expert on inns, about the accommodation on the road between London and Dover. Implicitly, his complaint describes what a traveller expected to find at an inn: a reasonably warm bed-chamber, a selection of tasty food and alcoholic drinks, a friendly landlord as well as sociable company, and all of this at an acceptable price. If Smollett, the grand tourist, enthused about classical and other famous sites in Italy and France, his profound bad humour often returned in reflections on accommodation.[3] The eighteenth century has been called the 'golden age' of the English inn.[4] Due to transport changes, growing commerce and increasing individual travel, by around 1700, England commanded over a network of rural and urban inns, which offered a range of facilities from food and accommodation to the changing of horses, although not always at the desired standards.

Like other sociable places – taverns, operas and pleasure gardens, to name just a few[5] – inns attracted the artistic and the writerly imagination. If research on the emergence of the public sphere in the eighteenth century has frequently focused on urban sociability (coffeehouses, theatres), little has been written about the country inn, although it was instrumental to the forging of a public sphere, which was by no means only urban, as for example William Hogarth's print *The Stage Coach or Country Inn Yard* (1747) shows. In literary texts, especially realist novels, with their programmatic focus on everyday details, inns are popular settings because they allow for expected and unexpected encounters across the barriers of social class and gender, facilitating intellectual debates as well as quarrels and love stories. Henry Fielding was intrigued by inns, coffee-houses, alehouses and other public meeting and drinking spaces, as his play *The Coffee-House Politician* (1730) as well as numerous episodes in his novels *Joseph Andrews* (1742) and *Tom Jones* (1749) show.[6] The famously ill-humoured Scotsman Smollett's novels and travelogues also lead the reader through an array of inns: carnivalesque haunts brimming with strange fellows in *Roderick Random* (1748), a veritable 'temple sacred to hospitality' in *Launcelot Greaves* (1762) and an assortment of places in *Humphry Clinker* (1771)[7] present him as a connoisseur of inns and other public institutions, which he judged meticulously by his own high standards. After a brief survey of the status of the country inn in eighteenth-century England, this contribution will turn to visual material: a print by Hogarth, depicting an inn, as well as the ubiquitous inn sign. I will then consider novels and travel writing by Scott, Fielding and Smollett.

Inns, Alehouses and Taverns as Spaces

In recent decades, sociable spaces and drinking venues have received attention from two academic fields in particular: history and literary criticism. Studies by the two historians Peter Clark (*The English Alehouse: A Social History*, 1983) and Beat Kümin (*Drinking Matters*, 2007) have mapped out with precision the types of establishments that existed and the range of functions they provided, while Steven Earnshaw's *The Pub in Literature* (2000) testifies to the omnipresence of drinking places in English literature, from Chaucer to Martin Amis.[8] Defining precisely what constitutes an 'inn' within the caste system of public drinking venues is not always easy. Kümin argues that central European public houses fall into 'two fundamental categories, depending on the availability or absence of lodgings and meals'.[9] Although *Drinking Matters* focuses on Bavaria and parts of Switzerland, many of his observations apply to English establishments, too. Inns would then be public houses offering food and accommodation. Clark's *The English Alehouse* distinguishes three types of public drinking venues: inns, taverns and alehouses, categories which can be traced back to the sixteenth century.[10] The exact differences between them are sometimes difficult to discern, especially as the terms varied from region to region and were sometimes used synonymously. The word 'alehouse' describes a drinking house which sold ale, beer, wine, spirits and some food and was frequented by the lower orders of society, for example by farmers and working men. Alehouses could be ordinary houses whose private quarters overlapped with the public drinking space, while inns, often purpose-built, aimed to attract the more well-to-do travellers.[11] Today's 'pub' is the successor of the former 'alehouse'. In this hierarchy of drinking places, taverns stood between alehouses and inns. Larger than alehouses, they sold a wider range of drinks (for example wine) but could not compete with inns when it came to providing extensive lodgings and stables.[12] A 1577 survey of twenty-seven counties found around 2,000 inns and 300 taverns in England, while it can be estimated that the number of alehouses was at least 14,000 – possibly more since alehouses often operated without being licensed.[13] An estimate by John Chartres suggests that at the beginning of the eighteenth century, England had around 6,000 to 7,000 inns.[14] Prior to this type of recent research, several older survey studies appeared, which nostalgically evoke the image of the old English inn. Frederick W. Hackwood's *Inns, Ales, and Drinking Customs of Old England* (1909) is one example: it idealizes 'the traditional homeliness and freedom of the inn', imbues it with national values and celebrates the male sociability of times gone by.[15]

As already noted, in terms of size and importance, inns were at the upper end of the spectrum, while alehouses ranked much lower. Two episodes in Fielding's *Joseph Andrews* exemplify this difference. First, when Mr Tow-wouse, master of an inn, pities the robbed and beaten hero Joseph, allowing him to stay, although this generosity may leave him with an unpaid bill, Mrs Tow-wouse protests: "'Why doth not such a Fellow go to an Ale-house?'"[16] And second, later during their journey, Joseph and Adams rest in an establishment which, as the narrator discloses, is a mere alehouse, yet it sports a sign with the words '*The New Inn*', thereby misleading the weary travellers, who are offered nothing but bread, cheese and ale.[17] Inns were usually associated with the local social and political elite, in any case, with affluent and well-reputed customers. In 1787, the German traveller Johann Wilhelm von Archenholz praised the splendid English country inns and stated that rural innkeepers even played a role in parliamentary elections.[18] As rural inns were the arrival and departure points for coaches, they attracted guests travelling over long distances, while alehouses predominantly catered for local farmers and working men.

Due to a system of stage coaches, English inns grew in importance from the second half of the seventeenth century, until the railway expansion in the mid-nineteenth century, which fundamentally changed the conditions of transport. Inns could be found along the major provincial roads and in London, often close to the principal roads that led into the capital.[19] Even though the number of London's inns, which were usually bigger than country inns, was not huge in comparison to other urban public drinking places, they were important institutions. Both in London and the provinces, larger inns could be business complexes, which hosted shops and offered storage facilities. Most inns had courtyards around which the function rooms (guest rooms, stables, kitchens) were grouped. In many inns, roofed outside galleries provided access to these rooms. The stage coaches stopped inside the courtyards, where horses were changed, passengers left or alighted and goods were loaded and unloaded.

Sadly, the role of public eating and drinking places has been neglected in Jürgen Habermas's canonical study, *The Structural Transformation of the Public Sphere* (1962), which locates the emergence of an urban public sphere in eighteenth-century society.[20] Although Habermas's book has been very influential, it has been heavily criticized for its conceptual shortcomings, to which one should add his disregard for rural and lower-class institutions. Unlike urban coffeehouses, regrettably, inns, taverns, alehouses and pubs, whatever their name or size, are not considered to be agents in this transformation; the drunken brawling, the fights, the gambling and the uproar sometimes associated with such places did not fit into the scheme of reasonable public discourse. Nor do areas outside London play a role in Habermas's *grand récit* of the history of the enlightened public. The rural inn, however, ought to find consideration among the meeting-places listed in *The Structural Transformation of the Public Sphere*.[21] As spaces of business, sociability, news-mongering, convivial conversation, heated argument, play, entertainment or political campaigning, country inns were central to the formation of the public sphere. Maybe the supposed backwardness of rural areas led to the omission of inns from this cult book of Enlightenment history.

Although, in the authorities' view, public drinking places, alehouses and taverns rather than inns, could be linked to political sedition and violence,[22] these venues were vital to establishing communication structures, especially as they enabled members of different social strata to meet. In this sense, they added to rather than disrupted order. If drinking spaces possess a potential for political activities, even upheavals, they nevertheless ought to be seen as stabilizing, as contributing to community-building on a micro-level. Of course, violence and the public consumption of alcohol could go hand in hand, as legal records show, but not all drunken arguments necessarily had a political cause. Despite all unruly tendencies associated with public drinking, people flocked to such places for social interaction and entertainment on various levels: public dances, weddings, theatre performances, card games etcetera. Guests at inns were likely to meet and engage in conversation with individuals from varying social backgrounds, different regions and different professions. Therefore, inns have always been attractive settings in literature, allowing characters to meet and mingle.

As literary settings, inns have achieved notoriety over the centuries. Chaucer's *Canterbury Tales* commence in an inn, the Tabard in Southwark. In literature, inns can be cast as microcosms of society, as Utopian spaces of ideal pre-modern, pre-urban humanity, but also as mirrors of a mercantile society obsessed with money, or the lack of it, as dens of vice, gambling, illicit sexual activities or accidental sexual encounters. They are often the scenes of eavesdropping or of burlesque fights. The rural inn especially is a space where different concepts of modernity and rural backwardness might clash, where oppositions like old-fashioned country life and fashionable city manners meet, where the rural journeyman encounters the urban gentleman. Inns appear in picaresque novels, where they allow the *picaro* to encounter all strata of society. Eighteenth-century novels like Smollett's *Launcelot Greaves* document through the election scenes alone that rural inns and towns belong to the emerging public sphere, where travellers and locals exchange views and news or negotiate their status. To resort to a recent theoretical paradigm, the so-called 'spatial turn':[23] the country inn, situated by the road and offering to host and feed travellers, is itself a space that is transitory, inviting travellers to remain only for a short time, for a drink or a meal, possibly for a night or two. In his essay 'Of Other Spaces', Michel Foucault claims the relevance of space as a category and coins the term 'heterotopia'. Such heterotopias, among which I would count the roadside inn, are, in the French philosopher's words, 'capable of juxtaposing in a single real place several spaces, several sites that are in themselves incompatible'.[24] And this is precisely what the roadside inn does by letting journeyman and squire, urban fop and country bumpkin come together.

William Hogarth, *The Stage Coach or Country Inn Yard* (1747) and the Inn Sign

Hogarth's *The Rake's Progress* and *The Harlot's Progress*, *Beer Street* and *Gin Lane*, all showing urban drinking places, are far better-known than his satirical print *The Stage Coach or Country Yard Inn*, which depicts the courtyard of a country inn.[25] Although it can be analysed as a comment on the upcoming election, it originally seems to have been prepared without this topical focus in mind. Hogarth's print is relevant on two levels: it is a detailed visual and informative representation of an inn courtyard, and it is imbued with an allegorical dimension. In this, it resembles literary descriptions of inns, which combine a programmatic realism with an allegorical and symbolic dimension. Hogarth shows a busy and crowded courtyard, from where a coach is about to depart. Refreshments are offered. The section of the large courtyard we see is framed by a huge, multi-storey building. The two lower floors possess the already mentioned roofed galleries, from which the customers could access various function rooms. The inn is populated by a crowd, a fairly large force; at the end of the courtyard, an election parade is visible. This may be a comment on current political events and on the role of the people, the masses, who have situated themselves as observers on the first-floor gallery. Inns sometimes played an important role in elections, simply because they were large enough to accommodate a fair number of people and to provide the necessary catering. In the foreground, a coach is about to depart. In truly Hogarthian fashion, some grotesque figures appear, like the woman who is squeezed into the vehicle. The beholder is invited to scrutinize her large, round backside, which is at the very centre of the print and mirrors the round wheel to her right. She is in effect 'turning her back' on the elections, as Ronald Paulson argues.[26] The election remains a 'background' event,[27] since the travellers, that is, in a wider sense, the English, are predominantly interested in their own business. This impression is furthermore conveyed by a group of characters in the front, who talk without showing any awareness of the election. On top of the coach, possibly as a comment on the War of Austrian Succession, two figures are seated, an English sailor and a Frenchman, who are engaged in a private argument.[28] While alluding to current politics, Hogarth presents the inn as a microcosm of society, of life and of Britain. Some of the characters in the foreground, outside the coach, who belong to different age groups, may be intended to represent the stages of life. Thus, implicitly, he refers to a popular eighteenth-century metaphor: life as an inn.[29] Among the many objects in the print, which carry symbolic meaning, is an inn sign, on which an angel and the words 'Old Angle In' (correctly spelt: 'Old Angel Inn') are visible. Religious symbols sometimes gave their names to inns frequented by pilgrims. Moreover, the words 'Old Angle In' can also be understood as a corrupted version of 'Old England'.[30] In such a reading, the inn would be a mirror of England.

That the inn was considered fundamentally English is obvious from an event which occurred fifteen years after Hogarth's print appeared: an exhibition of inn and shop signs. While in 1762, two exhibitions of paintings, one organized by the Society of the Artists of Great Britain, the other by the Society for the Encouragement of Arts, Manufactures and Commerce, took place in London, the journalist Bonnell Thornton organized the display of around 110 inn, tavern and shop signs in what presumably was a sarcastic comment on the fashion of high art, especially portrait painting under French influence, and the connoisseurship that accompanied it. Thornton's exhibition also included signs painted by Hogarth.[31] Although no original signs seem to have survived, the eleven-page exhibition catalogue, which unfortunately shows no illustrations, has. The positions at stake were not only high art versus popular craftsmanship, 'real' painting done by artists versus painting done by craftsmen. This exhibition also staged a conflict over French versus English culture, sarcastically commenting on French fashions undermining English essence. Many of the signs exhibited in the 'Grand Room' seem to have been inn or tavern signs. The catalogue lists their names and supplies brief descriptions, for example: '1. Portrait of a justly celebrated Painter, though an Englishman, and a Modern'. Other signs show 'The Good Woman', 'The Hog in Armour', 'A Buttock of Beef', 'The Irish Arms', 'The Gentleman of

Wales', 'The Robin Hood Society', 'The Vicar of Bray'.[32] In view of French tastes and influences, the descriptions sketch a programme of Englishness, a celebration of 'Old' England, which in a wider sense includes Wales and Ireland.

That the painting of shop and inn signs continued to be held in low esteem is also shown in Sir Walter Scott's *The Bride of Lammermoor* (1819). In the frame narrative, the talented Dick Tinto, a tailor's son, who had trained to become a sign-painter, opts to do more prestigious portraits and landscapes instead. Despite being 'discovered and appreciated'[33] in Edinburgh and later in London, he eventually fails as an artist. When the first-person narrator encounters him, Tinto has withdrawn from the local society because he has secretly returned to the less prestigious craft of sign-painting, which, however, helps him to earn his living. One comic climax in this story is the description of a sign for an inn or alehouse, painted by Tinto early in his career, which depicts a five-legged horse. Tragically, Tinto is unaware of the service he renders to the rural community. Again, sign-painting stands for honest yet sadly underrated British native crafts, whereas the foreign fashions of portrait and landscape painting are cast as hollow and pretentious: despite his skills, all that is in store for Tinto is an early grave. Thus, British (here: Scottish) rural hospitality and sociability, symbolized by public spaces like inns, emerge as more humane than the modern cities.

Henry Fielding, *Joseph Andrews* (1742)

Fielding's novel *Joseph Andrews*, which presents a lower-class version of the home tour, features the servants Joseph and Fanny and the comic Parson Adams as travellers, yet without the backdrop of the magnificent sights and classical ruins found in travelogues about Italy and France. What Fielding exuberantly presents, however, is an array of social and literary types: local gentry, clergymen, businessmen, a bookseller, a poet, jilted lovers, young rakes and others. Inns figure both as places of rest and sociability and as dense symbols, which work on several levels: inns serve to reflect about the nature of the new genre, the novel, they help to establish intertextual references, they allow Fielding to demonstrate an aesthetic programme of realism through attention to detail, they function as mirrors of society, and, finally, they support the author's political views, namely a praise of Englishness.

Since the popular realist novel was a fairly new genre, Fielding justified his mode of narration not only in his famous preface but also throughout the story, in the shape of authorial interventions, especially at the beginning of new sections. In the first chapter of book II, the narrator reflects about formal aspects of the novel, its division into books and chapters: 'those little Spaces between our Chapters may be looked upon as an Inn or Resting-Place, where he [the reader] may stop and take a Glass, or any other Refreshment, as it pleases him'.[34] The short descriptions above each chapter are likened to 'Inscriptions over the Gates of Inns', which inform the traveller of what he can expect.[35] Fielding's other great novel, *Tom Jones* (1749), frequently compares reading to a journey and repeatedly incorporates the inn into this extended metaphor. In book I, chapter 1, the narrator likens the author to 'one who keeps a public ordinary', while the process of reading through the chapters is captured in the image of enjoying a meal consisting of several courses.[36] Book II, chapter 1 compares the plot to a 'stagecoach', while the author figures as a traveller.[37] The last book (XVIII) begins with a farewell to the reader, comparing readers, characters and author to the mixed company one encounters during a ride in a stage coach.[38] Furthermore, the image of the inn establishes continuous intertextual references. The title page mentions *Don Quixote* as the model for Fielding's 'comic Epic-Poem in Prose', as *Joseph Andrews* is called in the 'Preface'.[39] Encounters at inns are frequent in Cervantes's novel, too: they bring individuals from varying social backgrounds together and exemplify the differences between them. If Sancho Panza likes to stay at inns, Don Quixote is sometimes not even aware of the worldly events occurring in such places. Thus, inns symbolize the way in which characters open themselves up to the world. Adams's benevolence but also his lack of practical skills are often highlighted in the inn scenes, for example when he is unable to pay his bills. His idealism makes him a rustic eighteenth-century version of Don Quixote, while Joseph, his Sancho Panza, continuously gets into scrapes, too, yet is more worldly-wise than his mentor.

Fielding's inns reflect his realist programme because they differ from the fantastic spaces of the romances he criticizes so severely.[40] Inns are not only devoid of ghosts but contain a large number of items and substances: furniture, pots and pans, money (which is regrettably scarce), food and drink. Other individual objects which are related to the characters – Adams's pipe, his handwritten copy of Aeschylus or Joseph's piece of gold, which gets him into trouble – all become significant during stays at inns. Attention is paid to detail: Adams wrongly believes that he has nine volumes of sermons in his luggage. Some items and substances are pleasant, like wine, others are not, like the 'Pan full of Hog's-Blood', which the mistress of one inn pours over Adams.[41]

Spaces in *Joseph Andrews* function as microcosms of society and present exemplary modes of living, both in a positive and in a negative sense. Parson Trulliber's home, where the profit raised through the breeding of pigs is assigned more importance than benevolence towards humans, is a negative example,[42] whereas Wilson's household, where honesty and productivity are held in high esteem, is worth emulating. It is only through Adams's and Joseph's overnight stays at inns that they learn about these contemporaries, and it is there that they meet a further array of characters from various backgrounds and occupational groups. Urban and rural values are contrasted: Adams, unquestioned authority in his own rural parish, learns through a bookseller at an inn that his sermons, which he would like to see in print, may not interest the urban reading public, which prefers plays.[43] The inns provide settings for social order as well as disorder. Disruptive forces are greed, sexual violence and miscarriage of justice, whereas benevolence and honesty set things right. Adams in particular finds himself engaged in several fights while staying at inns, yet these normally have a purifying function. Since disorder in Fielding's novels can mean vitality, the fights and arguments lead to solutions, to a better human understanding. Inns also help to unite characters: Adams meets Joseph at an inn, and they both meet Fanny some chapters later. Adams's reunion with his horse ironically reverses this narrative pattern.

Moreover, the inns represent a programme of Englishness at a time that saw numerous debates about luxury items, concerning, for example, food, clothes and china.[44] Fielding advocates a plain and rural lifestyle over urban luxuries. Wilson, the reformed rake, originally appears as the victim of a fashionable urban lifestyle, yet as he repents, he is rewarded with rural bliss. Leonora, the heroine of another embedded story, who prefers the superficial and wealthy French admirer Bellarmine over the honest Englishman Horatio, is punished by losing both men. In the eighteenth century, luxury was frequently coded as urban and French.[45] In the popular perception, Frenchified manners made English men effeminate and English women coquettish and heartless. Fielding not only questions the need for foreign luxuries but also the value of exploring France and Italy; several chance encounters with travellers who have done the grand tour prove its limited educational benefit.[46] Fielding's country inn is an epitome of English society: rough and plain, yet honest and without the affectation he regards as a sin. And thus, it is only appropriate that in an age of travel writing, Parson Adams's educational journey is no grand tour to the beauties of Italy and France but a rural English alternative.[47]

Tobias Smollett, *Roderick Random* (1748), *Launcelot Greaves* (1762) and *Humphry Clinker* (1771)

Smollett, himself a frequent traveller, author and compiler of travel writing, is concerned with various types of accommodation in *Roderick Random*, *Launcelot Greaves* and *Humphry Clinker*, all novels structured by geographical and, ultimately, biographical journeys. In *Roderick Random*, the hero is a young man who makes his way into the world, gets into scrapes, voluntarily and involuntarily tries his hands at several jobs, has his flirts, marries his great love and, like in a fairy tale, ends up a wealthy man. Like few other eighteenth-century novels, *Roderick Random* presents a large number of sociable spaces, both rural and urban, in Britain, Europe and elsewhere. In the early part of the novel, Roderick travels from Scotland to London and acquaints himself with the city before he is forced to enlist and work on a ship. This geographical journey runs parallel with a social and educational one: when travelling with his friend Strap, Roderick visits inns, alehouses and taverns; later in London he frequents venues like a cook's shop, a boiling cellar, a gin-shop and other public eating and drinking places. While the novel is frequently concerned with money, or rather the lack of it, the hero is cheated more than once: the inns, alehouses and taverns mirror his ups and downs and familiarize him with a world in which he will, after many trials and tribulations, finally succeed.

Inns figure on his first major journey from Scotland to London, during which he is initiated into the mysteries of travelling. As his surname suggests, much of his geographical and social travelling is conducted without a clear aim. Roderick starts his journey on foot and must learn how to travel by waggon; he is also taught to distinguish between the lower-class alehouses and the better equipped inns through frequenting them. Little is said about interiors; the focus is on the many absurd scenarios. The inns Roderick and Strap visit are rural meeting-places for local gentlemen and vicars; as in *Joseph Andrews*, they are veritable microcosms of society.[48] The mingling of classes and the toning down of aristocratic codes becomes most obvious when a duel with razors is suggested, a weapon which Strap, the barber, would be able to use.[49] One characteristic these establishments share is that nothing is as it seems. This concerns not only financial transactions but also human encounters. Friendly interaction suddenly metamorphoses into hidden attacks on other characters' physical integrity or financial interests: a gambling curate, for example, uses his superior skills to win money from uneducated farmers.[50] Individual, social, legal and economic confusion reign. The inns' and taverns' potential to deceive climaxes one night when the two friends believe that they see ghosts: 'At that instant, a monstrous overgrown raven entered our chamber, with bells at its feet, and made directly towards our bed'.[51] Smollett uses a stock element from supernatural fiction only to discover to the reader that the apparition is the landlord's old father accompanied by his tame animal. Later in the novel, after returning from the navy, Roderick engages in another type of sociable occasions: 'plays, operas, masquerades, drums, assemblies and puppet-shews',[52] entertainments which are urban and fashionable, open to the middle and upper class and frequented by women, too; he also visits coffeehouses, leaving the institution of the country inn behind, both geographically and psychologically.

Unlike *Roderick Random*, Smollett's *Launcelot Greaves* does not recount a life in many episodes but focuses on a period of a few months, during which the hero is reunited with his true love. Sir Launcelot and his squire, who fight against a corrupt world, are modelled on *Don Quixote*. Sir Launcelot is roaming around the country and helps people exposed to various villainies, for example miscarriages of justice, while trying to regain his Aurelia, whose guardian tries to put obstacles between them and even briefly manages to get the lovers locked up in a madhouse. *Launcelot Greaves* is an early example of a serialized and illustrated novel by a major novelist; it appeared between January 1760 and January 1762 in the *British Magazine*, a journal edited by Smollett himself.[53] Unlike *Roderick Random*, *Launcelot Greaves* describes the inns' interiors in more detail, for example in the opening scene:

> It was on the great northern road from York to London, about the beginning of the month of October, and the hour of eight in the evening, that four travellers were by a violent shower of rain driven for shelter into a little public house on the side of the highway, distinguished by a sign which was said to exhibit the figure of a black lion. The kitchen, in which they assembled, was the only room for entertainment in the house, paved with red bricks, remarkably clean, furnished with three or four Windsor chairs, adorned with shining plates of pewter, and copper sauce-pans nicely scoured, that even dazzled the eyes of the beholder; while a cheerful fire of sea-coal blazed in the chimney. Three of the travellers, who arrived on horseback, having seen their cattle properly accommodated in the stable, agreed to pass the time, until the weather should clear up, over a bowl of rumbo, which was accordingly prepared: but the fourth, refusing to join their company, took his station at the opposite side of the chimney, and called for a pint of two-penny, with which he indulged himself apart. At a little distance, on his left hand, there was another groupe, consisting of the landlady a decent widow, her two daughters, the elder of whom seemed to be about the age of fifteen, and a country lad, who served both as waiter and ostler.[54]

This introductory paragraph, which is of a highly visual quality, introduces the characters. Smollett chose a small inn as his setting to appeal to his readers. The serialization necessitates an episodic rhythm, which is tied to the various inns as the characters' regular meeting-places. Unlike in *Roderick Random*, the inns are cast in a more positive light ('domestic temple of good society, and good fellowship', 'temple sacred to hospitality').[55] They often appear as homely places where Sir Launcelot meets friends and has important chance encounters, for example with the disguised Aurelia, whose rejection of his love, as he eventually finds out, has never occurred. The novel's intricate love plot would not be possible without inns. Moreover, inns also enable meetings between characters of varying social status: Sir Launcelot, the attorney Tom Clarke, Captain Crowe, servants and landladies. Inns remain the necessary nodal points in the plot until the very end when yet another error is cleared up: Dolly Cowslip, Aurelia's faithful servant, not only proves to be of genteel birth but is even related to Sir Launcelot. It is only through the inn hostess's intervention that Dolly is awarded the place in life that she is entitled to. The institution of the inn enables Sir Launcelot and his squire to pursue their Quixotic ideals, their code of honour, in the world, yet since different social groups meet, the knights in armour are not restricted to their own social class.

Inns and accommodation are a constant theme also in *Humphry Clinker*, an epistolary novel with several letter writers and thus shifting points of view, which narrates the story of a trip through England and Scotland, another instructive British home tour as opposed to the grand tour. Smollett, himself Scottish, made Scotland one of the settings. Since the group, led by the squire Matthew Bramble of Brambleton-hall, has sufficient means for this journey, they can afford to reside in comparatively comfortable spaces. In some towns they visit, for example in Bath, they rent houses, yet occasionally resort to inns. Inns are mentioned when the horses are changed or when the party takes a rest. However, if inns are interesting and desirable in *Joseph Andrews* and *Launcelot Greaves*, they are less-than-ideal solutions in *Humphry Clinker*. The ill-humoured Bramble complains: 'We therefore departed in the evening, and lay at an inn, where I caught cold'.[56] Describing a visit to squire Burdock, whose house fails to please him, Bramble moans: 'The house, though large, is neither elegant nor comfortable. – It looks like a great inn, crowded with travellers, who dine at the landlord's ordinary',[57] and compares the footmen to insolent waiters. Bramble, both misanthropic and generous, is rarely satisfied with any accommodation. Yet it is telling that he uses the word 'inn' more than once to denote his displeasure, while coffee-houses, mentioned more often than inns, appear in a more positive light. Unlike in *Launcelot Greaves*, the inns in *Humphry Clinker* are less central to the plot. It is at an inn where the company first meets Lismahago, while other important encounters, for example with the titular hero, occur on the road.

Eighteenth-century writers and artists had a tendency to imbue the country inn and the inn sign, its best-known visible representation, with associations of a mythical rural Englishness that was supposedly anti-luxurious, sociable, socially all-encompassing and occasionally carnivalesque. Inns were often cast as micro-cosms of society and of human experience. They were certainly nodal points of communication and continued the 'levelling' of society of which coffeehouses had been accused in the seventeenth century.[58] That this trope of the inn as a symbol of Englishness survived into the nineteenth and twentieth centuries may be due to the nostalgic need to recreate an ideal state at a time when railways and motorways allowed speedier travelling and reduced the need for but also the frisson of giving oneself up to an unknown host or hostess at a country inn. With the spread of the hotel, further differentiation set in, and travellers from different social and occupational groups were less likely to encounter one another.

6 DRINKING, FIGHTING AND WORKING-CLASS SOCIABILITY IN NINETEENTH-CENTURY BRITAIN

John Carter Wood

Introduction

Although it has become 'well established' by researchers that alcohol 'facilitates' violence, the precise relationship between intoxication and aggression remains unclear.[1] Since the late 1960s, some have emphasized cultural expectations rather than biochemical reactions. In 1969, Craig MacAndrew and Robert Edgerton argued that 'the way people comport themselves when they are drunk', including violent behaviour, 'is determined not by alcohol's toxic assault upon the seat of moral judgment, conscience, or the like, but by what their society makes of and imparts to them concerning the state of drunkenness'.[2] Their social-constructionist analysis of drunkenness as a 'time out' that allows one to ignore – within limits – behavioural norms was popular and has remained influential among anthropologically-minded alcohol researchers.[3] However, alcohol's physical effects have become better understood, and the most promising perspectives on alcohol and aggression consider a combination of physiological, social and cultural factors.[4] Here, I provide a historical perspective by examining alcohol and male fighting in nineteenth-century Britain. While there were other relevant contexts of violence, such as family abuse or rioting, male fighting was public, much commented-upon and often alcohol-related. A study of late nineteenth- and early twentieth-century English assault cases found that 'men were twice as often (27 per cent) involved in conflicts where both parties were drunk than women (13 per cent)'.[5] And, importantly, both fighting and drunkenness were becoming less tolerated in the nineteenth century.

The criminal justice system provides sources for investigating connections between drinking and violence. Those used here include, first, courtroom testimony from London's main criminal court for serious crime, the Old Bailey, which are now available online and have been sampled in years between 1830 and 1875. The trial reports in the *Old Bailey Proceedings* range from brief references to types of crime and verdicts (and, if appropriate, sentences) to extensive descriptions of criminal acts and their contexts.[6] A second, related set of sources are witness depositions from the south-eastern circuit of the 'assizes' – the main courts for adjudicating serious crime – between the 1820s and the 1870s. They contain information broadly similar to that in the *Old Bailey Proceedings* but deal with areas outside of metropolitan London.[7]

The most extensively described violent crimes were those that ended fatally, and I focus here on homicide cases, especially those ending in 'manslaughter' verdicts. The absence of intention to kill on the part of the accused and the presence of provocation by the victim made a 'manslaughter' (rather than 'murder') verdict likely: when fights ended fatally, manslaughter verdicts were common. Incidents of male fighting arose from disputes and what were referred to in contemporary legal texts as 'amicable contests'.[8] Dispute-related violence resulted from disagreements or challenges to one's reputation or honour. Drinking establishments, as key arenas of male sociability, were not only favoured locations for settling scores but also for 'amicable contests'. Such fights might sometimes have a recognizable goal (for example, determining who would buy whom a beer), but they were often also related to gaining or maintaining masculine honour. Indeed, there was often a remarkable amount of sociability between the participants before (and sometimes after) fights. Alcohol-linked violence was not only male: in 1835, for instance, Mary Ann Welch was convicted of manslaughter after killing Mary Watson outside the Oxford Arms public house in Deptford, where both had been drinking.[9] However, fighting in contexts of alcohol-related sociability was such a normal aspect of masculine behaviour as to have developed a set of explicit (if unwritten) cultural expectations that guided behaviour and allowed bystanders to judge its legitimacy.

Declining Tolerance for Drunkenness and Violence

The prevalence and legitimacy of serious violence, however, declined in the nineteenth century, continuing a downward trend since the late Middle Ages.[10] Despite periodic reverses and geographic anomalies, this was a significant trend.[11] However, it affected different classes at varying rates. Already in the eighteenth century, the middle and upper classes were withdrawing from aspects of a culture – previously shared across classes – in which public violence was acceptable for many reasons, such as establishing and defending a widely held notion of (predominantly male) 'honour'. 'Young gentlemen', Robert Shoemaker observes, 'shifted from the social group most likely to be accused of murder at the Old Bailey to the least'.[12] While all social groups were becoming *less* violent, there was a continuing tradition towards the lower end of the social scale for men to solve disputes, assert their masculinity and entertain themselves through fighting rituals.[13] A legacy of this fact is the continuing predominance of the unemployed and working-class men in fatal, dispute-related violence.[14]

There were customary expectations that fistfights would take place according to informally understood rules, framed by rituals of challenge and reconciliation.[15] Actual conduct did not necessarily follow cultural expectations: sometimes people 'broke the rules', fights might get out of hand and particularly enraged (or intoxicated) men started swinging without any of the standard preliminaries.[16] Despite its traditional legitimacy, the state was increasingly willing to prosecute violence (especially male violence) from the late eighteenth and throughout the nineteenth century.[17] For example, whereas eighteenth-century coroners' inquests judged fatalities resulting from fights as 'accidental', such deaths were treated more often as crimes by the 1820s and 1830s; judges, meanwhile, encouraged juries to convict, although punishments for consensual, 'fair' fights remained minor and often symbolic.[18]

Like violence, drunkenness faced increasing legal and social sanctions. Although there had been secular laws against it since the early seventeenth century (the 1606 Act governing the operation of alehouses described drunkenness as leading to 'Bloodshed, Stabbings, Murder, Swearing, Fornication, Adultery and such like'[19]), it was only in the early nineteenth century that it was substantially prosecuted, partly as a result of the development of modern police forces (though arresting drunks was not a task that the police always eagerly undertook) and of summary prosecutions at magistrates' courts.[20] In Salford, near Manchester, in the late 1840s, more than a third of arrests were for alcohol-related offences.[21] Licensing Acts in 1872 and 1902 both clarified the definitions of prohibited behaviour and gave the police and magistracy more power, bringing peaks in prosecution in the 1870s and the Edwardian period.[22] As is well known, the Victorian era saw cultural pressures towards respectability, changing gender expectations – particularly the idealization of restrained forms of masculinity – and the development of new forms of leisure. Excessive consumption of alcohol and participation in public violence were critiqued by those who saw themselves as 'respectable' and 'civilized', and both activities were targeted by a justice system that put changing social attitudes into action. Drunkenness and violence appear to have been declining for much of the century; however, what did the connection between alcohol and fighting look like?

Connections between Drink and Violence

Modern surveys suggest that alcohol is a factor in between 57 and 79 per cent of violent crimes in North America and Europe.[23] Nineteenth-century trials show that alcohol contributed to accidents, family conflict and child neglect. In 1850,

74 *Drink in the Eighteenth and Nineteenth Centuries*

for example, a woman was tried in London for killing her husband during a quarrel (he had told her she drank too much).[24] She blamed the victim: 'My husband was very much in the habit of ill-using me, and was very much addicted to drinking, and seldom or ever sober'. In another London case in 1870, a man and woman were charged with manslaughter for causing the death of the woman's child through neglect as they would often leave the children to go out drinking.[25] There were also cases of drunk driving, but the extent of carriage drivers' intoxication was often disputed.[26] Alcohol not only made the streets more dangerous. In 1830, four-year-old Mary Ann Nunen, who lived in Clerkenwell, London, died after drinking 'more than half a glass of rum' given her by a neighbouring tailor. 'I did not object to it', stated her mother, 'for the men who work for my husband have been in the habit of giving the children liquor from their infancy'. The prisoner defended himself by saying the child 'was in the habit of taking more than I gave her, and it never took the least effect – I did it merely from good nature; I and other men have given her more than she had then; the father and mother often saw her take more'.[27] In February 1875, William Corley came home drunk in Deptford, south-east of London. 'He was tipsy, he had been drinking ever since Christmas time', said one witness. He damaged a paraffin lamp, starting a fire, and a witness's description of his efforts to put it out would be comical had the result not been so tragic (the fire killed his daughter):

> It was smoking and in a blaze, he took it in his hand and tried to blow it out, but that made it worse, and when he found it was alight he threw it on the bed where we laid and set it all alight – there was a pail of water under the bed and he chucked the water, pail, and all into the bed, and then walked away and was not seen any more.[28]

While both men and women drank and became involved in violence, drink-related violence in public spaces was particularly common among men. Drinking substantial quantities of alcohol was an important and normal part of working-class male socialization. A witness in a London homicide trial expressed this nicely: 'The deceased was not', he testified, 'more addicted to drink *than men ordinarily are* – he was not a drunkard'.[29] Not all fights took place among intoxicated men, and much drinking took place peacefully; nonetheless, most fatal fighting cases appear to have involved some drinking, and many arose out of escalating confrontations in 'public houses', 'alehouses', 'taverns', 'beershops' or other, non-specified types of drinking establishments. Contemporary laboratory research has shown that even small amounts of alcohol can make subjects, particularly men, more easily and intensely provoked.[30] A review of relevant studies has pointed out that the 'prototypic violent event sequence is drinking – provocation – violence, where the provocation is most frequently in the form of a verbal argument'.[31]

A few nineteenth-century London trials suggest a similar pattern. I shall detail three such cases here: At the skittle ground at The Bell public house, Abraham Pomroy had been drinking with Richard Dukes and others for about three hours in June 1830. As a witness put it, 'they were a little fresh, but they knew what they were doing'. At some point, 'Pomroy took up a pot of beer, and stood before the skittle-ground to prevent their playing'. He then 'threw the pot of beer across the ground, and bent the pot nearly double'. The dispute escalated: 'Dukes said, "Don't throw that beer away, you did not pay for it" – Pomroy then said he had paid for as much as [Dukes]; Pomroy then gave [Dukes] a shove – they had a scuffle together, and they both fell'.[32] Pomroy died of internal bleeding caused by a fractured skull. In October 1850, a fight broke out in The Ship in Limehouse between James Northeast and William Arnold.[33] 'A few words passed' between Arnold and Northeast, who were both drunk. 'The prisoner was rather in liquor', said a witness, and 'the deceased was intoxicated'. Arnold had provoked Northeast: 'As soon as Arnold came in he began blackguarding, singing, and dancing, and making use of very bad language'. (A witness described Arnold as 'a very drunken dissipated little fellow'.) Northeast dragged Arnold into the street, striking him fatally. A surgeon testified that Arnold's 'concussion of the brain' may have been 'caused by a fall'. 'Drunken persons', he added, 'have a good many falls'. Finally, The Zetland Arms, South Kensington, was the scene of a fatal brawl in April 1875.[34] Comments, or possibly insults, about the Devonshire origins of some people in the pub caused a general 'scuffle'. A policeman cleared the bar, later testifying that 'twelve or fourteen of the people in the public-house were the worse for liquor'. Once outside, fighting resumed, causing the death of John Damerell from a fractured skull.

Of course, even completely sober men issued and responded to insults and challenges, and some drunken fights were the culmination of long-simmering tensions that had nothing to do with drink.[35] After a fight at a fair in Hertfordshire in 1830 that led to the death of John Walding, a witness recounted that Thomas Owen had approached Walding while he was drinking in a public house: 'some conversation ensued between Owen and Walding about a quarrel they had had in the winter. The deceased then struck Owen and they went on to the Green to fight'.[36] Similarly, a fatal brawl at a public house in Woolwich in 1827 began when John Rice challenged Thomas Stevens:

> Rice said to Stevens, who was acting as a waiter, 'I understand that last Saturday night you degraded my character,' and Stevens said he would be damned if he had ever said a word against his character, and other words passed between them, and Rice said to Stevens he (Rice) was a man, and Stevens said the same to Rice, and Rice struck Stevens with his fist on the mouth which knocked Stevens down on his breech.[37]

This sort of fighting was a common way for working-class men to settle disputes.

In cases of so-called 'amicable contests' no provocation was necessary. A petition seeking a reduced sentence for John Langley, imprisoned six months for fatally striking William Thorp, suggested the atmosphere in which they arose:

> In September 1835, a number of agricultural labourers had been drinking in a neigh-
> bouring parish, and (as is too often the case) two men, John Langley and William
> Thorp, both intoxicated, agreed to fight 2 rounds without any quarrel whatever. To
> be brief, at the 2nd blow William Thorp fell & in about an hour died.[38]

They were 'old friends', and the deceased's brother spoke in the accused's favour at the trial and signed his petition. Such fights were seen as normal, even playful.[39] A carpenter noticed two young men fighting at his work site, later recalling, 'they were scuffling with one another and I thought at play': one of them later died.[40] Such impromptu fights gathered enthusiastic crowds at fairs, and some men fought several times.[41] The fight that killed John Walding was not his first: a labourer had seen him fighting earlier with a man named Job Stone. 'I saw Stone knocked him down three or four times', the witness said, noting that he had seen the fighters surrounded by a 'crowd'.[42]

The reference to the crowd here reminds us that this type of fighting was only culturally relevant and legitimate in public: it was a performance, and one must take into account not only the impact of the alcohol itself but also of the expectation that violence would be a likely outcome of drinking in certain places. Historical sources are fragmentary; however, the influence of social pressure is clear: men felt obliged to respond to challenges or insults to 'save face'. Contemporary research has shown that 'social pressure, even when subjects were intoxicated, significantly increased aggressive behavior'.[43] But whether sober or drunk, fighters were expected to respect certain limits. The legitimacy of a fight did not depend on observance of all the formal customary rules (with a ring, rounds and 'seconds' for each fighter), but 'fairness' – which mainly meant refraining from using 'foul blows', hitting a man while he was down or employing weapons – was important even if men had been drinking. Strikingly, even very drunk men did often abide by such expectations.[44] Robert Shoemaker reports a half-hour fight between two men in 1751, which ended with them shaking hands: 'Given the fact that the participants were so drunk "that as they went to strike at each other they missed their blows"', he observes, 'their adherence to the rules is even more remarkable'.[45]

Ethnographic research emphasizes the cultural shaping of intoxicated aggression. David Riches has noted that, even when drunk, Eskimo men in Canada respected certain limits; later, they blamed their behaviour on drunkenness, thereby avoiding the full consequences of their actions (that is losing a job or state benefit).[46] A study of intoxicated violence within an Australian aboriginal community has similarly shown how cultural expectations influence violence: rather than alcohol spontaneously causing conflict, drinking – especially group drinking – is part of a strategy for dealing with existing conflicts.[47]

In nineteenth-century England, physical aggression in drinking contexts, while expected, was not necessarily seen as ideal. A defence of pugilism contended that 'men ought not to be encouraged to fight while their blood is up;

because when their blood is up their reason is down, and that state of irritation mostly happens when they are in drink'. The 'office of true humanity', therefore, was to 'dissuade men from fighting when their blood is up, and to persuade them to wait until the next day, or some after period, when it has become cool'.[48] A participant in one 1827 fight suggested postponing it until he and his adversary would both be 'solid and sober together'; his opponent, however, was 'in the humour' and wanted to continue.[49] 'The disorder of drunkenness, even its violence', Martin Wiener concludes, 'was accepted as virtually inevitable, particularly for the poor'.[50]

Alcohol was also an accompaniment to reconciliation. One man claimed he had sought to interrupt a fight at a fair in 1830 in just this way. 'They fought about an hour and ten minutes', he testified, but 'neither of them wished to give over. I recommended them to give over and go and have a pot of beer together'.[51] His suggestion was ignored, but it did sometimes work out that way. At the trial of Thomas Owen for killing John Walding, Job Stone testified that he had not only known the deceased but even fought him himself: 'After fighting we drank together and shook hands. We sat together at the Coach and Horses about half an hour'.[52] On balance, however, it is doubtful that alcohol was more often a solution than a cause of conflict. Britain's authorities, certainly, saw it as a threat.

Alcohol, Violence and Criminal Justice

As Dave Marteau notes, 'moral disapproval of alcohol became just about hysterical in the second part of the nineteenth century', as 'criminality, sloth, violence and licentious[ness] were all put at alcohol's door'.[53] 'Drink', Martin Wiener observes, 'became perhaps the leading explanation for crime'.[54] The reform of this situation was part of a broader effort to 'civilize' the working class. Support for 'temperance' came from evangelicalism and liberalism. It appealed to 'temperate, self-improving, respectable, and socially responsible citizens of all classes in the interests of progress', who attacked 'reactionary defenders of the status quo, those involved in drink, in betting, in brutal sports or lacking sexual restraint'.[55] The temperance movement's impact is uncertain, though likely marginal, but the policing of drunkenness became far more intensive.

Those charged with maintaining law and order clearly viewed pubs as cradles of vice and a major cause of violence. In 1836, a correspondent to the Secretary of State, referring to an assault on two Leamington constables at an inn, complained: 'these assaults are continuously taking place of a *Sunday* in public houses'.[56] Concerns about alcohol and violence increased in the second half of the century. In 1868, the Chief Constable of Leeds wrote that 'an extended closing of public houses on Sunday would lead to the promotion of good order'. 'I am sure', he added, 'that so long as the working classes imbibe the decoctions of bar sellers there will not only be drunkenness and poverty but crimes of open violence among us'.[57] Such complaints were prominent in a government report on 'brutal assaults' in 1875. Justice Keating asserted: 'I believe nine-tenths of the crimes of violence committed throughout England originate in public houses, and are committed under circumstances which exclude all reflection'.[58] A judge urged the strict suppression of drunkenness: drinking was 'in many cases actually causing, and in many more accompanying, the commission of these offenses'.[59] Senior police officials pointed to increased leisure and higher wages. The Chief Constable of Staffordshire reported: 'I consider this increase [in brutal assaults] to be attributable to the great increase of wages and to the shorter hours of labour, the former leading to increased drunkenness, and the latter to increased time and opportunity for domestic and out-door brawling'.[60] Another chief constable explained:

> It is difficult to attribute this increase [in brutal assaults] with certainty to any particular cause, but, as intoxication is generally shown to have existed at the time of the assault, and is usually pleaded in mitigation of punishment, it is fair to presume that the higher rate of wages lately obtained has afforded a rough and uneducated class greater opportunities for excessive drinking, and has so led to the increased commission of the offenses recorded in this return.[61]

The status of intoxication as a legal defence (because it prevented the formation of malicious intent) had long been controversial. Some judicial rulings (and many juries' decisions) legitimized a 'drink defence',[62] and drunkenness had often led to milder sentences. Such tolerance diminished after the mid-nineteenth century: reflecting this shift, John Stuart Mill argued that people who demonstrated a tendency to violence when drinking alcohol should be prosecuted if found drunk: 'The making himself drunk in a person whom drunkenness excites to do harm to others is a crime against others', he claimed, arguing that punishments for their violent offences 'should be increased in severity'.[63] However, as Wiener notes,

> ever-more-firmly reiterated principles of strict personal responsibility and the intolerability of violent behaviour, as they gained power in determining verdicts and ultimate dispositions, had in practice to compromise with the continuing inclination of most men – whether we call it pragmatism, resentment of teetotal preachiness, humanitarianism or (in the case of domestic violence) male chauvinism – to see drunkenness as some mitigation of a homicide.[64]

Indeed, a witness at one homicide trial said the accused 'was in such a state of intoxication as to make him incapable of doing any injury to any man'; combined with other circumstantial evidence, this may have contributed to his acquittal.[65] If the intoxication coincided with other mitigating factors, such as provocation, 'fair' fighting, or good character, it was relevant. But the opposite was also true. A father's letter to the Home Office in 1838 seeking a lesser punishment for his son in a non-fatal case of 'cutting and wounding' argued that the affair arose 'at a late hour in the evening' when his son 'was in liquor': he was 'satisfied if he had not been so the unfortunate affair would never have occurred'.[66] That a weapon was used in the dispute (and that the victim was a police officer) contributed to the harsh sentence of fifteen-years' transportation and to the petition's denial. It would likely have had even less chance later in the century, with the declining acceptance of intoxication and violence in the late Victorian 'assault on aggressive masculinity'.[67]

The acceptability of the 'drink defence' varied across the United Kingdom. Judges condemned the notion that any 'rowdy, drunken ruffian was to be let off scot free simply because he made himself too drunk to understand what he was doing'; however, English, Welsh and especially Irish juries were less likely to convict if both fighters were drunk. Scottish justice, by contrast, saw drunkenness as an aggravating rather than a mitigating factor.[68] In England and Wales, as Carolyn Conley notes, drunkenness had a complicated impact on verdicts (reached by juries) and sentences (set by judges) in homicide cases: 'Though English and Welsh juries were less likely to return *murder* convictions if the killers had been drunk, judges were harsher in sentencing'. 'English authorities', she concludes 'may have been more concerned about drunken violence than were middle-class jurymen who were rarely threatened by it'.[69] A survey of the Home Office's implementation of 'bureaucratic mercy' reveals that 'the factor of drunkenness had become increasingly irrelevant ... and, by 1900 the "rule" in this respect was that it only became a consideration when its symptoms could be equated with permanent insanity'.[70]

However, in a homicide trial, the *victim's* drunkenness might also be relevant. A surgeon testifying in a London case in 1850 gave a remarkable description of the victim's fragile state: 'I attribute the cause of death to this, I think the man was lying down on a bench and had been drinking, and got his head exceedingly congested or full of blood, and a very slight blow in that state would produce death'. Cross-examined, he stated: 'everybody who gets thoroughly drunk is in a state *very nearly approaching apoplexy every moment he lives* – the least stimulant is likely to cause it, they are always subject to it'.[71] The accused was acquitted; however, in a fatal fighting case among women, a surgeon's testimony that the cause of death was 'apoplexy' caused by alcohol did not prevent a conviction.[72] Such testimony was common.[73]

Conclusion

As contemporary debates show, the relationship between alcohol and violence is complex. Research has pointed, however, to the relevance of 'highly scripted rituals of drinking' among groups of young males in bars, highlighting 'the importance of studying naturally occurring aggressive behaviour' outside of laboratory contexts.[74] Historical evidence provides only partial insights, but offers potentially useful contextual and comparative information on the interrelationship between intoxication and aggression, especially since the need to develop a multi-causal model taking into account social, cultural and situational factors alongside alcohol's basic pharmacological effects has become clear. Alcohol was an ingredient in working-class fighting in the nineteenth-century;-however, it was rarely its sole cause. Sober fights were similar to drunken ones, and even when drunk, men often observed customary constraints. The extent to which men chose to seek out (and resolve) their disputes in pubs and taverns involves both alcohol itself as well as expectations of what drinking it entails.

However, while emphasizing the important role of culture, I think historical evidence raises questions about MacAndrew and Edgerton's notion, referred to in the introduction above, that alcohol provides an exemption, a 'time out' from social rules and expectations. In this I would agree with two points from J. H. Shore and P. Spicer's critique of that approach, based on their study of intoxicated violence within an Australian aboriginal community. First, although historical studies, like ethnographic ones, cannot directly explore alcohol's pharmacological effects, it is doubtful, as they point out, that drunken behaviour 'is almost purely socially constructed'.[75] A perspective combining biological and cultural insights will usefully contribute to a more interdisciplinary understanding of human psychology and behaviour. Secondly, the nineteenth-century context also recalls Shore and Spicer's finding that, 'rather than functioning as an excuse for behaviour, drunken comportment functions as a medium through which tensions and conflicts are played out'.[76] Instead of intoxicated violence providing an *escape* from social rules, as in the 'time out' model, it appears that it operates more as an *extension* of normal social relationships. Alcohol plays a role in much violence; still, we cannot, it seems, blame it all simply on the bottle. Continuing efforts to combine pharmacological, psychological, social, cultural and historical perspectives on the alcohol–violence connection is the most fruitful way of understanding this enduring phenomenon.

7 ROMANTIC RADICALISM AND THE TEMPERANCE MOVEMENT

Rolf Lessenich

Any reader of nineteenth-century novels, from Elizabeth Gaskell's *Mary Barton* (1848) to Emile Zola's *L'Assommoir* (1877), will be well aware of the literary probing into the causes of alcoholism among the poor. Self-indulgence, nervous disorders and social or genetic dispositions were among the explanations produced at the time.[1] Nineteenth-century literature teems with representations both of drunkenness and of temperance campaigns with a religious or medical motivation, culminating in the teetotalism campaign for abstinence not only from spirits, but from alcohol in general. In the age of gin palaces in the great industrial cities, temperance tracts and cheap repository tracts for the poor were legion. In earlier centuries, discoveries and conjectures in philosophy, medicine and science were published both in prose and poetry, and literati and psychologists explored new fields such as the unconscious simultaneously.[2] In the words of the Radical temperance advocate Erasmus Darwin, pioneering doctor of medicine, innovative scientist and advocate of a change of the *radix* (root) of the feudal structure of society, it was thought beneficent 'to inlist Imagination under the banner of Science'.[3] Hence, the fiction, poetry, diaries, letters, periodicals, sermons, tracts and medical treatises that deal with the consumption of various kinds of alcohol, interwoven as they often were with national and colonial discourses, must be brought into dialogue. Radicals like Erasmus Darwin, advocates of the egalitarian and republican ideals of the French Revolution in the sense of a return to what they believed to have been the original state of nature and man, thus tended to propagate fresh water and vegetarian food instead of alcohol and meat against old Tory-associated habits, for both ideological and medical reasons.

Drowning one's cares in alcohol has been a worrying cultural practice as old as mankind: witness the stigmatization of drunkenness, though not necessarily of wine consumed in moderation, in the world's Holy Books. In the Bible, for example, the comforting ritual drink during the Last Supper and the Eucharist are sharply distinguished from the destructive intoxication of Noah and Lot. Throughout the ages, a distinction has always been made between the beneficent

– 81 –

and the disastrous effects of alcohol, depending on the kind, ritual, occasion, form and quantity of consumption. William Hogarth's engraving *Gin Lane* (1751) shows the disastrous effects of drunkenness and its connection with poverty in a London street, whereas Hogarth's contrastive companion piece, *Beer Street* (1751), celebrates the benefit of plentiful consumption of native beer. Gin, that is, Dutch 'genever' spiced with juniper or *genévrier* berries, only came to England with the 'foreign' King William of Orange. The Gin Craze of the early eighteenth century, favoured by the over-production of grain due to agricultural reforms, led to widespread intoxication and crime, especially among the frustrated poor, as it took only two pence to get drunk on gin. The Gin Acts of 1736 and 1751, controlling and effectively reducing the consumption of gin, advanced the cause of the Tories and their idea of healthy Englishness.[4]

The disastrous effects of unhealthy nutrition were visible in the streets. As opposed to the poor, the 'middling and affluent classes'[5] tended to suffer from gout and therefore often stood in need of sedan chairs. It was argued to be their curse that they could afford plenty of meat and red wine; and red wine, gin and rum were un-English imports from France, Holland and the West Indian colonies, respectively. Eighteenth-century medical literature, in prose and verse, advanced various theories of ingestion that stood on a clearly ideological basis. They give a certain support to Michel Foucault's concept of power-knowledge, at least with regard to the rising social esteem of doctors in the late eighteenth century, who had formerly been standard butts of ridicule and now began to pose as regulators of the body politic.[6] There was a politics of drink just as there was a politics of sex, and both were hotly debated. Tories like Henry Fielding and Hogarth together with their successors in the Romantic Period, such as the editors of *Blackwood's Edinburgh Magazine* and its 'Noctes Ambrosianae' (1822–35), praised plentiful, especially native food and drink for pleasure, nervous stability and good company. When James Cobb and Stephen Storace, later the authors of the musical entertainment *The Doctor and the Apothecary* (1789), adapted the Marquis de Sade's sacrilegious play *La tour enchantée* (1788) as a burletta for the London stage, they flattered the censors by giving it a conservative turn in revolutionary times, adding merry songs in praise of the British navy and of native English beer, in disdain of foreign wines:

> As now we're met, a jolly set,
> A fig for sack or sherry;
> Our ale we'll drink,
> And our cans we'll clink,
> And we'll be wondrous merry.[7]

Drinking gin, however, remained a stigma associated with criminals and traitors. In a splendid anonymous anti-Romantic parody of Coleridge's 'Christabel' entitled 'Christabess' (1816), the heroine is not the expected virgin from a medieval castle, but a vulgar prostitute from a criminal area of London, badly in need of immediate sexual gratification. As she meets another woman in the forest she smuggles her home into her father's filthy den. Not only do the two women get drunk with gin, they also lapse into an orgy that replaces the magic devilry of Geraldine's embrace with openly avowed and intoxicated lesbian love. Even more devastating is the representation of gin in a political caricature of 1794, 'A Peace Offering to the Genius of Liberty and Equality' by Isaac Cruikshank, the father of George Cruikshank and a diehard Tory. It stigmatizes the advocates of a peace with revolutionary France as traitors who sacrifice healthy nourishing Whitbread ale to the French Marianne, a drunk and bloodthirsty prostitute with Medusa hair sitting on barrels of a foreign drink: gin, of course.[8] And a caricature by William Heath derogates the newly founded University College London (1826) and its Whig efforts aiming at academic education for the masses as a hotbed of revolution and drunkenness. The spirit in which the rebellious lower classes are here instructed is, again, gin.[9]

In contrast to this obvious Toryism, numerous Radical Whigs and Dissenters, later advocates of the French Revolution,[10] increasingly recommended a moderate and frugal diet for the sustenance of physical and mental health: vegetarian food and fresh water. It was from them that temperance as a nineteenth-century mass movement emerged in the 1820s and 1830s. The moderate John Edgar (1798–1866), who campaigned against strong liquors only, and the Radical Joseph Livesey (1794–1884), who as a 'teetotaller' campaigned against all alcoholic drinks, were Dissenters and abolitionists. Abolitionists campaigned not only against rum, but also against sugared tea, with a view to the exploitation of slaves in the West Indian sugar fields. A caricature by James Gillray, 'Anti-Saccharites or John Bull and his Family Leaving off the Use of Sugar', dating from 1792, shows how King George III and Queen Charlotte habituate their reluctant children (that is, their subjects) to drinking their tea without sugar.[11] In the history of nutritional medicine, these were old recommendations. But now they became charged with strong political overtones, linked with patriotism, religion, sensibility, abolition of slavery and the anti-colonial discourse of the day.

A similar paradox between approval and rejection of intoxicating drink can be observed in poetics. The Classical Tradition saw wine as a source of inspiration for the poet and asked the question of 'an vinum fit poetam' (whether wine makes a poet). Alexander Pope, for example, imagined the waters of Helicon as intoxicating wine in a notable paradox: 'There *shallow Draughts* intoxicate the Brain, / And drinking *largely* sobers us again.'[12]

By contrast, Radicals and Preromantic primitivists with their belief in the superior virtue and superior happiness of men at an early stage of civilization[13] tended to locate true imaginative poetry in the uncivilized past, when, as they believed, natural man had drunk clear spring water and had not yet invented the production of wine. Thomas Trotter, a well-known Radical Scottish physician, nerve theorist and close friend of Erasmus Darwin, wrote in his *Essay on Drunkenness* (1804):

> Poetry, the first of the fine arts, took its rise among shepherds in the early ages of society, when the manners of mankind, as well as their diet, were simple; when the fermentation of the juice of the grape was unknown, and when the vine itself, either sprung up spontaneously, or was only cultivated as a fruit tree.[14]

While both sides agreed on the pernicious nature of wine and spirits, Radical nutritionists were divided over the question of beer. Whereas wine was imported, beer was a national product and was widely regarded as healthy liquid bread. Hogarth's national discourse on wine and beer thus proved its endurance. Moreover, British and Germanic ancestors were known to have drunk stupendous quantities of beer, as detailed in *De Germania* by Tacitus. Trotter admitted that, in contradistinction to wine and spirits, beer was a 'wholesome drink', and he justified his cultural primitivism by pointing out that his ancestors had 'counteracted the effects of intoxication' by regular and intensive physical exercise.[15] The Radical printer, vegetarian and nutritionist George Nicholson supported Trotter's national-primitivist view of the wholesomeness of beer:

> Mead was formerly the favourite liquor of the Ancient Britons and Anglo-Saxons. It still retains it's [*sic*] place at country feasts in the western parts of this island ... Being a wholesome and pleasant beverage, it is far preferable to brandy, gin, or other pernicious spirits.[16]

Long before Trotter and Nicholson and their egalitarianism, abolitionism and politics of national nutrition, James Thomson had anticipated some of their positions in *The Seasons* (1726–30), where he describes primitivism, vegetarianism and animal rights as conducive to virtue and happiness. Thomson himself was well-known for his luxurious and lazy life in London and Richmond, featuring large quantities of alcohol and meat, no physical exercise and late hours. This Scottish Dissenter in religion was also an early Preromantic Dissenter in ethics and aesthetics, when his speaker, a 'man of feeling', meditates in solitude upon himself and the world's need for reforms. He indicts false luxury and commends early rising, healthy natural food and drink, and cathartic introspection of the soul. His association of clear plentiful water with bliss is already linked to an anti-colonial discourse, as colonialism spoils the happiness of both the colonized and the colonizers. In Thomson's view, the British colonies with their fresh water, from which un-British luxuries are imported, once were 'The seat of blameless Pan, yet undisturbed / By Christian crimes and Europe's cruel sons'.[17]

Whereas the Radical hygienists Thomas Trotter and George Nicholson concentrated on medical aspects of the consumption of alcoholic drinks, the Radical Joseph Ritson was a man of literature and an antiquary, famous for his view of Robin Hood as a primitive Anglo-Saxon rebel against the cultivated French Normans. In his *Essay on Abstinence from Animal Food as a Moral Duty* (1802), he frequently quoted from Thomson's *Seasons* as well as from numerous classical and modern authors in support of natural food and drink: water, milk, fruit berries and roots being the nourishment of his eleventh-century champion of *liberté, égalité, fraternité* in Sherwood Forest.

By contrast, advocates of Britain's mercantile progress praised the importation of foreign luxuries as cultural enrichment by interchange. The debate over the Italian opera in England at the time of Handel (1711–41) featured such ideas. In retrospect, Charles Burney's *History of Music* (1776–89) argued that, as the Romans imported fine arts from Greece, so the British legitimately import fine arts from the modern Romans, the Italians, the leading nation in music: 'This last art is a manufacture of Italy, that feeds and enriches a large portion of the people; and it is no more disgraceful to a mercantile country to import it, than wine, tea, or any other production of remote parts of the world'.[18]

Typical of early Preromanticism as it was, primitivism was often a mere dissenting pose, best exemplified by the gluttonous James Thomson. Yet this sense of theatricality changed into an ideology as Preromanticism turned into Radicalism. The well-known Radical nerve theorist Thomas Beddoes, father of the poet Thomas Lovell Beddoes and a major figure in the earlier phase of British Romanticism, peppered Thomson's criticism in his anti-colonial prose and verse. Sentimental egalitarianism was the basis of Beddoes's medical creed, as he saw both savages and madmen as fellow human beings and not as creatures of inferior rank and quality, as would have been customary in the eighteenth century. Nerves were healthy as long as the good instincts of man, his universal social sympathies, were educated and prevailed; shattered nerves were symptomatic of man's evil instincts. Taught to regard others with disrespect, he argued, colonialist soldiers can feel no sympathy, which rouses their greed as well as their cruelty and makes them deprive the colonized peoples of their natural resources such as sugar cane after initiating and habituating them to alcohol.

Lack of social sympathy, combined with excessive consumption of foreign food and drink, could not but undermine the colonizers' nervous health. Beside numerous medical treatises written in a simple and knowledge-sharing prose, Beddoes published *Alexander's Expedition* (1792), a didactic poem on the evil effects of colonialism on both the colonizers and the colonized, which, like Thomson's, linked alcohol with disease and water with health. Beddoes's indictment of Alexander's 'ardent thirst of Glory and of Power' moreover associates inordinate drinking with inordinate passion.[19] As usual in Romantic primitivism, the Classical Tradition of Greece and Rome with its cult of wine, orgies and expansion is disparaged in favour of a British tradition of sober contentment on one's own native soil. The teaching of Greek and Latin should be discontinued; native sentimental education should replace the classical education of British children.[20] Significantly, Beddoes attacked the Tory Prime Minister William Pitt the Younger, a strong advocate of the Classical Tradition and an addict to port, for poisoning the people, especially the frustrated poor, by promoting taxed alcohol, merely to fill the coffers of the state treasury in times of war: 'The distilleries alone – "those manufactories of disease which take their bread from the people and convert it into poison" – paid into the exchequer not much less than a million yearly'.[21] Moreover, in a public lecture on healthy living, the hygienist Beddoes attributed the gloom and spleen, a typically English disease, to 'the abuse of strong beer and wine' and recommended water as the best drink for the maintenance of the health of an Englishman's body and soul. A drinker of water, Beddoes claimed, was 'by no means deficient in cheerfulness' when compared with a 'bacchanalian' drinker of wine.[22]

Another Radical doctor by training and profession, the poet John Keats, though a sensualist who imaginatively wallowed in 'a beaker full of the warm South',[23] advocated fresh water instead of strong wine for similar medical and socio-political reasons. Touring the Lake District in preparation of his Scottish tour of 1818, Keats complained of the corruption of country people by their reading about the pampered life and feudal society of London; he likewise complained of Wordsworth's turn to Toryism, his drinking and dining at the table of the Earl of Lonsdale and his inviting of guests to his own lordly table 'instead of being in retirement'.[24] But Keats was glad to find remnants of healthy rural simplicity in the border inhabitants, as he wrote to his brother Tom in London: 'They are quite out of keeping with the romance about them, from a continued intercourse with London rank and fashion. But why should I grumble? They gave me a prime glass of soda water'.[25]

Keats belonged to the Radical circle of Leigh Hunt in rural Hampstead, together with William Hazlitt, Charles Lamb and Barry Cornwall. In a groundbreaking study of Keats, Nicholas Roe has produced evidence that Keats's teachers of medicine were actually Radical doctors, as Radical thought was widespread among English physicians.[26] As an antidote to the multiplying dirt and rapidly growing population of London and to the restored *ancien régime*, the Hampstead group advocated small circles of affectionate friends, greenery and fresh air, as well as the cult of the leveller Robin Hood, green being the old and new colour of protest against regimes in power. Keats's literary promoter Leigh Hunt himself called upon Englishmen to adopt a healthier country life near the modern city, and, with many Romantic physicians and the authority of Paracelsus, he diagnosed excess of food and drink as causing diseases of body and mind. In the 'Preface' to his collection of poems with the significant title of *Foliage* (1818), Hunt's *exemplum horrendum* was Germany, for centuries reputed to be the country of eating and drinking to excess. In Hunt's view, this excess explained the German penchant towards ponderousness, including the lingering sickly imagination of the German storm-and-stress poets. Modern thought had not taught the Germans to eat and drink less, not even the German Romantics such as Goethe and Schlegel:

> The body of the German people, though it had a good shake given it by the French revolution ... does not seem to have recovered yet from the nightmares of its old eating and drinking habits, and its sedentary school divinity.[27]

By contrast and in the wake of Preromantic sensibility and primitivism, the Romantic poets inclined more towards fresh water and vegetarian food, whereas their adversaries, advocates of the classical as well as political tradition of the Greeks, Romans and the *ancien régime*, raised the consumption of stupendous amounts of meat, wine and beer to the level of a show of political allegiance. Wordsworth's change of diet reflected his gradual change of politics around 1800, from Radicalism to Toryism. Keats intensely disliked Wordsworth for this and other reasons. He preferred to see himself in the tradition of the earlier Radical Romantic poet William Blake, whose central creed, Neoplatonist and Gnostic antinomian philosophy, was widespread, though Keats, Percy Shelley and others knew little if anything of him directly.[28] And Charles Lamb, a notorious alcoholic ever on the verge of madness, publicly regretted his addiction in *Confessions of a Drunkard* (1821), associating fresh water with childhood and original, natural, holy, uncorrupted living:

> O if a wish could transport me back to those days of youth, when a draught from the next clear spring could slake any heats which summer suns and youthful exercise had power to stir up in the blood, how gladly would I return to thee, pure element, the drink of children, and of child-like holy hermit.[29]

Following the equation of health and water, Preromantic psychiatry turned away from the Classical Tradition's use of wine as an anti-depressive. Instead, it treated patients by gradually diluting their 'wine, rum, brandy, or geneva' with water.[30] William Perfect, a Radical psychologist who built his asylum in the country (West Malling, Kent) instead of the city (London), saw one of the origins of insanity in overindulgence in luxuries, especially rich and foreign food and drink, and prescribed the reduction of such drink to nil. Interestingly enough he does not even mention native beer.

By contrast, Preromantic psychologists who treated their mad patients as fellow creatures rather than the pathological other did recommend moderate quantities of wine as medicine, in order to raise their depressive patients' spirits

Drink in the Eighteenth and Nineteenth Centuries

and to reintegrate them into social circles. According to Philippe Pinel, such so-called 'traitement moral', meaning mental treatment, assumed madmen to be quantitatively, not qualitatively deranged, and diagnosed the origin of the disease in the mind's suffering from social injustice and social exclusion, thus exhibiting a typically pre-revolutionary stance. These innovative psychologists were members of democratic philosophical and literary clubs in London, Manchester or Edinburgh, where science was as openly discussed as literature and politics. Here, drink was an indispensable habit of group formation and conviviality. Nevertheless, Andrew Duncan, professor in the medical faculty of the University of Edinburgh, reputed to be the best in Britain and one of the best in all Europe, saw himself obliged to excuse his recommendation of some wine both for mental patients and for himself in humorous Hudibrastics:

> From business and from sickness free,
> Aged precisely Sixty-three,
> I have resolv'd on this my birth-day,
> With generous wine to moisten stiff clay. [31]

Moderate quantities of wine were reputed not only to raise the spirit of mentally ill patients, but also to strengthen weak constitutions in cases of physical sickness. George Nicholson made a strong case against the regular consumption of fermented grapes by healthy people, identifying 'wines and spirits' as 'the curse of the Christian world', but allowed them as medicine: 'They [wines] are useful as medical potions to comfort those who are sick'.[32] In medical theory, medicine administered to health produces sickness.

This explains the exception in the 'pledge of *total* abstinence' formulated by the otherwise uncompromising teetotaller Joseph Livesey of the Preston Temperance Society of 1832: 'We agree to abstain from all liquors of an intoxicating quality whether ale, porter, wine or ardent spirits, except as medicines'.[33] The London Temperance Hospital, built by the National Temperance League in London's Hampstead Road in 1873, also allowed exceptions from the teetotalling rule when doctors thought wine or beer necessary for a depressive or weak patient's treatment.[34]

In the writings of Radical hygienists and poets, wine is mostly associated with poison and disease. Poisoned wine had long been a favourite motif. In the Gothic novel *Zofloya* (1806) by Charlotte Dacre, the daughter of a well-known Radical writer, the motif is elaborated to dominate the story. Poor Berenza, who, against the advice of his doctors, firmly believes in wine's restorative power, is slowly poisoned by his villainous wife Victoria.[35] It is only for short intervals that the wine raises the victim's spirits, only to herald worse collapses. In the Radical doctor John Keats's 'Ode to a Nightingale' (1819), the bubbles of the seemingly refreshing red wine are clearly linked to the consumptive poet's fits of blood-spitting, a desire for self-annihilation that confirms the mainstream Radical rejection of alcohol:

Oh, for a draught of vintage that hath been
Cooled a long age in the deep-delvèd earth,
Tasting of Flora and the country green,
Dance, and Provençal song, and sunburnt mirth!
Oh, for a beaker full of the warm South,
Full of the true, the blushful Hippocrene,
With beaded bubbles winking at the brim,
And purple-stainèd mouth,
That I might drink, and leave the world unseen,
And with thee fade away into the forest dim –[36]

Some Radicals, however, were jolly topers or even heavy drinkers, among them Robert Burns. Burns notably celebrated the drinking of alcohol both as a source of inspiration and as an anodyne for the poor and sick. The Scottish abolitionist, physician and Radical temperance activist James Currie, Burns's first posthumous editor and first biographer (1800), diagnosed intemperate drinking as the cause of his friend's early demise.[37] This, however, he formulated with extreme respect to the principle of *de mortuis nil nisi bene*, as a warning to all 'men of feeling' and poetic genius. What Keats and Burns had in common was not only their incurable illness and early death, but also the note of despairing defiance that clung to their verses in praise of intoxication. Dutch courage was needed to face the threat of poverty, hunger, pain, depression and death in a world full of disease and injustice, a serious thought even in the comical ballad of Burns's *Tam o' Shanter* (1791):

Inspiring bold *John Barleycorn*!
What dangers thou canst make us scorn!
Wi' tippeny, we fear nae evil;
Wi' usquabae, we'll face the devil![38]

Burns's poem 'Scotch Drink' (1786) was a response to his fellow Scots poet Robert Fergusson's Radical praise of fresh water versus liquor in 'Caller Water' (1773).[39] Decades before Keats, Burns mythologized alcohol in the wake of the Classical Tradition, in his case native whisky and ale in particular, as a muse inspiring the poet. Here, however, the muse is associated with disease and death:

O thou, my MUSE! guid auld SCOTCH DRINK!
Whether thro' wimplin worms thou jink,
Or, richly brown, ream owre the brink,
In glorious faem,
Inspire me ...[40]

Significantly, the verse epigraph to Burns's poem is a Scots adaptation of Proverbs 31:6–7: 'Give strong drink unto him that is ready to perish ... Let him drink and forget his poverty, and remember his misery no more'.

Apart from the occasional indispensability of alcohol for the medical treatment of depressive and debilitated patients, Radical doctors and Radical politicians often behaved in the way that Heinrich Heine satirized in his famous lines against the clergy: 'Ich weiß, sie tranken heimlich Wein, Und predigten öffentlich Wasser' (I knew they drank wine in secret and preached water in public).[41] With apostles of abstention including teetotallers in all cultures and at all times, public theory and secret practice often clashed or were viciously reputed to clash, as in the above-mentioned cases of the overweight poets James Thomson and Erasmus Darwin. Among the Radical politicians, Charles James Fox was known to be a jolly toper given to excessive sensual pleasures, including immoderate drinking and gambling, a fact smugly elaborated in numerous Tory satires and caricatures. For an issue of *The Anti-Jacobin* of 1798, George Ellis wrote a plebeian pub song ironically entitled 'Acme and Septimius, or, The Happy Union', suggesting a drinking bout and homosexual love affair between the Radicals Fox and John Horne Tooke, much in the manner of 'Christabess'.[42] And in 1783 the cartoonist James Sayers portrayed Fox as Carlo Khan, a lascivious and tipsy oriental potentate mounted on an elephant, suggesting that he sought to exploit the luxurious treasures of India with the support of Edmund Burke's India Bill.[43] It discredited the anti-imperial Radical as a surfeited sensualist and political turncoat. However, that whole campaign could not prevent the most un-Victorian Fox from later becoming the hero of Victorian liberals. The Romantic poets, whom most Tories collectively accused of Radicalism, stood even more open to such kind of satire than the Radical politicians. Their Neoclassical adversaries, heirs to the Augustan Neoclassicists, saw them as uncultivated proletarians or country clowns, as ignorant of rule and reason, as madmen, alcoholics and addicts to opium, the very contrary of original noble savages living healthily on vegetables, fruits and fresh water.[44] Thus it was easy to disparage them as mere hypocrites marketing themselves to a modern Radical fashion. One of the traditionalists' easy victims was the Radical Charles Lamb, whose *Confessions of a Drunkard* and addiction to gin were pinpointed by Dr Robert Gooch in the Tory *Quarterly Review* as a cause of the nervous disorder of a hypocritical Radical on the verge of madness.[45]

In sum, the eighteenth-century and nineteenth-century literary and hygienist discourse on the relative merits of water, beer, wines and spirits was highly complex. It mixed medical, religious, moral, national, social and political arguments with biographical polemics. The teetotalling movement of the Victorians and Edwardians, a powerful cultural voice or rather medley of dissonant voices throughout the nineteenth century, was clearly a result of the equally multivoiced Radical and Romantic campaign against refinement, colonialism, moral obtuseness and degeneration through progress.

8 THE MYTH OF 'MISERY ALCOHOLISM' IN EARLY INDUSTRIAL ENGLAND: THE EXAMPLE OF MANCHESTER

Gunther Hirschfelder

Plate 3 of William Hogarth's famous series of etchings, *A Rake's Progress* (1735), the realistic-cynical mirror of his age, shows the protagonist Tom Rakewell squandering his money in the company of prostitutes in London's Rose Tavern. Two prostitutes can be seen, spitting gin at each other; two more women on the right devote themselves to drinking: one holds the carboy in her hand, probably to refill the glass quickly, while the other woman is greedily swallowing from a huge cup or bucket.[1] The women's excessive drinking may be motivated by their occupation, prostitution, and the exploitation and dependence that come with it. Such images of 'misery alcoholism' have become part of our cultural memory since the beginning of the industrial era. In order to explain this concept, I shall begin with some basic considerations of the indicator value of alcohol consumption as well as its function and its prevailing assessment. Subsequently, two parameters will illustrate my theory of misery-alcoholism: occupational and gender-specific drinking habits. The concept of misery alcoholism presented here rests on the assumption that excessive alcohol consumption constitutes a reaction to stress: the wish to intoxicate oneself grows in proportion to difficult circumstances, to decreases in individual self-determination and to deteriorations of living and working conditions.

Hogarth's engraving reflects a change of paradigm in the assessment of drinking: during much of the pre-modern period, alcoholic intoxication had high social status. Until the mid-eighteenth century, alcohol was consumed by both the lower and the middle classes with the deliberate aim of causing intoxication. This intent and its implementation were not censured as long as the limits of acceptability were not transgressed. Towards the end of the eighteenth century, however, a more critical view prevailed in the public sentiment. With the arrival of Enlightenment ideas and with the growing desire of governments to exert control over society, individuals and especially the economy, alcoholic intoxication and its dangers began to generate public interest. Thus, intoxication underwent

– 91 –

a gradual change in assessment; moreover, new groups of consumers emerged. Socio-economic changes in the wake of early industrialization also transformed intoxication: from the early nineteenth century onwards, in the early industrial centres on the continent, alcohol intoxication became a stigma of the lower classes, while the middle and upper classes, who also continued to enjoy alcohol, concealed their own regular practices of drinking. Now, intoxication itself, not only its consequences, came under criticism. Various political influences and the debates kicked off by the temperance movement coincided with the interests of elites, who realized that alcohol consumption and high productivity would be difficult to reconcile. Culture, however, even the culture of drink, cannot be dictated from above – value shifts occur gradually. While intoxication, that is the act of getting drunk, had become discredited among the middle and upper classes, it retained its high value among the lower classes and even fulfilled an important function of which the consumer was not always aware.[2] To many a contemporary, the structural characteristics of the consumption of alcohol were barely known. Numerous sources suggest a correlation between dismal living standards and increased alcohol consumption.[3] One example of this is the physician Peter Gaskell's portrait of a young factory worker who is caught in a vicious cycle of alcohol and poverty. Gaskell's influential study *The Manufacturing Population of England* (1833) describes the worker's wife as follows: 'She is thin, pale, and badly dressed ... She too disappears for a time within the gin-shop, remains longer than her husband, but returns equally changed' – that is, also drunk.[4]

Much evidence of drunkenness among workers exists at least for the early industrial period, which began in England during the late eighteenth century and in continental Europe in the first decade of the nineteenth century.[5] When Friedrich Engels drew his polemic sketch of the Wuppertal area in 1839, he had early industrial regions in mind: 'Especially on Saturday and Sunday and in the evening at eleven o'clock' many drunkards would leave the pubs. He gave reasons: 'First of all, factory work is a key factor', and: 'Weavers, who have their own looms in their homes, bend over them from morning to evening, so that their spinal cords gets shrivelled up by the hot stoves. Those who do not succumb to mysticism get addicted to drinking brandy'.[6] Since the publication of George Bailey Wilson's classic *Alcohol and the Nation* (1940) and certainly since E. P. Thompson's 'The Moral Economy of the English Crowd in the Eighteenth Century' (1971),[7] scholars have agreed that workers in early factories drank enormous amounts of liquor, 'to be able to get through work at all', as Utz Jeggle put it.[8] This sounds reasonable at first, but if we take another look at the situation, we notice that the topics of misery and alcohol are not always directly related.

Stereotypes, unfortunately, can be very persistent, and simple answers, rather than complex explanations, sometimes linger on in academia. The discipline of folklore studies, which devotes special attention to stereotypes, provides the perspective and the methodological frame for further explorations.[9] This academic discipline, known in the German-speaking countries as folklore studies (*Volkskunde*) until the 1970s, has today consolidated its position as a hybrid discipline, named (comparative) European ethnology (*Vergleichende Kulturwissenschaft, Europäische Ethnologie*), empirical cultural studies (*Empirische Kulturwissenschaft*) or cultural anthropology. *Volkskundler* or folklorists study the culture of everyday life of the population in Europe since the Reformation. The discipline works historically as well as empirically, resorting to written sources, objects and visual material.

This essay stems from a research project conducted at the universities of Bonn and Trier,[10] which focused on alcohol consumption at the dawn of the industrial period in Manchester, the cradle of the industrial age.[11] The main interest of this project concerned cultural transitions during a period in which the essential constituents of everyday culture (*Alltagskultur*) that characterized this period of industrialization (and are in decline today) emerged. It is with reference to this time of transition that the German historian Reinhart Koselleck coined the influential term 'saddle period' (*Sattelzeit*).[12] Manchester, called 'the first factory town in the world' by Engels, played a crucial role in the Industrial Revolution.[13] Never before has the production of goods had such a profound impact on a region or a settlement, or on people and values, and left such a deep mark on culture. Throughout the last third of the eighteenth century, Manchester experienced its take-off: the switch from commerce to industry came rapidly. During the cotton boom, a large number of factories, some of them multi-storey buildings, emerged in the city centre. The population grew at a breathtaking rate, from about 22,000 residents in 1774 to 70,000 in 1779 and 227,000 in 1831.[14] Still, until the 1830s, this industrial area was managed and governed like a village. Hardly any restrictions on trade existed. Within one generation, an industrialized, export-oriented factory system based on an extensive division of labour had been developed. The first industrial city in the world was therefore also the place in which a new class appeared on the stage of history: the working class. Thus, Manchester, the nucleus of a new age, also saw the birth of a new type of society.

In an analysis of this social transformation, the consumption of alcohol must be considered as one important factor. Most of the time, alcohol was consumed in public. For regulatory and fiscal reasons, sources often give more information on alcohol consumption than on any other activities.[15] As an academic discipline, comparative European ethnology considers a combination of social attitudes and material conditions for the study of such phenomena. Food culture as well as alcohol consumption are influenced by an array of factors, ranging from climate to religion, from government regulations to popular traditions. Alcohol was one of the most important status symbols and elements of distinction of that time, although contemporaries usually did not have such a differentiated perspective.

More definitive insights can only be gained through the systematic analysis of different types of sources throughout the varying archives in the Manchester area.

Among the most important sources are police files and the extensive reports of government commissions of inquiry. From a pool of about 2,000 documents, some striking examples, which provide paradigmatic insights, will be presented.[16] A study of the extremely heterogeneous working class needs to consider occupation while also tracing longer social and economic developments alongside levels of alcoholism. First of all, terminology is problematic: most employees worked in short-term and temporary employment, and at least until the middle of the nineteenth century, it is impossible to refer to a homogeneous class. Furthermore, economic conditions could make a continuously increasing consumption of alcohol impossible. As the consumption of alcohol was an important status symbol, it happened in public spaces. According to Ulrich Tolksdorf's classification, alcohol acted as a 'prestige object'.[17] And workers who had enjoyed it in good times tried to maintain their patterns of consumption through bad times. We might explain this tendency with reference to the theory of cultural fixation (*Kulturfixierungstheorie*).[18] However, especially in northern England, the fixation of a cultural pattern must have been extremely difficult because the region went through various crises: dramatic economic cycles, underemployment and falling wages. There is evidence of extreme recessions for the years 1808–12, 1819, 1824–6 and 1837.[19] In all likelihood, oppressive poverty, hunger and thirst would not necessarily drive the unemployed, whose food situation was often critical, to alcohol. Hence, alcohol could play a central role only as long as people were able to afford it.

In order to dismantle the generalizing and undifferentiated myth of misery alcoholism, drinking habits specific to certain occupational groups (weavers, craftsmen, railwaymen, policemen) need to be considered. The largest group of industrial workers between the late eighteenth and the beginning of the nineteenth century were the spinners, yet there is hardly any evidence relating to their consumption of alcohol. Like the spinners, the weavers initially received high wages. Evidence indicating that well-paid weavers who spent their free time together consumed alcohol is available from the late eighteenth century onwards. When wages began to drop at the beginning of the nineteenth century while the workload increased, hardly enough money was left to live on.[20] In 1816, Thomas Whitelegg, a Manchester businessman, described the everyday life of weavers, who lived and worked in cellars: 'Sometimes they do nothing on the Monday, and then they work on the other days very hard'.[21] To the question 'Are the weavers at Manchester addicted to frequent public houses?' he replied in the positive.[22] This, however, soon changed: in 1833 a commission analysed the social milieu in Lancashire and concluded that, of roughly 7,000 people in Bolton who were still working with outdated looms, only a few could afford alcohol every now and again.[23] When the weaver Richard Needham was asked if there was any evidence supporting the perception of weavers as habitual drinkers, he stated: 'No; it is in others that have more wages'. When the interviewing commission expressed doubt, Needham agreed that a weaver might drink the occasional 'glass of gin' or 'pot of beer'. Furthermore, he suggested that there was a general feeling of despair among the weavers that had nothing to do with alcoholism.[24] Considering the large number of weavers, there is hardly any evidence concerning alcohol consumption and none that points to excessive drinking.

This, however, leaves a question open: to whom did the stereotypical reports about drinking workers refer? At this point, we need to consider craftsmen, who benefited from the economic boom and found themselves on the winning side. Increasing demand, which resulted in high wages for tailors as well as butchers, ensured that individuals who belonged to these groups soon were among the most important customers of the music halls. This trend was even more significant among brick burners and those highly specialized craftsmen who manufactured the spindles used in cotton factories. Witnesses simply refer to them as 'drunken men'.[25] Likewise, those who attracted attention because of their abuse of alcohol belonged to high-wage occupational groups. According to police reports from the 1840s, crimes involving excessive drinking were especially likely to be committed by file-cutters, pin-makers and foundry men. The file cutters were notorious as, according to one report, a 'very drunken set of men'.[26] According to the Children's Employment Commission, the most severe drinking took place at specific times: 'Whenever they have work and get most money they drink the most'.[27]

This relation between high wages and increased consumption of alcohol is also apparent in the transportation business. The economic boom of the 1830s brought huge profits to the carters, who consequently attracted attention because of their drinking. Railwaymen, the heroes of the Industrial Revolution, had enormous prestige, which they were eager to express. After the first railway line in the world, running from Manchester to Liverpool, had been put into operation in 1830, conflicts between train conductors and their employers surfaced quickly.[28] Percival Hall was fired because of repeated drunkenness on the locomotive in March 1831, and only a few days later the same happened to a group of firemen. Shortly afterwards, a 'fireman' called Blackburn was dismissed. Sources reveal that the machine operator Simon Fenwick had sometimes given his instructions 'in a state of intoxication'.[29] Obviously, the railwaymen could scarcely accept that they were forbidden to drink – how could they have proved their status, their superiority and their manliness without alcohol? Yet members of this occupational group were repeatedly dismissed for being drunk on duty. Here, however, the concept of misery alcoholism does not apply. One last group are the merchants, who had high incomes while remaining comparatively safe from crisis. Ego-documents and literary sources prove that merchants consumed alcohol at similarly high rates.[30] Police records, too, indicate higher consumption among merchants but hardly any instances in which merchants were sanctioned accordingly.

Finally, the police must be mentioned. Policemen received high wages and possessed extensive privileges. They were also involved in numerous conflicts. John Richardson, for example, was found asleep in the police station in 1829 'in a complete state of intoxication' and 'not able to speak'.[31] Again and again, measures were taken against alcohol consumption among policemen, but with little impact. According to an internal police authority record, 239 night watches were penalized for drinking while on duty between October 1831 and October 1832 alone. These figures reached their peak in 1838–9.[32] Change only arrived with the Manchester Police Act of 1844.[33] Previously, poor training, frequent temptations and, especially, the high prestige connected to demonstrating one's manliness were responsible for problems caused by drunken policemen.

Women also played an important role in the discussions about misery alcoholism. Women who were occupied as homeworkers shouldered a significant burden of proto-industrialization and later industrialization. This pattern accelerated in the nineteenth century. In 1835, almost 50 per cent of the workforce in Lancashire factories was female and over thirteen years of age.[34] Maxine Berg noted in 1994: 'If we compare the situation of women in the new manufacturing households to their former position within the peasant family economy, their status *may* have improved'.[35] In fact, the concept of women's specific place outside the men's sphere only emerged with the development of the middle classes.[36] The transformation of an agrarian society's cultural patterns into those of an industrial society occurred in a short transitional period. Soon, gender-specific drinking habits changed dramatically. In 1832, Simeon Cundy, who had worked in several factories in the area between 1793 and 1812, reported 'that since he became connected with Manchester, the morals of the operative class have undergone a very extensive change for the worse – that drinking has been a growing evil in both sexes'. According to Cundy, three quarters of the female factory workers between fourteen and twenty became unchaste as a consequence of drinking.[37] In the nineteenth century, young working women in particular infuriated the authorities as well as bourgeois morality by drinking and having sexual relations; in the late eighteenth century, such behaviour had only been known from those who were relatively prosperous, for example female artisans or widows of artisans.[38]

The industrialization of the Manchester area led to far-reaching changes in women's social position, affecting female members of the lower classes in particular. They were part of the workforce in the growing factories, had to carry the burden of housework, were the first to feel the effects of short-time work and unemployment, and, together with their little children, suffered most from inadequate dwellings and excessive pollution. If women became destitute, they were often worse off than men because of their lower social position. In addition, factory women had to put up with bourgeois men's mockery. 'Lancashire has long been celebrated for the beauty of its women. "The Lancashire witches" being a standing toast in all private and public convivialities'. Thus, Peter Gaskell chaffed about these women in 1836: factory work had made them ugly.[39] Moreover, Lancashire's women had a questionable reputation in other respects as well. In 1834, a Mr Buckingham complained in a pamphlet about the increasing drunkenness of women and children. He came to the conclusion: 'In Manchester and the surrounding towns, the increase of spirit shops and spirit drinkers is greater perhaps than in any part of England'.[40]

How do these impressions compare with more solid evidence? According to the police report of Manchester's twin town Salford, 1,624 individuals were taken into custody in the years between 1848 and 1849. Of these arrests, 34 per cent were related to the consumption of alcohol, an additional 20 per cent to intoxication. Among the drunken arrested 25.8 per cent were female.[41] Most of the offences were committed by drunken delinquents. But while the interplay between alcohol and industrialization developed into a dangerous, explosive force, inebriated aggression remained a predominantly male phenomenon.

While prostitutes' drinking habits had received less attention in the eighteenth century, they excited more public interest and the attention of the authorities in the early nineteenth century. Frequently, the difference between common inns and brothels was not obvious. Peter Gaskell, considered an authority on all questions of Manchester's social life, characterized the establishments situated in this large grey area as

> receptacles for every thing that is wicked and degraded ... The mother with her wailing child, the girl in company with her sweetheart, the mother in company with her daughter, the father with his son, the grey-haired grandsire with his half-clad grandchild, all come here – herding promiscuously with prostitutes, pickpockets, the very scum and refuse of society – all jumbled together in a heterogeneous mass of evil, to the ruin of every thing chaste and delicate in woman, and the utter annihilation of all honourable or honest feeling in man.[42]

Gaskell concluded that the combination of prostitution, violence and criminality was so dangerous because of the ubiquitous drunkenness. The frequently used term 'prostitute keeping' gives a clearer idea of these women's situation, who were often forced to submit and were intoxicated in the process. Many prostitutes were the helpless victims of social conditions and the rapid change to which they were unable to adapt. In 1845, Engels complained about the morally corrupting influence of the kind of places they frequented.[43] The registers of the victims of the 1832 cholera epidemic testify to which degree women were ruined by alcohol and prostitution: all four prostitutes who died, sixteen, eighteen, twenty-two and thirty years old, were classified as alcoholics.[44] The lists also deal with the victims' nutrition and their way of life. Their analysis shows that 17 per cent of the cholera victims were alcoholics, 41 per cent of those were female.[45]

Women forced into prostitution as young girls were particularly often addicted to alcohol. In 1834, Charles Frederick Bagshaw, who had been 'Chaplain of the gaol of Salford' for four years, gave the following evidence to the Parliamentary Select Committee on Inquiry into Drunkenness: 'I have found in several instances children brought in the gaol, who have been given to habits of drunkenness and prostitution', many 'as young as 12 years of age'. After the passing of the Beer Act in 1830, John Horrocks had founded a beer shop in his hometown, Bolton. Bagshaw reported that Horrocks used this as a brothel and hired out his '12 or 13 years'-old daughter to customers. Bagshaw also stated that he had encountered many children addicted to drink, particularly prostitutes below the age of seventeen.[46] The situation in the smaller industrial towns was not better. In the mid-nineteenth century, the authorities' efforts to banish prostitution from inns and alehouses succeeded only temporarily and in few places.

My examples have shown that alcohol was central to the development of prostitution in Lancashire. It was given to young women who were forced into this occupation, as a narcotic and to make them tractable. They drank to cope with their unbearable situation; the places of drink were the places of prostitution. The source material makes the mechanisms of suppression perceptible: from the 1830s onwards, more and more women became victims, while the clients and procurers enjoyed the protection of the local elite.[47]

Apart from prostitutes, female workers' drinking habits can also be reconstructed through these sources. Admittedly, it is difficult to work out precise dividing lines between social classes. The first half of the nineteenth century was characterized by enormous economic fluctuation. For many women, social mobility meant instability and insecurity. An artisan's wife, for example, who moved to an industrial town, might soon find herself an unemployed widow, or a badly paid unskilled worker or a well-paid skilled worker. Whatever position she might achieve, she could not confidently rely on maintaining it.

Jakob Venedey, a German traveller, may have seen women belonging to each of these three groups when he wrote about Manchester's Shude Hill quarter in 1844:

> A people made up of vagabonds is living in these streets, not only the factory workers, but the rear guard of the factories' army. Despite the working hours, a lot of idle riff-raff was hanging around. Idle, usually dirty women were sitting or standing by their doors. I met a drunk and staggering mother, her baby on her breast. Singing and music was coming from the taverns. Many of the women, who were standing by the doors, were apparently prostitutes. Among them, some were drunk, maybe never without alcohol.[48]

The early factories employed mostly men. From the 1820s onwards, they gave more and more work to women, who provided more than half of the labour force in the mid-nineteenth century.[49] Thus, male workers had several decades to develop specific masculine industrial drinking patterns. Contemporary opinion on the drinking habits of the female workers as a new social class varied. Gaskell draws a graphic picture of male and female factory workers using alcohol as a remedy against hunger, monotony and depression. In Gaskell's view, it was common to take a mouthful of spirits from time to time: 'This habit of dram-drinking, so fatal in its consequences, is one of the most extensive prevalence. The labourers, male as well as female, swallow the pernicious draught, and bless it as the boon which relieves them from their harassed sensations'. He argues that such irregularities were on the increase because of the 'bringing together of the young of both sexes by the factory system'. Consequently, 'drinking became more habitual'.[50]

In 1849, Angus Bethune Reach, a well-known journalist, published a series of reports about Manchester. He picked out a Saturday evening in Oldham Road as one central topic: 'The street was swarming with drunken men and women; and with young mills girls and boys shouting, halloing and romping with each other'.[51] In 1844, the French traveller Léon Faucher wrote about Manchester's gin shops: 'Of all the buildings in Manchester, these open the earliest in the morning, and close the latest at night. From five or six, a.m., the operatives of both sexes visit the dram-shops before going to labour'.[52] The results of several parliamentary inquiry commissions corroborate the views of our three observers. In 1833, Titus Rowbotham was interrogated by one of those commissions. The fifty-one-year-old labourer had worked in several cotton mills since 1801. Titus agreed with Faucher. The moral condition, he felt, was bad: 'And then, the females, too, can't eat for exhaustion, and then they are led to drink, too'.[53]

Simeon Cundy, who had been working in Manchester since 1793, did not believe that permanent exhaustion led to more drinking among the factory girls. In 1833, he stated that 'drinking has been a growing evil in this place during the last fifteen years'. 'Drinking what?' he was asked: 'Spirits, in both sexes; and I think, upon oath, that one third of the distress and pressure in the poor-rates proceeds from the increase of this habit'. To the question: 'To what circumstance or circumstances do you attribute the increased habits of drinking spirituous liquors prevalent in Manchester?' he answered: 'To the circumstance that the overheat of factories debilitates the body, and causes persons to desire the temporary stimulus of liquor'. He could offer no other reasons for the hard drinking of 'both sexes'. Cundy contradicted himself in the very same statement: 'I have been up in the morning at four and five o'clock, and have followed men and women both to public houses, and have asked them why they took spirits, and they have told me that they could not get to the mill without in many scores of instances'.[54]

Undoubtedly, many female workers periodically drank alcohol in quantities that at least some people regarded as indecent. However, it is hard to say what led them to such levels of consumption. 'I am declined to believe that drunkenness has of late years very much increased in Manchester, and particularly spirit-drinking by females', mused the mill-owner James Bury in 1833.[55] For such cases, the changes caused by the 1830 Beer Act seem to have been of great significance. The Act led to an augmentation of the number of drinking places and a general increase in drunkenness. In 1833, the *Report from the Select Committee on Manufactures, Commerce, and Shipping* alleged that around 1818 there had been only six or eight 'spirit-vaults' in Stockport, one of the early industrial centres of the Manchester area, whereas in 1833 almost half of the licensed alehouses and beer-shops had their own vaults, 'many of them fitted up in a style of great splendour; and where they have not gin-shops, many of them practise the gin-shop trade at the bar'. Moreover, 'troops of young women that work in manufactories go to spirit-shops, that would have been ashamed of it some years ago'.[56] How can such a change be explained? James Turner, a workman, put his finger on it in 1834: 'One part of the evil is owing to the system of education, or rather the lack of it'. Furthermore, the long working hours were among the reasons for this development. In the factory where he worked, barely any of a number of recently married young female workers possessed simple domestic skills, 'but all could play at cards in a public-house'.[57] In 1853, the author of the *Second Annual Report of the Manchester and Salford Association for the Better Regulation of Public Houses* stated:

> Young girls of fifteen or twenty, who work in the factory, are seen without shame to go into the beerhouse three and four together. On one evening in June, I visited five beerhouses in my district, and found therein 157 persons, 83 males and 74 females, mostly under seventeen, and some under twelve years of age.[58]

Some working girls drank immoderately, but this was not the prevailing pattern. In 1833, a group of labourers told the *Factories Inquiry Commission*: 'Immorality and drunkenness are not more prevalent amongst persons employed in mills ... Females who work in mills are generally as prudent as any body of females working together'. They added: 'We have never heard of children, owing to faintness, fatigue, or any other cause, being driven to the dram-shop in this part of the country'.[59] A few weeks earlier, the Commission had interrogated a mill girl:

> Do you ever drink spirits? – No.
> Do you know any girls that do? – Some of the lasses does; but very few, I think.
> When do they drink it? – Chiefly to their tea; they think it does them good. Some has gin; some has rum.[60]

Working women did not develop their specific drinking habits until the second quarter of the nineteenth century. Repeatedly, very young girls attracted attention through their allegedly immoderate drinking. This group tried to express their demand for emancipation in a male-dominated industrial world by adapting to male patterns of behaviour and of drinking. The sources do not prove either that female workers on the whole drank more than other social groups or that their drinking habits were considered an urgent problem. Most of them drank seldom and imbibed little alcohol. It must be kept in mind that only behaviour that deviated from the norm was usually recorded. The sources quoted above stand in stark contrast to a statement by John L. Kennedy, who had investigated Manchester's social reality for years. In 1841, he reported: 'The mortality amongst the females may, perhaps, be taken as indicting most correctly the noxious influences of the places of residence, as they are more regular and temperate in their habits, and more constantly occupied at their homes than the men'.[61]

During industrialization, battles for membership in new social groups and classes arose. The analysis of drinking habits has shown that women of all classes were considered by many social observers to be the losers of this race. Within a single generation, women were excluded from forms of social life in which they had formerly participated. Liberal use of alcohol had developed into a stigma for working-class women, whereas hidden drinking, a new phenomenon, was characteristic among the middle and upper classes. Obviously, the purpose of consuming alcohol had changed as well. From being a stimulant and a pleasure it had developed into a common drug for all those who could not cope with the radical transformations of industrialization. Young women were particularly affected: their drinking, a result of helplessness and distress, was harshly judged and even punished. Society's attitude towards alcohol was schizophrenic. Men drank much more, the consequences of their drinking were more aggressive, and they utilized alcohol in their contact with women; but none of these factors were regarded as being of great social interest. Since the 1820s, drinking women gradually became emancipated. Interestingly, whereas young factory women created specific drinking-patterns, their bourgeois sisters were under pressure to appear as modest and passive.

The 'misery thesis' is an incomplete explanation for patterns in drinking. There were people who drank simply to escape their lives (then as now ...), but alcohol consumption was also a part of social interaction and a marker of status that was fully accepted within working-class communities. Hence it was necessary to consume it publicly. This public consumption, however, ran afoul of newer middle-class sensitivities about personal comportment, self-discipline and public order. The wealthier classes – who were also the employing and commenting classes – preferred more privatized forms of drinking. The continuing working-class attachment to public drinking – which for many workers was in fact a relatively rare occasion, not least for the simple reason that they lacked enough money to buy alcohol – thus appeared to 'outside' observers (and the state) as a social 'problem'.

9 ALCOHOL, SYMPATHY AND IDEOLOGY IN GEORGE GISSING'S *THE NETHER WORLD* (1889) AND *THE ODD WOMEN* (1893)

Anja Müller-Wood

Throw wide the doors of the temple of Alcohol! Behold, we come in our thousands,
jingling the coins that shall purchase us this one day of tragical mirth.
George Gissing, *The Nether World* (1889)[1]

I.

References to alcohol are ubiquitous in the work of the underrated and under-read late-nineteenth-century author George Gissing. Especially in his early novels, which deal almost exclusively with the working class, pubs and other establishments selling alcohol provide settings for character action and interaction. They are peopled by publicans, barmaids, and potboys and girls carrying jugs of beer to customers' homes; they contain cameo appearances of incorrigible drinkers in various states of inebriation and depict scenes of domestic violence committed under the influence; and even in Gissing's later work, with its focus on middle-class themes and concerns, there are still passing references to 'pledge cards' collected on mantelpieces and/or bedside tables, symbolizing characters' repeated failure to live up to their promise never to drink alcohol again.

It is tempting to explore such evidence of Gissing's interest in alcohol and its consumers for its contextual dimension, whether by connecting it to the cultural background at large or to the writer's personal experience. Indeed, alcohol had a topical significance in late Victorian public discourse, notably in the form of moral panics surrounding the issue of drink,[2] and such general concerns would have left their mark on the writing of any contemporary author, especially one as sensitive to the social issues of his day as Gissing. After all, Gissing had personal experiences with alcohol through his disastrous marriage with the Manchester prostitute Helen 'Nell' Harrison, an alcoholic whom he unsuccessfully tried to rescue from a life on the streets (becoming a convicted criminal in the process himself).[3] However, even if we concede, with John Halperin, that

– 103 –

'to read [Gissing's] books without a detailed knowledge of his biography is to read blindfolded',[4] the historicizing and contextualizing readings characteristic of contemporary Gissing criticism[5] present only one way of approaching the author's interest in drink and drinking. Aiming to extend the critical horizon, this essay is concerned less with how Gissing's representations of alcohol reflect upon the external reality in which he wrote and more with investigating how they are entangled in the internal structures of his plots. More precisely, it will address the aesthetic, emotional and ultimately ideological implications this entanglement involves, all of which come together in the figure of the reader, who in Gissing's work is granted a strikingly productive role. Therefore, although this analysis may seem to border on existing scholarship dedicated to the reception of literature, notably 1970s reader response criticism associated with names like Wolfgang Iser and Hans Robert Jauss,[6] its aim is to point beyond this critical school's focus on the text and to disclose the role Gissing accorded to the reader in the literary process. For unlike Iser, for whom reader responses were construed by gaps and indeterminacies in a narrative, Gissing acknowledged the readers' emotional contribution to this meaning-making process, thereby endowing them with a more substantial position of agency.

II.

Gissing's representations of drink and drinkers reveal the author's ambiguous relationship with these contemporary themes and illustrate what David Grylls has called the 'paradox of Gissing':[7] his simultaneous fascination with and yet detachment from, even hostility to, the low life he had encountered in Manchester and London.[8] On the whole, his view of alcohol abuse was a systemic or structural one comparable to that of Victorian reformers like Edwin Chadwick, Robert Owen and Charles Dickens,[9] and he continued to uphold the belief that alcoholism ought to be seen in light of environmental factors, even after his wife Nell's stubborn resistance to his civilizing influence.[10] Yet such personal experiences fed into the pessimistic stance he seemed to have developed in the early 1880s, when a Schopenhauerian notion of human society as being fundamentally atomistic and conflictual replaced his earlier positivist belief that human beings are products of their society and can be improved along with it.[11] Gissing's idealistic hope for social reform and his awareness that people often were immune to attempts at such reform generate a pervasive tragic tension in his work between ready spirit and weak flesh, between the determined wish to overcome human failings and the seemingly ingrained inability to do so.[12]

Gissing's depictions of plebeian debauchery warrant comparison with the grotesque realism of William Hogarth, whom Gissing admired greatly.[13] His first novel, *Workers in the Dawn* (1880), has been described as 'consciously Hog-

Alcohol, Sympathy and Ideology

arthian in its examination of the poorer classes',[14] and depictions of noxious Gin Lane excesses pervade other novels, too. The above-quoted epigraph testifies to Gissing's fascination with his satirical forefather. Taken from the opening of the notorious 'Io Saturnalia!' chapter in *The Nether World*, which depicts the violent excesses of a working-class binge on an August Bank Holiday with a scathingly realistic eye, it appears to confirm the narrator's sarcastic dismissal of plebeian life and pastimes. However, it also expands this narrow critical view, for the passing hint at tragedy in this quote ought to be taken seriously. Despite the 'conservative and anti-working-class bias'[15] of his 1880s novels, Gissing found tragedy in the lives of the London poor; the mix of 'revulsion and fascination'[16] that characterizes his attitude transformed into pity when his interest shifted to the suffering individuals constituting the intimidating labouring masses. Indeed, Gissing, David Trotter writes, 'could always, and always meant to, tell the difference'.[17] His awareness of 'human diversity'[18] led to a 'humanization' of his characters,[19] which in turn allowed him to engage readers' sympathies, albeit in a complex and far from unidirectional way.

This chapter will consider the way this humanization is played out in the representation of minor characters in two novels written and published fifteen years apart, which ostensibly represent very different issues and concerns. The first is the aforementioned *The Nether World*, in which John Hewett, a semi-skilled labourer, is struggling to keep himself and his family above the bread-line; the second is *The Odd Women*, which depicts the attempts of Virginia Madden, an impoverished spinster, to maintain an appearance of lower middle-class respectability on steadily diminishing funds. In the course of the novels, both characters become alcoholics and their demise is traced in protracted plots of great inevitability. Despite the obvious topographical and thematic differences between the two novels – the first set in the slums of Clerkenwell, the second addressing the problem of poverty among lower middle-class women in Chelsea and Battersea – both depict (at one level of the plot at least) a drunkard's progress of sorts and in doing so resort to very similar narrative strategies. In both texts, this progress is narrated in a patchy story line of individual tableaux, sometimes separated by more than a hundred pages. The patchiness of Gissing's character studies has in the past been targeted by critics, who have accused the author of stylistic inconsistency,[20] but a more reader-centred argument can contribute to a revision of these views. What from one perspective may appear as an aesthetic flaw might, from another, be seen as a token of Gissing's intentionally allusive style, which, by relying in substantial measure on the readers' abilities to make sense of fragmented data and string a coherent plot line out of presumably unconnected scenes, makes his novels particularly dramatic and emotionally and intellectually engaging.

Two related conclusions about Gissing's oeuvre in particular and the generation of literary meaning in general derive from the characteristically fragmented style of his narratives. First, and most importantly, Gissing's depiction of drink and drinkers sheds light on his perception of the reading process, revealing his implicit assumptions about the creation of textual meaning and the function of the reader within that process. Implicit in these assumptions is what could be called his psychology of reading. What his novels tell us is what he thought made his readers tick, that is, they reveal the novelist's view of their emotional concerns and interests as well as their interpretive abilities. A shift in focus on the audience would therefore provide a new angle on the long-acknowledged but ultimately underresearched emotional effects of Gissing's work. Several critics have emphasized the role of sympathy and suspense[21] in Gissing's writing, and indeed, in true Victorian fashion, Gissing was aware of the 'affective power of literature'[22]; nevertheless he was sceptical of exploiting this power through what he called the 'vile' method of serialization.[23] A focus on the way Gissing orchestrated reader responses would thereby highlight a level of continuity in his oeuvre usually disregarded by critics too focused on the changes and developments of his writing.

But the emotional dimension of Gissing's writing points to a second issue relevant to the discussion of his representation of drink and drinkers, that of literature's ideological content. In an insightful discussion of Gissing's work, Fredric Jameson warns against one-to-one comparisons between his novels and the reality in which they were written, however strongly such comparisons may suggest themselves. *The Nether World*, therefore,

> if it has documentary value at all, is best used as testimony, not on the state of Victorian slums, but rather on the narrative paradigms that organize middle-class fantasies about those slums, and about the unavoidable, yet only too disguisable, class structure of the world in which the Victorian reader reads.[24]

What can be gleaned from the novel, in other words, is not an image of workingclass reality, but a representation of contemporary middle-class ideologies taken in the broad Althusserian sense of the term: powerful, constructive fantasies constitutive of meaning and identity that provide the epistemic coordinates of human experience and coexistence. Internal contradictions and tensions in Gissing's representation of these fantasies, Jameson argues, hint at the limits of their influence, and this, he suggests, is a mitigating circumstance in our evaluation of the author's otherwise overtly conservative art. What makes Gissing so much more interesting and complex than other authors of the period, even those who endorse more liberal views, has to do with the way his middle-class assumptions reveal how this ideology works (and how it fails).[25]

Gissing's novels allow us to expand on this critical intervention, which – although undertaken in the author's defence – is no less flawed than the scholarly arguments thereby criticized. Jameson's argument relies on a monolithic, static and unrealistic notion of middle-class ideology[26] and ultimately reproduces the mimeticism he ascribes to other scholars. Although he warns against taking Gissing's novels as mirror images of lower-class *reality*, he is quite happy to interpret them as perfect reflections of middle-class *ideas*. More, Jameson's thematic critique of ideology disregards the emotional dimension of Gissing's work with which the present article is concerned. Jameson focuses on the ideological *content* of Gissing's novels, not on the question of *how* this content is transmitted, let alone what else this transmission might tell us, be it about the author's understanding of literary communication, or the role of the reader in this process.

This is not to deny that Gissing's novels do transmit certain fixed beliefs that are illustrative of the snobbism often ascribed to the author.[27] However, the close consideration of their narrative patterning reveals that this transmission is not, as Jameson appears to suggest, a simple one-way process. Christine Devine has observed that Gissing's narrative perspective differs from the 'traditional/omniscient narrator's normative bourgeois stance' in that it sends ambiguous messages; these create a potentially unsettling 'double vision' for the reader.[28] By extension, Gissing's novels are not static repositories of *actual* beliefs, but elicitors of *potential* responses external to the text. The latter are ultimately unpredictable, but what *can* be read out of Gissing's novels is that the author saw his readers as active participants in the literary process, who could be appealed to with the aid of a variety of textual strategies.

This is also suggested by Gissing's own commentaries on literary art. In a telltale comment in his *Commonplace Book* on the function of time in Shakespeare's *Cymbeline*, he emphasizes the audience's contribution in fleshing out the play's bare backbones:

> An instance of Shakespeare's imaginative treatment of time on the stage. – Imogen is told by her maid that it is nearly *midnight*; thereupon she goes to sleep. Iachimo comes out of the trunk, makes his soliloquy, & in retiring hears the clock strike *three*. Of course, the reader, or spectator, is to imagine this lapse between Imogen's sleeping & Iachimo's coming forth.[29]

This note suggests that for Gissing the audience is crucial in the process of making sense of a dramatic artefact, bridging the gaps between presumably discontinuous events and completing the imperfect picture provided by the author. Although Gissing here refers to drama, the implications of his observation may be extended to include prose and its ability to elicit reader imagination and emotion even when a text is fragmented and incomplete. To introduce a critical category that once enjoyed considerable currency in German literary scholarship, Gissing understood the principle of 'sympathy steering' ('Sympathielenkung') and deliberately sought to exploit it.[30] His novels suggest that he was aware of reading as an interactive process determined not only by the text, but ultimately by the reader. Such a view would defy the equation of sympathy steering with manipulation, emphasizing that literature can be persuasive only to the extent that its recipients are inclined to be persuaded by it.[31] In beckoning towards this possibility, Gissing also takes into account an aspect that later theorists of literary reception would ignore.[32] As we will see, in his depiction of drink and its users, Gissing relied in great measure on his readers' contributions to the literary process, and his writing is most powerful when it allows potential reader attitudes to unfold in tune with the subtle and strategic release of sometimes incomplete information, not when it bluntly and disingenuously enumerates prevailing clichés and prejudices.

III.

In *The Nether World* the depiction of John Hewett, a middle-aged, semi-skilled labourer drifting in and out of employment and increasingly unable to sustain his family, speaks to such clichés and prejudices. The character first appears in a chapter significantly entitled 'A Superfluous Family', in which Hewett has just failed to secure a menial job in a remote part of London; in a desperate bid to increase his value on the labour market he has dyed his hair to appear younger than he is. The self-emasculation entailed in this gesture, together with Hewett's middle-age and general feeling of despair, invite the readers' pity and acceptance of the anger with which he responds to his failure as a paterfamilias. His feeling of rejection and the concomitant inability to care for his family exacerbate the natural rebelliousness that is his trademark. In this attitude, his two oldest children, Bob and Clara, seem to take after him, with Clara's rebellion presenting a major source of conflict in the family. No less headstrong than her father and somewhat ambitious, she breaks with his notions of respectability when she takes up work as a barmaid. Hewett's immediate unease about this decision is confirmed when he learns that Clara, after a tiff with her employer, has abandoned her post and has vanished. On the August Bank Holiday that other working-class characters spend getting drunk at the Crystal Palace, the event depicted in the 'Io Saturnalia!' chapter on which this article has opened and which precedes the events discussed here, a stone-cold sober Hewett sets out on a desperate yet fruitless search for his daughter and ends up outside a public house that provides 'a wide door and a noisy welcome' for anybody looking for distraction or solace:

> At such a door, midway in the sultry afternoon, John Hewett paused. To look at his stooping shoulders, his uncertain swaying this way and that, his flushed, perspiring face, you might have taken him for one who had already been drinking. No; it was only a struggle between his despairing wretchedness and a lifelong habit of mind. Not difficult to foresee which would prevail; the public-house always has its doors open in expectation of such instances. With a gesture which made him yet more like a drunken man he turned from the pavement and entered .... (p. 119)

The passage concludes on a spectacular cliff hanger identified typographically by four dots, the visible markers of a significant but undescribed event that feature in many of Gissing's novels. Given that on the whole the novelist did not shirk from graphic depictions of working-class drinking and that the passage in question follows hard on the unflinchingly realistic depiction of a holiday binge in the 'Io Saturnalia!' chapter, it may seem surprising that the narrator here cuts himself short. Yet apart from signalling respect, even sympathy for the character, this particular instance of narrative discretion has further implications.

One of these implications is that for a brief moment the space mapped out by the four dots opens up different options as to how the plot may proceed after Hewett has entered the pub: he may or may not consume alcohol there, and this desperate act may or may not climax in a catastrophe. Already in the next paragraph, this momentary openness is curtailed, however, as we learn how Hewett's fruitless search for his daughter ends. In this final section of the chapter, which is separated from the scene above by a line break, a drunk John Hewett returns home at nine o'clock in the evening, cursing his daughter and collapsing on his bed: "'Let her go to the devil! She cares nothing for her father." He threw himself upon the bed, and soon sank into drunken sleep' (p. 119). This conclusion may of course not come as a surprise. Prepared by the passage immediately following Hewett's entering the pub, in which the reader has learnt that in the meantime at home John's wife has pacified her restless baby with an unspecified, but no doubt alcoholic, 'sleeping-dose' (p. 119), this ending has already been anticipated by the working-class excesses described in the preceding 'Io Saturnalia!' chapter. Together, the consecutive chapters establish a powerful sense of inevitability that casts doubt over the individual worker's ability to withstand the temptations of drink, to which his class, the novel suggests, is particularly susceptible.

Superficially seen, this is the ideological *content* of the passage, yet it is complicated by the way it is presented. As has already been pointed out, the narrator refrains from criticizing Hewett directly. While in the 'Io Saturnalia!' chapter the narrative voice oozes sarcasm, in this instance the position *vis-à-vis* the working-class drinker is far less clear. In the description of John Hewett outside of the pub, the source of the information remains unidentified; when the narrator comments on the character's 'struggle between his despairing wretchedness and a lifelong habit of mind' and claims that it is 'not difficult to foresee which would prevail', he not only refrains from stating explicitly what will happen, but also whose opinion these words reflect. A similar stance can be detected in the narrator's suggestion, repeated twice, that Hewett resembles a drunken man, which might be taken as a manipulative signal to the reader. However, the pronoun 'you' used here is ambiguous, and the formulation 'You might have taken him for one who had already been drinking' could be read as a direct, second-person address to the reader and to whatever preconceived notions of the symptoms of intoxication he or she might have. The *narrator*, then, is careful not to pass judgement on Hewett's actions. Rather than endorsing a particular ideological stance, he refrains from actively commenting on the scene, thereby teasing out a response from the reader.

This productive narratorial reticence is also underlined by the suspension of the Hewett plot line for several chapters after this scene, which presents a sharp contrast to the theatricality with which the character's incipient alcoholism is introduced. In the chapter that follows the one in question, we are told that three years have passed since Hewett's alcoholic apoplexy, but curiously the narrator avoids pursuing this story line further. Any possible suspicion on the part of the readers about Hewett's alcoholism is confirmed only three chapters later, as the narrator announces in passing that 'John was confirmed in a habit of drinking' (p. 141). Subsequently, Hewett's moral decline is depicted in a number of scenes that show him in different emotional states ranging from near madness (p. 182) to one almost of infantilization (p. 291), when he is entirely dependent on handouts by his well-meaning friend Sidney Kirkwood. The narrative voice remains distant and unconcerned throughout, allowing readerly attitudes to unfold independent of any narratorial input.

This is not to say, however, that Gissing's narrator supports whatever sense of moral superiority he thereby allows his readers to develop. He finally breaks with the reader, whose prejudices have cunningly been nourished up to this point, when one hundred pages after Hewett's debauch the intrusive narrator suddenly and expressly sides with the character he has allowed his readers to judge and stigmatize:

> The day's work had tired [John] exceptionally, doubtless owing to his nervousness, and again on the way to Sidney's he had recourse to a dose of the familiar stimulant. With our eyes on a man of Hewett's station we note these little things; we set them down as a point scored against him ... Poverty makes a crime of every indulgence. (p. 207)

Having allowed the readers to imagine a slum drinker's decline by feeding them patchy data about this process, the narrator turns the sorry tale construed with their aid against them; the moralistic story of a drunkard's 'progress' here becomes a comment on the readers' attitudes, rebutting those who have imagined John Hewett's downfall as prejudiced and petty.

The Nether World illustrates how Gissing, through an interplay of stark sensationalism and suspenseful silence, skilfully manages and probes readerly sympathies·and prejudices, only to expose them finally as ideologies. In that sense the novel is more an investigation into the minds and attitudes of its readers than into those of one of its characters, about whose psychological state the narrator's impassive account leaves us in the dark.[33] Gissing maintains such complex strategies of sympathy steering also in his later novels, considered more mature and sophisticated by many critics.[34] Structures and strategies similar to those detected in *The Nether World* can also be found in Gissing's 1893 novel *The Odd Women*. The topic of oddness announced in the title – which refers, among other things, to the demographic gender imbalance that makes finding a husband almost impossible for the women depicted in the novel – echoes the superfluity of the Hewett family and prophesies a similar tale of inevitable decline. Hewett's middle-class counterpart is Virginia Madden, one of three sisters around whose descent into poverty, frustration and despair the plot is arranged, and as in the earlier novel, the readers are co-opted to complete the sketchy story line that traces her decline.

A first hint of Virginia Madden's alcoholism is given in an early chapter in which she, after having bought a copy of John Keble's hortatory compendium *The Christian Year* as a birthday present for her younger sister, enters the 'refreshment room' at Charing Cross Station in a state of weary anxiety, whose source at this point remains obscure:

> A lady came out. Then again Virginia approached the door. Two men only were within, talking together. With a hurried, nervous movement, she pushed the door open and went up to a part of the counter as far as possible from the two customers. Bending forward, she said to the barmaid in a voice just above a whisper, –
> 'Kindly give me a little brandy.'
> Beads of perspiration were on her face, which had turned to a ghastly pallor. The barmaid, concluding that she was ill, served her promptly and with a sympathetic look.[35]

The reader does not know why Virginia behaves the way she does; apart from the barmaid's judgement there is no hint as to the nature of and reason for her condition. In fact, given the positive effect of the drink – which brings colour back into her cheeks, balances her emotionally and gives her an overall sense of 'delightful animation' (p. 23) – the reader might be inclined to share the barmaid's assessment that Virginia was physically unwell. Only the fact that on leaving the bar she sees Trafalgar Square in an entirely new light, 'like a person who stands there for the first time, smiling, interested' (p. 23), may appear suspicious and suggest that she might be intoxicated. However, a suspicion is indeed all the reader is allowed to develop. Throughout the novel Virginia's alcoholism remains a 'secret vice' (p. 327), depicted in coy euphemisms and narrative contortions that characterize all the other dramatic tableaux spread out across the novel to trace the character's decline.

This plot line is taken up again about a hundred pages later when Virginia is shown, this time through the eyes of her younger sister Monica, in a state of obvious disarray: 'Virginia had flushed cheeks, curiously vague eyes, and hair ruffled as if she had just risen from a nap. She began to talk in a hurried, disconnected way, trying to explain that she had not been quite well, and was not yet properly dressed' (p. 127). Her sister's comment on her strange brandy-like smell gives the reader a clue as to the cause of her state and puts in perspective both Virginia's explanation and the credulousness with which Monica responds: 'I don't want to alarm you, dear, but I felt rather faint'. The impression of reticence is even maintained in the much later scene in which the readers' suspicions are finally confirmed by Virginia's brother-in-law Edmund Widdowson, who detects in her 'an indisposition' whose 'cause [was] so strange that it seemed incredible' (p. 266).

The 'cause so strange' is never explicitly identified and named in the novel. In fact the narrator is so cautious about Virginia's condition that *The Odd Women's* most candid comment on her addiction is filtered through the eyes of another character, the staunchly sober feminist Rhoda Nunn, and even then formulated as a hypothesis:

> [Rhoda's] commiseration for Virginia was only such as she might have felt for any stranger involved in sordid troubles; all the old friendliness had vanished. Nor would she have been greatly shocked, or astonished, had she followed Miss Madden on the way to the railway station, and seen her, after a glance up and down the street, turn quickly into a public-house, and come forth again holding her handkerchief to her lips. A feeble, purposeless, hopeless woman; type of a whole class; living only to deteriorate –. (p. 322)

As in the earlier example from *The Nether World*, the narrative is broken off after having incited the readers' imagination enough to make them imaginatively anticipate the pitiable fate of Virginia (who, we learn later, voluntarily enters an institution (pp. 369–70)). Here, too, the narrator refrains from passing judgement on the character *directly* and instead deploys the narrative 'middle woman' Rhoda, a choice that invokes the special relationship between her and the Madden sisters, whom she had helped prepare for a life of self-respect and economic independence as teachers in their own school.

In light of this knowledge, Virginia's abandonment of a bright future 'for a temporary illusion of gin-soaked well-being'[36] carries particular significance; however, it is important that Rhoda has not even witnessed this scene herself, nor imagined it. In fact, the narrator merely imagines *her* 'follow[ing] Miss Madden on the way to the railway station', 'see[ing] her ... turn quickly into a public-house, and come forth again holding her handkerchief to her lips' and judging her on the basis of these potential observations. The hypothetic nature of the passage complicates its presumably straightforward representation of Virginia's alcoholism. At the same time as suggesting that information of this kind would confirm Rhoda's already sceptical view of the older woman, the statement undermines this claim by emphasizing that Rhoda did not actually witness Virginia entering and leaving a pub. Rhoda thus only seems to serve as a mouthpiece allowing Gissing to make a veiled statement about a social taboo. This reticence is underlined by the fact that in this scene Virginia's alcoholism is actually not the issue for Rhoda;

at stake is her (unwarranted) suspicion that Virginia's younger sister Monica is having an affair with Rhoda's fiancé Everard Barfoot, and her exasperation about Virginia has to do with what she presumes to be her involvement in this suspected relationship. Rhoda's misinterpretation of the general situation heightens the narrative secrecy of the passage and enables the narrator to divest himself from what is being said. These could be Rhoda's words, echoing her opinionated and outspoken nature in content and tone: 'A feeble, purposeless, hopeless woman; type of a whole class; living only to deteriorate –'. But as the narrator here resorts to free indirect discourse, leaving the thinker of these comments unidentified, it is the reader who is included as a potential source of these dismissive thoughts and, as in the case of *The Nether World*, is criticized for them.

Granted, the portrayal of Virginia's alcoholism and the narrative effects that it entails might be put down to the fact that Gissing is here tackling the tetchy issue of alcoholism among middle-class women – a topic that did not trouble him when he was writing about women from the working-class – but if anything, the sensitivity of the issue heightens the point made throughout this article. George Gissing employed the principle of narrative paucity in the knowledge, or at least expectation, that in doing so, he could rely on his readers, prejudiced and opinionated as he imagined them to be, to complete that which he did not want to make explicit.

IV.

In this article I have attempted to illustrate the narrative complexity of George Gissing's treatment of alcohol, to which merely contextual readings that seek to embed the author's depiction within a larger discursive frame, cannot do justice. In Gissing's work, drink is an emotionally charged topic and thus just as revealing about the novelist's aesthetics as about his social criticism.

In illuminating the intricacy of Gissing's craft, I have also sought to address the larger issues connected to his representation of alcohol: Gissing's understanding of the literary process, his view of his readers, his implicit acknowledgement of the psychological and emotional function of writing. From this perspective, drink and drinking are topics of particular emotional weight not because they possess this kind of quality in themselves, but because Gissing uses them to orchestrate readerly attitudes and prejudices to achieve an emotional effect. Having been given relevant but selective clues about characters who drink, readers fill the gaps the author has left in his narrative with the prejudices Gissing expected them to harbour. Importantly, therefore, these gaps do not construe a meaning, as other critical investigations of reader reception would have it, they merely facilitate the emergence of readerly attitudes authors presume to pre-exist before the text.

Gissing's harnessing of the reader to the creation of literary meaning and effect also sheds new light on the question of literary ideology, which earlier interpretations have linked merely to the content of his novels. If the examples discussed are anything to go by, then the ideological processes of Gissing's novels are more complex than critics accusing the writer of voicing bourgeois prejudices have been ready to acknowledge. If for Gissing, as I hope to have shown, reading is a reciprocal experience that relies in substantial measure on the readers' attitudes, expectations and emotional responses, then the same may be said for the ideological dimension of literary texts, which is by no means only located on the side of the narrative. In Gissing's novels, ideology emerges precisely in those instances in which the narrative's ideological content is at its most uncertain; rather than merely reiterating fixed ideological beliefs, they ultimately leave the realization of ideological responses to the readers.

10 LEGENDS OF INFERNAL DRINKERS: REPRESENTATIONS OF ALCOHOL IN THOMAS HARDY AND NINETEENTH-CENTURY BRITISH FICTION

Norbert Lennartz

I.

It is certainly a commonplace of cultural criticism to maintain that the nineteenth century was wary of most bodily pleasures. The Victorians' eating habits and their extreme reactions to food have been well documented,[1] but what tends to escape critical notice is the fact that representations of drinking were no less ambivalent at that time. A history of drinking in the nineteenth century, which still has to be written, should surely start with John Keats's sensual references to drinking as a source of inspiration in the 'Ode to a Nightingale' (1819). What, with its /b/-alliterations, looks like a eulogy of sparkling southern wine and, with its manifold synaesthetic implications, is only meant to serve the poet as a trajectory to leave the world, his body and all sensational stimuli behind:

> Oh, for a beaker full of the warm South,
> Full of the true, the blushful Hippocrene,
> With beaded bubbles winking at the brim,
> And purple-stainèd mouth,
> That I might drink, and leave the world unseen,
> And with thee [the nightingale] fade away into the forest dim –[2]

No sooner has Keats conjured up the image of red wine and its associations with Pegasus and the Muses than he discards it in the subsequent stanza and decides to replace Bacchus, the 'pards' and their connotations of riotous drinking with the promises of 'the viewless wings of Poesy'.[3] Keats's poem is thus an interesting case in point, since it sets the tone for many other nineteenth-century literary representations of drinking that unfold a variety of contradictory meanings: whereas drinking is a way to escape the corporeality of life with bird-like levity,

– 115 –

the 'purple-stainèd mouth' (l. 18) also suggests traces of blood and symptoms of consumption. That these ambivalent associations are also closely linked up with grotesque horses (*hippoi*), ferocious leopards and many other beasts which artists imagined as being in Bacchus's retinue is certainly another indication of Keats's conflicting ideas about drink. For Keats, who enjoyed claret and was not averse to drinking whisky when in Scotland in 1818,[4] but in 1819 was severely suffering from the limitations of his human condition, drinking alcohol, more than anything else, reflects man's liminality and is more than conducive to revealing his earthbound, anarchic and bestial sides.

Thus, Keats's poem is apparently closer to Cassio's insights into the animality of drinking in *Othello* than to Dickens's depictions of drinking and feasting in *David Copperfield*. The latter novel, with its mid-century representations of alcohol, was acknowledged by Hardy to be Dickens's best novel and a text that he was unconsciously indebted to.[5] When Mr Micawber, the antagonist of modern efficiency, turns the preparation of hot lemon punch into a ritualistic celebration of friendship, the first-person narrator temporarily takes the reader back into an atmosphere of conviviality and good life that is reminiscent of the eighteenth century, but conspicuously at odds with the threats of liminality that seem to be lurking everywhere in the novel.[6] Thus, it is not so much Uriah Heep's grotesque bestiality as the beast in the protagonist himself that, for a while, jeopardizes the concept of the *bildungsroman* and gives the novel an almost proto-Darwinian underpinning. In a night of dissipation with his friend and libertine Steerforth, David Copperfield drinks so much that he is not only dissociated from his self, but also re-transformed into the beast that he allegedly was.[7] In a feeling verging on disgust, he sees himself leaning out of his bedroom window, 'refreshing his forehead against the cool stone of the parapet' and turning what was labelled 'the pleasures of conversation and society' into the horrors of bestial retrogression. It is more than remarkable that, in one of his (unsent) apologies to Agnes the next day, David quotes Cassio's speech from *Othello* and thus aligns himself with the nineteenth-century discourse of temperance that is as remote from Mr Micawber's anachronistic delight in punch as the outlandish place that he is eventually sent to: "'Shakespeare has observed, my dear Agnes, how strange it is that man should put an enemy into his mouth'".[8]

II.

Alcohol as an enemy put into one's mouth, as a liquid that miraculously transforms the drinker into a monstrous *doppelgänger*, into a beastly inhabitant of infernal places, is also one of the leitmotifs in Thomas Hardy's fiction. His three major novels after 1885, *The Mayor of Casterbridge* (1886), *Tess of the d'Urbervilles* (1891) and *Jude the Obscure* (1895), must be accorded a prominent position in any history of drinking, given the fact that they foreground the consumption of alcohol to such an extent that it is a compellingly new approach to reconsider Hardy's concept of fatalism and to see the downfall of his Wessex characters as a consequence of the temptations of alcohol.

Right at the beginning of the first two novels, it is the lure of alcohol that triggers fate and transforms the pastoral locations into secular hells from which neither a Dickensian Agnes in *David Copperfield* nor Keats's viewless wings of poesy can offer a way of escape. Both novels are what Timothy M. Rivinus calls 'traged[ies] of the commonplace illness of alcoholism and its effect on off-spring'.[9] But what is more than ironic is that Tess's fall from paradise is brought about by two disastrous powers: that of alcohol and that of the village parson. While Tess is participating in a pagan feast in commemoration of Ceres, 'the local Cerealia',[10] her father, the haggler Durbeyfield, is accosted by the parson, who, acting on a whim, addresses him as Sir John, the descendant of an extinct noble family of Norman times. As a writer who in the wake of Heinrich Heine and Matthew Arnold saw mankind irreconcilably divided into Hebraists and Hellenists, Hardy gives the clergyman the role of the Old Testament serpent in the pagan paradise, which brings forth in its victim not only the deadly sins of pride and luxury, but also the vice of excessive drinking.

In Hardy's tightly woven narrative, which is a dense texture of prolep-tic hints, symbols and images, it is no coincidence that Tess's status as a 'pure woman' is endangered by both an old parson and a 'noggin o' rum' from an inn ambivalently named The Pure Drop. Situated at the end of the village, The Pure Drop Inn is a fully-licensed tavern which, however, seems to be deficient of the conspirative charms that Rolliver's inn, an alehouse with an off-licence, has. It is at the latter where the villagers furtively huddle around a 'gaunt four-post bedstead' and eventually submit to the illusion that they are sitting in front of 'the magnificent pillars of Solomon's temple' (p. 26). In his attack on alcohol-induced self-deception, Hardy also reverts to the Dickensian image of the family as a ship. However, in contrast to Peggotty's ark in *David Copperfield*, which on Yarmouth beach gives shelter to an odd assortment of abandoned or orphaned individuals, the 'passengers in the Durbeyfield ship' (p. 24) are at the mercy of many adversities and exposed to an alliterative list of dangers – 'difficulty, disas-ter, starvation, disease, degradation, death' (p. 24) – owing to the fact that the parental captains are constantly befuddled and in pursuit of an escape from the down-to-earth realities of rural life:

> A sort of halo, an occidental glow, came over life then. Troubles and other realities took on themselves a metaphysical impalpability, sinking to minor cerebral phenom-ena for quiet contemplation, in place of standing as pressing concretions which chafe body and soul. (p. 23)

Unlike various French Naturalists such as Zola, Manet or Toulouse-Lautrec, who in their novels (*L'assommoir* (1877), *La joie de vivre* (1884)) and paintings (*Le buveur d'absinthe* (1859/82)) focus on the physiological and moral consequences of alcoholism, Hardy is less interested in the scientifically faithful rendition of the drunkard's disintegration than in the way Tess is dependent on and victimized by people who prefer the fallacious moments of 'vinous bliss' (p. 25) to the imperative of the rational mind. Thus, as a result of being fatally linked with harebrained and inebriated parents and with growing up in a neighbourhood where 'systematic tippler[s]' go drunk to church, 'without a hitch in [their] eastings and genuflections' (p. 28), Tess's inevitable downfall is marked by numerous references to drink, potions and liquids, which others either imbibe or make her swallow. The horse's 'crimson drops' (p. 33) with which Tess is splashed from face to skirt after a collision with the mail-cart thus not only ironically echo The Pure Drop Inn, they also point to the fact that from then on, as in a moment of bloody initiation, the protagonist's body is a porous one, involuntarily soaked, impregnated by and exposed to liquids of various kinds.

It is not only the date of publication that Hardy's novel has in common with Oscar Wilde's *The Picture of Dorian Gray* (1891). The depiction of the dandy as a diabolic seducer in a triangular constellation of characters shows to what extent both writers translate the structure of the medieval morality play into a modern narrative. In Wilde's novel it is the Luciferic Lord Henry Wotton who, apart from instilling his seductive principles of New Hedonism into Dorian, treacherously invites him to have an iced drink, 'something with strawberries in it'.[11] Quite similar to Wotton's strategy of seduction, Alec d'Urberville, the dandyish villain in Hardy's novel, hypnotizes Tess into eating strawberries and thus proleptically makes her body pliant and open to his libertine influences in quite an etymological sense: to the potion that he compels her to drink in order to render her sufficiently soporific for the subsequent rape.[12]

This rape, the most critical and decisive point in her life, in which she is, as Hardy's narrator stresses, spellbound by evil and deserted by her guardian angel, is preceded by an episode in which alcohol and other intoxicating liquids are again the main cause of a ruthless chain of events. Accustomed to 'the dyspeptic effects of the curious compounds sold to them as beer' (p. 64), the ordinary working people in Trantridge are characterized as immoderate drinkers and seem to owe their existence to the people Hardy knew in Puddletown, a 'notoriously "wet" town'.[13] Having observed her fellows' riotous delights from a marginal position, from 'a corner by the tavern' (p. 64), and now following the 'serpentine courses' (p. 65) of women with the mysterious names Queen of Spades and Queen of Diamonds, Tess suddenly becomes the butt of an aggressive quarrel from which she is ironically saved by her future rapist. Flung into the grim game of life, checkmated by liminal figures of fate,[14] whose drunkenness affiliates them with snakes and other infernal beasts, Tess embodies an unprecedented form of ontological loneliness in a cosmos where drink has assumed theological dimensions, where 'weekly pilgrimages' (p. 64) are only associated with going to pubs and dubious taprooms and where help is only offered by devilish libertines. In contrast to David Copperfield, who even after a night of hedonistic excess can count on a wide range of friends, Tess is left stranded in a world of drinkers, ruffians and egotists; and while David is temporarily shown wavering between Agnes and Dora and later given the chance to correct his irrational choice, Tess is hopelessly locked in a dead-end situation between a mephisthophelean villain who attempts to pour sedative and seminal liquids into her and a fallen angel, whose Pauline soberness is of such a fundamentalist nature that it consigns her to the hell of Flintcomb-Ash and drives the other dairymaids to drink and despair.

III.

While the impact of alcohol on Tess's life is more than palpable, the misery of Jude, the protagonist of Hardy's final novel, seems to be brought about by man's futile rebellion against the hostility of fate and nature. But what is striking is the fact that the personification of this concept of fateful nature, Arabella Donn, is not only closely aligned with pigs and thus far more dangerous than Ursula, the pig woman in Ben Jonson's play *Bartholomew Fair* (first staged in 1614), she is also disconcertingly linked with the temptations of alcohol and shady bars. Spellbound by the magnetism of Arabella's sensuality, by the dimples that she can produce on her cheeks, but also stunned by the pig's penis that hits his face, Jude is rapidly drawn from his spiritual reveries into the depths of crude animality. The astounding facts that Arabella has 'the rich complexion of a Cochin hen's egg',[15] that she hatches eggs in her round, prominent and capacious bosom and that, in the pig-stabbing scene, she almost wallows in pigs' blood are remote from all indications of bucolic life and scarcely at variance with the urban side of her versatile existence, her life as a barmaid. More than in *Tess of the d'Urbervilles* and its iconography of hell, Hardy's last novel pinpoints the indissoluble link between drink and degeneration, between alcohol and the deterioration into bestial spheres. Placing Jude under the picture of Samson and Delilah and having him listen to the way Arabella flaunts her knowledge of the ingredients of beer – 'three or four ingredients that she detected in the liquor beyond malt and hops' (p. 47) – the narrator introduces this episode of Jude's *amour fou* by making several references to his downfall and descent. When the maidservant of the inn tacitly expresses her surprise at the fact that Jude, the self-taught student, 'should have suddenly descended so low as to keep company with Arabella' (p. 46), Jude's decline cannot only be defined in intellectual or social terms. His *liaison dangereuse* with a vulgar barmaid from Aldbrickham, who suddenly divests herself of a long tress of false hair, also has degenerative undertones, which are given a Shakespearean gloss when Arabella inadvertently quotes a line spoken by Lady Macbeth: 'What's done can't be undone' (p. 61). Although the intertextual reference to *Macbeth* (III.ii.11) at first glance seems to be implausible and barely compatible with Arabella's low-culture life, the reader cannot help remembering that, in her plot against King Duncan, Lady Macbeth relies heavily on the crude effects of alcohol and its capacity to transform men into beasts:

> ... his two chamberlains
> Will I with wine and wassail so convince,
> That memory, the warder of the brain,
> Shall be fume ...
> ... when in swinish sleep
> Their drenched natures lie, as in death,
> What cannot you and I perform upon
> Th' unguarded Duncan?[16]

Lady Macbeth's intention to use alcohol ('wine and wassail') to send Duncan's chamberlains into 'swinish sleep' is clearly echoed by Arabella, when, after a period of absence and bigamous life in Australia, she reactivates her Circean powers and spellbinds Jude with her crude animal charms. In a room above her father's 'small and precarious pork-shop' (p. 374), she manages to seduce Jude again, but now not so much with the attractions of her body as with the pernicious delights of liqueur. While she treacherously refrains from emptying her glass, she succeeds in refilling Jude's glass several times and causes him to lose his sense of control:

> Jude had the pleasure of being, as it were, personally conducted through the varieties of spirituous delectation by one who knew the landmarks well. Arabella kept very considerably in the rear of Jude; but though she only sipped where he drank, she took as much as she could safely take without losing her head. (p. 375)

Referring to Arabella as a conductor through the diversified field of (alcoholic) spirits, the narrator conjures up ideas of the mythological *psychogogos*, the guide of the souls. Keeping in the rear of Jude, she is not so much intent on leading him as on manipulating him and eventually leaving him in impenetrable darkness. '"It is as dark as pitch"' (p. 376), says Jude at the end of their journey into alcohol-induced monstrosity, and Arabella's offer to confide in her – '"Give me your hand, and I'll lead you"' (p. 376) – has strong overtones of demonic treachery and malice which Jude is no longer able to perceive.

With her blind yearning for economic welfare, she eventually turns out to be a deceiver deceived, because the 'bargain' (p. 384) she made in re-marrying Jude proves to be a negative one on account of her husband's aggravating symptoms of consumption. In this respect, she can only tenuously be compared to the long array of late nineteenth-century seducers who, like Henry Wotton and

Alec d'Urberville, take advantage of the shattering effects of alcohol to drag their victims into the hellish spheres of dissipation and monstrosity. But while most of her dandyish predecessors come to grief and fail in their schemes to corrupt their victims, in *Jude the Obscure* it is Arabella, the barmaid, who emerges triumphant and laughs to scorn all concepts of poetic justice. When, by the end of the novel, she is seen prowling the streets of Christminster in pursuit of a man who will replace the dying Jude, she even resorts to Alec's trick of using a potion to make the next candidate, the quack doctor and impostor Vilbert, pliant and responsive to her deceptiveness: "'O – a drop of wine – and something in it ... I poured your own love-philter into it, that you sold me at the Agricultural Show, don't you remember?'" (p. 401). Referring to *Macbeth* again – 'the race was lost and won' (p. 406)[17] – the narrator seems to insinuate that, like one of the Weird Sisters, Arabella remains the victorious epitome of equivocation, beyond the laws of the human condition and thus, in her animal affiliations, far more resilient than her antagonists, who not only lost touch with nature, but in moments of crisis proved to be too drunk: one 'gin-drunk' and the other 'creed-drunk' (p. 390).

IV.

While French decadent novels were experimenting with the mind-expanding effects of alcohol, exploring the soul of the wine, 'l'âme du vin', in the wake of Charles Baudelaire,[18] and, as in the case of Joris-Karl Huysmans,[19] willing to invent 'liquor organs' to indulge in the synaesthetic powers of spirits, Hardy never tires of reiterating the demonic potential of alcohol in his novels. Sergeant Troy in *Far from the Madding Crowd* (1874), the malicious intruder into Bathsheba Everdene's world, reduces the farm workers to puppets of a perilous *danse macabre* – 'the whole procession was not unlike Flaxman's group of the suitors tottering on towards the infernal regions under the conduct of Mercury'[20] – when he entices them into a fit of debauchery and makes them neglect their duties in the face of a storm; while Damon Wildeve's fatal love for the dark *femme fatale* Eustacia Vye in *The Return of the Native* (1878) is intricately linked with the fact that he, as the local keeper of a tavern, is a man of unstable disposition and with a propensity for excess.

There is, however, one novel in Hardy's oeuvre in which the personality-splitting potential of alcohol is so graphically depicted that it is strikingly in line with other narratives dealing with schizoid frames of mind, such as Robert Louis Stevenson's *The Strange Case of Dr Jekyll and Mr Hyde*, coincidentally also published in 1886: *The Mayor of Casterbridge*. Walking silently next to each other, Michael Henchard, his wife and their babbling child traverse an autumnal landscape which, in its ironic allusions to Shelley's 'Ode to the West Wind', prepares the reader for a period of imminent decline and irredeemable doom:

'the doomed leaves ... on their way to dingy, and yellow, and red'.[21] The voice of 'a weak bird singing a trite old evening song' (p. 5) is a further reference to Romantic poetry and its transcendental birds, but also a vague anticipation of Hardy's later darkling thrush, which with its 'blast-beruffled plume'[22] gives expression to at least some nondescript hope that this novel seems to be utterly devoid of. What is more, the 'total absence of conversation' (p. 4) in the expository chapter not only implies a threatening lack of communication between the couple, it also seems to underscore the fact that, beneath the veneer of sober and civilized silence, things are coming to a head and will eventually be discharged in a moment of shattering crisis. The very first pages clearly indicate that Henchard's human dignity is precariously on the cusp and that under his 'measured springless walk' there lurks a 'dogged and cynical indifference' (p. 3), which, because of the combination of the adjectives, is more than a hint at the dormant beast and ferocious dog (Greek *kýōn*) in his nature.

The place where Henchard's dubious personal integrity is severely put to the test and where he eventually yields to the imperative of the animal in himself is the heterotopian place of a country fair. As if crossing the threshold into a fantastic and infernal world, Henchard and his family enter the fairground and are instantaneously faced with chaos and a carnivalesque world teeming with 'peep-shows, toy-stands, wax-works, inspired monsters, disinterested medical men ... thimble-riggers, nick-nack vendors and readers of Fate' (p. 7). In spite of Hardy's relative reticence about Dickens's early novels, the reader cannot help being reminded of the grotesque characters in *The Old Curiosity Shop* (1840), in particular of Mrs Jarley's wax-works or the impish and canine Quilp. As in Dickens's universe, the demarcation line both between man and animal and between man and object is vexingly blurred. Man's loss of grip on ontological classifications of the nineteenth century thus becomes doubly apparent when, in the wake of Dickens and Darwin, human beings are suddenly shown as being closely related to animals, and wax-works seem to differ only in degree from inspired monsters. It is in this carnivalesque jumble of forms and monstrous figures that Henchard and his wife are treacherously faced with a choice which turns out to be a malicious manipulation of fate. Like two individuals at the crossroads, they stand in front of two refreshment tents, a new one offering 'Good Home-brewed Beer, Ale and Cyder', the other one, slightly ramshackle with the placard 'Good Furmity Sold Hear [*sic*]' (p. 7).

While Henchard does not take long to make up his mind and goes for the former tent, it is his wife who commits the tragic error of persuading him to choose the furmity booth: 'No – no – the other one', said the woman. 'I always like furmity; and so does Elizabeth-Jane; and so will you. It is nourishing after a long hard day' (p. 7). In a place where appearances are deceptive and liminal characters have paradoxically taken over central positions, Henchard's wife does

Legends of Infernal Drinkers   123

not suspect that furmity, a substantial traditional dish made from boiled, cracked wheat and often served with meat as a stew, has by now become something more intoxicating than nourishing. The pot, 'a large three-legged crock', over which a 'haggish creature of about fifty' (p. 7) presides, makes the reader aware of the fact that this refreshment booth has more in common with the witches' den in *Macbeth* than with an ordinary tavern. Quite consistent with the impression of the haggish monstrosity of the booth is that the dish is called a 'concoction' (8), meaning food that is deceptively fair and foul and whose nutritional value has been remarkably lowered by the surreptitious addition of a good quantity of rum. While his wife sees the adulteration of the meal with unease, Henchard fully approves of the seductive machinations that the demonic cook indulges in: 'he watched the hag's proceedings from the corner of his eye, and saw the game she played' (p. 8). Just as in *Tess*, the narrator refers to two familiar semantic fields: games and navigation. Thus, on the one hand, he makes it patently clear that in the weird company of witches, thimble-riggers, readers of Fate and dealers of alcohol, man is given the illusion of controlling a game in which he is, however, no longer an active *homo ludens*, but only a tragicomic *homo lusus*.[23] And this, on the other hand, perfectly fits the idea of man's life as a foundering ship. While in *Tess* the captains are constantly in a state of drunkenness and unable to navigate the family ship properly, in *The Mayor of Casterbridge* it is ironically Henchard's wife who by 'strenuously steering off the rocks of the licensed liquor-tent ... had only got into Maelstrom depths here amongst the smugglers' (p. 8).

As the 'Maelstrom depths' indicate, the longer the couple stay in this underworld, the more they will be ruled by laws and spells which will never allow them to get back to their daily reality. In contrast to Poe's narrator in 'The Descent into the Maelstrom', who finally evades the absorbing descent into the terrifying gyrations of the maelstrom by using his analytical powers, the Henchards are hopelessly trapped in the horrors brought about by the fiendish smuggling of alcohol into pots of furmity. Discarding his brooding sullenness and undergoing rapid metamorphoses from being jovial to being misogynistic and downright brutish, Michael Henchard provocatively starts to play the auctioneer and offers his wife – sarcastically called 'this gem of creation' (p. 10) – like a piece of meat in a sale: 'All I want is a buyer' (p. 10). When in the end Susan Henchard is sold for a five-pound note, it is meant to be an ironic twist that it is a sailor who rescues her from Henchard's shipwreck and immediately turns the scene of 'jovial frivolity' into one of 'tantalizing' agony (p. 12).

It is Hardy's grim philosophy that this alcohol-induced shift from jovial grandiloquence to tantalizing and infernal pain can never be remedied, that man's fall from Jove's grandeur to the underworld torments suffered by Tantalus is incorrigible. Having slept in the liminal precincts of the fairground on account of his drunkenness, Michael Henchard is astonished to find himself still confined to the carnivalesque world that is extended to a cosmos produced by the spokes of the wheels which are now 'elongated in shape to the orbit of a comet' (p. 16). What Henchard comes to learn is that this cosmos is inhabited not only by gypsies, hags and showmen, but also by dogs which, like him, the cynic, are characterized by a strange degree of hybridity: 'dogs of the mysterious breeds that vagrants own, that are as much like cats as dogs, and as much like foxes as cats' (p. 16).

Despite the fact that Henchard leaves this world of monstrosities and devilish temptations unhampered, he seems to be stigmatized by what Cassio's idea of 'the devil drunkenness' has made of him.[24] Modern studies concentrating on Hardy's representation of alcoholism analyse Henchard's behaviour in terms of his 'weak ego-structure ... his lack of impulse control, belligerence and aggressivity',[25] but the reader is well advised not to disregard the mythological overtones and instead to see the protagonist as the embodiment of intersections between myth, literature and anthropology. The next time the reader sees Henchard transgressing boundaries again, now entering the sanctuary of the altar space of a church in order to take a solemn oath, he/she is made to understand that the hope to get rid of the curse that all of Hardy's Ishmaelitish creatures are burdened with will never materialize, nor will there be any chance that the 'hardening mark' (p. 19), the Cain's mark imprinted on his wife's face, will ever be removed. The alcohol which Henchard could drink in huge quantities during the 'dog days' (p. 48) is thus not only 'a depressive drug',[26] but also a key which unlocks man's hidden and repressed reservoirs of animality. Even when Henchard has become mayor, the top representative of the town's chain of being, the atmosphere of precarious liminality never leaves him, and accepting the fact that the difference between an animal and a besotted human being is ever so small, Henchard does not seem surprised to see that the townspeople are constantly on the verge of turning into animals. In this world, which is strangely aligned with the heterotopian fairground and its furmity tent,[27] the aldermen sitting around him are not fundamentally different from the witch when they are 'sniffing and grunting over their plates like sows nuzzling for acorns' (p. 33), while inns like the King of Prussia and the Golden Crown have become the regal symbols of a new hierarchy of hybrid and animalized creatures. Since all ideas of sacredness and statemanship in Casterbridge have been transferred to the power of drink and even the concept of the trinity has become exclusively associated with 'port, sherry, and rum' (p. 34), it is only a question of time before Henchard, having lost his pre-eminent position and taken to drink again, discards his human dignity for the second time and lets the surface of his prosperous urbanity yield to 'the volcanic fires of his nature' (p. 232).

Now identified with the 'infuriated Prince of Darkness' (p. 269), bereft of his wealth and reputation and finally haunted by Captain Newson, a Nemesis figure who threatens to upset his little illusory haven of domestic happiness,

Henchard dies as a liminal character and re-embodiment of Cain, as 'an outcast and a vagabond' (p. 307), whom some critics not only consider to be superior to the swinish dignitaries in Casterbridge, but even on a par with tragic heroes such as the earlier Wessex figure King Lear.[28] Although the association between Henchard and Lear is very tenuous and more often than not confined to the fact that both die on the heath, disillusioned, debased and literally divested of their power, it is possible to detect some parallels between them, on condition that critics are prepared to demote Lear to the status of an anti-hero. Swayed by their unbalanced temperament, both Lear and Henchard unleash monstrosity and hardly become aware of the fact that they themselves are monsters surrounded by liminal creatures and centaurs, which have lost their theomorphic quality and no longer hide 'the sulphurous pit' of their satyr-like existence.[29] The fury that the transformation of the old king into a dragon brings about – 'Come not between the dragon and his wrath!' (I.i.123) – is certainly comparable to that of Henchard when he tries to take revenge on his rival Farfrae in a wrestling match. But while Lear epitomizes the deadly sin of wrath that, by the end of the tragedy, is miraculously neutralized by Cordelia's patience and her ability to 'outfrown false fortune's frown' (V.iii.6), Henchard remains impervious to entreaties and 'doggedly' (p. 288) tries to stem himself against a vision of domesticity in which he runs the risk of being reduced to the position of 'a fangless lion' (p. 303). In contrast to Lear, who dies in the midst of those who are called upon to restore 'the gored state' (V.iii.319), Henchard's life ends in a self-imposed state of liminality, in a hovel where he, as the modern Cain in a world turned upside down, is ironically nursed by a man called Abel. The will that he leaves behind with the grim injunctions that he must not be 'bury'd in consecrated ground & that no sexton be asked to toll the bell ... & that no man remember me' (p. 321) emphasizes the lasting otherness of the drunkard who, by once crossing the threshold of the fairground, has forever forfeited his chances of a peaceful family life.

V.

Consigned to the margins of society, flung into infernal places and exposed to monstrous creatures of liminality, Hardy's drinkers of alcohol have destroyed the myth of the merry eighteenth-century toper, who, as an anachronistic *revenant* in Dickens's *David Copperfield*, indulges in the convivial pleasures of a good bowl of punch. Invalidating the time-honoured idea that alcohol is a sign of civilization that blatantly contrasts with water drunk by the animals – "'we're not hanimals; we don't drink water'"[30] – Hardy's novels emphasize the degenerative and bestial side of alcohol, relentlessly showing the various metamorphoses that man undergoes under the influence of the strong liquors, which the Wessex people only on rare and 'sacred occasions' were ready to limit to 'half-a-pint'.[31] In the way Hardy's later novels illustrate Cassio's opinion that 'every inordinate cup is unblest, and the ingredience is a devil',[32] they continue the nineteenth-century interest in temperance, which surfaced briefly in Keats's poems, was juxtaposed with eighteenth-century nostalgia in Dickens's novels and received serious attention in Anne Brontë's delineation of Arthur Huntingdon in *The Tenant of Wildfell Hall* (1848). Referring to the 'infernal fire' that Huntingdon feels in his veins and 'that all the waters of the ocean cannot quench',[33] Brontë's narrator recaptures Shakespeare's image of alcoholism as a secularized hell and thus anticipates Hardy's manifold topographies of the underworld into which many of his characters are flung by the lure of the bottle. The 'general drama of pain',[34] in which man seems to be doomed to act and which reduces him to the tragic existence of a Cain, a Tantalus or a member of the numerous Ishmaelites in Hardy's novels, is, however, not always authored by the President of the Immortals or other embodiments of Hardy's agnosticism, which seem to spend their time dallying with man. Far from being puppets of demonic gods, Hardy's protagonists only too readily succumb to the fascination of alcohol and are thus instrumental in triggering off degenerative processes which reason and circumspection could have forestalled. And thus it is only a small step from Hardy's infernal drinkers to Freddy Malins in Joyce's 'The Dead' (1914) and to D. H. Lawrence's George Saxton in *The White Peacock* (1911), who continue the tradition of unholy and infernal drinkers into the post-Victorian age.

11 THE SPIRIT OF MEDICINE: THE USE OF ALCOHOL IN NINETEENTH-CENTURY MEDICAL PRACTICE

Jonathan Reinarz and Rebecca Wynter

In recent years international studies have highlighted the health benefits of moderate alcohol consumption.[1] A. S. St Leger, A. L. Cochrane and F. Moore have emphasized what has been described as the 'French Paradox': high fat and alcohol intake has resulted in a reduced rate of heart disease among the French population.[2] This was largely seen as being due to polyphenols in wine, such as resveratrol. However, the health benefits of flavonoids in stouts and dark beers have also been isolated and led University of Wisconsin researchers to reiterate the famous advertising slogan of the interwar period: 'Guinness is good for you.'[3] Claims are generally based on the antioxidant effects of these chemical substances, said to scrub the bodily system of free radicals, mitigating the threat of blood clots and even cancer.[4]

Such studies are part of a long tradition in the history of medicine. Almost sixty years ago, similar arguments were made by Salvatore Lucia, former professor of medicine and lecturer in medical history (Department of Preventive Medicine, San Francisco), in *Wine as Food and Medicine*, the title being suggestive of an earlier dual role for alcohol, which created tensions throughout the long nineteenth century.[5] Lucia's assertions equally involved isolating the health-giving constituents of wine, including aldehydes, ketones, esters and tannins.[6] This renewed interest in alcoholic beverages was stimulated by the repeal of the Eighteenth Amendment in 1933, ending American prohibition.[7] By 1963, like many others to research the subject, Lucia situated his work in deep-rooted practices. His book, *A History of Wine as Therapy*, charted this 'Oldest of Medicines' through continents and as far back as ancient Egypt.[8]

The place of wine in French medical heritage has since been researched more thoroughly than in any other national context by the historian Harry Paul. His study *Bacchic Medicine* (2001) also emphasizes the key place that wine has held in the *materia medica* of French and other European medical practitioners for several centuries.[9] Most treatises contain dozens of references to alcohol as a

– 127 –

menstruum for therapeutic herbs and substances.[10] However, Paul's work shows that it was also regularly highlighted as an appetite stimulant, a tonic for the stomach, a tranquilizer, an anaesthetic, astringent, antiseptic agent, vasodilator or an effective diuretic.

Many references to alcohol as a component of the medical practitioner's armamentarium cite wine rather than beer or stronger distilled liquors; and it is wine which, whilst popular throughout history, enjoyed its heyday as a remedy between the seventeenth and nineteenth centuries. This chapter will focus primarily on Britain and the 1800s, though it will also include the late eighteenth century. The chronology enables a concise survey of medical opinion and debate surrounding the medical use of wine and its place in practice, as well as the application of other alcoholic drafts. The diversity of opinion in this period largely related to the dosage prescribed to patients, just as continues to be the case today, especially when discussed in relation to pregnancy. Most recently, concern has resurfaced, with one senior British medical practitioner finding alcohol to be 'more dangerous than heroin'.[11] However, divisions have equally resulted from many other factors.

This chapter begins by assessing professional attitudes towards alcohol prescribing in the late eighteenth and early nineteenth centuries, when views were not yet polarized. It examines the way in which alcohol, especially wine, was discussed in the most popular *materia medica* treatises of that period, including that written by the leading Scottish Enlightenment physician William Cullen (1710–90). The next section will discuss the tensions between the views that alcohol was a cause of insanity and at the same time integral to curative techniques. Though some of Cullen's colleagues articulated a greater willingness to prescribe alcohol as a medicine, the gradual increase in its prescription occurred during the nineteenth century, both in regular medical practice and in the field of mental health. The final part of this chapter will consider the rise of the temperance movement in Britain, which ironically coincided with an increase in the medical use of alcohol, since associated with the London-based practitioner Robert Bentley Todd. While Todd's role in popularizing medicinal alcohol use has been researched previously, this chapter further aims to highlight other aspects of these debates, demonstrating the way in which discourse evolved differently in certain towns, yet also pivoted on professional networks; that many of the physicians deliberating the application of alcohol were Scottish and/or studied at Edinburgh can be no mere accident. As such, this essay is as much about paradigms and their dissemination, and it suggests that the survival and evolution of these debates were not entirely dependent on evidence drawn from individual experiment, but often very personal reasons, such as where one went to medical school. It is not a study concerning the rise of the concept of alcoholism, which emerged almost simultaneously, as this has been adequately researched previously,[12] but it will nevertheless allude to the influence of degeneration theories.

The chapter concludes with early twentieth-century discussions, when the medical professional became comfortable with more modern notions of alcohol's use in moderation, reflecting the practicalities of cost and the existence of pharmaceutical alternatives.

Alcohol and Medicine, *c.* 1770–1850

Many of the nineteenth-century views relating to the therapeutic use of alcoholic beverages were products of the late 1700s, if not an earlier era.[13] Throughout the eighteenth century, the issue of problem drinking was certainly 'medicalized' and no longer 'couched in purely religious terms'.[14] To a certain extent, medical practitioners were already divided on the subject; if some preached the cautious use of wine, others regarded it as the most useful of remedies. These assertions were enunciated in the *materia medica* lectures published in this period, which catalogued the remedies available. While numerous publications of this sort appeared, this section will outline the views of William Cullen alone, as he published one of the most popular series of lectures in this field.[15] It will also contrast Cullen's theories with those of his former pupil, John Brown (1735–88). Finally, it will examine the way in which these views played out on the wards of a single voluntary hospital: Edinburgh Royal Infirmary, where Cullen and his students taught.

In 1789, Cullen authorized the first official publication of his *Treatise of the Materia Medica*, which appeared in two volumes.[16] Volume 1 detailed the nature and production of medical ingredients and remedies, and, as such, included the production of alcoholic beverages and wines especially. It discussed the benefits of ripe versus old wines, the influence of climate and soil on grapes, and wine's potential to work as both a stimulant in the first instance and as a sedative over a longer period. Extolling less on the virtues of wine, perhaps because of earlier debates concerning the abuse of alcoholic substances, Cullen was a cautious advocate compared with other practitioners, including his compatriot William Buchan (1729–1805), who famously described wine as an 'excellent cordial medicine ... worth all the rest put together'.[17]

In volume 2 of his *Treatise*, Cullen outlines the medical uses of alcohol, and of wine in particular. He recognized wine's ability to make 'more agreeable medicine'.[18] From his entries for specific ailments, it is also clear that he recognizes certain therapeutic benefits. For example, alcohol is regularly noted as stimulating appetite, encouraging digestion and perspiration and is also recommended as a purgative. Compared with opium, a more effective stimulant, alcohol was more easily and accurately administered, due to its purity. Finally, in cases of fever – regularly encountered in eighteenth-century medical practice (especially gaol fever) – as noted by the Scottish military physician John Pringle (1707–82), it countered 'languor and debility in the system'.[19] The hazards Cullen associates with wine, however, are almost as numerous as its primary benefits. In particular, he discourages its use when headaches arise, when the patient is experiencing irritation or 'active haemorrhagies', as well as the potential for its consumption to become habit.[20]

While there were many practitioners who championed wine's use in medical practice, its most vocal advocate was Cullen's former pupil, John Brown. Like many physicians in this era, Brown's praise of wine therapy was upheld by a personal illness narrative. Diagnosed with gout and told to abstain from alcohol by Cullen, Brown worsened and subsequently modified his recommended treatment regime to include stimulants.[21] He developed these ideas into a simplified system which suggested that all disease was caused by excitability, or, more specifically, an excess or deficiency of stimulation. Too much excitability resulted in what he termed *sthenic* diseases, while too little led to *asthenic* conditions. In general, though patients could experience excitable states, humans had a natural tendency to 'disease and death' and were ultimately reduced to depletive states requiring stimulants, primarily alcohol and opium.[22] Advocating a case for the proactive physician, not nature, to heal, Brown's methods necessitated an attentive practitioner to monitor their patient's pulse, temperature and general condition, especially in the critical stages of disease. While his views altered practices, especially in Germany and Italy, their influence was 'far from clear cut'.[23]

Although the Brunonian system was not adopted evenly across Europe, practitioners for and against Brown's therapeutic approach also coexisted in communities and medical institutions. For example, historian Guenter Risse has demonstrated that there was an increase in the medical use of alcohol in Edinburgh Royal Infirmary in the years following the publication of Brown's system in *Elementa Medicinae* (1780). In the 1770s, the prescription of alcohol was modest and used 10 per cent of the time on the wards;[24] it tended to be prescribed in the form of beer, which Cullen found 'more nourishing than wines'.[25] Far more patients were the subjects of depletive remedies: purging and bleeding. By the 1790s, this changed, with purgatives and emetics in noticeable decline, whilst wine and opium use doubled. However, the increased consumption of these expensive items posed a new financial burden, and physicians were urged to restrict their application 'within proper bounds', a process aided by the introduction of a system of monthly reporting and the requirement that prescriptions be rewritten daily.[26]

In the early nineteenth century, the views of Cullen and Brown regarding alcohol's place in the sick room set the general parameters for its use among practitioners. These differences in prescribing are also evident in national pharmacopoeias. For example, the first *Pharmacopoeia of the United States of America* (1820) contained nine formulas for *vina medicate*; the Parisian *Pharmacopée Universelle* of 1840 listed 164 individual wine remedies.[27] The adulteration and luxury status of wine continued to restrict its routine medical use in these years.

There also existed a growing coterie of practitioners who can be described as early advocates of temperance; Dr Alexander Farquharson Henderson (1779/80–1863), a London-based Scottish physician and early historian of wine, has been noted as one of the most vocal.[28] The pioneer of occupational medicine, the Englishman Charles Turner Thackrah (1795–1833), likewise cautioned the readers of his *The Effects of Arts, Trades and Professions*, describing alcohol as 'the great bane of civilised life'.[29] John Darwall, Thackrah's contemporary and another of the earliest British practitioners interested in the impact of industry on health, also emphasized the dangers of alcohol.[30] This blossoming of concern around 1830 is unsurprising: the passage of the controversial Beer Act liberated the sale of beer and created 45,000 additional uncontrolled retail outlets for alcoholic beverages,[31] thereby placing more workmen of the burgeoning industrial nation in harm's way. As a result, the distinction between alcoholic drinks also appeared to evaporate and the idea of total abstinence, as opposed to temperance, gained greater numbers of supporters both inside and outside the medical community.[32]

Alcohol and Mental Health, *c.* 1770–1850

Excessive alcohol consumption was not only a danger to life and limb in a successful economy. One of the earliest specialists on 'nervous disorders' to warn about the hazards to the mind was Scottish physician George Cheyne, whose expertise, like that of Brown, was firmly rooted in experience. In 1733, he wrote that national prosperity had generated the '*Riot, Luxury ... and Excess*' which caused the 'English Malady'.[33] And Cheyne was no stranger to excess; upon qualifying as a physician and moving to London, he '[ate] lustily and [swallowed] down much *Liquor*',[34] and grew so fat on success that he weighed-in at over thirty-two stones (just over 203 kg). Consequently, Cheyne found himself '*short-breath'd, Lethargic* and *Listless*'.[35] The cure for his own malady, as well as that of the English nervous patient, was temperance.[36] Total abstinence was equally at the heart of the scientist-clergyman Stephen Hales's *Friendly Admonition* (1751).[37] Benjamin Rush (a physician and one of the US Founding Fathers) in 1784 and John Coakley Lettsom (the renowned British Quaker doctor) in 1789 respectively warned of the 'Effects of Ardent Spirits' and 'Hard Drinking'.[38] Both men described symptoms of delirium tremens. Lettsom also recognized what is now termed 'alcoholic psychosis'; while it is unclear whether Lettsom understood this could be precipitated by alcohol withdrawal,[39] he was unequivocal about the dire consequences of excess. Echoing Rush's 'Moral and Physical Thermometer' diagram, Lettsom's chart depicted the degrees of alcohol consumption and their effects. The consequences of intemperance included epilepsy, melancholy, madness and suicide, all of which were considered parts of the spectrum of insanity. Intemperance was at this point a description of excess, and, for many, the term was indicative of indulgence in 'bad' ardent liquors, which were contrasted with the health-giving cordials and tonics of beer, cider, wine and porter. 'Even Thomas Trotter', the Scottish naval physician, 'often feted as the discoverer of alcoholism [with his 1804 essay on drunkenness], advised that a 40-year old might take two glasses a day to raise his spirits, a 50-year old, four, and a 60-year old, six'.[40]

Alcohol was, then, an increasing part of the treatment armoury of medical men concerned with mental health. In 1724, Peter Shaw, later physician to 'mad' King George III, asserted that 'Wine [was] extraordinary in the Hippo [a term used for hypochondria or melancholy] and Hysterical Disease'.[41] Even John Wesley (1703–91), a founder of Methodism, follower of Cheyne's temperance and critic of drink and drunkenness,[42] prescribed alcohol for mental afflictions in his *Primitive Physic*, albeit as an ingredient of soothing ointments for the shaven-headed lunatic or as an ingredient of laudanum for the hysteric.[43] Meanwhile, the new breed of medical specialist that was emerging – the reputable mad-doctor – was quite clear on the uses and abuses of alcohol in the late eighteenth-century controversies surrounding the private asylum; for William Pargeter, drink could be an agent of normality for his disordered patients or a method by which unscrupulous madhouse proprietors stupefied the wrongfully confined.[44]

The emphasis on drink was indicative of a gradual shift in practice. Notions of necessary, brutalized custody and of the bestial maniac were losing ground. With Enlightenment mad-doctors came the idea of proactive intervention: lunatics were to be humanely treated and invested with self-control to inspire the restoration of reason. The York Retreat was founded in 1794 on the principles of this 'moral treatment'. Even here, at a place established by Quakers, alcohol was considered vital to a 'liberal and nourishing diet'.[45] Convalescents and melancholics were given additional wine or porter: 'attention of this kind [was] considered almost essential to ... recovery'.[46] Arguably, as there was little contemporary specialist training in mental illness and limited evidence of positive care outcomes, the influence of the Retreat was furthered among reformers and the small networks circling the few existing public asylums; the latter group included John Garrett, a young physician at the ancient Bethlem Hospital, London. The Retreat was therefore inspirational for many institutions founded in England after the permissive County Asylums Act of 1808. The fifth to open was Staffordshire County Lunatic Asylum, a facility for all social classes in the Midlands town of Stafford in 1818.

Other asylums, like the Northern Lunatic Hospitals at Manchester and Newcastle, seemed to rely on a 'low diet' based largely on gruel and milk, the theory being that this was a calmative and would mollify inmates.[47] As at the Retreat, at Stafford under Dr Garrett, its new superintendent, diet was the key to cure, though here it was used to fortify the body in preparation for more volatile or intrusive medical interventions, like the use of digitalis, antimony, mercury and 'water treatment'. Between 1818 and 1827, many admissions were emaciated through poverty, heroic remedies, mania, melancholy or delusions of poisoning. Even if such newcomers were agitated, restless or excited, they were immediately placed on a generous dietary, which supplemented the food and beer that all inmates received. 'Habits of intoxication' was one of many causes given for insanity, either directly or as an aggravating factor.[48] While earlier physicians recognized that women were just as prone to, as Trotter described, *'the habit of drunkenness* [as] *a disease of the mind'*[49] – foreshadowing the modern disease concept of alcoholism – at Stafford females were significantly less likely to be recorded as showing symptoms of what had recently been termed 'dipsomania', after the German Carl von Brühl-Cramer's study.[50] Four women were recorded with alcohol as a clear factor in their madness in comparison to twenty-three men, out of 304 and 388 patients respectively, that is, around 1 per cent and 6 per cent. Even so, many of these patients continued to be prescribed extra alcohol: wine, porter or, less frequently, brandy, to improve their physical health and thus address supposed somatic causes of insanity; or beer and ale as calmatives and soporifics for those whose mental afflictions meant they could not sleep at night.[51] Here then, drink was not necessarily used as a stimulant, though as many emaciated patients were also melancholic, alcohol served as a therapeutic agent on both counts.

Economy and Science, *c.* 1850–1910

The tension between alcohol as food and medicine, cause and cure – and between its suspension and use – was therefore felt most keenly in psychiatric practice. In many ways in Britain this was also due to public asylums being funded partly or fully by local rate-payers. For this reason, at Stafford (as at other nineteenth-century asylums), the reliance on beer made it economical to establish an on-site brewhouse, which was part-staffed by male inmates. Labour was considered integral to moral therapy by distracting lunatics from their disturbed thoughts and by introducing normality; it also became indispensable to the effective running of a large institution. Niall McCrae, a psychiatric researcher, has argued that in Victorian asylums, beer was used as an incentive for inmates to work.[52] Certainly, this would help explain why Staffordshire was successful in employing so many inmates,[53] and why the institution topped, by far, an official league table for alcohol expenditure at English asylums in 1858.[54] While these figures may be distorted by seasonal and gender issues,[55] it was precisely because of the expenditure of local rate-payers' money and associated polemics (like that of Sir George Strickland MP in 1861[56]) that the temperance movement began to influence asylum policy.

Interestingly, it was around this time that advocates of wine within the medical profession redoubled their use of alcohol in practice. As John Harley Warner has explained, a revolution in British medicine occurred between the early 1830s and 1850s, when therapeutics underwent a reversal, with fewer practitioners relying on depletive therapies, favouring instead stimulation with alcohol and nourishment; put succinctly, 'the brandy bottle replaced the lancet'.[57] In particular, alcohol became less a panacea than the chosen remedy for acute disease, including pneumonia, rheumatic fever and typhus. Whether or not this faith in alcohol legitimized its wider use, the public certainly favoured benign remedies over intrusive and painful treatments.[58] This new reliance on alcohol has been traced to Robert J. Graves (1796–1853), who was based at the Richmond Hospital in Dublin.[59] Graves challenged contemporary antiphlogistic or depleting therapies that were being advocated as remedies for fevers. Instead of bleeding and purging, Graves advocated the importance of a full diet and gained a reputation as the physician who 'fed fevers'.[60] Likewise, the Birmingham practitioner Peyton Blakiston implemented stimulants during epidemics and made a strong case for their use in his *Treatise on the Influenza of 1837*,[61] as did William Stokes, a colleague of Graves in Dublin. This suggests that there was a revival of the Brunonian system, though evidence for alcohol's use in practice before 1850 has been exaggerated.[62] The renewed support for wine therapy in mainstream medicine, however, would increase greatly during the late nineteenth century and was arguably owing to Graves's role as a medical educator in Dublin.

Robert Bentley Todd has been described as 'the most influential proselytizer of "alcoholic therapeutics" in mid-nineteenth-century Britain';[63] he was also a student of Graves before moving to London. Gaining popularity as a clinical lecturer at Aldersgate Street Medical School, Todd was appointed to King's College Medical School in 1833. He is best remembered for his *Cyclopaedia of Anatomy and Physiology*, the first volume of which appeared in 1843. On the subject of acute diseases, the massive fourth volume (1860), like Todd's mentor in Dublin, popularized those treatments that 'may excite, assist' or uphold the vital power of the patients during fever.[64] Alcohol, it was held at the time, produced heat and was, therefore, more effective than bleeding, calomel and other lower remedies when faced with acute cases such as typhus. Todd's arguments would also increase the tension between doctors and members of the temperance movement:

> Alcohol, in some form or other, is a remedy whose value can scarcely, I think, be overestimated, and one upon which, when carefully administered, I rely with the utmost confidence in a great number of cases of disease which are all amenable to treatment. Alcohol may be employed in all those diseases in which a tendency to depression of the vital powers exists, and there are no acute diseases in which this lowering tendency is not present.[65]

Todd 'made the liberal therapeutic use of alcohol fashionable and respectable', by grounding his views in modern physiology.[66] His death in 1860, as well as fresh evidence suggesting alcohol was excreted from the body unchanged, stimulated renewed debate. Among a flurry of work calling for the banishment of alcohol from medical practice, an influential paper by Scottish physician William T. Gairdner challenged the faith in brandy. Described by the editors of the *Lancet* as 'one of the most promising of the present generation of physicians in Scotland',[67] Gairdner undertook a study between 1861 and 1862 designed to test the efficacy of alcohol in the cure of typhus, 'the disease in which, of all others, it has been considered most important'.[68] Connected with the Glasgow Fever Hospital, Gairdner employed three degrees of stimulation on patients who then underwent treatment for typhus over an average of 20.5 days. One group received almost no stimulation – his preferred practice – another group received forty ounces of wine and seven ounces of spirit, as was common at the Glasgow Fever Hospital, while a final group endured 'extreme stimulation',[69] or half an ounce of brandy each hour in cases of fever, as had been practised by Todd at King's College Hospital. The resultant mortality levels were 10, 17.5 and 25 per cent respectively. Consequently, 'a most grave doubt' was said to have been thrown upon 'the wisdom of the practice'.[70] While the *Lancet*'s authors attributed the origin of alcohol's use in therapy to Todd, the responsibility for continuing this practice was seen to rest 'with the profession in London'.[71]

Rather than change their methods, most physicians continued to regard alcohol as essential to supporting the sick patient and stimulating the vital force. Embattled opponents continued to publicize and republish their views at conferences and in journals over the next decade. Gairdner, for example, presented his findings at the thirty-sixth annual meeting of the British Medical Association in Oxford in 1868. On this occasion, he did not argue for the abandonment of stimulants as remedies, 'but for their administration upon a much lower scale'.[72] Their use was also described as a 'wasteful' form of expenditure, which delayed recovery and often led to increased mortality levels. Nevertheless, it is the discussion which followed that proves most informative. Given that Gairdner had requested 'the pupils of Todd present' to correct any errors made in his paper, it is not surprising that his first question came from one such disciple, Dr Francis Anstie, who considered the cases quoted from Todd's practice exceptional. Moreover, he denied that Todd's pupils uniformly applied large amounts of alcohol and reiterated the fact that it saved 'vital force'. The action of alcohol as a food, he claimed, was proved by temperature, the effects of alcohol in delirium and its diminished excretion in urine. He also emphasized that cases varied very greatly in their requirements for alcohol.[73]

Since Todd's death, the subject had clearly become an emotive issue which now drew in a generation of students who had been taught both by the foremost exponent for medicinal alcohol and his opponents. Nevertheless, the response of Todd's former students appears to have remained rational, to judge by Anstie, 'the most vocal defender of the scientific integrity of Toddism'.[74] In his publications on the subject in the 1860s and 1870s, Anstie concentrated on some long-standing confusions in the prevailing debates concerning the dangers of alcoholic remedies. These included the question of alcohol content ('proof'), which remained as vague as it had been in texts some hundred years earlier.[75] Anstie introduced the clearly defined 'unit' still used today, the equivalent of 1.5 ounces of pure ethanol, to replace measures that potentially varied with glass size and the alcoholic content of the beverage.[76] Rather than considering proof alone, he also directed attention to the constituents of an alcoholic beverage, including sugar, acids and salts. Finally, he addressed the language of the debates, emphasizing that wine's use in medical practice had been 'established by wide-spread custom'; it was not just another medical fad or fashion which suggested quackery, but its role in therapy had a long tradition.[77] Like Todd, Anstie continued to emphasize that alcohol was essential in treating fevers, including typhus.[78] Like Brown, his writings invoked images of practitioners who attentively monitored changes in their patients' conditions. With the 1869 findings from Carl Binz's research laboratories in Bonn, Germany, suggesting that alcohol actually lowered temperature, rather than raising (or stimulating) it,[79] Anstie's side gained another very convincing justification to support their wine-fuelled practices. It was in these years, then, that wine's use in medical practice, not to mention its more general consumption,[80] peaked in Britain.

Alcohol therapy continued to divide medical practitioners. The case against alcohol, however, did not advance as a result of new research and sounded much as it had decades earlier. Nevertheless, the use of wine and beer in practice does appear to have started to decline, as is indicated by hospital records. Accounts documenting alcohol consumption between the 1860s and 1880s at the General Hospital, Birmingham, the city's largest hospital, are indicative of this trend. Table 11.1 depicts the levels of weekly consumption per patient of wine, spirits, beer and ale at the General Hospital, Birmingham for the years 1865–7 and 1881–4. They demonstrate that Todd's methods influenced practice in the largest teaching hospital in the Midlands in the 1860s. By 1881, however, consumption rates declined significantly. Interestingly, the hospital's minute-books also indicate that this decrease had little to do with arguments either for or against alcohol's use in practice. As at the Edinburgh Royal Infirmary in the 1790s, this dramatic decline was directly linked to the cost of wine and beer.[81]

Table 11.1: Alcohol consumption in the General Hospital, Birmingham, 1865–7 and 1881–4.

	Wine	Spirits	Beer	Ale
General Hospital (1865–7)	0.9 bottles	0.07 bottles	0.55 quarts	0.58 quarts
General Hospital (1881–4)	0.02 bottles	0.03 bottles	0.01 quarts	0.09 quarts

Source: BCLA, General Hospital, Birmingham, 'Medical Committee Minute Book, 1876–84', HC/GHB/68, 70.

During this same period, the perception that lunacy and drink were linked was strengthened through international exchange. By 1850, the modern term 'alcoholism' and a deeper clinical understanding of chronic drinking had been synthesized by Magnus Huss, a Swedish physician. His ideas and those of Trotter and French alienist J. E. D. Esquirol (1772–1840) came to influence US physician J. Edward Turner. Turner established the first inebriate asylum in New York in 1852.[82] The scheme coincided with theories of degeneration, and such asylums emerged in Europe and found especial advocates in France.[83] Where Huss had seen parents setting an example of inebriety, French alienist B. A. Morel considered them to be the innate cause.[84] In the 1860s and 1870s Victor Magnan, a pupil of Morel, went on to ensure that degeneration and drink were treated as synonymous in eugenic ideas. The work of the two French physicians would influence key British psychiatrists (including Henry Maudsley and Edinburgh-based David Skae and Thomas Clouston) and contributed to demarcate the young guns from the old guard.[85] Swimming against the tide was J. C. Bucknill, a doyen of the profession, who worked on alcohol during the late 1870s and questioned medically-managed inebriate homes.[86] While he also queried the leading alienist L. Forbes-Winslow's proclamations that one could ignite the fluid in the brain ventricles of many chronic drinkers during post-mortem – following Dr John Percy's 1839 anecdotal evidence that it was possible to smell, taste and light gin in the ventricles of someone who had drunk the spirit to excess – Bucknill quipped that 'it [pointed] to one use to which a drunkard might be applied: he might be distilled'.[87] Alcohol had, then, become the *bête noire* of European psychiatry. In Britain, the state intervened with the Habitual Drunkards Acts passed to facilitate their cure and control (1879) and to enable the establishment of retreats (1894), and the Inebriates Act (1894), which permitted local authorities to found reformatories.[88] Yet despite the promise of new facilities, statistics revealed that on average 14 per cent of the asylum population were interned because of drink.[89] The profound correlation, coupled with rate-payers' concerns and a burgeoning international shift in attitudes towards prophylactic 'mental hygiene', was enough to ensure that the use of alcohol as a food and medicine in asylums plummeted.[90]

The decline in alcohol consumption in British hospitals and asylums may have been associated with economy, but it also coincided with greater numbers of practitioners actively supporting the temperance cause. Many of these practitioners, like Benjamin Ward Richardson (1828–96), were leaders in their profession and shared similarities with their opponents. For example, Richardson resembled Anstie in several ways, not least in his interest in therapeutics and public health and his study of anaesthetics. Richardson had been identified as a rising star in medicine in the early 1870s, until he became a teetotaller in the mid-1870s. Like Anstie, he grew dissatisfied with the lack of precision when prescribing alcohol. After some years of running an alcohol-free practice, Richardson then joined the staff at the London Temperance Hospital, which opened in 1892.[91] He joined the British Medical Temperance Association (BMTA) and edited their journal, the *Medical Pioneer*.[92]

Richardson was succeeded by the equally eminent practitioner Victor Horsley, from the emerging discipline of neurology. Peak membership of the Association was 568, among a potential pool of 30,000 qualified British medical men.[93] Its journal continued but was renamed *Medical Temperance Review* (1898–1912). Drawing on popular eugenics and the laboratory work of German teetotal psychiatrist and 'father of psychopharmacology' Emil Kraepelin, *Alcohol and the Human Body* (1907) was Horsley's own influential publication in this area, co-written with Mary Sturge. The study naturally concluded that 'parental intoxication tends to produce impulsive degenerates and moral imbeciles'.[94] Three years later, Karl Pearson disseminated his own controversial views on the subject, which conflicted with those of temperance doctors. Interestingly, his work at the Eugenics Laboratory, University of London, with Ethel Elderton, actually suggested that 'the general health of the children of alcoholics appear[ed] on the whole slightly better than that of sober parents'.[95] Regardless of the accuracy of Pearson's and Elderton's conclusion, it has been seen to have contributed to overturning the consensus on the role of degeneration in psychiatry.[96] The BMTA was renamed the Medical Abstainers Association in 1921 and it is then that it disappears from view.[97] A similar fate was shared by inebriate asylums around the same time.[98]

Conclusion

The question of the use of alcohol divided the medical profession in the nineteenth century. At times described as a fashion in order to denigrate it in the eyes of the undecided, the practice was deeply rooted in medical tradition. Advocates for the use of alcohol in medical practice were easily found in ancient Greek literature by those who had written on the subject since Cullen's time, if not earlier. The debate concerning its benefits and its dangers in the mid-Victorian period consolidated around more contemporary individuals, including Graves and Todd, and was continued by the students of those central to defining the parameters of this controversial subject. In general, exponents of the temperance side were, first, experienced in issues of mental health and, second, tended to be political liberals. Though eminent men, their numbers tended to be few, as an openly stated support of the temperance cause could result in the kind of ostracism Richardson had experienced.[99] However, by the end of the nineteenth century, greater toleration appears to have entered these debates.[100]

By this time, however, those confronting this contentious issue had found a middle way. Moderation, as continues to be the case in recent decades, was a tenet practitioners could agree upon. Those writing on the subject also recognized that there was no absolute rule when it came to alcohol. Consequently, theories continued to vary, as they do today. That said, mainstream practice throughout the century, as Warner has demonstrated previously, was resilient to even the most convincing arguments for or against the prescription of alcohol. When institutional records indicate a clear decline in prescribing alcohol, the reason has more to do with cost than a change in prevailing theories. Neither should it be forgotten that many alternatives and more effective remedies than wine had also begun to emerge in these decades of debate and that experimental science was increasingly influential belief.[101]

12 'BEEN TO BARBADOS': RUM(BULLION), RACE, THE *GASPÉE* AND THE AMERICAN REVOLUTION

Eva-Sabine Zehelein

Ogden Nash, possibly the world's premium punster of all times, once infamously quipped: 'Candy / Is dandy / But liquor / Is quicker'.[1] And even when one specific part of world history is considered, one which connects Europe, Africa, the Caribbean and the American East Coast colonies, Nash's words seem to ring true. As soon as mankind had figured out that this grass, known as *saccharum officinarum* (or sugar cane, 'sugar of the apothecaries'), could be cultivated and processed to yield crystallized sweetness, things began to be high-proof, complex and global.[2] This chapter aims to highlight how sugar, molasses and, first and foremost, rum influenced world history in the sense that this drink became a crucial player in the British colonies' development towards and struggle for independence.

Sugar cane wants warmth and moisture. From the Canary Islands, Madeira and the Azores, sugar cane travelled with Columbus first to Hispaniola, where it was planted and grew with awesome rapidity and yield, and then on various Portuguese explorer vessels to other islands of the Caribbean and to the coasts of South America. The remarkable burgeoning of sugar cane initiated a growing demand for human labour, since its cultivation requires intensive toil and fast milling after harvest; it needs to be boiled quickly before the sugar content can diminish.[3] Neither the European discoverers and their audacious entourages nor the indigenous populations of the Caribbean islands could provide an adequate number of sturdy hands, and thus, slave labour was instituted in the Caribbean through large-scale imports of people from Africa. Pioneers were the Portuguese, soon to be copied by many seafaring and colonizing nations.[4] And although many British abolitionists protested against this development the best way they imagined they could, namely by refusing to add sugar to their tea, an inhumane system of organized exploitation and eradication was established.[5]

Over the decades, sugar transformed from a luxury article to an essential element of Western existence, cuisine and *savoir vivre*. Sugar became not only a sweetener for tea, coffee and chocolate, and a natural disaster for teeth, but helpful in various cooking situations, such as masking the taste of rancid meat. Within forty years, between 1660 and 1700, the per capita consumption of sugar in Britain quadrupled and doubled again within the next twenty-five years.[6] Demand increased, production followed, and the infamous connection between staple crop production and the exploitation of humans and their labour was sealed. In addition, ever more Western Europeans travelled to the far-away islands of the Caribbean in search of profit or became absentee owners of sugar plantations, as for example the British in Jamaica and Barbados. Here, the population soared within roughly thirty years from eighty to 75,000, primarily through the import of slaves but also through immigration.[7] African slaves outnumbered European settlers significantly; by 1750, at a ratio of four to one; Jamaica, by then Britain's chief sugar island, had a ratio of ten slaves to one European settler. Between 1640 and 1780, the islands of the Caribbean imported more than 1.2 million African slaves,[8] and a development that paralleled events on the American continents was initiated here: white owners and overseers moved into fortified mansions, exploited human labour, crushed the occasional rebellion and institutionalized slavery.[9]

Barbados not only has its place in the small group of venues which pioneered the 'peculiar institution' of slavery and became a key hub within the transatlantic slave trade, it also grew into the major producer and exporter of sugar cane and the richest colony in the British Empire, so that massive amounts of wealth were shipped back to England.[10] The following anecdote shows not only the growing self-confidence among Jamaican planters but also the impressive affluence brought to England by sugar trade. One day, King George III was riding with his Prime Minister Pitt near Weymouth and was pushed off the path by a colossal and extravagant carriage, accompanied by a lavishly dressed entourage. The King was informed that this convoy was that of a sugar planter from Jamaica. The King said: 'Sugar, sugar, hey? All *that* sugar! How are the duties, hey, Pitt, how are the duties?'[11]

Sugar was not only a sweetie-star in itself but also the ticket to a new and intoxicating success story. Various versions of the 'invention' of rum exist, just as there are differing theories on its geographical and epistemological roots; the most favoured geographical origin seems to be Barbados. Here, the first direct and much-quoted reference to rum was recorded in 1651: 'The chief fudling they make in the island is *rumbullion*, alias Kill-Devil, and this is made of sugar canes distilled, a hot, hellish and terrible liquor'.[12] Barbados still lays claim to fame for being home to the oldest rum-making distillery, Mount Gay, which celebrated its tercentenary in 2003 and features the slogan 'the rum that invented rum'.[13]

The 2013 official website of 'Mount Gay Rum' reveals an iconography in variations of amber and provides the viewer with a variety of essential ingredients of how rum wants to see itself. The setting is sunshine or a sunset on the white sands of a Caribbean beach, palm trees, water and the planks of a sailing vessel; a romantic atmosphere is created with the help of peppy music, which oscillates between a longing siren sing-song of a Southern black belle, who appears in the video, sensuously licking her lips before turning to the viewer, and a metropolitan beat. Amber and golden hues dominate the affective experience. Information on the product is sorely lacking, the focus is on the creation of feeling and images. The video serves to establish a brand platform. We are supposed to long for that beach, to be an imaginary guest at the party there while watching the sunset. And if we cannot travel to Barbados, the coral island of luxury, glamour and revelry, we should at least buy a bottle and imagine that we belong.

Whatever else we say about rum, it is the distillation of fermented industrial waste.[14] At first, no one wanted molasses, the waste product of sugar extraction. It was fed to cows and slaves, used as mortar, and some even thought it might cure syphilis. Besides, the first rums were terrible in taste, but they made the consumers happy and were often safer than water. This 'hot, hellish and terrible liquor' would, in various blends and versions known, for example, as the Barbadoes Waters or Jamaica Rum, become a genuinely American drink, a wheeler and dealer in American colonial times and a somewhat influential liquid throughout American history; it roamed the streets of Philadelphia as well as the cocktail bars of Havana and New York, it transformed from the kill-devil via the Hemingway Daiquiri (also known as the 'Papa Doble' in El Floridita, Havana)[15] to the Zombie (immortalized for example in T. C. Boyle's novel *The Inner Circle* (2004), which features Alfred Kinsey) and the Ginger Mojito.

Nutritionally, rum was beneficial because it is very caloric (ten times the calories of whole milk). Moreover, since issues such as diabetes, adiposity or AA membership were still unknown, and because drinking water was often not available in the early days, cider, beer, whisky and rum were the brews of the times. Never was the Puritan minister Increase Mather more popular, I suppose, than when he stated in 1673: 'Drink is in itself a creature of God'.[16] Rum was the ideal alcoholic beverage, particularly when the colonists considered their alternatives: cider requires a satisfactory apple crop, beer and whisky are both based on grain, and grain remained a very valuable and sometimes scarce commodity, which at times (during food shortages) was taken out of the distillation process by law. So rum would more often than not be the drink of the day. It did not take any agricultural product off the family dinner table but instead made wonderful use of a waste product. One option to acquire rum was to trade it for timber, yet with the technological know-how and surrounded by woods and forests, New England as a production site for rum made lots of sense, too. The taste was worse, but the price was lower than that of the imported rum from the West Indies. Soon, rum distillation became a very profitable business in the colonies and rum a major export article. By 1770, the American colonies had more than one hundred distilleries producing some 4.8 million gallons of rum per year on top of the imports. The colonial population in 1770 consisted of 1.7 million people, who, according to Williams, flushed down 7.5 million gallons of rum every year. If one discounts women and children, that amounts to approximately three pints of rum per week per adult male, an amount which certainly had its effects on livers and tempers.[17]

When members of the Continental Congress met in Philadelphia's City Tavern, they not only ordered, one must assume, a broad variety of drinks, such as the mimbo (shavings from a sugarloaf, rum and water), the sling (two parts water to one part rum), the bombo (which uses molasses instead of sugar, rum and water), the punch, or the calibogus (spruce beer and rum), a flip,[18] a blackstrap (a mix with molasses), or a stonewall (a mix with cider).[19] They also discussed that daring venture manifested in the *Declaration of Independence*. The taverns and inns were the meeting halls of the colonists; it is here that protest was voiced, inter-colonial resistance and communication organized, petitions were penned, and arguments for and against bitter resistance – or non-importation – were debated. The taverns were also the campaign grounds for politicians who aimed to win voters. One of their strategies was to throw rounds and rounds of liquor.[20] The militias also elected their colonels in the local taverns; one 'colonel from Rumford received his election on account of his incompetency. In a speech which he was obliged to make on receiving the office, he said, "I can't make a speech, but what I lack in brains I will try and make up in rum"'.[21]

Whichever way we look at it, sugar, slaves and rum fashioned an unholy trinity, which travelled the Atlantic Ocean on various journeys in a nodal network of globalized trade. The term 'triangular trade' can be misleading, since the trade movement was hardly ever really triangular; transatlantic trade was rather organized by shuttles, and there were many triangles between diverse 'corners'. The West Indies relied on imports of essentially everything but tobacco and sugar. From the North American colonies, above all from New England, came grain, meat, fish and lumber, especially to Antigua and Barbados. The processing of sugar required vast amounts of fuel so that the forests on the Caribbean islands were, by the beginning of the eighteenth century, eliminated. The Caribbean work force, slaves, came from Africa. Sugar and molasses for rum production were sent to New England, among other places. Some sugar travelled to England and was traded for manufactured items, which then went back to New England. Food, for example *bacalao*, rum and timber journeyed to southern Europe, namely Spain (Cadiz) and Portugal, wine and fruit to England, manufactures to the colonies.[22] Africa as a market was of small significance for colonial exports. And slave transportation was dominated by British rather than colonial vessels. Although the argument was made both by abolitionists and by teetotallers that rum figured in the slave trade of the American colonies – that slaves were brought from Africa and traded to the West Indies for molasses, that the molasses were used for rum distillation in New England and that the rum was then traded in Africa for more slaves – historians today estimate that the amount of rum shipped to Africa was rather small. The consumption of rum in the colonies was high, and when rum was exported from the North American colonies, it went to many different destinations, wherever New England wanted or needed to do trade.[23] Furthermore, colonial vessels were hardly ever directly involved in the slave trade – which is no defence or apology but helps to explain some convenient and therefore frequent misrepresentations.[24]

In Europe, Liverpool developed into an important slaving port and a centre for European–American trade. It was from here that rum was dripped into the European veins. By the end of the eighteenth century, countries such as Germany and parts of Scandinavia had taken to it. Flensburg became the rum capital of the north; it belonged to Denmark and thus profited from the Danish Virgin Islands' production after 1755. Flensburg was annexed by Prussia in 1864, and thus the originally Danish company Pott, one of the leading rum producers, established in 1848 by Hans Hinrich Pott and based in Flensburg, became German. Today, Flensburg hosts a rum museum, illustrating that more than thirty rum companies operated there at the end of the twentieth century.[25]

During the late eighteenth century, the colonies on the North American continent played an important part in Britain's political and economic theatre, namely that of a deliverer of staple crops and raw materials and of a market for British products.[26] This trade relationship proved to be rather beneficial for all involved, excluding competitors and securing regular and substantive income revenues for merchants on both sides of the transatlantic waterway. By the early 1760s, the American colonies were prospering and were developing into a pre-industrial consumer society.[27] Between 1720 and 1770, British exports to the American colonies more than doubled, so that contemporaries such as William Smith could remark: 'Our affluence, during the late war [Seven Years' War], introduced a degree of luxury in tables, dress, and furniture, with which we were before unacquainted'.[28] While the colonies prospered, the British Crown was tumbling into debt. As a consequence, it began to shift its attitude from benign neglect to enforcement of mercantilist policies with the ultimate aim of raising revenue. As part of the Trade and Navigation Acts, the Molasses Act (1733) had been passed by the British Crown in order to regulate the molasses trade. As a result of the intense political work by the West India lobby, with the Molasses Act, Britain had granted the British West Indies sugarcane growers a virtual monopoly as exclusive traders with the American British colonies by placing heavy duties upon the importation of molasses, sugar and rum from the French West Indies to the American colonies.[29] The simple reason for this was that the British West Indies could not absorb the mainland colonies' surplus. The Americans also sold their wares to the French West Indies, where traders were eager to sell their molasses, even at extremely low prices. The British sugar cane planta-tion owners, many of whom were absentee owners or investors in London, felt irritated in consequence and lobbied for protective legislation.

Smuggling had become an exceedingly lucrative business, and law enforce-ment was lax. In 1764, the Crown passed the Sugar Act, which lowered the tax on molasses but attempted a rigid implementation by restructuring and enlarging the customs service, forcing voluminous paper work on every captain entering any American port, sending more navy ships to patrol the coastlines and issuing writs of assistance to customs officials, which were search warrants requiring no proof of suspicion. In addition, the vice-admiralty courts denied the colonists trial by jury. With the notable exception of the Leeward Islands,[30] the sugar islands, particularly Barbados and Jamaica, acquiesced to the Sugar Act, likewise with the Stamp Act that followed in 1765.[31] The mainland colonists and protesters condemned the tameness of the sugar islands; the historian A. J. O'Shaughnessy illustrates how much vengeance and bitterness were expressed after the Sugar Act had been passed. The agitators on the American mainland suspected islanders' complicity in its passing – a suspicion surely enough not quenched or denied by Prime Minister George Grenville, who used this inner-colonial division for his own agenda. John Adams, who would later serve as America's second President, mused and moaned:

> Can no Punishment be devised for Barbadoes [sic] and Port Royal in Jamaica? For their base Desertion of the Cause of Liberty? Their tame Surrender of the Rights of Britons? Their mean, timid Resignation to slavery? Meeching, sordid, stupid Crea-tures, below Contempt, below Pity. They deserve to be made Slaves to their own Negroes. But they live under the scorching Sun, which melts them, dissipates their Spirits and relaxes their Nerves.[32]

And the *Boston Post-Boy & Advertiser*, 24 March 1766, printed an 'Extract of a Letter from New-London, March 13, 1766' whose author states unambiguously,

> The SLAVISH Islands of Barbados and Antigua – Poor, mean spirited, Cowardly, Das-tardly Creoles, I wish they may have neither Fresh or Salt Provision from any Son of LIBERTY on the Continent, and that they may like the Blacks, whom they now make Slaves of with Rigour, be deemed to wear the Infernal Badge of STAMPS about their Necks, 'till they like the brave Sons of LIBERTY on the Continent become FREE.[33]

Both the mainland colonies and the sugar islands detested and opposed the Stamp Act as well as the Sugar Act. The islands, with the exception of the Lee-ward Islands, however, accepted the constitutionality of these Acts and did not rise to arms, while the mainlanders did. The gulf between the mainland and the islands broadened and helped to foster opposition against Britain on the main-land. O'Shaughnessy argues,

The conciliatory response of Jamaica and Barbados was anathema to the mainland Sons of Liberty. To pay any stamp duty appeared to the mainland patriots to be both a tacit acknowledgment of Parliament's authority to tax the colonies and a fatal precedent for the future.[34]

While the islanders, nineteen colonies all in all, did not form committees of correspondence, pass non-importation agreements, boycott British imports or organize local resistance against crown officials, they secured for themselves for the coming years the status of a 'most favored nation' with Britain, which even exempted them from many new imperial policies as a just reward for their loyalty.[35] The West India lobby worked effectively,[36] despite its internal heterogeneity and diversity of interests. What united island agents in London, absentee owners, London merchants and members of Parliament with diverse connections to the West Indies were their economic interests. The islands fit perfectly into the existing economic scenery: they delivered tropical staple crops which were in high demand and relied on the import of all basic needs from Britain. The West Indies increased the number of agents they sent to London after 1760; in 1774, ten active agents represented the islands, in contrast to only three agents from North America.[37] During the 1760s, the West Indies' interests were bundled, and their bargaining and lobbying power concentrated in the Society of West Indies Merchants. This organization surfaced at a time when 'extensive British colonial policy initiatives and imperial reorganizations' emerged, in which the interests of the sugar islands were immediately affected.[38] In order to lobby effectually for their cause and interests, they used pamphlets, advertisements and anonymously published articles in various British newspapers.[39]

The American colonists on the other hand found diverse ways of protest and retaliation, for example by boycotting British goods. The first boycotts began as a reaction to the Stamp Act in 1765 and 1766 and were followed by more boycotts in the years 1768 to 1770 and 1774 to 1776. Every time, the boycotts became more efficient and the protest movement matured.[40] Over the years, the general opinion in the colonies shifted from a feeling of dependence on the mother country towards a notion that the British depended on the American consumer. Since the Crown had damaged the mercantilist equilibrium, the colonies questioned whether they were still bound to its provisions and jump-started their own manufactures to foster American independence from European imports. American colonists threatened non-consumption of British goods, non-delivery of their own commodities and crops as well as the construction of their own manufactures, thus practically terminating the (economic) relationship with Great Britain, which was framed in mercantilist terms and ideas, and as a consequence, an American self-confidence emerged.[41] In May 1770, Americans could read a call to boycott in the *Pennsylvania Gazette*:

> As we form a considerable, independent, and respectable Body of the People, we certainly have an *equal Right* to enter into Agreements and Resolutions *with others* for the public Good, in a sober, orderly Manner, becoming Freemen and loyal Subjects ... let us determine, *for the Good of the Whole*, to strengthen the Hands of the Patriotic Majority, by agreeing not to purchase *British Goods*.[42]

Moreover, the colonists reprimanded those Caribbean islands which had accepted the Stamp Act by simply discontinuing their trade relations with them.

The most famous historical moment of opposition to the Crown by agitated Americans is the torching of the British customs vessel *Gaspée* in Providence Harbor in June 1772, committed by respectable citizens of Rhode Island as an act of open resistance against British policies. The vessel's commander, Lieutenant William Dudingston, had quarrelled with the elected governor of Rhode Island, Joseph Wanton, over the superior authority in matters of controlling smuggling and law enforcement. Dudingston sent letters to Boston for adjudication, added twelve hogsheads of rum, which he had seized in Rhode Island as mollifier, and therewith enraged the Rhode Islanders, who not only lamented the loss of liquor but were about to be deprived of trial by jury in their own colony. Furthermore, Dudingston was, according to the *Providence Gazette*, 9 January 1773, accused of

> stealing Sheep, Hogs, Poultry, &c from the Farmers round the Bay, and cutting down their Fruit and other Trees for Firewood – In a Word, his Behaviour was as *piratical* and provoking, that Englishmen could not patiently bear it. This gave Rise to the unhappy Scheme of destroying the Gaspee, which though it has been represented by the King's Officers as an Affair preconcerted by the Inhabitants round Narraganset Bay, and that almost the whole Town of Providence were concerned in it, I say this Action was done by about forty People, in five or six Longboats, as the Gaspee's People declared on Oath the Day after she was destroyed.[43]

On 9 June 1772, the *Gaspée* had been patrolling for smugglers, chasing the sloop *Hannah*, and ran aground. Under cover of darkness, some concerned citizens of Rhode Island hurried to the ship, boarded, removed the crew and then set fire to the vessel. No witnesses could be found, despite the offer of the large reward of one hundred pounds sterling, and no charges could be made.

This rather minor and insignificant event has sometimes been considered the first act of violence triggering the American War of Independence, three years before the infamous 'shot heard round the world' was fired at Lexington. It was just after the burning of this schooner, in the aftermath of relative calm, since the Townshend duties had been repealed, that, in the face of this 'giant imperial conspiracy' against their liberties and rights, the American colonies began to organize inter-colonial committees of correspondence in order to monitor British activities. The British had ordered that individuals charged with the act of vandalism should be brought to England for trial, which was yet another violation of the idea of trial by jury. Emotions and tempers began to run high. From the *Gaspée*, it was only a small step to the Boston Tea Party[44] on 16 December 1773. Again, under cover of darkness, some concerned citizens hurried to a ship, boarded and threw some 342 chests full of tea overboard. George III lost his temper and reportedly cried out: 'The colonists must either submit or triumph!'[45] Yet that one third of the white male colonial population which openly advocated separation from England did its all to create a feeling of unity within and among the colonies. Patrick Henry would exclaim that he was no longer a Virginian, but an American,[46] and a disillusioned and ill-reputed British pastor, only recently transplanted to America after a dismissal from his flock and a trial for forgery, would also contribute to the 'war of words and ideas' in the colonies. Reverend John Allen, 'New England's Tom Paine',[47] told the congregation at the Second Baptist Church of Boston in December 1773:

> The King of England has no power to enact, or put in force any law that may oppress them [the Americans]; his very attempting to do it, at once destroys his right to reign over them ... You know that the King of England has no right, according to the laws of GOD and nature, to claim property of Americans without their consent. Liberty, my Lord, is the native right of the Americans; it is the blood-bought treasure of their Forefathers.[48]

The man who had begun his preaching career in Petticoat Lane, London, delivered fodder for the Revolutionary cause; the Crown was practising despotism, depriving the Americans of their rights and breaking the law. These *a prioris* would soon enter various pamphlets and statements, and, finally, the *Declaration of Independence*. Despite Lord North's best efforts, the colonies did triumph, after a longer process of unification, negotiation, arbitration and war.

Rum had been both a symbol and a fact.[49] It represented the North American colonies' gradual breaking away from the British motherland, an increasing self-reliance, the confidence in their own products and independent as well as active participation in the global trading game. It also accompanied the growing sense of political sovereignty and the 'can do' spirit, the courage to commit high treason and secede from Great Britain. It mirrors the general inbred psychological ups and downs of that nation America, as personified later by celebrities such as Poe and Al Capone, Hemingway and Fitzgerald (who introduced the Daiquiri into world literature in *This Side of Paradise*, 1920), and then also by the likes of Charlie 'the Battlin' Barfly' Bukowski, or Dylan '18 and Out' Thomas; or by Hunter S. Thompson, who said: 'I wouldn't recommend sex, drugs, or insanity for everyone, but they've always worked for me', or by Truman Capote: 'I'm an alcoholic. I'm a drug addict. I'm homosexual. I'm a genius'.[50] All these intellectuals and contemplators of American identity and exceptionalism have succumbed to fears and anxieties and doubts, not only about themselves and their idiosyncratic lives, but also about the American experiment. Today, we toast each other with Bacardi – a brand aiming to provide the quintessential lifestyle product in a society fallen prey to conspicuous consumption – yearning for the Bacardi feeling, and we try hard to ignore the impact the Bacardi family has had on Cuba and its political fate.[51] To sum up: rum was a multifunctional tool, a global player and a socio-political and cultural booster. Thus, it might indeed be 'the history of America in a glass',[52] rebellious, adaptable and pluralistic. At least it was, to use Bridenbaugh's phrase, the 'spirit of '76'.[53]

13 A BEVERAGE FOR THE MASSES: THE DEMOCRATIZATION OF COCOA IN NINETEENTH-CENTURY AMERICAN FICTION

Monika Elbert

To understand the history of cocoa and its consumption is to understand the politics of power and the economy of the privileged. Although the focus of this chapter will be power dynamics as reflected in nineteenth-century literary texts, I shall first give a brief history of the paradoxical meanings associated with chocolate – starting as a magical brew for the gods, beverage of the oppressed and exotic libation for the oppressor.

The value of cocoa and later of chocolate is inherently associated with power struggles and, as a result of its commodification, with social status and with exploitation. 'Chocolate' or 'cocoa' has its origins in 'Theobroma cacao', which is Latin and means 'food of the gods'. Since its inception as a word or as a concept, cocoa has been most problematic with its dual meanings of possession and dispossession. The origin of the word 'chocolate' dates back to the Aztecs in Mesoamerica, in whose culture 'xocoatal' means the bitter beverage derived from cocoa beans, and as cocoa was seen as magical, offerings of cocoa were often made to the gods. At the same time, Aztecs would offer sacrificial victims cocoa as a palliative beverage to drink before their death, so cocoa was associated with life-affirming practices as well as death rituals. With the conquest by Hernán Cortés, the sweet and bitter aspects of cocoa became even more apparent. There are early visual representations of Montezuma offering Cortés libations of cocoa, as the Spanish conquistador was thought to be a god, and this image captured the colonialist enterprise of the European conquest in the New World. The Spaniards, not caring for the bitter taste, tried to sweeten the cocoa with honey or sugar. What could not be sweetened was this dark episode of history and the destruction of the Aztec Indian culture that followed the Spanish conquest.

Later, too, the Cadbury's chocolate enterprise of England would be involved in a bitter episode of history as they turned a blind eye to the institution of slavery in Africa in an effort to increase profits from chocolate manufacturing to expand its already thriving chocolate empire. In the United States, Walter Baker,

– 151 –

of the famous Baker's chocolate, bragged in 1848 that it made its chocolate from the free island of Haiti and was quite proud of his 'Free Labor' chocolate during the American Civil War, but that did not stop him from doing business with *both* Northern abolitionists and Southern landowners, selling the latter cheap poor-quality cocoa for the slaves. The Baker company continued to import chocolate from Brazil, a country which did not abolish slavery until 1888.[1] The ongoing troubling power dynamics involved in the production and consumption of chocolate or cocoa can be seen in tense moments of economic history as well as in class conflicts presented in literary texts. An examination of changing attitudes towards cocoa and chocolate consumption as reflected in class dynamics lays the groundwork of this essay. Chocolate, an emblem of wealth, status or economic possibilities, became accessible to the American working class towards the late nineteenth century, and thus the gentrification of the product appears in Naturalist texts, where the disempowered populace could feel some claim to privilege or entitlement in their choice of cocoa as a desirable beverage associated with the niceties of the upper class and with social manners. In the process, cocoa often figures as a wholesome product, promoted by the woman of the household, even if it at times has some risqué qualities attached to it.

Using literary and cultural sources, I begin with an account of colonial America's attempts to resist the oppressor, England, by drinking cocoa and shunning tea. The fledgling nation quickly made its declaration of independence by creating its own cocoa company, Baker's, in Dorcester, Massachusetts. I will show how cocoa was first the province of the wealthy, both in Europe and in America. The gentrification of the underclass occurred with the inculcation of middle-class values and also tastes, as in the beverage of cocoa. Ingesting cocoa and later chocolate became a sign of aspiration to move up the social ladder, to advance from lowbrow to highbrow. Ironically, in the process, there are accounts of men resisting women who would civilize them with such beverages as cocoa (as in Frank Norris's *McTeague*, 1899) and of women breaking away from prescribed roles by connecting to the exotic or erotic side of cocoa and chocolate (as in the 'New Woman' works by Kate Chopin, Charlotte Perkins Gilman and Edith Wharton). On the negative side, cocoa or later chocolate pralines also began to stand for the baser qualities of the American consumer, who would guzzle down the beverage or binge on chocolates in a childlike manner. Indeed, Henry James saw and critiqued the ugly side of such overindulgence.

Chocolate in the Historical and Literary American Marketplace: From Colonial to Mid-Nineteenth-Century Times

Nineteenth-century writers of the American Renaissance often saw chocolate as a foreign commodity, one perhaps tainted by its association with European colonialism but not necessarily with similar American evils. The nineteenth-century author Nathaniel Hawthorne, in his early stint as editor of the encyclopedic

American Magazine of Useful and Entertaining Knowledge, maintained in his article on cocoa that Native Americans (and not Columbus, as Eurocentric culture would claim) discovered chocolate. The fondness for cocoa quickly became a sign of the European abuse of power and taste for riches, in the tyranny over those they conquered, as suggested by Hawthorne's declaration about Creole women, chocolate and slaves: 'Chocolate seems to have been first manufactured in Mexico, and the Creole ladies were for a long time so fond of the beverage that it was habitually served to them, even in church, by their slaves'.[2]

In colonial New England, cocoa was perceived alternately as beneficial and dangerous. In 1726, the Puritan Cotton Mather attributed healing powers to milk flavoured with cocoa, though an almanac published in Virginia in 1770 warned of the deleterious effects of novel-reading and chocolate-imbibing among members of the fair sex in spring, as it would arouse dangerous passions.[3] As early as 1825, the French gourmand Brillat-Savarin praised chocolate as a panacea for all sorts of maladies.[4] Benjamin Franklin, in eighteenth-century Philadelphia, touted the medicinal value of chocolate as an antidote to smallpox in the epidemic of 1764.[5] Other news stories suggest that chocolate could lead to suicide: one Boston chocolate grinder, in a state of delirium, threw himself out of a garret window. Further insidious side-effects included debauchery, robbery and attempted murder through poisonous tinctures.[6] But cocoa emerged as a patriotic beverage, when American colonists, after the Boston Tea Party in 1773, drank the American (New England) 'Baker's chocolate' instead of tea: Dorcester, Massachusetts, became the home of the Baker's cocoa enterprise. Baker's cocoa was later also the choice beverage of pioneering men in the West and Civil War soldiers from the North.[7] And Ghirardelli would go out West in 1849 for the Gold Rush but found a mine of wealth in chocolate instead![8] As the triumph of Baker's cocoa was a symbolic declaration of independence in culinary terms, advertisers marketed this brand of cocoa as quintessentially American. The victory of Baker's cocoa over European cocoa (three times at a Parisian exposition) was hailed as a great American achievement in a late nineteenth-century cocoa advertisement. In the *Ladies' Home Journal* in February 1903, the Baker's advert celebrated the quintessential democratic aspect of Baker's cocoa drinking: 'Walter Baker's Cocoa from Washington to Roosevelt, an American Cocoa, The Finest in the World'. Using images of George Washington and President Roosevelt, the advert proudly quotes from the *Confectioners' and Bakers' Gazette*: 'It might safely be asserted that every President of the United States from Washington to Roosevelt, has been a consumer of Baker's Chocolate'.

A glimpse at European history also shows that the consumption of cocoa was on the rise. But in late eighteenth-century Europe, drinking cocoa was associated with the indulgences and privileges of a lazy aristocratic class. 'Let them drink cocoa', might have been as flip a response to the masses as 'let them eat cake' in pre-Revolutionary France. Only the wealthy could afford the beverage, as was the case in the United States until the mid-nineteenth century. The association with cocoa production as a capitalist enterprise had a curious effect. Workers like the cocoa harvesters in Latin America or labourers in European or New England cocoa factories might be oppressed, but mass chocolate production during the Industrial Revolution would lead to easier access to cocoa for the common folks. Moreover, the price of cocoa decreased. The first chocolate factory was established by François-Louis Cailler in Vevey, Switzerland, in 1819, and the chocolate powder press was established by Coenraad Van Houten in Amsterdam. Along with the invention of Dutch chocolate and the improved less bitter and smoother cocoa taste came the popularization of cocoa houses in England and in Austria in the 1820s.[9]

Nineteenth-century American women writers of advice manuals and proponents of the 'Cult of True Womanhood' such as Catharine Beecher and Harriet Beecher Stowe decried cocoa as being a foreign and decadent beverage, consumed more often in Europe than in the United States. However, in their later edition of *American Woman's Home*, they attached health properties to cocoa and listed it as 'nourishing and healthful' because it contained no 'stimulating principles' associated with alcohol.[10] The British Romantics might have spent time being decadent (and creative) by imbibing alcohol or opium, but American Romantics were far more sedate in their choice of preferred beverages. Though Hawthorne was reputed to have enjoyed his Bourbon in college, and Melville wrote soulful letters to Hawthorne fantasizing about drinking champagne with him in heaven or conversing with him over 'the heroic drink, brandy', on earth, both men felt comforted by cocoa.[11] Herman Melville took great pleasure in imbibing cocoa at breakfast cafés on his travels through Italy, especially during his stay in Turin, which, Melville states, was best known for its cocoa.[12] Hawthorne is reputed to have enjoyed cocoa upon his return home to Salem after graduating from Bowdoin College, where he was known to have enjoyed drinking whiskey with his school chums. His sister Elizabeth draws quite a different portrait:

> His habits were as regular as possible. In the evening after tea he went out for about one hour, whatever the weather was; and in winter, after his return, he ate a pint bowl of thick chocolate (not cocoa, but the old-fashioned chocolate) crumbed full of bread: eating never hurt him then, and he liked good things.[13]

These Romantics, Hawthorne and Melville, could do well with either the hard liquor of taverns or the cozy comforts of coffeehouses, especially during their travels through Europe.

However, the utopian Transcendentalists of this period (Bronson Alcott, Thoreau, Emerson) actually warned against the dangers of stimulating drinks like coffee, tea and cocoa as agents that would thwart creativity. Emerson spoke out most vehemently against the unwholesome and intoxicating effects wrought by 'French coffee' on the imagination in his essay 'The Poet' (1844).[14] In fact, Bronson Alcott forbade cocoa in his utopia, Fruitlands, as one communal member complained: 'no butter nor milk, nor cocoa, nor tea, nor coffee. Nothing but fruit, grain, and water was hard for the inside'.[15] It is a small wonder that Louisa May

Alcott challenged her father's strict diet regimens with lovely festive scenes in her children's literature, which celebrated the glories of cocoa. In *A Week on the Concord and Merrimack Rivers*, which was published in 1849 but written during his stay at Walden, Thoreau extols the manly pleasures of drinking cocoa in the wild:

> Here we found huckleberries still hanging upon the bushes, where they seemed to have slowly ripened for our especial use. Bread and sugar, and cocoa boiled in river water, made our repast, and as we had drank in the fluvial prospect all day, so now we took a draft of the water with our evening meal to propitiate the river gods, and whet our vision for the sights it was to behold.[16]

At another juncture in *A Week*, Thoreau describes making a feast out of watermelon, bread and cocoa.[17] Perhaps here cocoa is idealized as Thoreau thinks nostalgically of his earlier 1839 trip with his now-deceased brother, while in *Walden* (1854) he speaks against the evils of stimulants. It may seem ironic that after Thoreau makes his great stand against the United States government's support of slavery during his night in Concord jail, he is offered cocoa for breakfast, perhaps in an infantilizing if not disrespectful gesture by the prison warden, as this was the time period in which Thoreau was recommending water as the most spiritual beverage, for example, in the 'Higher Laws' chapter of *Walden*.[18] Certainly, the sweetness of cocoa is in strange juxtaposition with the actual prison experience.

In the late Romantic period, in the United States, chocolate and cocoa were seen as infantilizing agents and often associated with children's wishes and whims, as in various episodes in Louisa May Alcott's *Little Women* (1868–9) as well as in other texts by her; in learning to overcome or curb their appetites for chocolate by sharing the beverage or candy, the children would learn a moral lesson about charity. Amy in *Little Women*, for example, plans a grand luncheon for her girlfriends, but everything goes wrong, and Hannah the servant has a catastrophic day in the kitchen: 'Hannah's cooking didn't turn out well; the chicken was tough, the tongue too salt, and the chocolate wouldn't froth properly'.[19] Moral deficits are apparent in the child's desire to hoard chocolate or overimbibe in cocoa, as in part two of *Little Women*, when Jo's small nephew Demi is drawn to Jo's fiancé, the German Professor Bhaer, as he carries with him a surplus of chocolate drops, which the boy too hurriedly eats. This leads to Bhaer's teaching him a lesson: 'Thou shouldst save some for the little friend; sweets to the sweet, mannling'.[20] And with that gesture, we hear that 'Mr. Bhaer offered Jo some with a look that made her wonder if chocolate was not the nectar drunk by the gods',[21] which brings us back to the original etymological meaning of 'cocoa'. Alcott's lesson is, of course, to share the cocoa and to be morally upright; this attitude would change in the Naturalist and Realist period.

Late Nineteenth-Century Changing Tastes: Codes of Cocoa and Chocolate Enjoyment

Chocolate as a gift to children and to women, especially as a token of love, would become increasingly important in trade cards and advertisements of the late nineteenth century. Let me turn once more to Alcott's use of cocoa, this time in the short story 'Silver Pitchers', in which three girls, with the nineteenth-century temperance cause on their mind, want to play a prank on their suitors for having spiked their coffee with brandy. These three middle-class girls, belles of the town, are seen plotting their revenge, as they are viewed together in a beautiful pose, 'nestled together on the lounge in dressing-gowns and slippers, with unbound hair, eyes still bright with excitement, and tongues that still wagged briskly'.[22] The most striking beauty is enjoying hot chocolate: 'Handsome Portia looked out from her blonde locks with a disgusted expression, as she sipped the chocolate thoughtful mamma had left' for her.[23] This image of the lovely middle-class girl who enjoys her independence and her cocoa became the mainstay of many literary and advertisement types, especially of the New Woman in the late nineteenth century, and the striking image of lovely gentrified young ladies lounging around in pristine dresses and imbibing cocoa represented, for good or evil, a class of privileged and carefree women. But for Alcott, drinking cocoa was also a decadent liberating event, not simply a middle-class sign of respectability, as for example, when the actress in her adult thriller, *A Long Fatal Love Chase* (written 1866, published posthumously, 1995), enjoys her freedom drinking cocoa in public, alone in a café.

Later Realist writers include an earlier sentiment of sweetness and nostalgia but also the pain of poverty in their depictions of cocoa consumption. The chapter 'The Garden Tea' of Sarah Orne Jewett's *Betty Leicester: A Story for Girls* (1890) focuses on a middle-class teenage girl enjoying an outdoor luncheon, where her aunt and a servant prepare an overly sweet table: 'there it stood presently, with its white cloth, and pink roses in two china bowls, all ready for the sandwiches and bread and butter and strawberries and sponge-cake, and chocolate to drink out of the prettiest cups in Tideshead'.[24] Enjoying cocoa is an experience beyond the common worker's grasp, as in Elizabeth Stuart Phelps's darker Naturalistic story, 'The Sacrifice of Antigone', where a desolate waif and hard-working girl, who studies Greek at night and does menial labour during the day, finds herself competing for an essay prize in the house of a wealthy benefactor. For a moment, the 'hot chocolate from the dining-room made her ravenously giddy',[25] and although she looks forward to enjoying intellectual sustenance along with the cocoa, she escapes before her identity as a menial labourer can be discovered: 'Poor Dorothy slipped away home – without even her chocolate – and cried and studied and shivered half the night in her dingy attic lodging. The other girls stayed and had a beautiful time'.[26] She cannot participate in the cocoa ritual, nor can she enjoy a middle-class education. Although she wins the composition prize, the fruits of her labour come to naught, as she dies shortly afterwards:

She had crawled home – no one ever knew how – after that last flaring flash of strength, in whose strong flame her fading life had gone out. She had managed to creep into her cold little cot, – too exhausted to save what was left of her scanty fire, – and there her landlady, a respectable, but indifferent matron, had found her, unconscious, at noon next day.[27]

Although the matronly sponsor of the composition prize brings Dorothy to her own stately mansion to die, the grucsome image of Dorothy's starvation is a far cry from the scheming cocoa-guzzling girls in Alcott's or Jewett's happy stories for girls.

If cocoa was a beverage for the wealthy in the early nineteenth century and then a child's preferred beverage in the mid-nineteenth century, it became more and more a fashionable woman's drink. It was also deemed a healthy beverage, so that drinking cocoa became a more universal practice. The change of logo within the Baker's advertisements illustrates this change in attitude. The Baker's advertisement, with its focus on good health, appeared in journals like the *Atlantic Monthly* and the *Century Magazine* from the late nineteenth century onwards; and the Baker's girl image could be found on many trade cards and in ads in other periodicals (see Figure 13.1). The manufacturer of Baker's chocolate was the most respectable in New England; Dr James Baker had begun production as early as 1780. His nephew, William Henry Pierce, took over the business in 1873 and adopted the trademark logo of 'La Belle Chocolatière', otherwise known as the 'Schokoladenmädchen', the 'chocolate girl', whose image was based on a 1745 legend from Vienna, in which a nobleman, Prince Dietrichstein, fell in love with a lowly waitress, Anna Baltauf, in a chocolate shop. The happy story ends with the nobleman marrying beneath him, reconciling the two classes. The image of Baltauf is immortalized in the Swiss-French Jean-Étienne Liotard's painting, who depicted her, at her husband's request, in her chocolate server's outfit.[28] Baker's nephew Pierce saw the Baltauf portrait at the Dresden Art Gallery, where it is still housed, and promptly co-opted the image for his chocolate empire.[29] The image of cocoa as a more egalitarian beverage for the masses, a sign of hope and optimism, in the last decades of the nineteenth century, coincided with Baker's 1883 appropriation of the Belle Chocolatière. Still, it is noteworthy that Anna Baltauf, the model for the Baker's girl, is eternalized as a woman in attendance, not a woman on par with her husband. And there is, indeed, a striking contrast in the late nineteenth century between the reality of the working girl and the decadent life of the wealthy imbiber, as evidenced in the ads of the German company Stollwerck, which depict the beautiful pristine consumers of cocoa in their frilly feminine dresses and, underneath, in a smaller image, the chocolate factory in Cologne, which employed many invisible female workers, who would never get a chance to embody the aristocratic traits associated with the beverage they were producing.[30] Pierce, representing The Baker Company, wanted to present a rags to riches story through the simulacrum of the 'Chocolate Girl' and simultaneously reconcile classes, so that the chocolate appealed to young, old, male, female, rich and poor.

Figure 13.1: Advertisement, Baker's Vanilla Chocolate and Breakfast Cocoa, *The Century Magazine* (1885). Author's collection.

In the late nineteenth century, cocoa became a sign of fraternization among the working class, or a way of having disparate classes connect, if only momentarily. Chocolate advertisements, in the United States (Baker's) and in England (Cadbury's), had various ages and classes fraternizing: children, muscular men and old men as well as members of the upper and the working class. Moreover, if alcohol had been the domain of men's fraternities and drinking clubs in earlier nineteenth-century literature, the consumption of cocoa and chocolate in Naturalist literature allowed the closing of the gender gap because it drew men and women together, at least fleetingly, in – strangely for Naturalist fiction – intimate and sentimental, domestic moments of *Gemütlichkeit*. Men actually started to acquire more of a taste for cocoa over alcohol, and this connected the world of the woman's parlour with that of the man's public space in the workplace. In a Baker's advertisement circulating in 1906, a version of the New Woman (though with some maternal softness, as a throwback to earlier times) pours out cups of cocoa for dashing young men, who seem athletic or academic. She is labelled 'La Belle Chocolatière', as a throwback to the Liotard painting, and this Americanized image of the lovely European waitress Baltauf is served to the men on their ornamental cocoa cups (see Figure 13.2). Along with the health-promoting value of cocoa, a bit of sexuality is being sold. Consumers of all classes and ages drinking cocoa could be united in their love of cocoa.

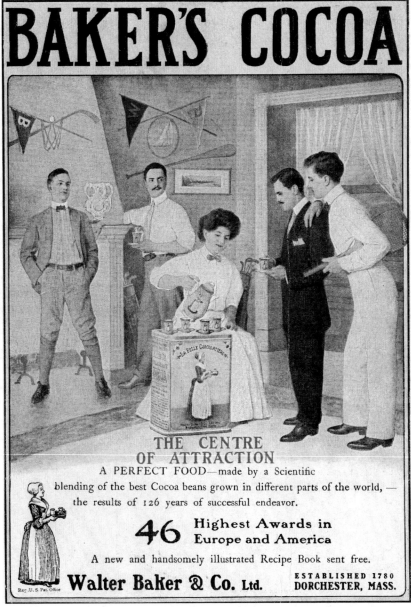

Figure 13.2: Advertisement, Walter Baker Chocolate Drink Cocoa, Dorcester, MA, 'La Belle Chocolatière', original print ad (1906). Author's collection.

In Naturalist fiction by Kate Chopin, Frank Norris, Charlotte Perkins Gilman and Edith Wharton, cocoa is an egalitarian beverage available to all, though several male characters seem averse to its increasingly feminine associations. The bonbon, however, is the particular province of women. 'Since milk chocolate appeared, women were assumed to yearn for it, and, despite, or perhaps because of chocolate's alleged power to stimulate erotic desires, it was marketed to them.'[31] In Chopin's *The Awakening* (1899), Edna Pontellier embodies middle-class decadence, self-centredly abusing power for pleasure rather than effecting change in a class system that elevates her above the Latina 'Mariequitas'. Dix and Piatti point out that Edna's predilection for sweets and the goods produced by poor labourers, such as her husband's gift of bonbons, marks her as oppressor and aligns her with the power dynamics of the former sugar plantation, the location of her summer home.[32] Edna becomes as oblivious to the working class as do her children, who delight in their father's gifts of chocolates. Furthermore, sweets serve to infantilize and prostitute Edna as she and her family accept such presents in lieu of her husband's emotional sustenance. But, importantly, Edna's growing sense of identity can be charted in her evolving relationship to sweets and chocolate. Her love affairs with Robert and Arobin diminish Edna's desire for chocolates, as she replaces candy with sex.

In her relationship with the musician Mlle Reisz, Edna develops an aversion towards chocolate, which she begins to associate with the spinster's undeveloped sexuality. But she also connects chocolate with the seductive Other, when she learns that the exotic Mariequita has flirted with her beloved Robert and his brother, who then brags about 'a Mexican girl who served [him] chocolate one winter in a restaurant in Dauphine Street'.[33] When Robert announces his intention to go to Mexico, Edna, who can 'think of nothing to say about Mexico or the Mexicans',[34] disconsolately sips her 'black coffee'. Though Edna's friend Mlle Reisz offers chocolates to placate her over Robert's departure and his flirtation with Mariequita, Edna begins to have a distaste for all chocolate – and for all that is typically feminine.

While the spinster Mlle Reisz associates the chocolates with good health: 'She habitually ate chocolates for their sustaining quality; they contained much nutriment in small compass',[35] Edna begins to associate chocolate pejoratively first with child's play and then jealously with perceived underclass promiscuity. While Edna initially rejects the wine offered by her undesirable husband, she begins to drink wine alone and then with her lovers. Her drinking escalates so that she finally rejects cocoa for brandy. At dinner parties, her maid offers guests 'liqueur, coffee, or chocolate, as they may desire';[36] privately, when visiting Mlle Reisz, who is forever boiling pots of chocolate on her stove, Edna prefers brandy. Edna mentally disengages from the (perceived) dangerously sexually free Mariequita and the dangerously independent and eccentric Mlle Reisz, both of whom she associates with chocolate. Instead, Edna refuses cocoa for the masculine beverage and drinks 'the liquor from the glass as a man would have done'.[37] In exchanging cocoa for brandy, Edna foregoes a female alliance and identifies with the liquor-drinking male oppressors: her boring husband, her manipulative seducers (Robert, Arobin) and even her patriarchal Southern Colonel father, who also imbibes at dinner parties. She can accept neither the chocolate associated with the sexualized foreign underclass (Mariequita), nor the spinster's innocuous cocoa (Mlle Reisz).

The gender roles are somewhat reversed in Frank Norris's novel *McTeague*, a brilliant Naturalist study of the deterioration of a man into beast, also published in 1899. The protagonist McTeague's choice of beverages, from cocoa to liquor, represents a spiralling down in social class and good taste. The atavistic McTeague vacillates between wanting to binge and wanting to improve his lot in life, and in the war between his desires for alcohol and cocoa, liquor finally triumphs, though he has nostalgia for the 'cocoa', which he associates with his bourgeois wife Trina. Initially, he is seen as a monstrous fleshy brute man whose 'only relaxations were to eat, to drink steam bear, and to play upon his concertina'.[38] With Trina, he begins to feel more cultivated. Trina is often seen sipping her chocolate, while he guzzles down beer and 'devours huge chunks of butterless bread'.[39] Put off by his uncouth behaviour, she impresses upon him more refined tastes so that he exchanges steam beer for bottled beer. At first, the marriage is good: there is plenty of food, such as a lunch of sausages, mashed potatoes, stew, herring, salad, and there is '*chocolate*, which Trina adored'.[40] When Trina wins a $5,000 lottery, the meals get more paltry as she becomes miserly; now lunch consists of stewed codfish, and Trina starts depriving McTeague of various pleasures, including finally his bottled beer, although she refuses to give up her own pleasure of drinking chocolate.[41] Obsessed with money, Trina forces McTeague to return to steam beer, and thus begins the regression of McTeague, who starts to spend Sundays not with her at the theatre or at her family events, but dining at the 'car conductor's coffee joint' and wasting the afternoon in bed, 'stupid, warm, smoking his huge pipe, drinking his steam beer'.[42] He nostalgically thinks about the better days, and the sentimental tableaux centre around imbibing good beverages: 'He missed the cabbage soups and steaming chocolate that Trina had taught him to like ... he missed the bottled beer that she had induced him to drink in place of steam beer from Frenna's'.[43] The lack of domestic comfort drives him into a state of stupor and beastliness: he finally takes to whiskey, and in a bitter drunken rage, he beats the life out of his cocoa-hoarding (and gold-hoarding) estranged wife. Norris's Darwinian world view shows that the niceties associated with the civilizing beverage, cocoa, are not in sync with more violent human emotions.

In Edith Wharton's wealthy world of old New York, similar dynamics exist between the possessed and dispossessed. Elitist parlour settings of old New York seep into one of her early books, *The Valley of Decision* (1901), her recreation of a historical romance about eighteenth-century aristocracy in Italy, who are portrayed as lolling about, being served cocoa by their domestics. The eighteenth century appears as the period during which only the prosperous could afford cocoa, but Wharton, coming from a wealthy family, was aware of the privileges and follies of the rich. The protagonist in *The Valley of Decision*, a woebegone Odo abandoned in the countryside, is reunited with his mother, who is living the life of nobility, and he wonders, 'how any one could be in want, who slept between damask curtains and lived on sweet cakes and chocolate'. One of the servants, seeing him so pale, exclaims that he needed 'his cup of chocolate'.[44] From that point on, he is always given cocoa as his morning beverage. But he is also aware of the grotesque implications of cocoa-drinking as he witnesses his mother's decadent aristocratic habits: 'He found his mother propped against her pillows, drinking chocolate, feeding her pet monkey and giving agitated orders to the maidservants'.[45] He also observes the wealthy enjoying their laziness: 'The tables before the coffee-houses were thronged with idlers taking their chocolate and reading their gazettes'.[46] And he is seduced in an episode revolving around cocoa: a young woman at court, telling the servant to get Odo his cocoa, closes the door and gives Odo his first kiss. The various conquests related to chocolate are alluded to quite clearly when Odo's friend sings to him about the pleasures of chocolate after the servant brings Odo his morning chocolate. The song is the abate Parini's 'satire of the Morning [which] apostrophizes the cup of chocolate which the lacquey presents to his master'. This was a popular eighteenth-century song that perversely celebrates the conquest of the Native Americans and the acquisition of chocolate:

> That Cortez and Pizarro should esteem
> The blood of man a trivial sacrifice
> When, flinging down from their ancestral thrones
> Incas and Mexicans of royal line
> They wrecked two kingdoms to refresh thy palate –[47]

In 'The Duchess at Prayer', a story Wharton wrote a year before *The Valley of Decision*, she similarly views the corruption of the nobility through the image of cocoa: there are 'kitchens and offices full of cooks and lackeys to serve up chocolate all day long to the fine ladies in masks and furbelows'.[48] Dukes and duchesses alike enjoy being served chocolate in their gazebos.

When Wharton records more modern life in her novel *Summer* (1917), she shows, as Chopin had in *The Awakening*, the power of seduction involved in chocolate transactions, and here solid chocolate and not cocoa becomes the selling point. The eligible bachelor Harney seduces the rustic girl from the Mountain, Charity, first with wine and then with chocolates. Although he seems to eat very little, as he just smokes cigarettes, he brings her 'tablets of chocolate' to their trysting place in the woods.[49] When her mother, who lives among the poverty-stricken people of the Mountain, falls ill, Charity runs away up the Mountain to be with her. Charity brings chocolate along with her for sustenance: first she had 'forced herself to swallow a glass of milk and eat a piece of bread; and she had put in her canvas satchel a little packet of the chocolate that Harney always carried in his bicycle bag'.[50] Chocolate is thus equated with Charity's sexual experimentation, and with a form of escape. But the excitement of chocolate together with the image of nourishing milk quickly turn into a nightmarish mirage as Charity finds her mother has suffered an impoverished, inhuman death: 'she lay there like a dead dog in a ditch'.[51] Not cocoa but coffee is the sobering drink Charity imbibes upon her descent down the Mountain.

Images of chocolate and cocoa converge in late nineteenth- and early twentieth-century Naturalist fiction, probably because after the 1870s, American producers of chocolate, like Lowney's of Boston and later Hershey's of Pennsylvania, started making chocolate bars and found that the market for such sweets was profitable. It seems curious that the very serious and politically-minded Charlotte Perkins Gilman wrote a testimonial advertisement for Lowney's in her progressive socialist journal, the *Forerunner*. Gilman composed most of the ads and stories, and then also copy-edited them. In the issue of 1 November 1909, the following advert appeared:

> I speak as one who has cared little for candy of any kind and less for chocolate candy.
> I don't like chocolate cake, nor chocolate blanc mange, nor chocolate pudding, nor chocolate to drink – unless it is cocoa, very hot, not too sweet, and strained carefully.
> Nevertheless, I fell in with friends, who feasted upon Lowney's; they beguiled me into feasting upon Lowney's, and since then my attitude has changed as to candy.[52]

It is telling that Gilman changes her mind regarding her distaste for chocolate, perhaps because of the greater popularity solid chocolate was attaining, with several expositions creating temples to chocolate – one at the 1876 Centennial Exposition in Philadelphia, and another at the Columbia Exposition in 1893 in Chicago, where Lowney's had a marvellous exhibit, as did the Stollwerck Brothers, who tried to outdo Lowney's by creating a pavilion and the statue 'Germania', all in chocolate – 30,000 pounds of chocolate![53] This might have been as decadent a gesture as the earlier consumption of cocoa by the nobility. In any case, both cocoa and chocolate made it to both expositions in the late nineteenth century and created a promise about the future through these modern pleasure temples. That is, perhaps, the reason why Gilman in her perfect utopia in her novel *Herland* (1915) makes cocoa the national beverage: 'There was water to drink, and a hot beverage of a most pleasing quality, some preparation like cocoa'.[54] In Gilman's utopia, cocoa is a vehicle for unity and an elixir for social ills.

Critics of the American scene, such as the expatriate Henry James in his *The American Scene*, published in 1905–6, a year after James's visit to United States, perceived a downward spiral for American culture, symbolized by the country's love affair with chocolate. The market for cocoa had given way to the market for solid chocolate by the early twentieth century, and with it appeared a larger variety of desserts and a growing number of producers and sellers. Visiting a Bowery Theater performance, James is appalled by the many 'munching' spectators and the 'little playhouse peddlers'.[55] He is struck by the 'wondrous consumption by the "people", over the land, of the most elaborate solid and liquid sweets, such products as form in other countries an expensive and select dietary'.[56] James questions this democratization process and the symbolic value attached to such consumption:

> These almost 'high-class' luxuries, circulating in such a company, were a sort of supreme symbol of the *promoted* state of the aspirant to American conditions. He, or more particularly she, had been promoted, and more or less at a bound, to the habitual use of chocolate-creams, and indeed, of other dainties, refined and ingenious.[57]

Questioning such cultural advancement, James asks how 'so much purchasing-power can flow to the supposedly superfluous'[58] and goes even further in critiquing American culture: 'The wage-earners, the toilers of old, notably in other climes, were known by the wealth of their songs; and has it, on these lines, been given to the American people to be known by the number of their "candies"?'[59] The classes mingling together in the theatre had ultimately nothing in common but the 'munching'.

Maybe Montezuma had his revenge by having a nation filled with sick or obese people who are drawn to the many 'candies' James describes. In a popular sense, cocoa and chocolate have been cheapened, and we can see that in various chocolate-centred film scripts. The magic on a deep spiritual level, which the Native Americans had celebrated, has disappeared with the obesity dilemma, but also with filmic images focusing on chocolate. In *Dinner at Eight* (1933), we can view a pouty Jean Harlow, playing the part of the socially ambitious but also blundering Kitty, who is lying in bed and devouring chocolates. Or, perhaps, Forrest Gump, who, in the movie of the same title of 1994, is intellectually backward but has a good heart to compensate and who has taken a very simple maxim from his mother as the basis for his life's journey: 'Life is like a *box of chocolates* ... you never know what you're gonna get'. These famous lines, spoken by Tom Hanks, which linger with us long after the movie is over, are part of that American popular culture of kitsch that James would have derided, in which the highbrow mingles with lowbrow. The film views the tumultuous 1960s both simplistically and romantically through a prism smaller than a cocoa bean or chocolate bonbon, while it projects a panoramic vision of personal and national history as well as infinite, though illusory, possibilities onto the silver screen.

14 THE POWER OF THE POTION: FROM GOTHIC HORROR TO HEALTH DRINK, OR, HOW THE ELIXIR BECAME A COMMODITY

Elmar Schenkel

Magical potions have been present in human culture ever since humans started to brew herbs and animal skins, taste fermented drinks or cook mushroom, rotten wheat or worms. In the Neolithic burial chamber Barclodiad y Gawres (*c.* 2000 BC) in north-western Wales, the following brew has been identified:

> The central area contained the remains of a fire onto which had been poured 'a strange stew consisting of wrasse, eel, frog, toad, grass-snake, mouse, shrew & hare', then covered with limpet shells and pebbles. The significance of this ceremony is unknown.[1]

From shamanism to Greek myths, from fairy tales to Shakespeare's *A Midsummer Night's Dream* (1590–6) and the *Harry Potter* (1997–2007) novels, magical drinks have been bridges into unknown dimensions, expanding life and consciousness, producing hallucinations and visions, creating or destroying love, distorting perception, transforming or killing bodies. The borderline between potion and poison is sometimes hard to spot, not only linguistically. Though they seem to be omnipresent in human cultures, the nineteenth century saw a return of these substances in the arts and especially in literature. It is here that we find the best close-up revealing the cultural dynamics at work. While the Victorians embraced the realist novel, fantasy also blossomed and revived archaic memories, and magical potions returned with a vengeance. Love potions and elixirs of life made their way into novels and short stories, from Honoré de Balzac to Edward Bulwer-Lytton, and magical food and drink invaded children's literature, as in *Alice's Adventures in Wonderland* (1865).

This essay, situated in the territory between literature and science, will demonstrate that a fundamental shift took place in the nineteenth century and that this shift can be studied closely in terms of the magical potions appearing in literary works. Potions in literature illustrate how folk medicine and ancient magical practices are turned into commodities and become part of the commercial system we call consumer culture. Potions lose their aura by becoming

– 167 –

reproducible on a large scale, thus resembling works of high art, about which Walter Benjamin wrote in his essay 'The Work of Art in the Age of Mechanical Reproduction' (1936).[2] After 1900, potions survive in sensational and popular novels as a literary commodity which we call cliché. Alternatively, they gain psychological significance, or else become modern, that is, are turned into the quack medicine and miracle drinks advertised in the mass media. Here H. G. Wells's novel *Tono-Bungay* (1909) will serve as a significant illustration. It shows that there still is great potential in magical potions – commercially speaking: magic and capitalism have always been on good terms. Obviously, literature does not reflect these events in synchronicity. On the contrary, it either anticipates this process or serves as a nostalgic reminder of a lost past. This tension is felt in the nineteenth century, the age that enthusiastically greeted science and technology, until the turn of the century more than at any other time.

The Elixir of Life

The first transition from folk to literary culture, that is, from potions as part of a pre-modern world to specialized uses reflecting unease in modernity, takes place in the Romantic period, a time that was the first to express a conflict Freud famously subsumed under the title *Civilization and Its Discontents* (1930). The Romantics were inspired by what they thought to be folklore and folk literature, and thus potions became part of this traffic between elite culture and popular culture.

The most productive author in this respect was certainly E. T. A. Hoffmann, in whose works brews and potions bubble quietly before they explode into significant events. Two of his works have to be singled out in this context: *Der Goldene Topf* (The Golden Pot; 1814) and *Die Elixiere des Teufels* (The Devil's Elixir; 1815–6). *Der Goldene Topf* is a story about a student who is led into a strange world of salamanders and serpents, of witchcraft and dreaming, which at the same time is the very bourgeois world of Dresden. The golden pot is the symbol of ultimate happiness, of the lost Atlantis and of the Philosopher's Stone. Mirrors, rings and stones serve as magical objects, as does a golden fluid in a vial. The bourgeois world, however, is represented by the *köstlicher Punsch* (savoury punch) the decent citizens of Dresden like to drink. When Anselmus, the student, makes a mistake as a copyist and spills ink over the manuscript, he is dispatched into a bottle – a hallucinatory experience which opposes life in a crystal world to the humdrum reality of Dresden.[3] While this narrative evolves within an alchemical setting and symbolism, *Die Elixiere* weaves potions into a Gothic tradition. The novel was influenced, as Hoffmann himself suggested, by Matthew Lewis's *The Monk* (1795–6), in which a potion sends a woman to sleep for forty-eight hours. In Hoffmann's text, the elixir first appears as a highly worshipped relic in a monastery, allegedly inherited from St Anthony, who was given this bottle by the devil when tempted in the desert. One day, the narrator opens the bottle, first only to sniff its wonderful odours. He finds a strange blue flame dancing on top. When he finally takes a sip, he feels as if he has inhaled a fiery stream, and this inspires his eloquence. He becomes the most popular preacher at the monastery, gaining more and more power until he succumbs to temptation. This opens a Pandora's Box of murders and doppelgängers, of blood, poison and madness until he finally retires to repent in another monastery.

The potion in this case is less part of a folk tradition than part of the Catholic relic culture. Catholicism, the inquisition and murderous priests are part and parcel of the Gothic tradition. In Hoffmann's *Elixiere*, however, the potion unleashes a new sense of self, one that might be called modern. Doubling and splitting personalities reappear at the end of the century, sometimes under the influence of a potion, as in Stevenson's *Strange Case of Dr Jekyll and Mr Hyde* (1886).[4] In Hoffmann's tale one can detect early signals of a threat to identity, which foreshadow modernity. The subject is under pressure and all actors 'are melted into air', as Prospero in Shakespeare's *The Tempest* (1611) would have it.[5] The narrator has visions of himself as a martyr and imagines his blood being replaced by a 'disgusting colourless juice', which will have to be re-transformed into blood again by his better self: 'It was *me* who had spoken, but as soon as I felt separated from my dead self, I realized that I had become the bodiless idea of my self, and I soon found myself to be the red substance floating in the ether'.[6] The impure water and the pure blood are two versions of the same substance. In any case, the self in *Elixiere* is liquefied, as Anselmus is bottled up in *Der Goldene Topf*, and both states signal an extreme sense of self-alienation.

Hoffmann's world is inspired by the ancient art of alchemy. Its symbols proliferate, whether in the laboratory of Archivarius Lindhorst or the witch's chamber (*Der Goldene Topf*), or in the Elixir of Youth and Eloquence (*Elixiere*). Alchemy is one of the sacred traditions of the West that was handed down by the Romantics and inscribed into a modern self. This is a feature often overlooked, since alchemy, as the chemists would say, lost its central position with the Scientific Revolution in the seventeenth century. While in the pre-revolutionary world of the *Ancien Régime*, alchemy still had a part to play – many sovereigns still had their private alchemists, including Frederick the Great – the nineteenth century only had a symbolical use for it. Even Goethe was sceptical, though he was apparently cured by an alchemist in Leipzig when seriously ill. Romantics and Symbolists, however, continued the tradition on another level. Indeed, a century before C. G. Jung they discovered the psychological dimension of the old art.[7]

Two traditions have to be distinguished in alchemy: gold making and the prolongation of life. While the Philosopher's Stone is related to the transformation of lower matter into gold and thus to the accumulation of worldly riches, the Elixir of Life belongs to the other alchemical tradition: the search for immortality. In this sense, it has often been associated with spiritual techniques. With the disillusionment of human ability to produce gold, popular interest shifted to the Elixir of Life. And longevity, or eternal youth, became an obsession. When Goethe wrote the first part of his *Faust* in the 1770s, the theme of the witch's potion rejuvenating the hero was still marginal, but when a century later Charles Gounod set *Faust* to music, he turned it into an opera on the theme of eternal youth, and as such it became a great success.[8]

The Elixir of Life also offered possibilities of exploring concepts of time, a fascination which reached a peak with H. G. Wells's *The Time Machine* (1895). In a sense the elixir could be seen as an alternative time machine since it stretched people's lives across centuries, expanding consciousness and memory in a way only a time traveller could experience.

Throughout the nineteenth century, authors resorted to this motif since it fitted in well with phenomena such as violent death, mystery and charlatanry. One of the best known practitioners in this respect was the obscure Count St Germain, who was surrounded by veils of alchemy, drank elixirs and was reputed to have survived centuries. Nor were writers like Alexandre Dumas or Honoré de Balzac ever averse to such popular themes. In Balzac's *L'Élixir de longue vie* (1830), the elixir, which was brought to Italy from the Orient, is used as an ointment with the help of which a dying person could be brought back to life. In the hands of young Don Juan it becomes a terrible weapon, and when used on himself, a cause of horror and disaster.[9]

Mary Shelley wrote a rather flimsy tale about the elixir called 'The Mortal Immortal' (1833), in which the narrator, aged 303, muses about his long life and tells us how it came about. In the seventeenth century, he had been the pupil of the alchemist Cornelius Agrippa von Nettesheim and had helped him with his potions. In love with Bertha, his playmate from infancy, he drinks an elixir which is meant to cure love but has the opposite effect. The potion is a delicious liquor, a flaming fluid with 'flashes of admirable beauty'.[10] The alchemist is furious since the labour of his life has been destroyed, but the narrator is deliriously happy and marries Bertha. When the alchemist dies five years later, the pupil takes hold of another elixir, now that of immortality. This leads to an interesting result: while his wife ages as expected, he becomes younger and younger. Since Bertha is growing ever more jealous of him, she buys him a grey wig and spreads the rumour that he suffers from a terrible illness, saying his 'youth was a disease'.[11] Immortals like the narrator, however, share the fate of Ahasver as they wander the centuries like a sailor without rudder or compass: they are lost between the times.[12] The only hope left to Shelley's narrator is that he drank only half of the potent potion and would therefore be only half-immortal. But how long does half an eternity last, he wonders: 'I often try to imagine by what rule the infinite may be divided'.[13]

Similar misadventures befall the protagonists in William Harrison Ainsworth's *Auriol or The Elixir of Life* (1844). Auriol, who – again – has stolen the elixir from the hand of his dying master, who had only just discovered it, is condemned to drift through the centuries, burdened as he is with guilt. In addition, every ten years he has to deliver a woman to a man who has entered into a contract with the devil. In this narrative, the potion both fuels the well-oiled Gothic machinery and helps to explain mental confusions:

> 'How else, if I were not mad, could I have believed that I had swallowed the fabled elixir vitae? And yet, is it a fable? for I am puzzled still. Methinks I am old – old – old – though I feel young, and look young. All this is madness. Yet how clear and distinct it seems! I can call to mind events in Charles the Second's time. Ha! – who told me of Charles the Second? How know I there was such a king? The reigning sovereign should be James, and yet I fancy it is George the Fourth. Oh! I am mad – clean mad!'[14]

As these lines show, it is at times quite unclear whether Auriol is not simply raving in a feverish dream and inventing his longevity.

Another writer whose work features longevity potions is Bulwer-Lytton. In both *A Strange Story* (1862) and *Zanoni* (1842), the reader is confronted with events exploding the limits of time and space.[15] At the root, there is often some potion based on Oriental recipes. Bilocation, telepathy and mesmerism (also known as animal magnetism) play an important role. The potion is part of this occult world and serves as a bridge between body and mind. Bulwer-Lytton devotes many pages of serious discussion to this topic, which is located between philosophy, physiology and mental science. In *A Strange Story*, the doctor and narrator Alan Fenwick is writing a book about the relationship between mind and matter. Furthermore, Bulwer-Lytton includes numerous fictitious footnotes explaining the state of research at the time of writing, thus making his discussion part of a broader philosophical and academic discourse and bridging the gap between scientific and fictional writing. The story revolves around a woman who is apparently controlled by an evil spirit and, as a result, alienated from her lover. She experiences many crises and trances as well as comatose sleep. Eventually, a great showdown occurs in the Australian outback, where the elixir for the revival of her evil persecutor is to be brewed as part of a magic ritual. However, in spite of terrible and even apocalyptic dangers, the evil man is finally killed while the woman returns to full consciousness and to her lover. The Gothic elements of the story are intertwined with psychological, physiological and philosophical annotations by the author. The doctor, who in the beginning is firmly footed in positive science, sees his beliefs shaken by age-old wisdom, non-rational states of being and dream visions. In the end, he even admits the possibility that dreaming can help with finding the right kind of medication.[16]

172 *Drink in the Eighteenth and Nineteenth Centuries*

The elixir, whose value is quite openly questioned at the end of *A Strange Story*, originates, as so often, in the mysterious East (Damascus, Aleppo, Syria), where it was first produced by an alchemist and dervish. The liquid is brewed in a cauldron supervised by a 'Veiled Woman' called Ayesha, who was to become more famous as a mythical woman in Rider Haggard's *She* (1887).[17] This is significant since the participation of a woman in the alchemical process is a novelty, as is the Australian location. This soil is very important for the experiment, the reader is told:

> In the old gold mines of Asia and Europe the substance exists, but can rarely be met with. The soil for its nutriment may there be well-nigh exhausted. It is here, where Nature herself is all vital with youth, that the nutriment of youth must be sought. Near this spot is gold.[18]

The process of producing the liquid is then described in great detail, including the horrors it arouses in the environment. Evil spirits in the form of gigantic eyes and feet threaten the completion of the process, but finally the obstacles are overcome and the fluid glows with flashes of ruby: 'Out from the mass of the molten red, broke coruscations of all prismal hues, shooting, shifting, in a play that made the wavelets themselves seem living things, sensible of their joy'.[19] These coruscations will eventually form the shape of a rose surrounded by emerald, diamond and sapphire flashes. Bulwer-Lytton has thus transported European Rosicrucianism to Australia. Interestingly, however, the experiment fails since the elixir is spilled and will now nourish plants and insects instead of helping humans with their destinies. As in Shakespeare's *The Tempest* (1611) or Tolkien's *The Lord of the Rings* (1954–5), the real alchemy takes place when the external rigging – magical wands, stones and elixirs – is abandoned in favour of moral transformation. Bulwer-Lytton's potion with its occult background recurs in twentieth-century literature, for example in Arthur Machen's *The Great God Pan* (1926) and Somerset Maugham's gruesome early novel *The Magician* (1908).

Much more light-hearted is Nathaniel Hawthorne's story 'Dr. Heidegger's Experiment' (1837), in which the worthy doctor offers his elixir to a club of elderly people, who get the sillier the younger they begin to feel.[20] The elixir, as Marty Roth has pointed out, is probably a good dose of alcohol which produces the illusion of being young.[21] Another spoof is *The Rejuvenation of Miss Semaphore: A Farcical Novel* (1897) by Hal Godfrey, the pseudonym of Charlotte O'Conor Eccles. The author herself notes that it was inspired by Hawthorne's story. Two sisters live in a London pension. One day, the older one finds an advertisement in the paper addressed to 'Ladies and Gentlemen of Means', in which the widow of

> an eminent explorer ... is compelled to offer for sale a single bottle of water from the Fountain of Youth, vainly sought in Florida by Ponce de Leon. Its marvellous rejuvenating properties cannot be exaggerated. By its means a person of seventy may regain, after six small doses, the age of eighteen.[22]

Miss Semaphore immediately sets out to get hold of the potion and finds out that the widow is a German lady by the telling name of Sophia Geldheraus (Out-With-Your-Money!). She buys the potion for a large sum and then begins the experiment. Unfortunately, the bottle breaks and, in order to prevent more spilling, she drinks more than she intended. Soon after, her sister next door is wakened by a crying baby and finds out that it is her sister who has reached this young age.[23] All kinds of complications arise from this turn of events, including suspicions that the sister is trying to conceal an illegitimate child. As things are coming to a head in court, the baby begins to grow quickly, reaching its previous age and maturity. 'The medical press took the matter up', we learn. 'Samples of the Water of Youth were called for to be analysed, but without avail, since Mrs Geldheraus and her mysterious potion had disappeared into the *Ewigkeit* [eternity]'.[24] Miss Augusta Semaphore, however, is set up as a wax model at Madame Tussaud's.[25]

In nineteenth-century literature, the Elixir of Life vacillates between Gothic horrors and absurdity, between Romantic striving and nonsensical adventures. But its continuous presence as a theme certainly suggests that questions of longevity and of an impending youth cult were topical throughout the century. At the same time, the phenomenon proved to be a perfect toy, a kind of biological time machine, in the hands of literary tricksters. There is no doubt that its appeal has survived into the twenty-first century. J. K. Rowling's *Harry Potter* series (1997–2007) and Stephenie Meyer's *Twilight* saga (2005–8) both testify to the enduring attraction of elixirs (or blood) promising immortality.

Transformation and Consumption:
Alice's Adventures in Wonderland and 'Goblin Market'

Children's literature is full of oral symbolism, of eating and drinking, or of being eaten. This oral trend begins with one of the early classics, Lewis Carroll's *Alice's Adventures in Wonderland*. The book, as has been noted by many a critic, is full of foods and drinks and oral activities. Many death jokes revolve around the fear of being eaten or swallowed. In this context, I will only concentrate on the first episode of drinking. When Alice falls down the hole, she finds herself in a hall with a number of doors around it. On a table she finds not only a golden key which unlocks one of the doors to a wonderful garden but later also a bottle, which, in the Victorian manner, is corked and has a paper label tied around its neck with the words: 'DRINK ME'.[26]

> It was all very well to say 'Drink me,' but the wise little Alice was not going to do *that* in a hurry. 'No, I'll look first,' she said, 'and see whether it's marked "*poison*" or not'; for she had read several nice little stories about children who had got burnt, and eaten up by wild beasts and other unpleasant things, all because they *would* not remember the simple rules their friends had taught them: such as, that a red-hot poker will burn you if you hold it too long; and that if you cut your finger *very* deeply with a knife, it usually bleeds.[27]

Alice is a civilized Victorian girl and thus cautious vis-à-vis any temptation. She is also very English in her understatements 'and she had never forgotten that, if you drink much from a bottle marked "poison," it is almost certain to disagree with you, sooner or later'.[28] Alice still trusts her world, though Wonderland should make one more suspicious:

> However, this bottle was *not* marked 'poison,' so Alice ventured to taste it, and finding it very nice, (it had, in fact, a sort of mixed flavour of cherry-tart, custard, pine-apple, roast turkey, toffy, and hot buttered toast), she very soon finished it off.[29]

As a result of drinking the potion, Alice shrinks. Why does the potion appear and why does she drink it without too many qualms? It is because she feels that in Wonderland, her desires simply must come true. For she had desired something that would lead her into the garden and found something that might change her completely or at least produce a sort of hallucination. Critics have pointed out that the experiments with the different sizes Alice is going through reflect a child's view of the world as it is used in Victorian books popularizing science for children[30] or Carroll's wishful projections on the female body.[31] They also reflect her difficulties in growing up, that is, of adjusting a growing body to the conventions of her world. Whatever the conscious or unconscious drives may be, it is the potion that makes her wish come true: she is telescoped into a dwarf, ten inches high. Shrinking is the first result of this drink and she does not even know whether she will go on shrinking:

> And so it was indeed: she was now only ten inches high, and her face brightened up at the thought that she was now the right size for going through the little door into that lovely garden. First, however, she waited for a few minutes to see if she was going to shrink any further: she felt a little nervous about this; 'for it might end, you know,' said Alice to herself, 'in my going out altogether, like a candle. I wonder what I should be like then?' And she tried to fancy what the flame of a candle looks like after the candle is blown out, for she could not remember ever having seen such a thing.[32]

If we take the garden to be an echo and emblem of paradise, the potion and the cake which makes her grow again are mirror reflections of what happened in Eden when Adam and Eve tasted a fruit, albeit a forbidden one, which drove them out of their lovely garden. The paradisiacal quality of the drink, which, of course, also carries overtones of seduction and temptation, is indicated by the mixture of flavours so palatable to a child. It is a child's dream come true, a glimpse of the land of Cockaigne, to which one might easily become addicted. It is also important to note that while drinking shrinks her, food will make her grow again. The message implied might be that food is more adult in the sense of being more defined, limited and solid, while drink is more archaic and closer to the suckling baby. The potion here initiates a transformation that is equivalent to living forms' adaptation to the environment, as described by Charles Darwin in *The Origin of Species* (1859). But first of all, it is a game which Alice enjoys, although she is also slightly disturbed by it. The potion is the liquid form of wish fulfilment: it helps her to be shut up like a telescope, and, in terms of taste, it provides emotional well-being. In its mixture of roast turkey and toffee, among other things, it also epitomizes a Victorian feast, such as a Christmas or birthday dinner. In this sense, the drink is momentarily the dreamt-of garden.[33]

Such wish fulfilment is also part of the psychological dynamics in Christina Rossetti's narrative poem 'Goblin Market' (1862). Here, the goblins tempt a girl with fruit and their juices to the extent that she seems to get addicted. The fruits have hallucinating qualities, which are translated into the mesmerizing advertising chant of the goblins:

'Look at our apples
Russet and dun,
Bob at our cherries,
Bite at our peaches,
Citrons and dates,
Grapes for the asking,
Pears red with basking
Out in the sun'[34]

The girl swoons and her sister takes it upon her to lick off the juice from her body – the lesbian connotation is obvious. Here, the potion, in this case the juice of wild fruit, is an emblem of suppressed desires, an almost bodily liquid. Apart from the erotic element, we should also pay attention to the 'Market' in the title of the poem, that is, the fact that these fruit are part of an advertising campaign trying to sell exotic fruits, 'not just common, home-grown English apples and cherries, but also a rich variety of gourmet fruits imported from foreign climes – pomegranates, dates, figs, lemons and oranges, "citrons from the South"'.[35]

While Alice's drink may also satisfy the repressed desire of the author to shrink and become one of the children himself, it is related to Rossetti's fruit juice through the dynamics of consumer culture. While falling through the hole, Alice studies marmalades on a shelf as if she were in a shop, as has been noted by Nancy Armstrong in her influential essay 'The Occidental Alice'.[36] Furthermore, the way she is suddenly in possession of a bottle and a cake points to an economy catering to the Victorian middle and upper classes by making products of the country and even Empire available at any point in time or space.[37] In this reading, the invisible hand putting commodities on a table for her is no longer a spirit like Ariel or a ghost, but the market itself. Biographically speaking, the drink and the cake are baits the author Carroll as a friend of young girls uses to entice his creature into his own fairy world. As the writer shapes and adjusts his fictional protagonist according to his purposes – Alice changes size no less than twelve times – drink and food serve as the material incentive for the imagination. Arguably, this kind of relationship between matter and spirit would be more complicated with adult fictional characters.[38]

Marketing the Potion: Wells's *Tono-Bungay*

Alice's Adventures in Wonderland prefigures the later use of potions at the turn of the century. Potions by then had become baits of a different, though related order: they are now firmly part of an industry that creates desires and offers to satisfy them at the same time. Advertising reached new heights towards the end of the century, and the motif of potions is taken up by writers as diverse as Anthony Trollope or H. G. Wells. Quack doctors had been a well-known phenomenon in reality and literature well before the nineteenth century, but they reach centre stage with the advent of the mass media and the enhanced possibilities of commercialization.

Take the example of Mrs Pinkham's Tonic, as described in a popular history of dubious medical cures:

> Women were encouraged to write for advice about their medical problems to Mrs Pinkham herself, who would reply with sage recommendations usually involving the purchase of large quantities of her tonic. This ruse worked excellently until in 1905 the *Ladies Home Journal* printed a picture of Lydia's grave, revealing she had died in 1883! Denying that she had been dispensing advice from beyond the grave, the company claimed that it was in fact her daughter Jennie Pinkham who had been answering the letters, a claim that was exposed as a further lie when it was revealed that a typing pool was employed to reply to the women who wrote in.[39]

Or, why not try Ryno's Hay Fever Cure, which 'was 99 per cent pure cocaine for "when the nose is stuffed up, red and sore"'?[40] The discovery of new drugs, combinations of drinks or synthesized forms of opium (morphine, heroine, cocaine) expanded the possibilities for commerce tremendously. Take coca wine: 'Coca-laced wine proved vastly popular. Amongst its devotees were Queen Victoria, Robert Louis Stevenson ... assorted popes and one John Pemberton, devotee of the coca leaf and inventor of Coca-Cola'.[41]

It is in this context of inflated language, inflated desire and inflated hopes and hypes that H. G. Wells set his masterly social novel *Tono-Bungay* (1909). Wells had long been interested in the effect of drugs upon the mind, an aspect so far underrated by criticism. In 'The Purple Pileus' (1896), he describes an unhappy man who turns into a local hero by accidentally eating a mushroom. In 'The Story of the Late Mr. Elvesham' (1896), the use of a little pinkish powder in a glass of 'Kummel' turns the drink into a heavenly potion and changes the drinker's identity. In *The First Men in the Moon* (1901), the two English explorers eat a moon fungoid, start to talk nonsense and then one of them begins to see the future of

British Imperialism on the moon. Thus Wells turns the Empire into a junkie's dream. In 'Under the Knife' (1896), a story about a near-death experience, the patient travels into the galaxy under the influence of chloroform. Wells's major drug story is certainly 'The New Accelerator' (1901), in which two men take a new drug that speeds up their perception. As a result, everything around them slows down to the extent that they become rich by working a one-armed bandit, while the tunes of a march band turn into a funeral hymn. Wells in a sense summarizes the drug experience of a century: the unmotivated mirth known by the users of nitrous oxide or laughing gas in the age of Romanticism,[42] the slowing down of movements and the grotesque phenomena as noted in Thomas De Quincey's *Confessions of an English Opium Eater* (1821), or Edgar Allan Poe's spatial distortions, as in his short story 'The Sphinx' (1846). 'The New Accelerator' can be considered the seed of *Tono-Bungay* since it not only has two protagonists like the novel, but Wells also tries to sketch in it the cultural function of drugs in general. The modern Mephisto who tempts the narrator with his experiment in time is very much aware of the signs of the age. It is the age of speed and modernization, and 'The New Accelerator' both celebrates and denigrates speed.[43]

In *Tono-Bungay*, the narrator George Ponderevo is a young man from a lower-class background, who after a difficult start in life collaborates with his uncle, a pharmacist, who is trying to market a new tonic he calls Tono-Bungay. Edward Ponderevo is a vigilant man, and his career resembles the career of Balzac's César Birotteau in the novel of the same title.[44] Like Birotteau, who believes in his magical hair growth tonic and finally ends up in debts and misery, uncle Ponderevo is half-educated, a nouveau riche with a knack for business, or at least this is how it seems:

> 'You see,' said my uncle in a slow confidential whisper, with eyes very wide and a creased forehead, 'it's nice because of the' (here he mentioned a flavouring matter and an aromatic spirit), 'it's stimulating because of' (here he mentioned two very vivid tonics, one with a marked action on the kidneys). 'And the' (here he mentioned two other ingredients) 'makes it pretty intoxicating. Cocks their tails. Then there's' (but I touch on the essential secret). 'And there you are. I got it out of an old book of recipes – all except the' (here he mentioned the more virulent substance, the one that assails the kidneys), 'which is my idea. Modern touch! There you are!'[45]

It is never quite clear whether the uncle believes in his patent-medicine. While his nephew is quickly disillusioned with the substance, which, as a matter of fact, does not exist, his uncle becomes carried away with his own advertising rhetoric, which tries to fuse the familiar and old-fashioned with the future:

> 'What I like about it all, Ponderevo, is its poetry ... And it's not your poetry only. It's the poetry of the customer too. Poet answering to poet – soul to soul. Health, Strength and Beauty – in a Bottle – the magic philtre! Like a fairy tale.'[46]

178   *Drink in the Eighteenth and Nineteenth Centuries*

Uncle Ponderevo is as much the victim of his own concoction as his custom-ers.[47] The cynical nephew, who is also engaged in other activities like building airplanes and later destroyers, views his own position in this process differently:

> My special and distinctive duty was to give Tono-Bungay substance and an outward and visible bottle, to translate my uncle's great imaginings into the creation of case after case of labelled bottles of nonsense, and the punctual discharge of them by railway, road and steamer towards their ultimate goal in the Great Stomach of the People.[48]

Tono-Bungay cures everything, it is the 'Secret of Vigour'.[49] On its basis they produce, like Birotteau, 'Tono-Bungay Hair Stimulant', '"Concentrated Tono-Bungay" for the eyes', 'Tono-Bungay Lozenges' and 'Tono-Bungay Chocolate'. Advertisements for the product show climbers hanging from awfully vertical cliffs or cyclists on the race track – an early anticipation of what was to happen to the Tour de France in more recent days – as well as soldiers in action, who show no signs of fatigue.[50]

> We also showed a dreadfully barristerish barrister, wig, side-whiskers, teeth, a hor-ribly life-like portrait of all existing barristers, talking at a table, and beneath, this legend: 'A Four Hours' Speech on Tono-Bungay Lozenges, and as fresh as when he began.' That brought in regiments of school-teachers, revivalist ministers, politicians and the like. I really do believe there was an element of 'kick' in the strychnine in these lozenges.[51]

George is well aware that deception is at the core of their enterprise, and thus he links the rise of Tono-Bungay with the decline of old English values which, by analogy, also appear to have been based on an illusion. Uncle Ponderevo is well aware of this dangerous yet alluring loss of substance in terms of both social and individual identity. This deficit becomes his great opportunity:

> 'The real trouble of life, Ponderevo, isn't that we exist – that's a vulgar error; the real trouble is that we *don't* really exist and we want to. That's what this – in the highest sense – muck stands for! The hunger to be – for once – really alive – to the finger-tips!'[52]

The quack potion here really responds to modernity and its discontents and is meant to relieve modern humanity from its many psychological ailments. This search for an antidote to the psychological losses through modernization is taken still further when Ponderevo's system begins to fail. He then turns to a new material with which he hopes to overcome his financial troubles: 'quap', a radio-active material he plans to sell to bulb factories for the production of better and cheaper filament. He sends his nephew on a mission to an African island, from which he is supposed to bring back large quantities of quap. They discover that the workers digging quap soon fall sick. George's murder of a native proves that quap also exerts a disastrous moral influence. When George returns with quap on board, the ship all but melts away and founders. Later on, he will find out that it was radioactivity that destroyed the wooden ship. Quap, the final potion, becomes a fatal patent-medicine. What is more, it is also a symbol of the decay of Western culture. As Wells put it, radium is just 'little molecular centres of dis-integration'[53] and 'radioactivity is a disease of matter'.[54] A few years later, Wells was to write the first novel about an atomic bomb: *The World Set Free* (1914).

We have followed the tortuous path from magical potions and elixirs to quack medicine and eventually to radioactivity and the atomic bomb. The magic quality, however, lives on, in whatever guise it may take, because humans have always been and will always be keen on miracles. Magical potions, be they elixirs or vitamin pills, touch on three core aspects of our existence: biological, political and religious. First, good health and longevity; second, power over ourselves and others; and third, access to a transcendent world, which some call paradise. Commercialized, the magical potion has been advertised as a key that is meant to help us find the 'right size', in other words, the harmony, between ourselves and a modern world increasingly difficult to understand and cope with. In this sense, it is not very different from what little Alice discovered in the rabbit-hole.

NOTES

Schmid and Schmidt-Haberkamp, 'Introduction'

1. J. Philips, *Cyder: A Poem in Two Books* (1708), bk 2, ll. 367–71, ed. J. Goodridge and J. C. Pellicer (Cheltenham: Cyder Press, 2001), p. 38.
2. See S. Schmid, 'Cider, Masculinity, and the Nation: Drink in Seventeenth-Century Britain', in *Anglistentag 2010 Saarbrücken: Proceedings*, ed. J. Frenk and L. Steveker (Trier: WVT, 2011), pp. 267–77, on pp. 271–3.
3. J. E. Fromer, *A Necessary Luxury: Tea in Victorian England* (Athens, OH: University of Ohio Press, 2008).
4. C. A. Wilson, *Food and Drink in Britain* (Harmondsworth: Penguin, 1975); A. Barr, *Drink: A Social History of America* (New York: Carroll and Graf, 1999); A. Jones (ed.), *Royston: Inns and Public Houses* (Royston: Royston and District Local Historical Society, 1990).
5. T. E. Brennan (general ed.), *Public Drinking in the Early Modern World: Voices from the Tavern, 1500–1800*, 4 vols (London: Pickering & Chatto, 2011); M. Ellis (general ed.), *Tea and the Tea-Table in Eighteenth-Century England*, 4 vols (London: Pickering & Chatto, 2010).
6. B. Cowan, *The Social Life of Coffee: The Emergence of the British Coffeehouse* (New Haven, CT: Yale University Press, 2005); M. Elbert and M. Drews (eds), *Culinary Aesthetics and Practices in Nineteenth-Century American Literature* (New York: Palgrave Macmillan, 2009).
7. J. Burnett, *Liquid Pleasures: A Social History of Drinks in Modern Britain* (London: Routledge, 1999), p. 179.
8. For example, Anon., *The Women's Petition Against Coffee* (London, 1674), p. 2.
9. J. Walvin, *Fruits of Empire: Exotic Produce and British Taste, 1660–1800* (Basingstoke: Macmillan, 1997).
10. D. Defoe, *Review of the State of the British Nation*, no. 43 (8 January 1713), in *Daniel Defoe: Review*, ed. J. McVeagh (London: Pickering & Chatto, 2011), vol. 9, pt 1, p. 168; see also F. W. Neumann, *Ned Wards London. Säkularisation, Kultur und Kapitalismus um 1700* (München: Fink, 2012), p. 161.
11. Anon., *The Character of a Coffee-House, with the Symptoms of a Town-Wit* (1673), in E. Mackie (ed.), *The Commerce of Everyday Life: Selections from* The Tatler *and* The Spectator (Boston, MA: Bedford/St Martin's Press, 1998), pp. 137–43, on p. 139; see S. Schmid, '"Hodge-Podge" of Unreason or the "Citizens Academy"? The London Coffee-House, 1652–1800', *Das Achtzehnte Jahrhundert*, 32 (2008), pp. 62–73, on p. 66.

182   *Notes to pages 4–11*

12.   J. Habermas, *The Structural Transformation of the Public Sphere: An Inquiry into a Category of Bourgeois Society*, trans. T. Burger with the assistance of F. Lawrence (Cambridge: Polity Press, 1989); for a summary of the debate, see J. A. Downie, 'Public and Private: The Myth of the Bourgeois Public Sphere', in C. Wall (ed.), *A Concise Companion to the Restoration and Eighteenth Century* (Oxford: Blackwell, 2005), pp. 58–79, and S. Schmid, *British Literary Salons of the Late Eighteenth and Early Nineteenth Centuries* (New York: Palgrave, 2013), pp. 11–15.

13.   N. Ward, *The London Spy*, ed. P. Hyland (East Lansing, MI: Colleagues Press, 1993), p. 64.

14.   S. Earnshaw, *The Pub in Literature: England's Altered State* (Manchester: Manchester University Press, 2000), p. 118. Earnshaw draws on this quotation by Ward, too. See also F. W. Neumann's contribution in this volume.

15.   H. Fielding, *Joseph Andrews* and *Shamela*, ed. J. Hawley (London: Penguin, 1999); R. Bradley, *The Virtue and Use of Coffee, With Regard to the Plague and Other Infectuous Distempers* (London: Matthews and Mears, 1721).

16.   M. Toussaint-Samat, *A History of Food*, trans. A. Bell (Oxford: Blackwell, 1992), p. 588.

17.   T. Trotter, *An Essay, Medical, Philosophical, and Chemical, on Drunkenness and Its Effects on the Human Body* (London, 1804).

18.   S. Warner, *The Wide, Wide World*, ed. J. Tompkins (New York: Feminist Press, 1987).

19.   Burnett, *Liquid Pleasures*, p. 142.

1 Harvey, 'Politics by Design: Consumption, Identity and Allegiance'

1.   F. Trentmann, 'Materiality in the Future of History: Things, Practices and Politics', *Journal of British Studies*, 48:2 (2009), pp. 283–307, on p. 287.

2.   C. Shammas, 'The Domestic Environment in Early Modern England and America', *Journal of Social History*, 14 (1980), pp. 3–24. The gendered account of Shammas has been qualified in L. Weatherill, 'A Possession of One's Own: Women and Consumer Behaviour in England, 1660–1740', *Journal of British Studies*, 25 (1986), pp. 131–56.

3.   See J. de Vries, 'Between Purchasing Power and the World of Goods: Understanding the Household Economy in Early Modern Europe', in J. Brewer and R. Porter (eds), *Consumption and the World of Goods* (London: Routledge, 1993), pp. 85–132; J. de Vries, 'The Industrial Revolution and the Industrious Revolution', *Journal of Economic History*, 54:2 (1994), pp. 249–70; J. de Vries, *The Industrious Revolution: Consumer Behaviour and the Household Economy, 1650 to the Present* (Cambridge: Cambridge University Press, 2008).

4.   See, for example, G. J. Barker Benfield, *The Culture of Sensibility: Sex and Society in Eighteenth-Century Britain* (Chicago, IL: University of Chicago Press, 1992); E. Kowaleski-Wallace, *Consuming Subjects: Women, Shopping, and Business in the Eighteenth Century* (New York: Columbia University Press, 1997).

5.   A. Vickery, 'Women and the World of Goods: A Lancashire Consumer and Her Possessions, 1751–81', in Brewer and Porter (eds), *Consumption and the World of Goods*, pp. 274–301.

6.   See K. Harvey, 'Barbarity in a Teacup? Punch, Domesticity and Gender in the Eighteenth Century', *Journal of Design History*, 21:3 (2008), pp. 205–21, for a discussion of how men became increasingly engaged with domesticity through the material culture of drinking over the eighteenth century. On men's consumption, see M. Finn, 'Men's Things: Masculine Possession in the Consumer Revolution', *Social History*, 25:2 (May 2000), pp. 133–54; K. Harvey, *The Little Republic: Masculinity and Domestic Authority*

in *Eighteenth-Century Britain* (Oxford: Oxford University Press, 2012), pp. 99–133; D. Hussey, 'Guns, Horses and Stylish Waistcoats? Male Consumer Activity and Domestic Shopping in Late-Eighteenth- and Early-Nineteenth-Century England', in D. Hussey and M. Ponsonby (eds), *Buying for the Home: Shopping for the Domestic from the Seventeenth Century to the Present* (Aldershot: Ashgate, 2008), pp. 47–69.

7. M. Johnson, *An Archaeology of Capitalism* (Oxford: Blackwell, 1996), p. 200.

8. N. McKendrick, J. Brewer and J. H. Plumb, *The Birth of a Consumer Society: The Commercialization of Eighteenth-Century England* (Cambridge: Cambridge University Press, 1982).

9. C. Campbell, *The Romantic Ethic and the Spirit of Modern Consumerism* (Oxford: Blackwell, 1987; York: Alcuin, 2005), esp. pp. 77–95; quotations on pp. 88, 180. See P. Glennie, 'Consumption Within Historical Studies', in D. Miller (ed.), *Acknowledging Consumption: A Review of New Studies* (London: Routledge, 1995), pp. 164–203, for a useful review of work in this area prior to the late 1990s.

10. D. Miller, 'Consumption as the Vanguard of History', in Miller (ed.), *Acknowledging Consumption*, pp. 1–57, on pp. 19, 50.

11. See, for example, K. Davies, 'A Moral Purchase: Femininity, Commerce and Abolition, 1788–1792', in E. Eger, C. Grant, C. Ó Gallchoir and P. Warburton (eds), *Women, Writing and the Public Sphere, 1700–1830* (Cambridge: Cambridge University Press, 2001), pp. 133–62.

12. T. H. Breen, *The Marketplace of Revolution: How Consumer Politics Shaped American Independence* (Oxford: Oxford University Press, 2004), p. xvii. See also T. H. Breen, 'Narrative of Commercial Life: Consumption, Ideology and Community on the Eve of the American Revolution', in L. Glickman (ed.), *Consumer Society in American History* (Ithaca, NY: Cornell University Press, 1999), pp. 100–29; M. Zakim, *Ready-Made Democracy: A History of Men's Dress in the American Republic 1760–1860* (Chicago, IL: University of Chicago Press, 2003).

13. M. Daunton and M. Hilton, 'Material Politics: An Introduction', in Daunton and Hilton (eds), *The Politics of Consumption: Material Culture and Citizenship in Europe and America* (Oxford: Berg, 2001), pp. 1–32.

14. For a study of eighteenth-century ceramic objects and nationalism, see A. Brooks, 'Building Jerusalem: Transfer-Printed Finewares and the Creation of British Identity', in S. Tarlow and S. West (eds), *The Familiar Past? Archaeologies of Later Historical Britain* (London: Routledge, 1999), pp. 51–65.

15. Harvey, 'Barbarity in a Teacup?', pp. 216–18.

16. See J. D. Griffin, *The Leeds Pottery 1770–1881* (Leeds: Leeds Art Collections Fund, 2005). This also contains a transcription of the letters; see vol. 1, pp. 282–4.

17. S. Richards, *Eighteenth-Century Ceramics: Products for a Civilised Society* (Manchester: Manchester University Press, 1999), pp. 92, 94.

18. M. Berg, 'The British Product Revolution of the Eighteenth Century', in J. Horn, L. N. Rosenband and M. Roe Smith (eds), *Reconceptualizing the Industrial Revolution* (Cambridge, MA: MIT Press, 2010), pp. 47–64, on p. 56; Wedgwood to Bentley, n.d., but written between February and September 1709, cited in M. Vickers and D. Gill, *Artful Crafts: Ancient Greek Silverware and Pottery* (Oxford: Clarendon, 1994), p. 27, cited in Berg, 'British Product Revolution', p. 56.

19. R. T. Cornish, 'Cartwright, John (1740–1824)', *ODNB*.

184   *Notes to pages 14–17*

20. R. Hemmings, *Liberty of Death: The Story of Thomas Hardy, Shoemaker, and John Cartwright, Landowner, in the Early Struggles for Parliamentary Democracy* (London: Lawrence and Wishart, 2000), p. 30.

21. See British Library English Short Title Catalogue, http://estc.bl.uk/ [accessed September 2010]. Also see N. C. Miller, 'Major John Cartwright and the Founding of the Hampden Club', *Historical Journal*, 17:3 (1974), pp. 615–19, for details on Cartwright's published works.

22. J. W. Osborne, *John Cartwright* (Cambridge: Cambridge University Press, 1972), pp. 29–35.

23. Hemmings, *Liberty of Death*, p. 30; J. P. W. Ehrman and A. Smith, 'Pitt, William (1759–1806)', *ODNB*.

24. J. Burke and J. B. Burke, *The Encyclopaedia of Heraldry, or General Armory of England, Scotland, and Ireland* (London: Henry G. Bohn, n.d.).

25. Letter from J[ohn] Cartwright, 7 November 1783, Letter inserted in 'Original Drawing Book no. 1', Hartley, Green & Co, Victoria and Albert Museum, E.576–1941. My sincere thanks to Hilary Young, who first made me aware of these letters. Of the surviving letters Cartwright wrote in the winter of 1783, only those to Hartley, Green & Co. discuss the bowl designs. Letters from this year survive in Birmingham City Archives, Duke University Library, Yale University Library and the Centre for Kentish Studies. I thank in particular Josh Rowley at Rare Book, Manuscript and Special Collections Library, Duke University, and Neil Chambers of Sir Joseph Banks Archives Project, Nottingham Trent University, for their assistance.

26. Letter from J[ohn] Cartwright, 7 November 1783, Letter inserted in 'Original Drawing Book no. 1', Hartley, Green & Co.

27. See Harvey, 'Barbarity in a Teacup?', and K. Harvey, 'Ritual Encounters: Punch Parties and Masculinity in the Eighteenth Century', *Past and Present*, 214:1 (2012), pp. 165–203, on the exotic connotations of punch.

28. See, for example, L. L. Lipski, *Dated English Delftware: Tin-Glazed Earthenware 1600–1800* (London: Sotheby Publications, 1984), numbers 1141 and 1186; L. B. Grigsby, *The Longridge Collection of English Slipware and Delftware*, 2 vols (London: Jonathan Horne, 2000), vol. 2.

29. Letter from J[ohn] Cartwright, 7 November 1783, Letter inserted in 'Original Drawing Book no. 1', Hartley, Green & Co.

30. Ibid. On the significance of keys and locked furniture, see A. Vickery, 'An Englishman's Home Is His Castle? Thresholds, Boundaries and Privacies in the Eighteenth-Century London House', *Past and Present*, 199:1 (2008), pp. 147–73.

31. John Cartwright to Thomas Hallet Hodges, 17 October 1777, Kent History and Library Centre, U49 C13/77.

32. Ibid.

33. John Cartwright to Thomas Hallet Hodges, 20 October 1777, Kent History and Library Centre, U49 C13/78.

34. John Cartwright to Thomas Hallet Hodges, 17 October 1777, Kent History and Library Centre, U49 C13/77.

35. Letter from J[ohn] Cartwright, n.d., Letter inserted in 'Original Drawing Book no. 1', Hartley, Green & Co.

36. Letter from J[ohn] Cartwright, 9 November 1783, Letter inserted in 'Original Drawing Book no. 1', Hartley, Green & Co. I have not been able to locate a source for either version this poem, so believe it to be original.
37. [John Cartwright,] *A Declaration of the Rights of Englishmen* ([London], [*c.* 1784]), p. 2.
38. Letter from J[ohn] Cartwright, n.d., Letter inserted in 'Original Drawing Book no. 1', Hartley, Green & Co.
39. 'An Abstract of the Title of John Cartwright, Esq. to Hopp-ground in Woodcoats in the parish of Fledborough in the County of Nottingham' (1784), Nottinghamshire Archives, DD/WM/7/40, p. 9.
40. J. Cartwright, *Take Your Choice! Representation and Respect: Imposition and Contempt. Annual Parliaments and Liberty: Long Parliaments and Slavery* (London, 1776), p. viii.
41. Ibid., p. xvi.
42. Ibid., p. 20.
43. Ibid., pp. 88–9.
44. Ibid., p. 91.
45. R. Rompkey, 'Jenyns, Soame (1704–1787)', *ODNB*.
46. J. Cartwright, *Internal Evidence; or An Inquiry How Far Truth and the Christian Religion have been Consulted by the Author of Thoughts on a Parliamentary Reform* (London, 1784), p. 34.
47. Ibid., pp. 40–1, on p. 40.
48. Cartwright, *Take Your Choice!*, p. 2.
49. Cartwright, *Internal Evidence*, p. 62.
50. Kowaleski-Wallace, *Consuming Subjects*, p. 58.
51. M. Vincentelli, *Women and Ceramics: Gendered Vessels* (Manchester: Manchester University Press, 2000), p. 112; Richards, *Eighteenth-Century Ceramics*, p. 39.
52. C. Shammas, *The Pre-Industrial Consumer in England and America* (Oxford: Oxford University Press, 1990), p. 187.
53. S. Gray Detweiler, with C. Meadows, *George Washington's Chinaware* (New York: Harry N. Abrams, Inc., 1982), p. 9.
54. 'General Washington's Economy', in 'R. Mathews Commonplace book' (*c.* 1780s), Henry E. Huntington Library, HM694, f.142.
55. John Cartwright to Joseph Banks, 5 June 1783, f1. JSB940124/015.21783, Sir Joseph Banks Archives Project, Nottingham Trent University. Original in Sir Joseph Banks Papers, Manuscripts and Archives, Yale University Library (MS 58).
56. John Cartwright to Joseph Banks, 14 May 1784, f1. JSB940111/004.21784, Sir Joseph Banks Archives Project, Nottingham Trent University. Original in Sir Joseph Banks Papers, Manuscripts and Archives, Yale University Library (MS 58), f 1, f1–2.
57. Harvey, 'Ritual Encounters', pp. 180–96.
58. For a review of the history of masculinity in this period, see M. Cohen, '"Manners" Make the Man: Politeness, Chivalry, and the Construction of Masculinity, 1750–1830', *Journal of British Studies*, 44:2 (2005), pp. 312–29; K. Harvey, 'The History of Masculinity, circa 1650–1800', *Journal of British Studies*, 44:2 (2005), pp. 296–311.
59. See Harvey, *Little Republic*, pp. 122–4.
60. M. Berg, 'Women's Consumption and the Industrial Classes of Eighteenth-Century England', *Journal of Social History*, 30:2 (1996), pp. 415–34.
61. 'Copy of the Will of John Cartwright', 9 June 1824, Gloucestershire Archives, D1245/CF10, 10a, 1824.

186 *Notes to pages 21–5*

62. 'Memorandum, the 9th of June 1824', supplement to the Will of John Cartwright, Gloucestershire Archives, D1245/CF10, 10a, 1824.
63. J. Epstein, 'Radical Dining, Toasting, and Symbolic Expression in Early Nineteenth-Century England', *Albion*, 20:2 (1988), pp. 271–91.
64. Ibid., p. 290.
65. Ibid., pp. 290, 278.
66. Harvey, 'Ritual Encounters', pp. 196–203.

2 Rosenthal, 'Drinks, Domesticity and the Forging of an American Identity in Susan Warner's *The Wide, Wide World* (1850)'

1. R. Barthes, 'Toward a Psychosociology of Contemporary Food Consumption', in C. Counihan and P. van Esterik (eds), *Food and Culture: A Reader* (New York: Routledge, 1997), pp. 28–35, on p. 29.
2. D. Grigg, 'The Worlds of Tea and Coffee: Patterns of Consumption', *GeoJournal*, 57 (2003), pp. 283–93.
3. S. Warner's *The Wide, Wide World* was reissued and introduced by Jane Tompkins with the Feminist Press in 1987. All parenthetical references are to this edition.
4. F. O. Matthiessen, *The American Renaissance: Art and Expression in the Age of Emerson and Whitman* (London: Oxford University Press, 1964).
5. Ibid., p. vii.
6. Ibid., p. ix.
7. M. S. Cummins, *The Lamplighter*, ed. N. Baym (New Brunswick, NJ: Rutgers University Press 1988); E. D. E. N. Southworth, *The Hidden Hand* (CreateSpace Independent Publishing Platform, 2009). On sentimental fiction or the domestic novel, i.e. texts written exclusively by women in America between the 1820s and the 1870s, see N. Baym, *Women's Fiction: A Guide to Novels by and about Women in America, 1820–1870* (Ithaca, NY: Cornell University Press, 1978). For facts on the publication of Warner's book, see E. H. Foster, *Susan and Anna Warner* (Boston, MA: Twayne, 1978).
8. On the development of separate spheres in the nineteenth century and the designation of the domestic realm to women and the public realm to men, see for example, M. Kelley, *Private Women, Public Stage: Literary Domesticity in Nineteenth-Century America* (New York: Oxford University Press, 1984), and L. K. Kerber, 'Separate Spheres, Female Worlds, Woman's Place: The Rhetoric of Women's History', *Journal of American History*, 75:1 (June 1988), pp. 9–39.
9. J. Tompkins, 'Afterword', in S. Warner, *The Wide, Wide World* (New York: Feminist Press, 1987), pp. 584–608; J. Tompkins, 'The Other American Renaissance', in W. B. Michaels and D. Pease (eds), *The American Renaissance Reconsidered* (Baltimore, MD: Johns Hopkins University Press, 1989), pp. 34–57.
10. Hawthorne in a letter to W. D. Ticknor (19 January 1855), in *The Letters, 1853–1856*, ed. T. Woodson, J. A. Rubino, L. N. Smith and N. H. Pearson, *Centenary Edition*, vol. 17 ([Columbus], OH: Ohio State University Press, 1987), p. 304; quoted in F. L. Mott, *Golden Multitudes* (New York: Macmillan 1947), p. 122.
11. H. N. Smith, *Democracy and the Novel* (New York: Oxford University Press, 1978), p. 12.
12. J. Tompkins, *Sensational Designs: The Cultural Work of American Fiction, 1790–1860* (New York: Oxford University Press, 1985).
13. Tompkins, 'The Other American Renaissance', p. 39.

14. Ibid., p. 36.
15. See D. G. Myers, 'The Canonization of Susan Warner', *New Criterion*, 7:4 (1988), pp. 73–8.
16. Tompkins, 'Afterword', p. 594.
17. See H. Hoeller, 'Hunger, Panic, Refusal: The Gift of Food in Susan Warner's *The Wide, Wide World*', in M. Elbert and M. Drews (eds), *Culinary Aesthetics and Practices in Nineteenth-Century American Literature* (New York: Palgrave Macmillan, 2009), pp. 173–87, on pp. 175–6.
18. In this context see J. Butler, 'Gender is Burning: Questions of Appropriation and Subversion', in A. McClintock, A. Mufti and E. Shohat (eds), *Dangerous Liaisons: Gender, Nation, and Postcolonial Perspectives* (Minneapolis, MN: University of Minnesota Press, 1997), pp. 381–95.
19. Grigg, 'Worlds of Tea and Coffee', p. 292.
20. Hoeller, 'Hunger, Panic, Refusal', p. 181.
21. Ibid., p. 177.
22. See for example L. Naranjo-Huebl, '"Take, Eat": Food Imagery, the Nurturing Ethic, and Christian Identity in *The Wide, Wide World*, *Uncle Tom's Cabin*, and *Incidents in the Life of a Slave Girl*', *Christianity and Literature*, 56:4 (2007), pp. 597–631.
23. S. W. Mintz, 'Eating American', in *Tasting Food, Tasting Freedom: Excursions into Eating, Culture, and the Past* (Boston, MA: Beacon Books, 1997), pp. 106–24.
24. M. Elbert and M. Drews, 'Introduction', in Elbert and Drews (eds), *Culinary Aesthetics*, pp. 1–18, on p. 1.
25. Henry David Thoreau already called the activity of collecting wild berries to go 'a-huckleberrying' in *Walden* (New Haven, CT: Yale University Press, 2006), p. 166; see also Thoreau's later essay 'Huckleberries', in *Wild Apples and Other Natural History: Essays by Henry D. Thoreau,* ed. W. Rossi (Athens, GA: University of Georgia Press, 2002), pp. 166–202.
26. L. M. Child, *The American Frugal Housewife* (1829; New York: Dover Publications, 1999).
27. In a passage that mirrors the tea ceremony at the beginning of the novel, Ellen makes breakfast when her aunt is sick. In this scene, she prepares coffee, not tea, and does it less religiously but with a lot of laughter and heartiness (pp. 363–4).
28. C. O'Connell, '"We *Must* Sorrow": Silence, Suffering, and Sentimentality in S. Warner's *The Wide, Wide World*', *Studies in American Fiction*, 25 (Spring 1997), pp. 21–39.
29. R. W. Emerson, 'The American Scholar', in P. Lauter et al. (eds), *The Heath Anthology of American Literature* (Lexington, MA: Heath, 1990), vol. 1, pp. 1499–1511.
30. L. L. Damon-Bach, 'To Be a "Parlor Soldier": Susan Warner's Answer to Emerson's "Self-Reliance"', in M. M. Elbert (ed.), *Separate Spheres No More: Gender Convergence in American Literature, 1830–1930* (Tuscaloosa, AL: University of Alabama Press, 2000), pp. 29–49; I. White, 'Anti-Individualism, Authority, and Identity: S. Warner's Contradictions in *The Wide, Wide World*', *American Studies*, 21:2 (1990), pp. 31–41; G. A. Hovet and T. R. Hovet, 'Identity Development in S. Warner's *The Wide, Wide World*: Relationship, Performance and Construction', *Legacy*, 8:1 (1991), pp. 3–16.
31. A. Kaplan, 'Manifest Domesticity', *American Literature*, 70:3 (1998), pp. 581–606, on p. 601.
32. Ibid., p. 582.

3 Cowan, '*Café* or Coffeehouse? Transnational Histories of Coffee and Sociability'

1. T. Judt, 'Europe vs. America', *New York Review of Books*, 52:2 (10 February 2005), http://www.nybooks.com/articles/archives/2005/feb/10/europe-vs-america [accessed 3 February 2013].
2. B. Simon, *Everything But the Coffee: Learning about America from Starbucks* (Berkeley, CA: University of California Press, 2009).
3. B. Cowan, *The Social Life of Coffee: The Emergence of the British Coffeehouse* (New Haven, CT: Yale University Press, 2005); W. S. Haine, *The World of the Paris Café: Sociability among the French Working Class, 1789–1914* (Baltimore, MD: Johns Hopkins University Press, 1996); H. B. Segel, *The Vienna Coffeehouse Wits 1890–1938* (West Lafayette, IN: Purdue University Press, 1993); S. Bauschinger, 'The Berlin Moderns: Else Lasker-Schüler and Café Culture', in E. Bilski (ed.), *Berlin Metropolis: Jews and the New Culture 1890–1918* (Berkeley, CA: University of California Press, 1999), pp. 58–83.
4. For example, D. Woolf, *A Global History of History* (Cambridge: Cambridge University Press, 2011); D. Armitage and S. Subrahmanyam (eds), *The Age of Revolution in Global Context, c. 1760–1840* (Basingstoke: Palgrave, 2010); C. A. Bayly, *The Birth of the Modern World 1780–1914: Global Connections and Comparisons* (Malden, MA: Blackwell, 2004).
5. B. W. Higman, *How Food Made History* (Malden, MA: Wiley-Blackwell, 2012); A. Nützenadel and F. Trentmann (eds), *Food and Globalization: Consumption, Markets and Politics in the Modern World* (Oxford: Berg, 2008); J. M. Pilcher (ed.), *The Oxford Handbook of Food History* (Oxford: Oxford University Press, 2012); J. Pilcher, *Food in World History* (London: Routledge, 2006).
6. J. Habermas, *The Structural Transformation of the Public Sphere: An Inquiry into a Category of Bourgeois Society*, trans. T. Burger and F. Lawrence (Cambridge, MA: MIT Press, 1989); T. Blanning, *The Culture of Power and the Power of Culture: Old Regime Europe 1660–1789* (Oxford: Oxford University Press, 2000); J. van Horn Melton, *The Rise of the Public in Enlightenment Europe* (Cambridge: Cambridge University Press, 2001).
7. M. Jacob, *Radical Enlightenment: Pantheists, Freemasons and Republicans* (London: Unwin, 1981); M. Jacob, *Strangers Nowhere in the World: The Rise of Cosmopolitanism in Early Modern Europe* (Philadelphia, PA: University of Pennsylvania Press, 2006), p. 99.
8. An unpersuasive attempt to do so may be found in D. Lord Smail, *On Deep History and the Brain* (Berkeley, CA: University of California Press, 2008), esp. pp. 179–97.
9. B. Cowan, '*Publicity and Privacy* in the History of the British *Coffeehouse*', *History Compass*, 5:4 (2007), pp. 1180–213; Segel, *Vienna Coffeehouse Wits*; V. De Grazia, *Irresistible Empire: America's Advance through Twentieth-Century Europe* (Cambridge, MA: Harvard University Press, 2005), p. 469.
10. R. S. Hattox, *Coffee and Coffeehouses: The Origins of a Social Beverage in the Medieval Near East* (Seattle, WA: University of Washington Press, 1985); S. A. Özkoçak, 'Coffeehouses: Rethinking the Public and Private in Early Modern Istanbul', *Journal of Urban History*, 33:6 (September 2007), pp. 965–86.
11. A. Mikhail, 'The Heart's Desire: Gender, Urban Space and the Ottoman Coffee House', in D. Sajdi (ed.), *Ottoman Tulips, Ottoman Coffee: Leisure and Lifestyle in the Eighteenth Century* (London: Tauris, 2007), pp. 133–70; see also A. Çaksu, 'Janissary Coffee Houses in Late Eighteenth-Century Istanbul', pp. 117–32, in the same volume.
12. A. Cowan, 'Rosee, Pasqua (*fl.* 1651–1656)', *ODNB*; M. Ellis, *The Coffee-House: A Cultural History* (London: Weidenfeld & Nicolson, 2004), pp. 25–38.

Notes to pages 38–41

13. T. Wijsenbeek, 'Ernst en Luim: Koffiehuizen tijdens de Republiek', in P. Reinders and T. Wijsenbeek (eds), *Koffie in Nederlands* (Zutphen: Walburg, 1994), pp. 32–54, esp. pp. 36–7.

14. Ellis, *Coffee-House*, pp. 79–80; J. Leclant, 'Le café et les cafés à Paris (1644–1693)', *Annales: Histoire, Sciences Sociales*, 6:1 (January–March 1951), pp. 1–14.

15. F. de Vivo, *Information and Communication in Venice: Rethinking Early Modern Politics* (Oxford: Oxford University Press, 2007), pp. 105–6; Ellis, *Coffee-House*, p. 82. The often repeated claim that a Venetian café was opened in 1645 has not been substantiated by reliable evidence.

16. Van Horn Melton, *Rise of the Public*, pp. 240–1; Segel, *Vienna Coffeehouse Wits*, pp. 8–9.

17. Wijsenbeek, 'Ernst en Luim', p. 39.

18. Leclant, 'Le café et les cafés à Paris'.

19. S. Schmid, '"That Newfangled, Abominable, Heathenish Liquor called COFFEE": Türkeibilder in englischen Texten über den Kaffee', in B. Schmidt-Haberkamp (ed.), *Europa und die Türkei im 18. Jahrhundert/Europe and Turkey in the 18th Century* (Göttingen: V & R unipress, 2011), pp. 161–75, points out that this putatively Turkish character has some oddly Jewish characteristics. Such indiscriminate views were not uncommon in early modern English ethnic satire.

20. Compare Cowan, *Social Life of Coffee*, with B. Kümin, *Drinking Matters: Public Houses and Social Exchange in Early Modern Central Europe* (Basingstoke: Palgrave, 2007); and P. Clark, *The English Alehouse: A Social History, 1200–1830* (London: Longman, 1983).

21. J. Houghton, *Collection for the Improvement of Husbandry and Trade*, no. 461 (23 May 1701); [T. Jordan], *The Triumphs of London* (London: J. Macock, 1675), scoffs at the coffeehouses as 'So great an university ... In which you may a scholar be, For spending of a penny', p. 23; see also Cowan, *Social Life of Coffee*, pp. 99–101.

22. U. Heise, *Coffee and Coffee-Houses*, trans. P. Roper (1987; West Chester, PA: Schiffer Publishing, 1997), p. 106.

23. Cowan, *Social Life of Coffee*, p. 169.

24. Z. C. von Uffenbach, *London in 1710*, trans. W. H. Quarrell (London: Faber, 1934), p. 27; see also pp. 70, 97, 142, 149, 151, 188.

25. R. Paulson, *Hogarth: The 'Modern Moral Subject', 1697–1732* (New Brunswick, NJ: Rutgers University Press, 1991), p. 14; R. Paulson, *Hogarth's Harlot: Sacred Parody in Enlightenment England* (Baltimore, MD: Johns Hopkins University Press, 2003), pp. 65–7.

26. Cowan, *Social Life of Coffee*, pp. 100, 282 n. 31, 99.

27. J. Strang, *Germany in 1831*, 2 vols (London: T. Foster, 1836), vol. 2, p. 243.

28. J. Macky, *A Journey through England in Familiar Letters from a Gentleman Here to His Friend Abroad*, 2 vols (London: J. Hooke, 1722–4), vol. 1, p. 172.

29. M. Ellis, 'Coffee-House Libraries in Mid-Eighteenth-Century London', *Library*, 10:1 (2009), pp. 3–40.

30. P. Fritzsche, *Reading Berlin 1900* (Cambridge, MA: Harvard University Press, 1996), p. 281 n. 40; S. Wobick-Segev, 'Buying, Selling, Being, Drinking: Jewish Coffeehouse Consumption in the Long Nineteenth Century', in G. Reuveni and S. Wobick-Segev (eds), *The Economy in Jewish History: New Perspectives on the Interrelationship Between Ethnicity and Economic Life* (Oxford: Berghahn, 2011), pp. 115–34, see esp. pp. 127–8; M. Constantin, *Histoire des cafés de Paris: extraite des mémoires d'un viveur* (Paris: Desloger, 1857), p. 121, my translation.

190   *Notes to pages 41–4*

31. É. Goudeau, *Dix Ans de Bohème*, ed. M. Golfier and J.-D. Wagneur (1888; Paris: Champ Vallon, 2000), p. 88; my translation, adapted from M. Gluck, *Popular Bohemia: Modernism and Urban Culture in Nineteenth-Century Paris* (Cambridge, MA: Harvard University Press, 2005), pp. 124–5.
32. *Spectator*, ed. D. F. Bond, 5 vols (Oxford: Oxford University Press, 1965), vol. 1, p. 44.
33. S. Zweig, *The World of Yesterday*, trans. anon. (London: Cassell, 1943), p. 41.
34. *Collection for the Improvement of Husbandry and Trade*, 461 (23 May 1701); also cited and discussed in Cowan, *Social Life of Coffee*, pp. 99, 282 n. 30.
35. *Spectator*, ed. Bond, vol. 1, p. 210; see also B. Cowan, 'Mr. Spectator and the Coffeehouse Public Sphere', *Eighteenth-Century Studies*, 37:3 (2004), pp. 345–66; L. Klein, 'Property and Politeness in the Early Eighteenth-Century Whig Moralists: The Case of *The Spectator*', in J. Brewer and S. Staves (eds), *Early Modern Conceptions of Property* (London: Routledge, 1995), pp. 221–33.
36. M. Ellis, 'Coffee-Women, "The Spectator" and the Public Sphere in the Early Eighteenth Century', in E. Eger, C. Grant, C. Ó Gallchoir and P. Warburton (eds), *Women, Writing and the Public Sphere, 1700–1830* (Cambridge: Cambridge University Press, 2001), pp. 27–52, on pp. 44–5. Habermas's public sphere ideal was shaped by the politics of post-war Germany, a point that is developed at length in M. G. Specter, *Habermas: An Intellectual Biography* (Cambridge: Cambridge University Press, 2010); see also B. Cowan, 'English Coffeehouses and French Salons: Rethinking Habermas, Gender and Sociability in Early Modern French and British Historiography', in A. Vanhaelen and J. P. Ward (eds), *Making Space Public in Early Modern Europe: Performance, Geography, Privacy* (London: Routledge, 2013), pp. 41–53.
37. G. Newman, *The Rise of English Nationalism: A Cultural History, 1740–1830*, rev. edn (Basingstoke: Macmillan, 1997); L. Colley, *Britons: Forging the Nation* (New Haven, CT: Yale University Press, 1992); D. Bell, *The Cult of the Nation in France: Inventing Nationalism, 1680–1800* (Cambridge, MA: Harvard University Press, 2003); I. Berlin, 'Nationalism: Past Neglect and Present Power', in *Against The Current: Essays in the History of Ideas* (Princeton, NJ: Princeton University Press, 2001), pp. 333–55. For a critical survey of this problematic, see the essays in L. Scales and O. Zimmer (eds), *Power and the Nation in European History* (Cambridge: Cambridge University Press, 2005).
38. S. Pincus, *1688: The First Modern Revolution* (New Haven, CT: Yale University Press, 2009), pp. 76–7.
39. A. L. Beier and R. Finlay, 'Introduction: The Significance of the Metropolis', in *London 1500–1700: The Making of the Metropolis* (London: Longman, 1986), pp. 1–33, esp. pp. 2–4; see also R. O. Bucholz and J. P. Ward, *London: A Social and Cultural History, 1550–1750* (Cambridge: Cambridge University Press, 2012); L. Lees and A. Lees, *Cities and the Making of Modern Europe, 1750–1914* (Cambridge: Cambridge University Press, 2007).
40. Cowan, *Social Life of Coffee*, pp. 154–8, esp. p. 154; C. Jones, *The Great Nation: France from Louis XIV to Napoleon* (New York: Columbia University Press, 2002), pp. 180–1; Van Horn Melton, *Rise of the Public*, p. 240, gives figures for Paris in 1720, 1750 and 1789. Precise figures for London in the same period have not been calculated but probably ranged between 1,000 and 3,000 over the century, if unlicensed coffeehouses are taken into consideration: see Cowan, *Social Life of Coffee*, p. 154.
41. H. E. Bödeker, 'Le café allemand au XVIIIe siècle: une forme de sociabilité éclairée', *Revue d'histoire moderne et contemporaine*, 37:4 (1990), pp. 571–88, esp. p. 574; Cowan, *Social Life of Coffee*, p. 154.

42. C. Kirli, 'Coffeehouses: Public Opinion in the Nineteenth-Century Ottoman Empire', in A. Salvatore and D. F. Eickelman (eds), *Public Islam and the Common Good* (Leiden: Brill, 2004), pp. 75–97, esp. p. 76.

43. C. M. S. Johns, 'Did the King take Coffee with the Pope? Charles III, Benedict XIV and the Quirinale Caffeaus', paper given at the ASECS 2008 conference in Portland, Oregon.

44. B. Cowan, 'The Rise of the Coffeehouse Reconsidered', *Historical Journal*, 47:1 (2004), pp. 21–46.

45. Kümin, *Drinking Matters*.

46. A. Franklin, *La Vie privée d'autrefois: le café, le thé et le chocolat* (Paris, 1893), pp. 297–301; Cowan, *Social Life of Coffee*, p. 188.

47. Strang, *Germany in 1831*, vol. 1, pp. 247–8.

48. J. W. von Archenholz, *A Picture of England*, trans. anon., 2 vols (1785 reprint; London: E. Jeffery, [1789]), vol. 2, pp. 107–8.

49. Cowan, 'Publicity and Privacy in the History of the British Coffeehouse', pp. 1194–6.

50. P. Langford, *Englishness Identified: Manners and Character 1650–1850* (Oxford: Oxford University Press, 2000), p. 253. For a more nuanced study of a similar theme in a later period, see P. Mandler, *The English National Character: The History of an Idea from Edmund Burke to Tony Blair* (New Haven, CT: Yale University Press, 2006).

51. M. Knights, 'Harris, Benjamin (c. 1647–1720)', *ODNB*. As early as the 1670s, one Dorothy Jones had obtained a license to sell coffee in Boston, but it is not clear that she sold it in a coffeehouse; see S. V. Salinger, *Taverns and Drinking in Early America* (Baltimore, MD: Johns Hopkins University Press, 2002), p. 288 n. 43.

52. B. A. Weinberg and B. K. Bealer, *The World of Caffeine: The Science and Culture of the World's Most Popular Drug* (London: Routledge, 2001), pp. 181–4; D. S. Shields, *Civil Tongues and Polite Letters in British America* (Chapel Hill, NC: University of North Carolina Press, 1997), pp. 56–7, 60–3.

53. M. Eamon, 'The Quebec Clerk Controversy: A Study in Sociability, the Public Sphere, and the Eighteenth-Century Spirit of Enlightenment', *Canadian Historical Review*, 90:4 (2009), pp. 609–38. See also M.-C. Poliquin, *Les aubergistes et les cabaretiers montréalais entre 1700 et 1755* (MA thesis, McGill University, 1996); Y. Briand, *Auberges et cabarets de Montréal (1680–1759): Lieux de sociabilité* (Mémoire, Faculté des études supérieures, Université Laval, Québec, December 1999).

54. W. S. Seton-Karr (ed.), *Selections from Calcutta Gazettes of the Years 1784, 1785, 1786, 1787, and 1788, Showing the Political and Social Condition of the English in India Eighty Years Ago* (Calcutta: Military Orphan Press, 1864), pp. 28–9, 286; [P. Gibbs], *Hartly House, Calcutta*, 3 vols (London: J. Dodsley, 1789), vol. 1, pp. 103–4.

55. Shields, *Civil Tongues and Polite Letters*, pp. 56, 61.

56. I. T. Berend, *History Derailed: Central and Eastern Europe in the Long Nineteenth Century* (Berkeley, CA: University of California Press, 2003), pp. 86, 232; J. Lukacs, *Budapest 1900: A Historical Portrait of a City and Its Culture* (New York: Weidenfeld, 1988), pp. 14–15, 151–2.

57. S. Barrows, 'Nineteenth-Century Cafés: Arenas of Everyday Life', in B. S. Shapiro (ed.), *Pleasures of Paris: Daumier to Picasso* (Boston, MA: Museum of Fine Arts, 1991), pp. 17–26; F. Torberg, *Tante Jolesch or the Decline of the West in Anecdotes*, trans. M. P. Bauer (1975; Riverside, CA: Ariadne Press, 2008); R. F. Allen, *Literary Life in German Expressionism and the Berlin Circles* (Ann Arbor, MI: UMI Research Press, 1983), esp. pp. 67–74.

4 Neumann, 'Claret at a Premium: Ned Ward, the True Tory Defender of Fine Wines?'

1. See the preface to H. Troyer's *Ned Ward of Grub Street: A Study of Sub-Literary London in the Eighteenth Century* (1946; London: Cass, 1968), p. vii, until recently the only monograph on Ned Ward. Mine has followed suite: F. W. Neumann, *Ned Wards London. Säkularisation, Kultur und Kapitalismus um 1700* (München: Fink, 2012).

2. W. Besant, *London in the Eighteenth Century* (London: Black, 1903), p. 276.

3. Discussing the booming cultural studies industry at the helm of which they themselves operate in Germany, Ansgar and Vera Nünning complain about an expansion on both sides of the Atlantic, which according to their diagnosis, is programmatic rather than substantial, eclectic rather than systematic, and most of all, more polemical than methodical; see 'Kulturwissenschaften: Eine multiperspektivische Einführung in einen interdisziplinären Diskussionszusammenhang', in Nünning and Nünning (eds), *Einführung in die Kulturwissenschaften. Theoretische Grundlagen – Ansätze – Perspektiven* (Stuttgart: Metzler, 2008), pp. 8–9.

4. For P. Rogers on 'Grubstreeters', see his *The Augustan Vision* (London: Weidenfeld and Nicholson, 1974), p. 112.

5. See Neumann, *Ned Wards London*, pp. 12–13, and in the context of material culture and the related epistemology, C. Huck, *Fashioning Society, or, The Mode of Modernity: Observing Fashion in Eighteenth-Century England* (Würzburg: Königshausen & Neumann, 2010), pp. 85–7, on the 'restraints of representation' in Ward and Defoe. Ward's representation of the metropolis seems to be widely accepted; see P. Ackroyd, *London: The Biography* (London: Chatto & Windus, 2000), pp. 147–8, 187, 349, 360, 450, 471, 556, 664.

6. On the qualities of the cuisine at the time, see Ward, *The London Spy*, ed. P. Hyland (East Lansing, MI: Colleagues Press, 1993), p. 219. See also Ward's poem *The Delights of the Bottle* (London, 1720) or the prose narrative *A Frolick to Horn-Fair* (London, 1699).

7. For Swift's familiarity with Ward, whom he mentions in one breath with prominent figures of the period like Gildon and Dennis, see *A Complete Collection of Genteel and Ingenious Conversation, according to the Most Polite Mode and Method now Used at Court, and in the Best Companies of England* (1738), in *The Prose Works of Jonathan Swift, in 12 Volumes*, ed. T. Scott (London, [*c.* 1900]), vol. 11, p. 221.

8. J. Swift, *A Proposal for Correcting, Improving and Ascertaining the English Tongue; in a Letter to the Most Honourable Robert Earl of Oxford and Mortimer, Lord High Treasurer of Great Britain* (London, 1712), p. 12; like Ned Ward, Tom Brown was a chronicler of contemporary London life, notably in his *Amusements Serious and Comical* (1700). For the connection with Pope, see Pope on 'Pert Style', *Peri Bathous: or, Martinus Scriblerus His Treatise of the Art of Sinking in Poetry* (1728), in *The Prose Works of Alexander Pope*, vol. 2: *The Major Works, 1725–1744*, ed. R. Cowler (Oxford: Blackwell, 1986), pp. 220, 267.

9. See for example A. C. Partridge, *Tudor to Augustan English: A Study in Syntax and Style from Caxton to Johnson* (London: Deutsch, 1969), p. 219.

10. S. Johnson, *The Lives of the Poets*, ed. R. Lonsdale, 4 vols (Oxford: Clarendon, 2006), vol. 2, p. 124.

11. To E. Partridge, Ward's writings were a mine of information on colloquial language; see his *Dictionary of Historical Slang* (1937; abridged edn, Harmondsworth: Penguin, 1977).

12. See R. Posner, 'Kultursemiotik', in Nünning and Nünning (eds), *Einführung in die Kulturwissenschaften*, pp. 39–71, on pp. 58–61.

Notes to pages 49–51

13. Ward's strategy of semiotic dysfunctionalism is a case in point to apply Posner's concept of 'cultural garbage' ('Kulturschrott', my translation); see Posner, 'Kultursemiotik', p. 61.
14. Ward, *The London Spy*, p. 11.
15. For Butler's popularity, see U. Broich, *The Eighteenth-Century Mock-Heroic Poem* (Cambridge: Cambridge University Press, 1990), pp. 17–21.
16. For the concept of 'conspicuous' consumption and material culture, see N. McKendrick, J. Brewer and J. H. Plumb, *The Birth of a Consumer Society: The Commercialization of Eighteenth-Century England* (London: Hutchinson, 1983), pp. 1–6.
17. Ward, *London Spy*, p. 11.
18. Troyer, *Ned Ward of Grub Street*, pp. 33–58, had already emphasized the guide-book quality of the sequels of *The London Spy*.
19. For the premises Ward bought, see Troyer, *Ned Ward of Grub Street*, pp. 169–88. 'For Men of Sense must own 'tis better / To live by Malt, than starve by meter', thus Ward autobiographically in *The Hudibrastick Brewer*, in *A Collection of Historical and State Poems, Satyrs, Songs and Epigrams. Being the (fifth) Volume of Miscellanies. By the Author of The London Spy* (1714; London, 1717), p. 36.
20. For this term, see C. B. Macpherson, *The Political History of Possessive Individualism: Hobbes to Locke* (Oxford: Clarendon, 1962).
21. P. Dillon, *The Much-Lamented Death of Madam Geneva: The Eighteenth-Century Gin Craze* (London: Review, 2002), p. 18; on the targets of the Societies for the Reformation of Manners, see ibid., pp. 45–6.
22. See L. E. Klein, 'Coffeehouse Civility, 1660–1714: An Aspect of Post-Courtly Culture in England', *Huntington Library Quarterly*, 59:1 (1996), pp. 30–51; L. E. Klein, 'Politeness for Plebes: Consumption and Social Identity in Early Eighteenth-Century England', in A. Bermingham and J. Brewer (eds), *The Consumption of Culture, 1600–1800: Image, Object, Text* (London: Routledge, 1997), pp. 362–82.
23. J. C. Drummond and A. Wilbraham, *The Englishman's Food: Five Centuries of English Diet* (1939; rev. edn London: Pimlico, 1994), p. 197; for a survey, see J. Warner, *Craze: Gin and Debauchery in the Age of Reason* (New York: Four Walls Eight Windows, 2002).
24. This political mechanism was anticipated in Ward's 'The Contending Candidates: or, The Broom-Staff Battles, Dirty Skirmishes, and other Comical Humours of the Late Southwark Election', in *The Wand'ring Spy: or, The Merry Travellers*, Part II (London, 1724), pp. 21–2.
25. See Dillon, *The Much-Lamented Death of Madam Geneva*, on how Sir Robert Walpole was trained to drink at his father's table (p. 18).
26. See L. W. Cowie, *The Wordsworth Dictionary of British Social History* (Ware, Hertfordshire: Wordsworth Editions, 1996), *s.v.* Claret: 'the name given in England to the red wines of Bordeaux for the past 600 years. These were especially popular in the country when the English kings ruled over Bordeaux and Gascony.'
27. For the price difference, see J. Hunter, 'English Inns, Taverns, Alehouses and Brandy Shops: The Legislative Framework, 1495–1797', in B. Kümin and B. A. Tlusty (eds), *The World of the Tavern: Public Houses in Early Modern Europe* (Aldershot: Ashgate, 2002), pp. 65–87, on pp. 77–8; for prices of wine at the end of Queen Anne's reign, see G. Rudé, *Hanoverian London, 1714–1808* (Stroud: Sutton, 2003), p. 70; on wine C. C. Ludington, '"Be Sometimes to your Country True": The Politics of Wine in England, 1660–1714', in A. Smyth (ed.), *A Pleasing Sinne: Drink and Conviviality in Seventeenth-Century England* (Cambridge: Brewer, 2004), pp. 89–106, with an excellent survey of

194 *Notes to pages 51–3*

import figures and political distinctions, and especially on Richard Ames, a poet frequently copied by Ward.

28. See G. Stedman, *Cultural Exchange in Seventeenth-Century France and England* (Farnham: Ashgate, 2013), p. 255.

29. It was Ames and not Ward who declared claret 'Naturaliz'd'; see his *A Dialogue between Claret and Darby-Ale, A Poem* (London, 1691), p. 9. As Troyer, *Ned Ward of Grub Street*, pp. 213–14, had already argued, this poem was erroneously attributed to Ward. This error was spread by D. Wing (comp.), *Short-title Catalogue of Books Printed in England, Scotland, Ireland, Wales, and British America and of English Books Printed in Other Countries: 1641–1700*, 2nd edn (New York: MLA, 1988), vol. 3; see also S. Schmid, 'Cider, Masculinity, and the Nation: Drink in Seventeenth-Century Britain', in J. Frenk and L. Steveker, *Anglistentag 2010 Saarbrücken: Proceedings* (Trier: WVT, 2011), pp. 267–77, on pp. 275–6.

30. For Ward and Ames, see A. D. Francis, *The Wine Trade: The Merchant Adventurers* (London: Black, 1972), pp. 103–4.

31. Richard Ames was distinctly Whig. Ludington describes him as 'a claret-loving Whig' valiantly attempting 'to break the link between claret and the Tories'; Ludington, '"Be Sometimes to your Country True"', p. 94. Ames's poem *The Search after Claret; or, A Visitation of the Vintners, a Poem in Two Cantos* (London, 1691) had three sequels.

32. *Spectator*, 24 (28 March 1711), in *The Spectator*, ed. D. F. Bond, 5 vols (Oxford: Clarendon, 1965), vol.1, pp. 100–4, on p. 101.

33. Ibid., p. 181.

34. For George's coffee-house, see B. Lillywhite, *London Coffee Houses: A Reference Book of Coffee Houses of the Seventeenth, Eighteenth and Nineteenth Centuries* (London: Allen & Unwin, 1963), p. 226. The location was 'the upper end of Haymarket'.

35. *Spectator*, ed. Bond, vol. 1, pp. 181–2.

36. See Troyer, *Ned Ward of Grub Street*, p. 262, for the context of Thomas Brooke's *Petition to Parliament concerning the Duties on Wines* (London, 1710), however without further evidence.

37. Ward, *British Wonders: or, A Poetical Description of the Several Prodigies and Most Remarkable Accidents that have Happen'd in Britain since the Death of Queen Anne* (London, 1717), p. 38. *British Wonders* is Ward's satirical version of Abel Boyer's *History of the Reign of Queen Anne, Digested into Annals* (London, 1703–13). For 'chip and dash', see M. R. Best, 'The Mystery of Vintners', *Agricultural History*, 50 (1976), pp. 362–76. Ward obviously alludes to *In Vino Veritas, or A Conference betwixt Chip the Cooper and Dash the Brewer, (Being both Boozy) Discovering Some Secrets in the Wine-brewing Trade* (London, 1698). In *Tatler*, 131 (9 February 1710), Addison mentions 'Subterraneous Philosophers' who can 'squeeze *Bourdeaux* out of the *Sloe*, and draw *Champagne* from an *Apple*'; *The Tatler*, ed. D. F. Bond, 3 vols (Oxford: Clarendon, 1987), vol. 2, pp. 259–64, on pp. 259–60. See also T. Tryon, *The Way to get Wealth: or, A New and Easie Way to Make Twenty Three Sorts of Wine, Equal to that of France, with their Vertues* (London, [c. 1701]).

38. A. Pope, 'Windsor-Forest' (1713), ll. 15–16, in *The Poems of Alexander Pope*, ed. J. Butt (London: Routledge, 1963), pp. 195–210, on p. 195.

39. Ward, *The Humours of a Coffee-House. A Comedy. As it is Daily Acted at Most Coffee-Houses in London* (1707), in *A Collection of the Writings of Mr. Edward Ward, Vol. II*, 5th edn (London, 1717), pp. 334–5.

40. Ward, 'The Wine Bibber's Wish', in *The Fourth Volume of the Writings of the Author of The London Spy* (London, 1709), p. 6.

41. James Nayler and George Fox were the leading Quakers of the revolution period; the very rare expression 'poz roz' may refer to 'possibly roseate' or 'rosined'. The connotation of 'roz' (resin, rosin) may describe the state of inebriation. Syntactically, 'poz roz' seems to be a derogatory variation of 'dull stuff' (*OED*).

42. Ward, *The Merry Travellers: or, A Trip upon Ten-Toes, from Moorfields to Bromley* (London, 1721), quoted from *The Wandering Spy; or, The Merry Observator ... being the Sixth Volume of Miscellanies* (1724), p. 15.

43. Ibid.

44. Ward, *The London Spy*, p. 65.

45. See 'Wine beyond Love, or the Bottle before Beauty', *The Fourth Volume of the Writings*, pp. 115–16: 'Love and Beauty you may ask, / Give me the cheerful Flask, / ... I'll no Woman's Bubble be, / Love for you and Wine for me'.

46. Ward, *The Amorous Bugbears: or, The Humours of a Masquerade* (London, 1725), p. 27. See T. Castle, 'Eros and Liberty at the English Masquerade, 1710–90', *Eighteenth-Century Studies*, 17 (1983–4), pp. 156–76; Castle, *Masquerade and Civilization: The Carnivalesque in Eighteenth-Century English Culture and Fiction* (Stanford, CA: Stanford University Press, 1986); see also Lillywhite, *London Coffee Houses*, p. 427.

47. The motifs used by Ward are close to the stereotypes of Samuel Butler's *Hudibras* as illustrated by Hogarth; see R. Paulson, *Hogarth: The 'Modern Moral Subject', 1697–1732* (New Brunswick, NJ: Rutgers University Press, 1991), pp. 141–50.

48. *A Journey to H****: or, A Visit Paid to, &c. A Poem. Part II. Both Parts by the Author of the London-Spy* (London, 1700), canto vi.

49. *The Delights of the Bottle* (London, 1720), pp. 22–3.

50. B. de Mandeville, *The Grumbling Hive, or Knaves Turn'd Honest* (London, 1705), which was integrated into *Fable of the Bees: or, Private Vices, Public Benefits* (London, 1714).

51. R. Williams, *The Country and the City* (London: Chatto & Windus, 1973), p. 176.

52. Ibid., p. 179.

53. A. Geertz, 'Thick Description: Toward an Interpretive Theory of Culture', in J. Munns and G. Rajan (eds), *A Cultural Studies Reader: History, Theory, Practice* (London: Longman, 1995), pp. 237–56, on p. 251.

5 Schmid, 'Eighteenth-Century Travellers and the Country Inn'

1. T. Smollett, *Travels Through France and Italy*, ed. F. Felsenstein (Oxford: Oxford University Press, 1999), p. 3; see also A. A. Warden, 'The Old English Inn', *British Medical Journal*, 1:3978 (3 April 1937), p. 732.

2. G. M. Kahrl, *Tobias Smollett: Traveller-Novelist* (1945; New York: Octagon, 1978).

3. Ibid., p. 99.

4. J. Chartres, 'The Eighteenth-Century Inn: A Transient "Golden Age"?', in B. Kümin and B. A. Tlusty (eds), *The World of the Tavern: Public Houses in Early Modern Europe* (Aldershot: Ashgate, 2002), pp. 205–26.

5. G. Russell, *Women, Sociability and Theatre in Georgian London* (Cambridge: Cambridge University Press, 2007).

6. H. Fielding, *The Coffee-House Politician; or, the Justice Caught in his Own Trap. A Comedy* (London: Watts, 1730). H. Fielding, *Joseph Andrews* and *Shamela*, ed. J. Hawley (London: Penguin, 1999); H. Fielding, *Tom Jones*, ed. R. P. C. Mutter (London: Penguin, 1999).

196   *Notes to pages 60–3*

7. T. Smollett, *The Adventures of Roderick Random*, ed. P.-G. Boucé (Oxford: Oxford University Press, 2008); T. Smollett, *The Life and Adventures of Sir Launcelot Greaves*, ed. B. L. Fitzpatrick (Athens, GA: University of Georgia Press, 2002), p. 105; T. Smollett, *The Expedition of Humphry Clinker*, ed. L. M. Knapp, rev. P.-G. Boucé (Oxford: Oxford University Press, 2009).

8. P. Clark, *The English Alehouse: A Social History, 1200–1830* (London: Longman, 1983); B. Kümin, *Drinking Matters: Public Houses and Social Exchange in Early Modern Central Europe* (Basingstoke: Palgrave Macmillan, 2007); S. Earnshaw, *The Pub in Literature: England's Altered State* (Manchester: Manchester University Press, 2000).

9. Kümin, *Drinking Matters*, p. 17.

10. Clark, *English Alehouse*, p. 5.

11. P. Fumerton, 'Not Home: Alehouses, Ballads, and the Vagrant Husband in Early Modern England', *Journal of Medieval and Early Modern Studies*, 32:3 (2002), pp. 493–518, on p. 495; Clark, *English Alehouse*, pp. 273, 195.

12. Clark, *English Alehouse*, pp. 5, 11–14. See also S. Schmid, 'Cider, Masculinity, and the Nation: Drink in Seventeenth-Century Britain', in *Anglistentag 2010 Saarbrücken: Proceedings*, ed. J. Frenk and L. Steveker (Trier: WVT, 2011), pp. 267–77, on p. 269.

13. P. Clark, 'The Alehouse and the Alternative Society', in D. Pennington and K. Thomas (eds), *Puritans and Revolutionaries: Essays in Seventeenth-Century History Presented to Christopher Hill* (Oxford: Clarendon Press, 1982), pp. 47–72, on pp. 49–50; Clark, *English Alehouse*, pp. 41–59.

14. Chartres, 'Eighteenth-Century Inn', p. 207.

15. F. W. Hackwood, *Inns, Ales, and Drinking Customs of Old England* (London: Unwin, 1909), p. 237. Other studies of this type are: A. E. Richardson, *The Old Inns of England* (London: Batsford, 1934); W. Gaunt, *Old Inns of England in Colour* (London: Batsford, 1958).

16. Fielding, *Joseph Andrews*, p. 93.

17. Ibid., p. 254.

18. J. W. von Archenholz, *England und Italien*, 3 vols (Leipzig: Dyckische Buchhandlung, 1787), vol. 2, pp. 50–1.

19. On the functions see J. A. Chartres, 'The Capital's Provincial Eyes: London's Inns in the Early Eighteenth Century', *London Journal*, 3:1 (1977), pp. 24–39.

20. J. Habermas, *The Structural Transformation of the Public Sphere: An Inquiry into a Category of Bourgeois Society*, trans. T. Burger with the assistance of F. Lawrence (Cambridge: Polity Press, 1989).

21. For a critique of Habermas, see Kümin, *Drinking Matters*, pp. 185–9; for a summary of the debate see also J. A. Downie, 'Public and Private: The Myth of the Bourgeois Public Sphere', in C. Wall (ed.), *A Concise Companion to the Restoration and Eighteenth Century* (Oxford: Blackwell, 2005), pp. 58–79.

22. Clark, 'Alehouse and Alternative Society', pp. 57–8. Kümin discusses the stabilizing as well as the subversive potential of drinking places; Kümin, *Drinking Matters*, pp. 126–42.

23. J. Döring and T. Thielmann (eds), *Spatial Turn: Das Raumparadigma in den Kultur- und Sozialwissenschaften* (Bielefeld: Transcript, 2008).

24. M. Foucault, 'Of Other Spaces', trans. J. Miskowiec, *Diacritics*, 16:1 (1986), pp. 22–7, on p. 25.

25. For a detailed contextual analysis of this print, see R. Paulson, '"Country Inn Yard at Election Time": A Problem in Interpretation', *Yearbook of English Studies*, 14 (1984), pp. 196–208.

Notes to pages 64–70

26. Ibid., p. 208.
27. Ibid. On Hogarth and election scenes, see also R. Paulson, *Hogarth: His Life, Art, and Times*, abr. by A. Wilde (New Haven, CT: Yale University Press, 1974), pp. 322–9.
28. Paulson, "'Country Inn Yard'", p. 201.
29. Ibid., p. 200.
30. Ibid.
31. J. Conlin, "'At the Expense of the Public': The Sign Painters' Exhibition of 1762 and the Public Sphere', *Eighteenth-Century Studies*, 36 (2002), pp. 1–21. The catalogue survived: *A Catalogue of the Original Paintings, Busts, Carved Figures, etc. etc. etc.* (London: Becket, [1762]). See also J. Larwood and J. C. Hotten, *The History of Signboards, from the Earliest Times to the Present Day* (London: Hotten, 1867), for a survey of signs; see pp. 512–26 on Thornton's exhibition.
32. *Catalogue of the Original Paintings*, p. 7. 'The Vicar of Bray' is a satirical song about a religious turncoat.
33. W. Scott, *The Bride of Lammermoor*, ed. F. Robertson (Oxford: Oxford University Press, 2008), p. 19.
34. Fielding, *Joseph Andrews*, p. 119; see also p. 361.
35. Ibid., p. 120. On Fielding and inns see also Earnshaw, *Pub in Literature*, pp. 145–56.
36. Fielding, *Tom Jones*, pp. 51–2.
37. Ibid., p. 87.
38. Ibid., pp. 813–14.
39. Fielding, 'Preface' in *Joseph Andrews*, pp. 49–54, on p. 49.
40. Ibid., pp. 50, 54.
41. Fielding, *Joseph Andrews*, p. 144.
42. Ibid., pp. 181–8.
43. Ibid., pp. 111–14.
44. See M. Berg and E. Eger (eds), *Luxury in the Eighteenth Century: Debates, Desires and Delectable Goods* (Basingstoke: Palgrave Macmillan, 2003).
45. See for example, *Spectator*, 45 (21 April 1711), in *The Spectator*, ed. D. F. Bond, 5 vols (Oxford: Oxford University Press, 1965), vol. 1, p. 191–5.
46. See for example Fielding, *Joseph Andrews*, pp. 145–6, 247.
47. It is hardly surprising that Hackwood's *Inns, Ales, and Drinking Customs* takes Fielding's and Smollett's inns as examples in his nostalgic look back.
48. For example, Smollett, *Roderick Random*, pp. 39–42, 49–56.
49. Ibid., p. 54.
50. Ibid., p. 39.
51. Ibid., p. 60.
52. Ibid., p. 294.
53. On the serialization see R. D. Mayo, *The English Novel in the Magazines 1740–1815* (Evanston, IL: Northwestern University Press, 1962), pp. 274–88.
54. Smollett, *Launcelot Greaves*, p. 3. For an analysis see J. C. Beasley, *Tobias Smollett: Novelist* (Athens, GA: University of Georgia Press, 1998), pp. 151–83: R. Folkenflik, 'Introduction', in Smollett, *Launcelot Greaves*, pp. xvii–liv.
55. Smollett, *Launcelot Greaves*, pp. 30, 105.
56. Smollett, *Humphry Clinker*, p. 171.
57. Ibid., p. 165.
58. See, for example, Anon., *The Character of a Coffee-House, with the Symptomes of a Town-Wit* (London, 1673), p. 3.

6 Wood, 'Drinking, Fighting and Working-Class Sociability in Nineteenth-Century Britain'

1. P. R. Giancola et al., 'Diverse Research on Alcohol and Aggression in Humans', *Alcoholism: Clinical and Experimental Research*, 27 (2003), pp. 198–208, on p. 199.
2. C. MacAndrew and R. Edgerton, *Drunken Comportment: A Social Explanation* (Chicago, IL: Aldine, 1969), p. 165.
3. J. S. Blocker, D. M. Fahey and I. R. Tyrrell (eds), *Alcohol and Temperance in Modern History: A Global Encyclopedia* (Santa Barbara, CA: ABC-Clio, 2003), pp. 45–8. For comment and critical evaluation of MacAndrew and Edgerton, see J. H. Shore and P. Spicer, 'A Model for Alcohol-Mediated Violence in an Australian Aboriginal Community', *Social Science & Medicine*, 58 (2004), pp. 2509–21.
4. K. Graham et al., 'Current Directions in Research on Understanding and Preventing Intoxicated Aggression', *Addiction*, 93 (1998), pp. 659–76; S. T. Chermack and P. R. Giancola, 'The Relation between Alcohol and Aggression: An Integrated Biopsychosocial Conceptualization', *Clinical Psychology Review*, 17 (1997), pp. 621–49.
5. B. S. Godfrey, S. Farrall and S. Karstedt, 'Explaining Gendered Sentencing Patterns for Violent Men and Women in the Late-Victorian and Edwardian Period', *British Journal of Criminology*, 45 (2005), pp. 696–720, on p. 705.
6. Old Bailey trials will be cited via their reference number at the *Old Bailey Online* (OBO), www.oldbaileyonline.org [accessed 2 April 2013]. For this essay, I have examined OBO manslaughter cases from 1830, 1835, 1850, 1870 and 1875. When helpful for clarity, minor changes in punctuation to OBO and archival sources have been made.
7. Depositions were collected during my research for my book: J. C. Wood, *Violence and Crime in Nineteenth-Century England: The Shadow of Our Refinement* (London: Routledge, 2004).
8. C. A. Conley, *The Unwritten Law: Criminal Justice in Victorian Kent* (Oxford: Oxford University Press, 1991), p. 49.
9. OBO t18350817–1888. Watson's death may have in part associated with an 'apoplexy' brought on by intoxication.
10. J. S. Cockburn, 'Patterns of Violence in English Society: Homicide in Kent, 1560–1985', *Past and Present*, 130 (1991), pp. 70–106; M. Eisner, 'Long-Term Historical Trends in Violent Crime', *Crime and Justice: A Review of Research*, 30 (2003), pp. 83–142.
11. P. King, 'The Impact of Urbanization on Murder Rates and on the Geography of Homicide in England and Wales, 1780–1850', *Historical Journal*, 53 (2010), pp. 671–98. For suggestions of a 'wave of violence' ('Welle der Gewalt') in Manchester in the 1820s and 1830s, see G. Hirschfelder, *Alkoholkonsum am Beginn des Industriezeitalters (1700–1850). Vergleichende Studien zum gesellschaftlichen und kulturellen Wandel*, vol. 1: *Die Region Manchester* (Köln: Böhlau, 2003), p. 269.
12. R. Shoemaker, *The London Mob: Violence and Disorder in Eighteenth-Century England* (London: Hambledon and London, 2004), p. 174. Gentlemen 'virtually disappear from Old Bailey murder cases': R. Shoemaker, 'Male Honour and the Decline of Public Violence in Eighteenth-Century London', *Social History*, 26 (2001), pp. 190–208, on p. 205.
13. On fighting connected to alcohol, see also Hirschfelder, *Alkoholkonsum*, vol. 1, pp. 270–2.
14. F. Brookman, 'Confrontational and Revenge Homicides among Men in England and Wales', *Australian and New Zealand Journal of Criminology*, 36 (2003), pp. 34–59, on pp. 38–9.
15. On the 'rules' of male fighting in the nineteenth century, see Wood, *Violence*, pp. 70–94.

16. For example The National Archives (TNA) ASSI 36/4 Kent Winter 1843, *R. v. Watts*; ASSI 36/1 Surrey Lent 1827, *R. v. Rice*; ASSI 36/1 Essex Summer 1825, *R. v. Goodday*; ASSI 36/16 Norfolk 1870, *R. v. Neave*.

17. P. King, 'Punishing Assault: The Transformation of Attitudes in the English Courts', *Journal of Interdisciplinary History*, 27 (1996), pp. 43–74; M. Wiener, 'The Victorian Criminalization of Men', in P. Spierenburg (ed.), *Men and Violence: Gender, Honor and Rituals in Modern Europe and America* (Columbus, OH: Ohio State University Press, 1998), pp. 197–212.

18. M. Wiener, *Men of Blood: Violence, Manliness, and Criminal Justice in Victorian England* (Cambridge: Cambridge University Press, 2004), pp. 51–2.

19. J. R. Gusfield, *Contested Meanings: The Construction of Alcohol Problems* (Madison, WI: University of Wisconsin Press, 1996), p. 86.

20. D. Taylor, *Hooligans, Harlots and Hangmen: Crime and Punishment in Victorian Britain* (Santa Barbara, CA: Praeger, 2010), pp. 59–64.

21. About a quarter of those arrested were women; see G. Hirschfelder, 'Women's Drinking Usages on the Eve of the Industrial Revolution: The Example of Manchester', in M. Hietala and L. Nilsson (eds), *Women in Towns: The Social Position of European Urban Women in a Historical Context* (Helsinki/Stockholm: Finnish Historical Society/Stadsoch kommunhistoriska institutet, 1999), pp. 70–1.

22. B. Harrison, 'Religion and Recreation in Nineteenth-Century England', *Past and Present*, 38 (1967), pp. 98–125.

23. A cross-cultural review has documented that about 63 per cent of violent offenders were drinking at the time that they committed their crimes. See summary and citations of this research in Chermack and Giancola, 'Alcohol and Aggression', p. 623.

24. OBO t18500408–769.

25. OBO t18701121–36.

26. For example, OBO t18300415–168 and t18300916–252.

27. OBO t18300708–65.

28. OBO t18750405–291.

29. OBO t18500408–769; emphasis added.

30. P. F. Tremblay et al., 'Role of Motivation to Respond to Provocation, the Social Environment, and Trait Aggression in Alcohol-Related Aggression', *Aggressive Behavior*, 33 (2007), pp. 389–411, on p. 390. Some laboratory studies conclude alcohol has no impact on women's aggression: Giancola et al., 'Diverse Research', p. 200. Other research has shown a contextual rather than pharmacological link: for example, A. Rolfe et al., 'Alcohol, Gender, Aggression and Violence: Findings from the Birmingham Untreated Heavy Drinkers Project', *Journal of Substance Use*, 11 (2006), pp. 343–58, and R. L. Collins, B. Quigley and K. E. Leonard, 'Women's Physical Aggression in Bars: An Event-Based Examination of Precipitants and Predictors of Severity', *Aggressive Behavior*, 33 (2007), pp. 304–13.

31. R. O. Pihl and J. Peterson, 'Drugs and Aggression: Correlations, Crime and Human Manipulative Studies and Some Proposed Mechanisms', *Journal of Psychiatry & Neuroscience*, 20 (1995), pp. 141–9.

32. OBO t18300708–71. Another witness said: 'I was present, but not playing; Pomroy threw down a pot of beer, and interrupted the play, that was the cause of the dispute – they called each other shufflers as to which had paid for the most beer, and Pomroy pushed the prisoner, hit him, and gave him a black eye; there were two or three scuffles, not regular fighting'.

33. OBO t18501125–52.

200   *Notes to pages 75–8*

34. OBO t18750605–402.
35. TNA ASSI 36/1 Essex Summer 1825, *R. v. Payne*.
36. TNA ASSI 36/1 Herts. Summer 1830, *R. v. Owen*.
37. TNA ASSI 36/1 Surrey Lent 1827, *R. v. Rice*, William Becket's deposition.
38. TNA HO 17/65 Lw 33 John Langley, Norfolk Lent assizes March 1836. Letter written by Henry Jex to the Secretary of State.
39. C. A. Conley, *Certain Other Countries: Homicide, Gender, and National Identity in Late Nineteenth-Century England, Ireland, Scotland, and Wales* (Columbus, OH: Ohio State University Press, 2007), pp. 78–9.
40. TNA ASSI 36/10, Sussex December 1863, *R. v. Andrews*.
41. See TNA ASSI 36/1 Essex Summer 1825, *R. v. Speller* and ASSI 36/1 Herts. Summer 1830, *R. v. Owen*.
42. TNA ASSI 36/1 Herts. Summer 1830, *R. v. Owen*, deposition of George Berton.
43. Chermack and Giancola, 'Alcohol and Aggression', p. 629.
44. TNA ASSI 36/1 Surrey Lent assizes 1827, *R. v. Rice*; TNA ASSI 36/1 Sussex Lent 1830, *R. v. Hewitt*; TNA ASSI 36/1 Hertfordshire summer, 1830, *R. v. Griffiths*; TNA ASSI 36/1 Hertfordshire summer, 1830, R. v. Owen; TNA ASSI 36/2 Surrey Summer Assizes, 1832, *R. v. Chapman*.
45. Shoemaker, *The London Mob*, p. 195.
46. D. Riches, 'The Phenomenon of Violence', in D. Riches (ed.), *The Anthropology of Violence* (Oxford: Blackwell, 1986), pp. 1–27, esp. pp. 15–20.
47. Shore and Spicer, 'Model for Alcohol-Mediated Violence'.
48. B. Beaumont, Middlesex magistrate, letter to the *Morning Post*, 18 September 1829, quoted in O. Swift, *The Handbook to Boxing; Being a Complete Instructor in the Art of Self-Defence* (London, 1840), p. 6.
49. TNA ASSI 36/1 Surrey Lent 1827, *R. v. Rice*.
50. Wiener, *Men of Blood*, p. 255.
51. TNA ASSI 36/1 Hertfordshire summer, 1830, *R. v. Griffiths*.
52. TNA ASSI 36/1 Hertfordshire summer, 1830, *R. v. Owen*.
53. D. Marteau, 'Binge Drinking: Some Not-So-Dry Facts', *Criminal Justice Matters*, 65 (2006), pp. 32–3.
54. M. Wiener, *Reconstructing the Criminal: Culture, Law and Policy in England, 1830–1914* (Cambridge: Cambridge University Press, 1990), p. 79.
55. M. J. Huggins, 'More Sinful Pleasures? Leisure, Respectability and the Male Middle Classes in Victorian England', *Journal of Social History*, 33 (2000), pp. 585–600, on p. 586.
56. TNA HO 17/105 pt. 1, Tw 40; original emphasis.
57. R. Storch, 'The Policeman as Domestic Missionary: Urban Discipline and Popular Culture in Northern England, 1850–1880', *Journal of Social History*, 9 (1976), pp. 481–509, on p. 485.
58. Parliament, *Reports to the Secretary of State for the Home Department on the State of the Law Relating to Brutal Assaults, &c.* (London, 1875), p. 12.
59. Ibid., p. 17.
60. Ibid., p. 160. See similar sentiments from the Deputy Chief Constable of Northumberland (p. 157).
61. Chief Constable of Worcestershire, ibid., p. 165.
62. M. Wiener, 'Judges v. Jurors: Courtroom Tensions in Murder Trials and the Law of Criminal Responsibility in Nineteenth-Century England', *Law and History Review*, 17 (1999), pp. 467–506.

Notes to pages 78–83

63. J. S. Mill, *On Liberty* (1859; London: Penguin, 1985), p. 167.
64. Wiener, *Men of Blood*, p. 270.
65. OBO t18350706–1682.
66. TNA HO 17/75 pt 1 Ny 8; original trial: OBO t18380402–980.
67. Godfrey, Farrall and Karstedt, 'Gendered Sentencing Patterns', p. 715.
68. Conley, *Certain Other Countries*, pp. 26, 81.
69. Ibid., p. 25.
70. G. R. Chadwick, 'Bureaucratic Mercy: The Home Office and the Treatment of Capital Cases in Victorian England' (PhD dissertation, Rice University, 1989), p. 456.
71. OBO t18500107–358; emphasis added.
72. OBO t18350817–1888.
73. TNA ASSI 36/2 Norfolk Summer 1834, William Seaman: a surgeon's report noted the victim was prone to 'apoplexy' and that it was very easy to provoke a potentially fatal fit of apoplexy in a drunken man. See also OBO t18750605–402, in which testimony by a surgeon that a fatal wound had been caused by a fall (rather than the punch that occasioned it) led to an acquittal.
74. Graham et al., 'Current Directions', p. 668.
75. Shore and Spicer, 'Model for Alcohol-Mediated Violence', p. 2519.
76. Ibid.

7 Lessenich, 'Romantic Radicalism and the Temperance Movement'

1. See G. Hirschfelder, *Alkoholkonsum am Beginn des Industriezeitalters (1700–1850). Vergleichende Studien zum gesellschaftlichen und kulturellen Wandel*, vol. 1: *Die Region Manchester* (Köln: Böhlau, 2003).
2. R. Lessenich, 'Romanticism and the Exploration of the Unconscious', in M. Meyer (ed.), *Romantic Explorations: Selected Papers from the Koblenz Conference of the German Society for English Romanticism* (Trier: WVT, 2011), pp. 185–97.
3. E. Darwin, 'Advertisement', *The Botanic Garden, Part II, containing The Loves of the Plants* (Lichfield, 1789), n.p. For Erasmus Darwin's strong opposition to all alcoholic drink, see D. King-Hele, *Doctor of Revolution: The Life and Genius of Erasmus Darwin* (London: Faber, 1977), p. 68.
4. P. Dillon, *The Much-Lamented Death of Madam Geneva: The Eighteenth-Century Gin Craze* (London: Review, 2002); J. Warner, *Craze: Gin and Debauchery in an Age of Reason* (New York: Four Walls Eight Windows, 2002, and London: Profile, 2003).
5. T. Beddoes, *Hygeia, or, Essay Moral and Medical on the Causes Affecting the Personal State of Our Middling and Affluent Classes*, 3 vols (Bristol, 1802).
6. M. Foucault, 'The Politics of Health in the Eighteenth Century', in C. Gordon (ed.), *Power/Knowledge: Selected Interviews and Other Writings, 1972–1977*, trans. C. Gordon et al. (New York: Pantheon Books, 1980), pp. 166–82, on p. 177, quoted in M. Faubert, *Rhyming Reason: The Poetry of Romantic-Era Psychologists* (London: Pickering & Chatto, 2009), p. 119.
7. J. Cobb and S. Storace, *The Haunted Tower: A Comic Opera, as Performed at the Theatre Royal, Drury Lane* (Dublin, 1790), p. 49.
8. I. Cruikshank, 'A Peace Offering to the Genius of Liberty and Equality', coloured etching, 1794.
9. W. Heath, 'Cockney College', 1816.

10. The 'Radical Whigs' were levellers and republicans of the Cromwell succession who, like the later 'Jacobins', advocated a change of the *radix* or root of society from a feudal to an egalitarian structure and later opposed Britain's wars with the American colonies. Called 'Commonwealth Men', they existed throughout the late seventeenth and the early eighteenth centuries, even during the Whig Supremacy 1714–60, and increased in number towards the time of the French Revolution (John Wilkes, Charles James Fox, Lord Byron). See also M. S. Zook, *Radical Whigs and Conspirational Politics in Late Stuart England* (University Park, PA: Pennsylvania State University Press, 1999).

11. J. Gillray, 'Anti-Saccharites or John Bull and his Family Leaving off the Use of Sugar', coloured etching, 1792. See also E. Abbott, *Sugar: A Bittersweet History* (London: Duckworth, 2009), pp. 239–42.

12. A. Pope, *An Essay on Criticism* (1711), ll. 217–18, in *The Poems of Alexander Pope*, ed. J. Butt (London: Routledge, 1963), pp. 143–68, on p. 151.

13. L. C. Whitney, *Primitivism and the Idea of Progress in English Popular Literature of the Eighteenth Century* (Baltimore, MD: Johns Hopkins Press 1934); A. O. Lovejoy, G. Chinard, G. Boas and R. S. Crane, *A Documentary History of Primitivism and Related Ideas* (Baltimore, MD: Johns Hopkins Press, 1935) was unfortunately left unfinished.

14. T. Trotter, *An Essay, Medical, Philosophical, and Chemical, on Drunkenness and Its Effects on the Human Body* (London, 1804), pp. 161–2.

15. T. Trotter, *A View of the Nervous Temperament* (London, 1807), in T. Morton (ed.), *Radical Food: The Culture and Politics of Eating and Drinking 1790–1820*, 3 vols (London: Routledge, 2000), vol. 3, pp. 560–677, on p. 564.

16. G. Nicholson, *On Food* (1803), in Morton (ed.), *Radical Food*, vol. 1, pp. 41–142, on p. 135.

17. J. Thomson, *The Seasons*, 'Summer', ll. 854–5, in *Poetical Works*, ed. J. L. Robertson (1908; London: Oxford University Press, 1961), pp. 52–120, on p. 83.

18. B. Burney, *A General History of Music*, 4 vols (London, 1776–89), vol. 4, p. 221.

19. T. Beddoes, *Alexander's Expedition Down the Hydaspes and the Indus to the Indian Ocean* (London, 1792), l. 220, p. 26.

20. See Faubert, *Rhyming Reason*, pp. 145–58.

21. T. Beddoes, *Essay on the Public Merits of Mr Pitt* (London, 1796), p. 112.

22. T. Beddoes, *A Lecture Introductory to a Course of Popular Instruction on the Constitution and Management of the Human Body* (Bristol, 1798), p. 46.

23. J. Keats, 'Ode to a Nightingale' (1819), l. 15, in *The Poems of John Keats*, ed. M. Allott (London: Longman, 1970), pp. 523–32, on p. 526.

24. J. Keats, Journal 25–27 June 1818, Letter to Tom Keats, in *The Letters of John Keats 1814–1821*, ed. H. E. Rollins, 2 vols (Cambridge, MA: Harvard University Press, 1958), vol. 1, pp. 298–301, on p. 299.

25. Ibid.

26. N. Roe, *John Keats and the Culture of Dissent* (Oxford: Oxford University Press, 1997; rev. edn 1998), pp. 160–81.

27. L. Hunt, 'Preface', in *Foliage* (1818), in *Leigh Hunt's Literary Criticism*, ed. L. H. Houtchens and C. W. Houtchens (New York: Columbia University Press, 1956), pp. 129–42, on p. 142.

28. W. J. Bate, *John Keats* (Cambridge, MA: Harvard University Press, 1964), p. 327.

29. C. Lamb, *Confessions of a Drunkard* (1821), republished in *Last Essays of Elia* (1833), in *The Works of Charles Lamb*, ed. W. MacDonald, 12 vols (London: Dent, 1903), vol. 2, pp. 195–207, on p. 204.

Notes to pages 87–91   203

30. W. Perfect, *Cases of Insanity, the Epilepsy, Hypochondriacal Affection, Hysteric Passion, and Nervous Disorders Successfully Treated*, 2nd edn (Rochester, 1785), p. 45.

31. A. Duncan, *Miscellaneous Poems: Extracted from the Records of the Circulation Club at Edinburgh*, ll. 53–6 (Edinburgh, 1818), p. 26. See also Faubert, *Rhyming Reason*, p. 103.

32. Nicholson, *On Food*, p. 126.

33. J. Weston, *Joseph Livesey: The Story of His Life, 1794–1884* (London, 1884), p. 51.

34. National Archives, Hospital Records Database, http://www.nationalarchives.gov.uk/a2a/records.aspx?cat=2102-nth&cid=0 [accessed 8 February 2013].

35. B. Dacre, *Zofloya: or, The Moor*, ed. K. I. Michasiw (1997; Oxford: Oxford University Press, 2008), pp. 157–85.

36. Keats, 'Ode to a Nightingale', ll. 11–20, pp. 525–6. Compare the imagery of drinking 'hemlock' and 'some dull opiate', ibid., ll. 1–4, pp. 525–6, as well as the formulations 'poisonous wine' and 'ruby grape of Proserpine', connecting wine with death instead of (traditionally) the recovery of health, in 'Ode on Melancholy' (1819), ll. 2 and 4, p. 539.

37. *The Works of Robert Burns, with an Account of his Life and a Criticism on his Writings*, ed. J. Currie, 4 vols (London: T. Cadell & W. Davies, and Edinburgh: W. Creech, 1800), vol. 1, pp. 250–3.

38. R. Burns, 'Tam o' Shanter' (1791), ll. 105–8, in *Burns: Poems and Songs*, ed. J. Kinsley, 3 vols (Oxford: Oxford University Press, 1968), vol. 2, pp. 557–64, on p. 560.

39. R. Fergusson, 'Caller Water' (1773), in *The Poems of Robert Fergusson*, ed. M. P. MacDiarmid, 3 vols (Edinburgh: Blackwood, 1954–6), vol. 2, pp. 106–8. For the connection of Burns and Fergusson in poetics and politics, see L. McIlvanney, *Burns the Radical: Poetry and Politics in Late Eighteenth-Century Scotland* (East Linton: Tuckwell, 2002).

40. R. Burns, 'Scotch Drink' (1786), ll. 7–12, in *Burns: Poems and Songs*, ed. Kinsley, vol. 1, pp. 173–6, on p. 173. Worms, meaning the long spiral tubes at the head of a whisky still, also has a death association.

41. H. Heine, *Deutschland ein Wintermärchen* (1844), I.31–2, in *Werke*, ed. P. Stapf, 3 vols (Berlin: Tempel-Verlag 1957), vol. 1, pp. 610–69, on p. 610.

42. G. Ellis in the *Anti-Jacobin*, 13 (5 February 1798), pp. 452–5.

43. J. Sayers, *Carlo Khan's Triumphal Entry into Leadenhall Street* (1783), repr. in S. E. Jones (ed.), *The Satiric Eye: Forms of Satire in the Romantic Period* (Basingstoke: Palgrave Macmillan, 2003), p. 21.

44. For the survival and vitality of Neoclassicism in the Romantic Period and its indictment of Romantic irrationality, see my recently published *Neoclassical Satire and the Romantic School 1780–1830* (Göttingen: V&R unipress, 2012).

45. J. Cutmore, *Contributors to the Quarterly Review* (London: Pickering & Chatto, 2008), p. 222.

8 Hirschfelder, 'The Myth of "Misery Alcoholism" in Early Industrial England: The Example of Manchester'

1. See D. Bindman, F. Ogée and P. Wagner (eds), *Hogarth: Representing Nature's Machines* (Manchester: Manchester University Press, 2001); B. Hinz (ed.), *William Hogarth 1697–1764, Katalog zur Ausstellung der Neuen Gesellschaft für Bildende Kunst e. V. in der Staatlichen Kunsthalle Berlin vom 28.6. bis 10.8.1980* (Gießen: Anabas, 1980). My thanks go to my Regensburg colleagues Birgit Berger, Karin Lahoda, Gerda Maiwald, Ben Tendler and Jonas Thanner for helping me, especially with the translation. This essay

204   *Notes to pages 92–3*

summarizes parts of my book-length study: G. Hirschfelder, *Alkoholkonsum am Beginn des Industriezeitalters (1700–1850). Vergleichende Studien zum gesellschaftlichen und kulturellen Wandel*, vol. 1: *Die Region Manchester* (Köln: Böhlau, 2003).

2. G. Hirschfelder, 'Die Betäubung der Sinne. Die Suche nach dem Rausch zwischen kulturellem Zwang und individueller Freiheit', in D. von Engelhardt and R. Wild (eds), *Geschmackskulturen. Vom Dialog der Sinne beim Essen und Trinken* (Frankfurt: Campus, 2005), pp. 219–37, esp. pp. 233–4.

3. J. W. Petersen, *Geschichte der deutschen Nationalneigung zum Trunke*, ed. K. Hitzegrad (1782; Dortmund: Harenberg, 1979); J. S. Roberts, *Drink, Temperance and the Working Class in Nineteenth-Century Germany* (Boston, MA: Allen & Unwin, 1984); G. Schreiber, *Deutsche Weingeschichte. Der Wein in Volksleben, Kult und Wirtschaft* (Köln: Rheinland-Verlag, 1980); G. Völger and K. von Welck (eds), *Rausch und Realität. Drogen im Kulturvergleich*, vol. 1 (Reinbek: Rowohlt, 1982). For a survey see G. Hirschfelder, 'Bemerkungen zu Stand und Aufgaben volkskundlich-historischer Alkoholforschung der Neuzeit', *Rheinisch-westfälische Zeitschrift für Volkskunde*, 39 (1994), pp. 87–127.

4. P. Gaskell, *The Manufacturing Population of England, its Moral, Social and Physical Conditions, and the Changes Which Have Arisen from the Use of Steam Machinery; with an Examination of Infant Labour* (1833; New York: Viking Press, 1972), p. 120.

5. D. Ziegler, *Die Industrielle Revolution* (Darmstadt: Wissenschaftliche Buchgesellschaft, 2005).

6. F. Engels, 'Briefe aus dem Wuppertal', *Telegraph für Deutschland*, 49 (1839), pp. 417–19, esp. p. 417, repr. in *Karl Marx, Friedrich Engels, Werke*, vol. 1 (Berlin: Dietz-Verlag, 1962), pp. 413–32, esp. p. 417; my translation.

7. G. B. Wilson, *Alcohol and the Nation: A Contribution to the Study of the Liquor Problem in the United Kingdom from 1800 to 1935* (London: Nicholson and Watson, 1940); E. P. Thompson, 'The Moral Economy of the English Crowd in the Eighteenth Century', *Past and Present*, 50 (1971), pp. 76–136.

8. U. Jeggle, 'Alkohol und Industrialisierung', in H. Cancik (ed.), *Rausch – Ekstase – Mystik* (Düsseldorf: Patmos-Verlag, 1978), pp. 78–94, esp. pp. 85–6. See also Roberts, *Drink, Temperance and the Working Class*; H. Spode, *Die Macht der Trunkenheit. Kultur- und Sozialgeschichte des Alkohols in Deutschland* (Opladen: Leske + Budrich, 1993).

9. H. Gerndt (ed.), *Stereotypenvorstellungen im Alltagsleben. Beiträge zum Themenkreis Fremdbilder – Selbstbilder – Identität. Festschrift für Georg R. Schroubek zum 65. Geburtstag* (München: Münchner Vereinigung für Volkskunde, 1988); J. Konrad, *Stereotype in Dynamik. Zur kulturwissenschaftlichen Verortung eines theoretischen Konzepts* (Tönning: Der Andere Verlag, 2006).

10. Hirschfelder, *Alkoholkonsum*, vol. 2: *Die Region Aachen* (Köln: Böhlau, 2004).

11. F. Vigier, *Change and Apathy: Liverpool and Manchester during the Industrial Revolution* (Cambridge, MA: MIT Press, 1970); S. Hylton, *A History of Manchester* (Chichester: Phillimore, 2003).

12. R. Koselleck, 'Einleitung', in O. Brunner, W. Conze and R. Koselleck (eds), *Geschichtliche Grundbegriffe* (Stuttgart: Klett Cotta, 1979), vol. 1, pp. xiii–xxvii, on p. xv.

13. F. Engels, *Die Lage der arbeitenden Klasse in England*, in *Marx, Engels, Werke* (Berlin: Dietz-Verlag, 1957), vol. 2, pp. 225–506, on p. 285; H. Schmidtgall, *Friedrich Engels' Manchester-Aufenthalt 1842–1844* (Trier: Karl-Marx-Haus, 1981), pp. 86–101.

14. Vigier, *Change and Apathy*, pp. 138, 198; see also Hirschfelder, *Die Region Manchester*, pp. 18–20.

Notes to pages 93–6

15. G. Hirschfelder, 'Gaststättenwesen und Alkohol als Indikatoren kulturellen Wandels. Bemerkungen zur ethnographisch-historischen Alkoholforschung', *OTIUM: Journal of Everyday Life History*, 4:1–2 (1996), pp. 131–48.

16. Compare sources in Hirschfelder, *Die Region Manchester*, pp. 22–4; L. L. J. Faucher, *Manchester in 1844: Its Present Condition and Future Prospects* (1844; London: Cass, 1969).

17. U. Tolksdorf, 'Nahrungsforschung', in R. W. Brednich (ed.), *Grundriß der Volkskunde*, 3rd edn (Berlin: Reimer, 2001), pp. 229–42, on p. 235.

18. G. Wiegelmann, 'Die schwedische "Kulturfixierungstheorie" in der internationalen Diskussion', in Wiegelmann (ed.), *Theoretische Konzepte der Europäischen Ethnologie. Diskussionen um Regeln und Modelle* (Münster: Lit-Verlag, 1991), pp. 90–111.

19. See Hirschfelder, *Die Region Manchester*, p. 202.

20. Ibid., pp. 202–7.

21. *Report of the Minutes of Evidence Taken before the Select Committee on the State of Children Employed in the Manufactories of the United Kingdom, House of Commons Parliamentary Papers*, 397 (London: House of Commons, 1816), p. 148.

22. Ibid., p. 155.

23. Hirschfelder, *Die Region Manchester*, p. 208. See D. Kift, 'Mary Barton, "The Oldham Weaver" und die Star Music Hall in Bolton. Handweberkultur in der Industrialisierung', in K. Ditt and S. Pollard (eds), *Von der Heimarbeit in die Fabrik. Industrialisierung und Arbeiterschaft in Leinen- und Baumwollregionen Westeuropas während des 18. und 19. Jahrhunderts* (Paderborn: Schöningh, 1992), pp. 388–408.

24. *Report from the Select Committee on Manufactures, Commerce, and Shipping; with Minutes of Evidence, and Appendix and Index, House of Commons Parliamentary Papers*, 690 (London: House of Commons, 1833), p. 704.

25. *Appendix, Part I, Children's Employment Commission: Second Report of the Commissioners. Trade and Manufactures, House of Commons Parliamentary Papers*, 431 (1843; London: Clowes, 1842), p. b 47, *Appendix, Part II, House of Commons Parliamentary Papers*, 432 (1843), p. m 30; Hirschfelder, *Die Region Manchester*, pp. 210–11.

26. *Appendix, Part I, Children's Employment Commission: Second Report, House of Commons Parliamentary Papers*, 431 (1843), p. b 39; Hirschfelder, *Die Region Manchester*, pp. 211–12.

27. *Appendix, Part I, Children's Employment Commission: Second Report, House of Commons Parliamentary Papers*, 431 (1843), p. b 40.

28. For early railway history, see S. Hylton, *The Grand Experiment: The Birth of the Railway Age 1820–1845* (Hersham: Ian Allan, 2007).

29. R. H. G. Thomas, *The Liverpool & Manchester Railway* (London: Batsford, 1980), p. 144; Hirschfelder, *Die Region Manchester*, pp. 216–17.

30. Hirschfelder, *Die Region Manchester*, pp. 217–18.

31. *Records of the Manchester Police Commissioners. Minute Books of the Watch, Nuisance and Hackney Coach Committee 1828–1831*, pp. 78–9 (Manchester Central Library, M9/30/5/1).

32. Hirschfelder, *Die Region Manchester*, p. 221.

33. A. Redford and I. S. Russell, *The History of Local Government in Manchester* (London: Longmans Green, 1940), vol. 2, p. 86.

34. J. K. Walton, 'Die Baumwollindustrie und die Arbeiterklasse von Lancashire: Lebensformen, Lebensstandard und Politik in der Region von Manchester 1770–1860', in Ditt and Pollard (eds), *Von der Heimarbeit in die Fabrik*, pp. 364–87, on p. 383; on the women's

206 *Notes to pages 96–8*

role in factories, see J. Lown, *Women and Industrialization: Gender at Work in Nineteenth-Century England* (Minneapolis, MN: University of Minnesota Press, 1990); D. Valenze, *The First Industrial Woman* (New York: Oxford University Press, 1995), pp. 85–94.

35. M. Berg, *The Age of Manufactures 1700–1820: Industry, Innovation and Work in Britain* (London: Routledge, 1994), p. 160, see also pp. 136–65.

36. L. Davidoff and C. Hall, *Family Fortunes: Men and Women of the English Middle Class, 1780–1850* (Chicago, IL: University of Chicago Press, 1987), pp. 30–1; L. Zedner, *Women, Crime, and Custody in Victorian England* (Oxford: Oxford University Press, 1991), p. 12. Criminal women were more stigmatized; ibid., pp. 40–6; J. M. Battie, 'The Criminality of Women in Eighteenth-Century England', *Journal of Social History*, 8 (1975), pp. 80–116.

37. *Manchester Statistical Society. Appendix to Minutes. Analysis of the Evidence Taken before the Factory Commissioners* (Manchester, 1833), p. 25 (Manchester Central Library, Archives, Ms 310.6 M5/6).

38. For more examples see J. H. Young, *St. Mary's Hospitals Manchester 1790–1963* (Edinburgh: Livingstone, 1964), pp. 9, 16–17.

39. P. Gaskell, *Artisans and Machinery: The Moral and Physical Condition of the Manufacturing Population Considered with Reference to Mechanical Substitutes for Human Labour* (London: Parker, 1836), p. 186.

40. Buckingham, *Drunkenness: Speech of Mr. Buckingham on the Extent, Causes, and Effects of Drunkenness* (1834), p. 4 (Manchester Central Library, Archives, P.1239.11).

41. S. Neal, *The Chief Constable's Report to the Watch Committee, comprising the Criminal and Statistical Returns in Connection with the Police Force, for the Year ending August 31st, 1849* (Salford, 1849), table 1. See also J. Clay, *Chaplain's 24th Report of the Preston House of Correction* (Preston, 1847), p. 31.

42. Gaskell, *Manufacturing Population*, pp. 118, 150; Gaskell, *Artisans and Machinery*, p. 125.

43. Engels, *Lage der arbeitenden Klasse*, p. 354.

44. H. Gaulter, *The Origin and Progress of the Malignant Cholera in Manchester* (London: Longman, 1833), pp. 178, 196, 201, 205.

45. In Manchester, between May and August 1832, 200 people died of the cholera. It was Gaulter who described these cases. He was particularly interested in the nutrition and in the victim's previous way of life. In sixty-eight cases (forty men, twenty-eight women), he mentioned alcohol. He classified forty-four individuals (65 per cent) (among them twenty-two women) as *hard drinker, drunkard, tippler, sot* etc. and fifteen (22 per cent) as *occasional drunkard* etc. Five individuals (7 per cent) drank only occasionally, for example a pint of ale with their dinner. Four individuals (6 per cent) were *formerly drunkards*; Gaulter, *Origin and Progress*; for the registers, see pp. 168–206.

46. *Report from the Select Committee on Inquiry into Drunkenness, with Minutes of Evidence and Appendix, House of Commons Parliamentary Papers*, 559 (London: House of Commons, 1834), p. 359. See B. Harrison, *Drink and the Victorians: The Temperance Question in England, 1815–1872* (Pittsburgh, PA: University of Pittsburgh Press, 1971), pp. 64–86; R. Wilson, 'The British Brewing Industry Since 1750', in L. Richmond and A. Turton (eds), *The Brewing Industry: A Guide to Historical Records* (Manchester: Manchester University Press, 1990), pp. 1–22, on p. 3.

47. On prostitution and its function as an analytical indicator of society, see P. Schuster, *Das Frauenhaus. Städtische Bordelle in Deutschland 1350–1600* (Paderborn: Schöningh, 1992); S. Kienitz, *Sexualität, Macht und Moral. Prostitution und Geschlechterbeziehung*

Notes to pages 98–103   207

Anfang des 19. Jahrhunderts in Württemberg. Ein Beitrag zur Mentalitätsgeschichte (Berlin: Akademie-Verlag, 1995); Valenze, *First Industrial Woman*, p. 25.

48. J. Venedey, *England* (Leipzig: Brockhaus, 1845), vol. 3, p. 285, my translation; Schmidt-gall, *Friedrich Engels' Manchester-Aufenthalt*, pp. 102–9, 135.

49. Walton, 'Baumwollindustrie', p. 383; Lown, *Women and Industrialization*.

50. Gaskell, *Manufacturing Population*, p. 116; Gaskell, *Artisans and Machinery*, p. 301.

51. A. B. Reach, *Manchester and the Textile Districts in 1849*, ed. C. Aspin (Helmshore: Helmshore Local History Society, 1972), p. 61.

52. Faucher, *Manchester in 1844*, p. 51.

53. *Factories Inquiry Commission: First Report of the Central Board, of His Majesty's Commissioners Appointed to Collect Information in the Manufacturing Districts, as to the Employment of Children in Factories, and as to the Propriety and Means of Curtailing the Hours of their Labour: with Minutes of Evidence, and Reports by the District Commissioners, House of Commons Parliamentary Papers*, 450 (London: House of Commons, 1833), D1, pp. 48–9.

54. *Factories Inquiry Commission: Employment of Children, House of Commons Parliamentary Papers*, 450 (1833), D1, p. 57.

55. *Factories Inquiry Commission: Employment of Children, House of Commons Parliamentary Papers*, 450 (1833), D2, p. 64.

56. *Report from the Select Committee on Manufactures, Commerce, and Shipping, House of Commons Parliamentary Papers*, 690 (1833), p. 624; see P. M. Giles, *The Economic and Social Development of Stockport 1815–1836* (MA thesis, Manchester, 1950), pp. 499–500 (Stockport Central Library, S/H/10).

57. *Report from the Select Committee on Inquiry into Drunkenness, House of Commons Parliamentary Papers*, 559 (1834), p. 372.

58. *The Second Annual Report of the Manchester and Salford Association for the Better Regulation of Public Houses and other Places of Entertainment* (Manchester, 1853), p. 9.

59. *Factories Inquiry Commission: Employment of Children, House of Commons Parliamentary Papers*, 450 (1833), D1, p. 130.

60. *Factories Inquiry Commission: Employment of Children, House of Commons Parliamentary Papers*, 450 (1833), p. 78.

61. *Appendix, Part I, Children's Employment Commission: Second Report, House of Commons Parliamentary Papers*, 432 (1843), p. B 48.

9 Müller-Wood, 'Alcohol, Sympathy and Ideology in George Gissing's *The Nether World* (1889) and *The Odd Women* (1893)'

1. G. Gissing, *The Nether World* (1889; Oxford: Oxford University Press, 1999), p. 104. All parenthetical references are to this edition.

2. B. Harrison's *Drink and the Victorians: The Temperance Question in England 1815–1872*, 2nd edn (Keele: Keele University Press, 1994), remains a seminal treatment of this topic. Further helpful investigations are D. Marteau, 'Binge Drinking: Some Not-So-Dry Facts', *Criminal Justice Matters*, 65 (2006), pp. 32–3, and M. Wiener, *Reconstructing the Criminal: Culture, Law and Policy in England, 1830–1914* (Cambridge: Cambridge University Press, 1990), p. 79. The consumption of alcohol and its abuses are addressed at greater length in John Carter Wood's essay in this volume.

208   *Notes to pages 103–5*

3. Gissing had met Harrison when he was a student at Owen College in Manchester. After he was caught stealing for her from his fellow students, he was sentenced to a month of hard labour in a Manchester prison and subsequently sent to the United States by his family, who probably hoped that he would start a new life there. Gissing returned from America in 1877, having failed to establish himself there, and again took up relations with Nell. They married in 1879, but their marriage was plagued by her alcoholism, and Gissing separated from Nell in 1882; she died in 1888. Their disastrous relationship is the source of the Arthur Golding and Carrie Mitchell plot in Gissing's *Workers in the Dawn* (1880) and has been retold by different Gissing scholars. See P. Delany, *George Gissing: A Life* (London: Weidenfeld and Nicholson, 2009); J. Halperin, *George Gissing: A Life in Books* (Oxford: Oxford University Press, 1987); J. Korg, *George Gissing: A Critical Biography* (Brighton: Harvester, 1963).
4. Halperin, *George Gissing*, p. 6.
5. Recent examples of this trend are M. Allen, *Cleansing the City: Sanitary Geographies in Victorian London* (Athens, OH: Ohio University Press, 2008); D. Harrison, 'The Deadliest Enemy of the Poor?', *Gissing Journal*, 38:3 (July 2002), pp. 14–26; E. Liggins, *George Gissing, the Working Woman, and Urban Culture* (Aldershot: Ashgate, 2006).
6. For a good survey of this school, see chapter 2 of T. Eagleton, *Literary Theory: An Introduction* (Oxford: Blackwell, 1996).
7. D. Grylls, *The Paradox of Gissing* (London: Allen & Unwin, 1986), p. xi.
8. D. Trotter, *Cooking With Mud: The Idea of Mess in Nineteenth-Century Art and Fiction* (Oxford: Oxford University Press, 2000), p. 249.
9. See Harrison, *Drink*, p. 340.
10. See the oft-cited diary entry from the day after Nell's death, in which Gissing depicts himself standing by her bed and promising never to cease 'to bear testimony against the accursed social order that brings about things of this kind' (Gissing, Diary, 1 March 1888; quoted in Delany, *George Gissing*, p. 136). The 'things of this kind' of course refer to Nell's death in abject poverty.
11. See R. Edmonds, 'The Conservatism of Gissing's Early Novels', *Literature and History*, 8 (1978), pp. 48–69.
12. On this conflict, see D. Grylls, 'Determinism and Determination in Gissing', *Modern Language Quarterly*, 45:1 (1984), pp. 61–84; R. L. Selig, *George Gissing* (Boston, MA: Twayne, 1983), p. 23, and Halperin, *Gissing*, pp. 5–6.
13. J. Sloan, *George Gissing: The Cultural Challenge* (Basingstoke: Macmillan, 1989), p. 16, and Halperin, *Gissing*, pp. 32–3.
14. Halperin, *Gissing*, p. 32.
15. Edmonds, 'Conservatism', p. 48.
16. F. Jameson, *The Political Unconscious: Narrative as a Socially Symbolic Act* (Ithaca, NY: Cornell University Press, 1981), p. 189.
17. D. Trotter, 'The Avoidance of Naturalism: Gissing, Moore, Grand, Bennett, and Others', *The Columbia History of the British Novel*, ed. J. Richetti (New York: Columbia University Press, 1994), pp. 608–30, on p. 612. This leads him to perceptively state in another context that '*The Nether World* ... could quite justifiably have been called *Nether Worlds*' (Trotter, *Cooking*, p. 250).
18. Sloan, *George Gissing*, p. 56.
19. Allen, *Cleansing the City*, p. 162.
20. See M. C. Donelly, *George Gissing: Grave Comedian* (Cambridge, MA: Harvard University Press, 1954), on the character Arthur Peachey in *The Year of Jubilee*, p. 171.

Notes to pages 106–8 209

21. Sloan points out Gissing's indebtedness to a Dickensian 'appeal to sympathy' (*George Gissing*, p. 56); Trotter detects a 'faith in the power of imaginative sympathy' in Gissing's writing that he explains casually as something 'typically English' (Trotter, 'Naturalism', p. 612); Grylls foregrounds the author's 'deftly handled psychological suspense' ('Determinism', p. 67).

22. J. King, *Tragedy in the Victorian Novel: Theory and Practice in the Novels of George Eliot, Thomas Hardy and Henry James* (Cambridge: Cambridge University Press, 1978), p. 2. For instance, Gissing repeatedly claimed to have been overwhelmed by emotion during the writing of his novel *Thyrza* (1887): 'I cried myself into illness over a chapter as I wrote it, and this cannot be balderdash' (28 December 1886). A few days later, having completed the novel, he proclaimed almost triumphantly that its 'last chapters drew many tears'. See *Letters of George Gissing to Members of his Family*, ed. A. and E. Gissing (New York: Haskell House, 1970), pp. 188, 189.

23. *The Collected Letters of George Gissing*, ed. P. F. Mattheisen, A. C. Young and P. Coustillas (Athens, OH: Ohio University Press, 1992), vol. 3, p. 196, quoted in F. Nesta, *The Commerce of Literature: George Gissing and Late Victorian Publishing, 1880-1903* (PhD dissertation, University of Wales, 2007), p. 159, online edn, http://cadair.aber.ac.uk/dspace/handle/2160/645 [accessed 20 October 2013]; Gissing, *Collected Letters*, vol. 3, p. 193. Gissing's view of serialization was more ambiguous than this judgement may suggest, however, he was aware of the financial advantages of this format and voiced his frustration when publishers did not serialize his work or did not market the few novels that were serialized aggressively enough (Nesta, *Commerce*, pp. 90–4).

24. F. Jameson, 'Authentic Ressentiments: The "Experimental" Novels of Gissing', *Nineteenth-Century Fiction*, 31:2 (1976), pp. 127–49, on p. 130.

25. Ibid., pp. 147–8.

26. M. Huggins emphasizes that 'Victorian society was large, ramshackle, complex and diverse, embracing a multiplicity of cultural traditions'; Huggins, 'More Sinful Pleasures? Leisure, Respectability and the Male Middle Classes in Victorian England', *Journal of Social History*, 33:3 (2000), pp. 585–600, on p. 585.

27. See the chapter on Gissing in J. Carey's *The Intellectuals and the Masses: Pride and Prejudice among the Literary Intelligentsia, 1880–1939* (London: Faber, 1992).

28. C. Devine, *Class in Turn-of-the-Century Novels of Gissing, James, Hardy, and Wells* (Aldershot: Ashgate, 2005), p. 28.

29. *George Gissing's Commonplace Book*, ed. J. Korg (New York: New York Public Library, 1962), p. 35.

30. On the term 'Sympathielenkung' and its operations, see M. Pfister, 'Zur Theorie der Sympathielenkung im Drama', in W. Habicht and I. Schabert (eds), *Sympathielenkung in den Dramen Shakespeares* (München: Fink, 1978), pp. 20–34.

31. A point made by Pfister in 'Theorie der Sympathielenkung', p. 25. Literature's dependence on the recipient may be true of other forms of literary expression potentially based on literature's proto-form of dramatic mimesis. See H. P. Abbott, 'The Evolutionary Origins of the Storied Mind: Modeling the Prehistory of Narrative Consciousness and Its Discontents', *Narrative*, 8 (2000), pp. 247–56, on p. 249.

32. Iser's reception theory, for instance, despite its nominal interest in the reader, ultimately refrains from defining or identifying this facet of the process. For Iser, the reader is a textual construct by the same gaps in the text to which he or she is meant to respond, rather than an independently existing entity that makes the meaningful deployment of such textual gaps possible in the first place. See his article 'Interaction Between Text and

210 *Notes to pages 108–18*

Reader', in S. R. Suleiman and I. Crosman (eds), *The Reader in the Text: Essays on Audience and Interpretation* (Princeton, NJ: Princeton University Press, 1980), pp. 106–19, on pp. 118–19. As Hamilton and Schneider put it, Iser's work 'plays up the agency of the text at the apparent expense of the agency of the reader'; C. A. Hamilton and R. Schneider, 'From Iser to Turner and Beyond: Reception Theory Meets Cognitive Criticism', *Style*, 36:4 (2002), pp. 640–58, on p. 645.

33. I here differ from critics who have pointed to Hewett's awareness and understanding of his alcoholism; see, for example, Harrison, 'Deadliest Enemy', p. 14.

34. See, for instance, A. Matz, 'George Gissing's Ambivalent Realism', *Nineteenth-Century Literature*, 59:2 (2004), pp. 214–48, on p. 213, and Selig, *George Gissing*, p. 41. This is also reflected in the critical responses to the novels on publication. While *The Nether World* was greeted with mixed reviews, the response to *The Odd Women* was more enthusiastic. See Halperin, *George Gissing*, pp. 120–1, 188–9.

35. G. Gissing, *The Odd Women* (Oxford: Oxford University Press, 2000), p. 23. All parenthetical references are to this edition.

36. Selig, *George Gissing*, p. 77.

10 Lennartz, 'Legends of Infernal Drinkers: Representations of Alcohol in Thomas Hardy and Nineteenth-Century British Fiction'

1. For the wider context, see M. Gymnich and N. Lennartz (eds), *The Pleasures and Horrors of Eating: The Cultural History of Eating in Anglophone Literature* (Göttingen: V & R unipress, 2010), esp. S. Mergenthal, 'Dining with the Brontës: Food and Gender Roles in Mid-Victorian England', pp. 205–19, and N. Lennartz, 'The *bête humaine* and Its Food in Nineteenth-Century Naturalist Fiction', pp. 255–71.

2. J. Keats, 'Ode to a Nightingale', ll. 15–20, in *The Poems of John Keats*, ed. M. Allott (London: Longman, 1970), pp. 523–32, on p. 526.

3. Ibid., l. 32, p. 527.

4. For this piece of biographical information, I am indebted to N. Roe, who has recently published his biography of Keats; Roe, *John Keats: A New Life* (New Haven, CT: Yale University Press, 2012), p. 307.

5. See N. Page's entry on 'Dickens' in the *Oxford Reader's Companion to Hardy*, ed. N. Page (Oxford: Oxford University Press, 2001), pp. 100–1.

6. N. Lennartz, 'Aspects of Darwinian Liminality: The Precarious Relationship between Man and Animals in *David Copperfield* and Other Victorian Fiction', *Literaturwissenschaftliches Jahrbuch*, 52 (2011), pp. 279–93.

7. See C. Dickens, *David Copperfield*, ed. J. Tambling (London: Penguin, 2004), p. 371.

8. Ibid., p. 373; see W. Shakespeare, *Othello*, II.iii.286.

9. T. M. Rivinus, 'Tragedy of the Commonplace: The Impact of Addiction on Families in the Fiction of Thomas Hardy', *Literature and Medicine*, 11 (1992), pp. 237–65, on p. 250.

10. T. Hardy, *Tess of the d'Urbervilles*, ed. T. Dolin (London: Penguin, 1998), p. 13. All parenthetical references are to this edition.

11. O. Wilde, *The Picture of Dorian Gray*, ed. I. Murray (Oxford: Oxford University Press, 1998), p. 16.

12. In the MS of the novel, Hardy has Tess drink from a 'large wicker-cased jar', which Alec produces from under the seat of a gig and which contains strong spirits intended for

Notes to pages 118–26   211

'household purposes'. Thus the link between Tess's rape and alcohol was originally much clearer; Hardy, *Tess of the d'Urbervilles*, notes, p. 415.

13. Rivinus, 'Tragedy of the Commonplace', p. 238.

14. The combination of these two embodied playing cards is vaguely associated with war and the underworld; see J. C. Cooper, *An Illustrated Encyclopaedia of Traditional Symbols* (London: Thames and Hudson, 1978), pp. 29–30. In the 1875 opera *Carmen* (III.2), spades and diamonds are clearly related to death.

15. T. Hardy, *Jude the Obscure*, ed. D. Taylor (London: Penguin, 1998), p. 39. All parenthetical references are to this edition.

16. W. Shakespeare, *Macbeth*, I.vii.64–71.

17. 'When the hurlyburly's done, / When the battle's lost and won', *Macbeth*, I.i.3–4.

18. C. Baudelaire, 'L'âme du vin', l. 1, *Les fleurs du mal*, in *Œuvre complètes*, ed. C. Pichois (Paris: Gallimard, 1975), vol. 1, pp. 7–145, on p. 105. 'L'âme du vin' is the first poem of a series of poems entitled 'Le vin' (pp. 105–10).

19. See A. Kupfer's more general survey *Göttliche Gifte. Kleine Kulturgeschichte des Rausches seit dem Garten Eden* (Stuttgart: Metzler, 1995), p. 128. Hardy is inexplicably missing in this overview.

20. T. Hardy, *Far from the Madding Crowd*, ed. R. Morgan (London: Penguin, 2003), p. 223.

21. T. Hardy, *The Mayor of Casterbridge*, ed. K. Wilson (London: Penguin, 2003), p. 4. All parenthetical references are to this edition.

22. T. Hardy, 'The Darkling Thrush', l. 21, in *The Complete Poems of Thomas Hardy*, ed. J. Gibson (1976; London: Macmillan, 1991), p. 150.

23. The term *homo ludens* is derived from Huizinga's 1938 book *Homo ludens: A Study of the Play-Element in Culture*, which implies that man is an active participant in social rituals based on games. In Hardy's novels, man is increasingly reduced to a passive plaything, a creature played upon and never winning.

24. Shakespeare, *Othello*, II.iii.291.

25. J. Lilienfeld, '"I Could Drink a Quarter-Barrell to the Pitching": The Mayor of Casterbridge Viewed as an Alcoholic', in J. Lilienfeld and J. Oxford (eds), *The Languages of Addiction* (London: Macmillan, 1999), pp. 225–44, on p. 229.

26. Ibid., p. 233.

27. For this parallel and for the pagan context, see A. Radford, *Thomas Hardy and the Survivals of Time* (Aldershot: Ashgate, 2003), p. 123.

28. See M. Thorpe's entry on 'Shakespeare' in *The Oxford Reader's Companion to Hardy*, pp. 395–7, on p. 396.

29. Shakespeare, *King Lear*, IV.vi.124.

30. S. Maugham, *Liza of Lambeth* (London: Penguin, 1967), p. 36.

31. Hardy, *Mayor of Casterbridge*, p. 228.

32. Shakespeare, *Othello*, II.iii.302–3.

33. A. Brontë, *The Tenant of Wildfell Hall*, ed. G. D. Hargreaves (London: Penguin, 1988), p. 265.

34. Hardy, *Mayor of Casterbridge*, p. 322.

212   *Notes to pages 127–30*

11 Reinarz and Wynter, 'The Spirit of Medicine: The Use of Alcohol in Nineteenth-Century Medical Practice'

1.   By moderate consumption, most researchers mean one to four units of alcoholic beverage, or ten to forty grams of alcohol, daily.
2.   A. S. St Leger, A. L. Cochrane and F. Moore, 'Factors Associated with Cardiac Mortality in Developed Countries with Particular Reference to the Consumption of Wine', *Lancet*, 313 (12 May 1979), pp. 1017–20.
3.   See the report, 'Guinness could really be good for you', http://news.bbc.co.uk/1/hi/3266819.stm [accessed 9 June 2013].
4.   J. Fehér, G. Lengyel and A. Lugasi, 'The Cultural History of Wine – Theoretical Background to Wine Therapy', *Central European Journal of Medicine*, 2:4 (2007), pp. 379–91, on pp. 379–80, 384.
5.   S. P. Lucia, *Wine as Food and Medicine* (New York: Blakiston, 1954).
6.   S. P. Lucia, *A History of Wine as Therapy* (Philadelphia, PA: J. B. Lippincott, 1963), p. 6.
7.   Ibid., p. 9.
8.   Ibid., p. 3.
9.   H. Paul, *Bacchic Medicine: Wine and Alcohol Therapies from Napoleon to the French Paradox* (Amsterdam: Rodopi, 2001).
10. Lucia, *History of Wine as Therapy*, p. 4.
11. 'Alcohol "more harmful than heroin" says Prof David Nutt', http://www.bbc.co.uk/news/uk-11660210 [accessed 9 June 2013]; S. Boseley, 'Alcohol "more harmful than heroin or crack"', *Guardian*, 1 November 2010, http://www.guardian.co.uk/society/2010/nov/01/alcohol-more-harmful-than-heroin-crack [accessed 9 June 2013].
12. See, for example, R. M. MacLeod, 'The Edge of Hope: Social Policy and Chronic Alcoholism, 1870–1900', *Journal of the History of Medicine and Allied Sciences*, 22:3 (1967), pp. 215–45; J. Sournia, *A History of Alcoholism* (Oxford: Basil Blackwell, 1990); S. Tracy, *Alcoholism in America: From Reconstruction to Prohibition* (Baltimore, MD: Johns Hopkins University Press, 2007).
13. J. Nicholls, *The Politics of Alcohol: A History of the Drink Question in England* (Manchester: Manchester University Press, 2009), pp. 34–50.
14. Ibid., p. 59.
15. W. F. Bynum, 'William Cullen (1710–1790)', *ODNB*.
16. W. Cullen, *A Treatise of the Materia Medica*, 2 vols (Edinburgh, 1789), vol. 1, p. v.
17. W. Buchan, *Domestic Medicine* (London, 1800), p. 740; see also W. Sandford, *A Few Practical Remarks on the Medicinal Effects of Wine and Spirits; With Observations on the Oeconomy of Health* (Worcester: J. Tymbs, 1799).
18. Cullen, *Treatise*, vol. 2, p. 69.
19. Ibid., pp. 235, 316.
20. Ibid., pp. 103, 318.
21. G. Risse, 'Brunonian Therapeutics: New Wine in Old Bottles', *Medical History Supplement*, 8 (1988), pp. 46–62, on p. 47.
22. W. F. Bynum, *Science and the Practice of Medicine in the Nineteenth Century* (Cambridge: Cambridge University Press, 1994), p. 17.
23. Risse, 'Brunonian Therapeutics', pp. 54–9.
24. Ibid., p. 51.
25. Cullen, *Treatise*, vol.1, p. 420.
26. Risse, 'Brunonian Therapeutics', p. 52.

27. Lucia, *History of Wine as Therapy*, p. 145.
28. Ibid., p. 159.
29. A. T. Thackrah, *The Effects of Arts, Trades and Professions on Health and Longevity* (London: E. & S. Livingstone, 1957), p. 211.
30. J. Reinarz and A. N. Williams, 'John Darwall MD (1796–1833): The Short Yet Productive Life of a Birmingham Practitioner', *Journal of Medical Biography*, 13:3 (2005), pp. 150–4.
31. T. R. Gourvish and R. Wilson, *The British Brewing Industry, 1830–1980* (Cambridge: Cambridge University Press, 1994), pp. 21–2.
32. Nicholls, *Politics of Alcohol*, pp. 99–101.
33. G. Cheyne, *The English Malady: Or a Treatise of Nervous Diseases of all Kinds, as Spleen, Vapours, Lowness of Spirits, Hyperchondriacal and Hysterical Distempers, etc.* (London, 1733), p. 49; original emphasis.
34. Ibid., p. 326; original emphasis.
35. Ibid.; original emphasis.
36. For dietary advice, see ibid., throughout pp. 284–364.
37. Nicholls, *Politics of Alcohol*, p. 65.
38. A. Rush, *Inquiry into the Effects of Ardent Spirits on the Human Body and Mind* (Philadelphia, PA, 1784); J. C. Lettsom, *A History of Some of the Effects of Hard Drinking* (London, 1789).
39. K. J. B. Rix, 'John Coakley Lettsom and Some of the Effects of Hard Drinking', *Alcohol and Alcoholism*, 11:3 (1976), pp. 97–103, on p. 99.
40. T. Trotter, *An Essay, Medical, Philosophical, and Chemical, on Drunkenness, and its Effects on the Human Body*, 2nd edn (London: Longman, Hurst, Rees, and Orme, 1804), p. 156, quoted from R. Porter, 'The Drinking Man's Disease: The "Pre-History" of Alcoholism in Georgian Britain', *British Journal of Addiction*, 80 (1985), pp. 385–96, on p. 387.
41. P. Shaw, *The Juice of the Grape; or, Wine Preferable to Water. A Treatise Wherein Wine is Shewn to be a Grand Preserver of Health, with a Word of Advice to the Vintners* (1724), pp. 40–51, as quoted in A. Ingram (ed.), *Patterns of Madness in the Eighteenth Century: A Reader* (Liverpool: Liverpool University Press, 1998), pp. 69–72, on p. 69.
42. J. Wesley, 'Word to a Drunkard', *The Beauties of the Rev. John Wesley containing the Most Interesting Passages Selected from his Whole Works* (Philadelphia, PA, 1817), pp. 232–3.
43. J. Wesley, *Primitive Physic: or, An Easy and Natural Method for Curing Most Diseases*, 21st edn (London, 1785), pp. 42, 77.
44. W. Pargeter, *Observations on Maniacal Disorders* (Reading, 1792), pp. 28–34, 49–53 and 123–9, in Ingram, *Patterns of Madness*, pp. 179–86, on pp. 183, 185.
45. S. Tuke, *Description of the Retreat, an Institution near York for Insane Persons of the Society of Friends* (York, 1813), p. 125.
46. Ibid., p. 128.
47. K. Jones, *Lunacy, Law and Conscience, 1744–1845: The Social History of the Care of the Insane* (London: Routledge & Kegan Paul, 1955), p. 55; L. Smith, *Lunatic Hospitals in Georgian England, 1750–1830* (London: Routledge, 2007), p. 144.
48. Staffordshire County Record Office (SCRO), 'Male and Female Case Book, 1818–1827', D4585/6.
49. Trotter, *Essay*, p. 179; original emphasis.
50. For details, see F.-W. Kielhorn, 'The History of Alcoholism: Brühl-Cramer's Concepts and Observations', *Addiction*, 91:1 (1996), pp. 121–8.
51. SCRO, 'Male and Female Case Book', D4585/6.

214   *Notes to pages 133–6*

52. N. McCrae, 'The Beer Ration in Victorian Asylums', *History of Psychiatry*, 15:2 (2004), pp. 155–75.
53. Surviving figures from between 1836 and 1863 run at an average of 66 per cent of all asylum inmates as employed (R. Wynter, 'Diseased Vessels and Punished Bodies: A Study of Material Culture and Control in Staffordshire County Gaol and Lunatic Asylum, c. 1793–1866' (PhD dissertation, University of Birmingham, 2007), p. 265), compared to Peter Bartlett's number of 'about half' at Leicester (P. Bartlett, 'The Asylum, the Workhouse, and the Voice of the Insane Poor in 19th-Century England', *International Journal of Law and Psychiatry*, 21:4 (1998), pp. 421–32, on p. 424).
54. Parliamentary Papers, *Twelfth Annual Report of the Commissioners in Lunacy*, 1858, Appendix C., p. 34 (340 XXIII, pp. 542–639, on p. 583).
55. Wynter, 'Diseased Vessels and Punished Bodies', p. 297.
56. G. Strickland, *A Letter to the Rate-Payers of England on Asylums, Their Management and Expenses*, 3rd edn (York, 1861).
57. J. H. Warner, 'Physiological Theory and Therapeutic Explanation in the 1860s: The British Debate on the Medical Use of Alcohol', *Bulletin for the History of Medicine*, 54 (1980), pp. 235–57, on p. 236.
58. A. K. Warsh, 'Medicine, Alcohol as', in J. S. Blocker Jr, D. M. Fahey and I. R. Tyrell (eds), *Alcohol and Temperance in Modern History: An International Encyclopedia*, 2 vols (Santa Barbara, CA: ABC Clio, 2003), vol. 2, p. 407.
59. Warner, 'Physiological Theory', p. 240, n. 17.
60. A. M. Crawford, 'Typhus in Nineteenth-Century Ireland', in G. Jones and E. Malcolm (eds), *Medicine, Disease and the State in Ireland, 1650–1940* (Cork: Cork University Press, 1999), pp. 121–37, on p. 133.
61. P. Blakiston, *A Treatise on the Influenza of 1837, Containing an Analysis of 100 Cases Observed in Birmingham Between the 1st of January and 15th of February* (London: Longman, 1837).
62. S. E. Williams, 'The Use of Beverage Alcohol as Medicine, 1790–1860', *Journal of Studies in Alcohol*, 41:5 (1980), pp. 543–66, on p. 543; Nicholls, *Politics of Alcohol*, p. 112.
63. Warner, 'Physiological Theory', p. 240.
64. D. Power, 'Robert Bentley Todd', in Sir D'Arcy Power (ed.), *British Masters of Medicine* (Manchester, NH: Ayer Publishing, 1969), p. 116.
65. R. B. Todd, *Clinical Lectures* (Philadelphia, PA, 1860), p. 280.
66. Warner, 'Physiological Theory', p. 244.
67. 'Use of Alcohol in Disease', *Lancet*, 83 (26 March 1864), pp. 357–8, on p. 357.
68. Ibid., p. 358.
69. Ibid.
70. Ibid.
71. Ibid.
72. 'On the Limits of Alcoholic Stimulation in Acute Disease', *British Medical Journal* (22 August 1868), pp. 198–9, on p. 198.
73. Ibid., p. 199.
74. Warner, 'Physiological Theory', p. 252.
75. A. E. Anstie, *Uses of Wine in Health and Disease* (London: Macmillan, 1877), pp. 4–9.
76. A. D. Baldwin, 'Anstie's Alcohol Limit: Francis Edmund Anstie 1833–1874', *American Journal of Public Health*, 67:7 (1977), pp. 679–81.
77. Anstie, *Uses of Wine*, p. 7.
78. Ibid., p. 53.

79. C. Binz, 'On the Influence of Alcohol upon the Temperature of the Body', *Practitioner*, 3 (1869), pp. 137–47.

80. J. Simpson, 'Selling to Reluctant Drinkers: The British Wine Market, 1860–1914', *Economic History Review*, 57:1 (2004), pp. 80–108, on pp. 82, 84.

81. Birmingham Central Library and Archive (BCLA), 'General Hospital, Birmingham, Medical Committee Minute Book, 1876–84', HC/GHB/68, 70.

82. E. M. Brown, '"What Shall We Do with the Inebriate?" Asylum Treatment and the Disease Concept of Alcoholism in the Late Nineteenth Century', *Journal of the History of the Behavioural Sciences*, 21:1 (1985), pp. 48–59.

83. W. F. Bynum, 'Alcoholism and Degeneration in 19th-Century European Medicine and Psychiatry', *British Journal of Addiction*, 79:1 (1984), pp. 59–70, on p. 60. For details on French alcohol concerns, inebriety and treatment, see P. E. Prestwich, 'Drinkers, Drunkards and Degenerates: The Alcoholic Population of a Parisian Asylum, 1867–1914', *Histoire Sociale/Social History*, 27:54 (1994), pp. 321–35; P. E. Prestwich, 'Female Alcoholism in Paris, 1870–1920: The Response of Psychiatrists and Families', *History of Psychiatry*, 14:3 (2003), pp. 321–36.

84. Bynum, 'Alcoholism and Degeneration', p. 60.

85. Ibid. For discussion of Clouston, see M. Thompson, 'The Wages of Sin: The Problem of Alcoholism and General Paralysis in Nineteenth-Century Edinburgh', in W. Bynum, R. Porter and M. Shepherd (eds), *The Anatomy of Madness: Essays in the History of Psychiatry*, vol. 2: *The Asylum and its Psychiatry* (London: Tavistock, 1988), pp. 316–40.

86. J. C. Bucknill, 'On Some Relations between Intemperance and Insanity', *British Medical Journal* (3 March 1877), pp. 254–5. See also J. C. Bucknill, *Habitual Drunkenness and Insane Drunkards* (London: Macmillan, 1878).

87. J. C. Bucknill, 'Habitual Drunkenness: A Vice, Crime or Disease?', *Contemporary Review*, 29 (1877), pp. 431–47, on p. 438. See J. Percy, *An Experimental Inquiry, Concerning the Presence of Alcohol in the Ventricles of the Brain, after Poisoning by that Liquid; Together with Experiments, Illustrative of the Physiological Action of Alcohol: for which, a Gold Medal was Awarded by the Medical Faculty of the University of Edinburgh* (London: Hamilton, Adams & Company, 1839), p. 4.

88. For details, see G. Johnstone, 'From Vice to Disease? Concepts of Dipsomania and Inebriety, 1860–1908', *Social and Legal Studies*, 5:1 (1996), pp. 37–56.

89. P. McCandless, '"Curses of Civilization": Insanity and Drunkenness in Victorian Britain', *British Journal of Addiction*, 79:4 (1984), pp. 49–58, on p. 50.

90. V. Horsley and M. D. Sturge with A. Newsholme, *Alcohol and the Human Body: An Introduction to the Study of the Subject, and a Contribution to National Health* (London: Macmillan, 1907), p. 10; R. Hunter and I. MacAlpine, *Psychiatry for the Poor: 1851 Colney Hatch Asylum-Friern Hospital 1973: A Medical and Social History* (Folkestone: Dawsons of Pall Mall, 1974), pp. 120–1.

91. B. W. Richardson, *Vita Medica: Chapters of Medical Life and Work* (London: Longmans, 1897), p. 369.

92. K. Pearl, 'British Medical Temperance Association', in Blocker Jr, Fahey and Tyrell (eds), *Alcohol and Temperance*, pp. 112–14, on p. 113.

93. Ibid.

94. Horsley and Sturge, *Alcohol and the Human Body*, p. 320.

95. Bynum, 'Alcoholism and Degeneration', p. 68.

96. Ibid., pp. 68–9.

216   *Notes to pages 138–42*

97. Nicholls, *Politics of Alcohol*, p. 175. For details on the fall of temperance physicians, see J. Woiak, '"A Medical Cromwell to Depose King Alcohol": Medical Scientists, Temperance Reformers, and the Alcohol Problem', *Histoire Sociale/Social History,* 27:54 (1994), pp. 337–65.
98. Nicholls, *Politics of Alcohol*, p. 175.
99. Richardson, *Vita Medica*, pp. 357–8, 377.
100. Ibid., p. 374.
101. Paul, *Bacchic Medicine*, p. iii.

12 Zehelein, '"Been to Barbados": Rum (Bullion), Race, the *Gaspée* and the American Revolution'

1. O. Nash, 'Reflections on Ice-Breaking', in *The Best of Ogden Nash*, ed. L. N. Smith (Lanham, MD: Ivan R. Dee, 2007), p. 282.
2. See, for example, A. C. Hannah and D. Spence, *The International Sugar Trade* (Cambridge: Woodhead, 1996). For a more recent analysis of sugar and the global sugar market, see S. Gudoshnikov, L. Jolly and D. Spence, *The World Sugar Market* (Cambridge: Woodhead, 2004). Both books were published in association with the International Sugar Organization.
3. I. Williams, *Rum: A Social and Sociable History* (New York: Nation Books, 2005), pp. 11, 19.
4. Ibid., p. 20.
5. See, for example, K. A. Sandiford, *The Cultural Politics of Sugar: Caribbean Slavery and Narratives of Colonialism* (Cambridge: Cambridge University Press, 2000), and R. B. Sheridan, *Sugar and Slavery: An Economic History of the British West Indies, 1623–1775* (Kingston, Jamaica: Canoe Press, 1974). Recent scholarship on slavery has emphasized that slavery was highly variable, depending on time, space and specific socio-cultural and economic conditions, and that thus also the slaves' experiences varied decisively. Kolchin therefore suggests speaking of slaveries (P. Kolchin, 'Introduction: Variations of Slavery in the Atlantic World', *William and Mary Quarterly*, 59:3 (July 2002), pp. 551–4). See also M. M. Smith, *Debating Slavery: Economy and Society in the Antebellum American South* (New York: Cambridge University Press, 1998), or I. Berlin, *Many Thousands Gone: The First Two Centuries of Slavery in North America* (Cambridge, MA: Belknap Press, 1998).
6. W. Curtis, *And a Bottle of Rum: A History of the New World in Ten Cocktails* (New York: Three Rivers Press, 2006), p. 17.
7. Ibid., p. 18.
8. R. S. Dunn, 'Servants and Slaves: The Recruitment and Employment of Labor', in J. P. Greene and J. R. Pole (eds), *Colonial British America: Essays in the New History of the Early Modern Era* (Baltimore, MD: Johns Hopkins University Press, 1984), pp. 155–94, on p. 172.
9. In her article, 'Zones of Law, Zones of Violence: The Legal Geography of the British Atlantic, circa 1772' (*William and Mary Quarterly*, 60:3 (July 2003), pp. 471–510), E. H. Gould shows 'the tension between periphery and center' (pp. 473–4) of a legal geography, in which Britons at home had a different status from Britons abroad, a condition which would soon become crucial in the case of the North American colonies.

10. On the historical background of Barbados, see R. B. Sheridan, *Sugar and Slavery*; for current statistics see *The CIA World Factbook* at https://www.cia.gov/library/publications/the-world-factbook [accessed 13 March 2013].
11. Quoted in S. W. Mintz, *Sweetness and Power: The Place of Sugar in Modern History* (New York: Penguin, 1985), p. 156.
12. The quotation is from a manuscript description of Barbados; see L. Spitzer, 'Anglo-French Etymologies', *Modern Language Notes*, 59:4 (April 1944), pp. 223–50, on p. 244; see also A. M. Earle, *Customs and Fashions in Old New England* (New York: Charles Scribner, 1894), p. 94. According to Spitzer, rumbullion 'is an English dialectal word originating in French, in fact a derivative from *bouillon* (to which Weekley once referred in his tentative explanation of *rumbullion* as equivalent to *rum* "good" + Fr. *bouillon* "hot drink"). Now *rum* is distilled "from the *fermented* skimmings of the sugar-boilers and molasses, together with sufficient cane juice to impart the necessary flavor" (*Univ. Dict.*); and *rebulhir* "to ferment" (FEW s.v. *bullire*, I, 622) has been developed, for example in the South of France, from the word family *rebouiller* "to boyle once more, or over again, or boyle the second time", *rebouillonner* "to bubble, surge, or wamble often, or over again" (Cotgrave): thus *rumbullion* is a*rebouillon or *rembouillon ... As for the other meaning of *rumbullion* ("tumult"), we find that in French *bouillonner, bouillonnement* are still said of an "ebullition of passion"; thus it is possible that *rumbullion*, in the language of sailors, meant originally both "uproar, tumult" and "distillation from fermented skimmings" – without the one being necessarily prior to the other' (p. 245).
13. See http://www.mountgayrum.com/ [accessed 9 February 2013].
14. Curtis, *And a Bottle of Rum*, p. 24.
15. See for example http://www.liquoranddrink.com/Drinks/344-Hemingway-Daiquiri-%28Original%29/ [accessed 13 March 2013].
16. Quoted in Curtis, *And a Bottle of Rum*, p. 70. Williams also quotes an early recipe for an artichoke brew, 'boiled with the scores of roots and herbs, with birch, spruce or sassafras bark, with pumpkin and apple parings, with sweetening of molasses or maple syrup, or beet tops and other makeshifts' (p. 63).
17. Williams, *Rum*, p. 86. See also J. J. McCusker, 'The Rum Trade and the Balance of Payments of the Thirteen Continental Colonies, 1650–1775', *Journal of Economic History*, 30:1 (March 1970), pp. 244–7. McCusker argues: 'The importation and internal sale of rum and molasses thus occupied a significant area of colonial economic activity, significant enough to be worth defending by the peaceful protests and petitions of the mid-1760's against restrictive English legislation' (p. 247). See also J. J. McCusker, *Rum and the American Revolution: The Rum Trade and the Balance of Payments of the Thirteen Continental Colonies*, 2 vols (New York: Garland, 1989).
18. Curtis explains: 'Mix one cup of beer (a stout like Guinness), 2 tablespoons of molasses, and 1 ounce of Jamaica-style rum into a mug. Heat a loggerhead to red hot in an open fire, then thrust into the drink. Keep loggerhead in place until foaming and sputtering ceases. Drink hot' (Curtis, *And a Bottle of Rum*, p. 65).
19. Ibid., p. 4.
20. See also P. Thompson, *Rum Punch and Revolution: Taverngoing and Public Life in Eighteenth-Century Philadelphia* (Philadelphia, PA: University of Pennsylvania Press, 1999).
21. The Town of Waterford, *The History of Waterford, Oxford County, Maine* (Portland, ME: Hoyt, Fogg & Donham, 1879), p. 189. In the Caribbean, rum was also consumed in large quantities, as F. H. Smith has shown in *Caribbean Rum: A Social and Economic History* (Gainesville, FL: University Press of Florida, 2005).

Notes to pages 144–7

22. See the wonderful study by R. Grafe, *Distant Tyranny: Markets, Power and Backwardness in Spain, 1650–1800* (Princeton, NJ: Princeton University Press, 2012).

23. See, for example, McCusker, 'The Rum Trade': 'Rum did not go "mostly to Africa". At the outside the colonists sold 25 percent of it to the fishermen of Newfoundland. The Indians beyond the frontier consumed perhaps 30,000 gallons out of 30 times that amount. The colonists' best export customers were their nearest English neighbors in North America. Some of our cherished ideas about the directions of the colonial rum trade (and colonial trade in general) need to be reassessed in the light of this evidence' (p. 245).

24. The Atlantic slave trade has been the subject of various studies over the last two decades; see, for example, T. Hugh, *The Slave Trade: The History of the Atlantic Slave Trade, 1440–1870* (London: Phoenix, 2006); A. C. Bailey, *African Voices of the Atlantic Slave Trade: Beyond the Silence and the Shame* (Boston, MA: Beacon, 2003); D. Eltis, S. D. Behrendt, D. Richardson and H. S. Klein (eds), *The Trans-Atlantic Slave Trade: A Database on CD-ROM* (Cambridge: Cambridge University Press, 1999).

25. For information on the rum producer Pott, see www.pott.de; for information on Flensburg's Rum Museum, see for example http://www.flensburg-online.de/museum/rum-museum.html [both accessed 13 March 2013].

26. See, for example, M. Kammen, *Empire of Interest: The American Colonies and the Politics of Mercantilism* (Philadelphia, PA: Lippincott, 1970), pp. 45–50.

27. See C. Shammas, *The Pre-Industrial Consumer in England and America* (Oxford: Clarendon, 1990).

28. W. Smith, *The History of the Late Province of New-York, from its Discovery to the Appointment of Governor Colden, in 1762* (New York: New York Historical Society, 1829), vol. 1, p. 277. See also T. H. Breen, 'Narrative of Commercial Life: Consumption, Ideology, and Community on the Eve of the American Revolution', *William and Mary Quarterly*, 50:3 (July 1993), pp. 471–501, on p. 483.

29. See R. B. Sheridan, 'The Molasses Act and the Market Strategy of British Sugar Planters', *Journal of Economic History*, 17:1 (March 1957), pp. 62–83. See also J. Brewer, *The Sinews of Power: War, Money and the English State, 1688–1783* (London: Unwin Hyman, 1989), esp. pp. 192–251.

30. A. J. O'Shaughnessy, 'The Stamp Act Crisis in the British Caribbean', *William and Mary Quarterly*, 51:2 (April 1994), pp. 203–26. See also an early precursor to this analysis, one of the few ever conducted: D. J. Spindel, 'The Stamp Act Crisis in the British West Indies', *Journal of American Studies*, 11:2 (August 1977), pp. 203–21.

31. See, for the case of Jamaica, T. R. Clayton, 'Sophistry, Security, and Socio-Political Structures in the American Revolution; or, Why Jamaica Did Not Rebel', *Historical Journal*, 29:2 (June 1986), pp. 319–44.

32. L. H. Butterfield (ed.), *The Diary and Autobiography of John Adams*, 4 vols (New York: Athenaeum Press, 1964), vol. 1, p. 285.

33. 'Extract of a Letter from New-London, March 13, 1766', *Boston Post-Boy & Advertiser* [Boston, MA], 449 (24 March 1766), p. 3 (*Readex American Historical Newspapers*, www.readex.com/content/americas-historical-newspapers [accessed 28 April 2013]); see also O'Shaughnessy, 'Stamp Act Crisis', p. 217.

34. O'Shaughnessy, 'Stamp Act Crisis', p. 224.

35. Ibid., p. 225.

36. See here O'Shaughnessy, 'The Formation of a Commercial Lobby: The West India Interest, British Colonial Policy and the American Revolution', *Historical Journal*, 40:1 (March 1997), pp. 71–95.

Notes to pages 147–50

37. See M. Kammen, *A Rope of Sand: The Colonial Agents, British Politics, and the American Revolution* (Ithaca, NY: Cornell University Press, 1968), p. 282.
38. O'Shaughnessy, 'The Formation of a Commercial Lobby', p. 79.
39. Ibid., p. 80.
40. Breen, 'Narrative of Commercial Life', p. 486.
41. See also E. S. Morgan and H. Morgan, *The Stamp Act Crisis: Prologue to Revolution*, rev. edn (New York: Collier, 1962).
42. Quoted in Breen, 'Narrative of Commercial Life', p. 488.
43. *Providence Gazette and Country Journal* [Providence, RI], 10 (9 January 1773), p. 2 (*Readex American Historical Newspapers*, www.readex.com/content/americas-historical-newspapers [accessed 28 April 2013]). See also W. R. Leslie, 'The Gaspee Affair: A Study of its Constitutional Significance', *Mississippi Valley Historical Review*, 39:2 (September 1952), pp. 233–56, on p. 235.
44. The English East India Company was on the verge of bankruptcy, being unable to sell their vast amounts of tea. The Americans boycotted British tea and drank the smuggled tea from Holland instead. With the Tea Act, the Company could bypass American wholesalers, thus making the tea cheaper for the customer. But the Americans feared a monopoly and a conspiracy. The Tea Party was followed by the Coercive Acts.
45. As quoted for example in W. Stahr, *John Jay: Founding Father* (New York: Continuum, 2005), p. 47.
46. C. Bridenbaugh, *The Spirit of '76: The Growth of American Patriotism Before Independence, 1607–1776* (New York: Oxford University Press, 1975), pp. 3–4.
47. J. M. Bumsted and C. E. Clark, 'New England's Tom Paine: John Allen and the Spirit of Liberty', *William and Mary Quarterly*, 21:4 (October 1964), pp. 561–70. Allen's *Oration* was a true best-seller of the time, with seven editions in four cities between 1773 and 1775.
48. J. Allen, *An Oration, Upon the Beauties of Liberty, or The Essential Rights of the Americans: Delivered at the Second Baptist-Church in Boston. Upon the Last Annual Thanksgiving. Humbly Dedicated to the Right-Honourable the Earl of Dartmouth. Published by the Request of Many*, 3rd edn (Boston, 1773), pp. xvii–xviii, quoted in Bumsted and Clark, 'New England's Tom Paine', p. 566, and in Bridenbaugh, *The Spirit of '76*, p. 144.
49. A. W. Taussig, *Rum, Romance and Rebellion* (New York: Minton, Balch, 1928), p. 225; quoted in Williams, *Rum*, p. xiv.
50. For Charles Bukowski, see http://bukowski.net/, for Dylan Thomas, http://www.dylanthomas.com/. It is interesting to note how many writers and intellectuals of the twentieth century were into gin: think of Dorothy Parker ('One more drink and I'll be under the host'), F. Scott Fitzgerald ('First you take a drink, then the drink takes a drink, and then the drink takes you'), Raymond Chandler, Tom Lehrer, also Anne Sexton and Joan Didion. For details, see http://www.worldsbiggestcookbook.com/drinks/rich-famous/ [all accessed 13 March 2013].
51. See U. L. Voss, *Die Bacardis: Der Kuba-Clan zwischen Rum und Revolution* (Frankfurt: Campus, 2005); P. Foster, *Family Spirits: The Bacardi Saga of Rum, Riches, and Revolution* (Toronto: Macfarlane, Walter and Ross, 1990).
52. Curtis, *And a Bottle of Rum*, p. 4.
53. Bridenbaugh, *The Spirit of '76*.

220   *Notes to pages 151–4*

13 Elbert, 'A Beverage for the Masses: The Democratization of Cocoa in Nineteenth-Century American Fiction'

1. Recently, the media have shown a multitude of chocolate company empires who have resorted to illegal child labour in Africa. The history of cocoa and of chocolate is recounted in many significant studies, among them: S. D. Coe and M. D. Coe, *The True History of Chocolate*, 2nd edn (London: Thames and Hudson, 2007); L. K. Fuller, *Chocolate Fads, Folklore & Fantasies: 1,000+ Chunks of Chocolate Information* (New York: Harrington Park Press, 1994); L. E. Grivetti and H.-Y. Shapiro (eds), *Chocolate: History, Culture, and Heritage* (New York: Wiley, 2009); C. L. McNeil (ed.), *Chocolate in Mesoamerica: A Cultural History of Cacao* (Gainesville, FL: University Press of Florida, 2009); M. Norton, *Sacred Gifts, Profane Pleasures: A History of Tobacco and Chocolate in the Atlantic World* (Ithaca, NY: Cornell University Press, 2008); L. J. Satre, *Chocolate on Trial: Slavery, Politics, and the Ethics of Business* (Athens, OH: Ohio University Press, 2005). See also the following website: http://exhibits.mannlib.cornell.edu/chocolate/theaztecs.php (Cornell University, Albert R. Mann Library) [accessed 8 June 2013].
2. N. Hawthorne, 'The Cacao-Tree and its Products', *American Magazine of Useful and Entertaining Knowledge*, 1:2 (October 1834), pp. 55–6, on p. 56.
3. L. E. Grivetti, 'Medicinal Chocolate in New Spain, Western Europe, and North America', in Grivetti and Shapiro (eds), *Chocolate*, pp. 67–88, on p. 78. See also the study by H. Ellis, who maintained that 'women are friandes rather than gourmandes, loving special foods, chiefly sweets' (H. Ellis, *Man and Woman: A Study of Human Secondary Sexual Characters* (London: Walter Scott, 1894), p. 240).
4. J. A. Brillat-Savarin, *The Physiology of Taste, or, Meditations on Transcendental Gastronomy*, trans. M. F. K. Fisher (1825; New York: Knopf, 2009), p. 120. According to Brillat-Savarin, cocoa is preferable to coffee because it does not 'cause the same harmful effects to feminine beauty'. He feels that cocoa is healthy, 'nourishing', 'easily digested' and that it can resolve stomach issues and other chronic health problems. Using slogans that Baker's chocolate would later employ (see below), Brillat-Savarin shows it to be universally appealing: 'it is above all helpful to people who must do a great deal of mental work, to those who labor in the pulpit or the courtroom, and especially to travelers'.
5. Grivetti, 'Chocolate and the Boston Smallpox Epidemic of 1764', in Grivetti and Shapiro (eds), *Chocolate*, pp. 89–97, on p. 90.
6. Grivetti, 'Medicinal Chocolate', p. 80.
7. For the history of Baker's chocolate, in terms of its use during the American Revolution and the American Civil War, see L. E. Grivetti, 'Boston Chocolate: Newspaper Articles and Advertisements, 1705–1825', and 'Blue and Gray Chocolate: Searching for American Civil War References', in Grivetti and Shapiro (eds), *Chocolate*, pp. 359–73 and pp. 731–41.
8. B. Kimmerle, *Chocolate: The Sweet History* (Portland, OR: Collectors Press, 2005), pp. 106–7.
9. Ibid., p. 35; A. H. de Lemps, 'Colonial Beverages and the Consumption of Sugar', in A. Sonnenfeld (ed.), *Food: A Culinary History from Antiquity to the Present* (New York: Columbia University Press, 1999), pp. 382–93, on pp. 385–6. It was only in the mid-nineteenth century that solid chocolate was produced and consumed. Fry's developed the first edible (i.e. solid) chocolate in England in 1847, followed by inventions by chocolatiers such as Cadbury's, Lindt, Tober and, in the United States, Hershey's and Lowney's; see E. Abbott, *Sugar: A Bittersweet History* (New York: Duckworth Overlook, 2009), pp. 362–5.

Notes to pages 154–61

10. C. E. Beecher and H. Beecher Stowe, *The American Woman's Home: Principles of Domestic Science* (1869; Bedford, MA: Applewood Books, 2010), p. 111. Beecher and Stowe also take pride in the quality of American cocoa; even though it was traditionally seen as a 'French' or 'Spanish' article, the American brand is 'every way equal to any which can be imported from Paris' (p. 144).

11. See letters from Melville to Hawthorne, 1 June 1851, 29 June 1851, in *The Portable Melville*, ed. J. Leyda (New York: Penguin, 1978), pp. 429–34, 434–6.

12. H. Melville, 11 April 1857, in *Journals*, vol. 15, ed. H. Hayford (Chicago, IL: Northwestern University Press, 1989), p. 50.

13. J. Hawthorne, *Nathaniel Hawthorne and His Wife* (Boston, MA: Houghton Mifflin, 1894), p. 125.

14. R. W. Emerson, 'The Poet', in *Ralph Waldo Emerson: Essays and Lectures*, ed. J. Porte (New York: Library of America, 1983), pp. 447–68, on pp. 460–1.

15. F. B. Sanborn, *Bronson Alcott at Alcott House, England, and Fruitlands, New England (1842–44)* (Cedar Rapids, IA: Torch Press, 1908), p. 50.

16. H. D. Thoreau, *A Week on the Concord and Merrimack Rivers* (1849; New York: Library of America, 1985), p. 33.

17. Ibid., p. 270.

18. H. D. Thoreau, 'Higher Laws', in *Walden*, ed. R. Sayre (New York: Library of America, 1985), pp. 387–587, on pp. 490–500. In his most famous political essay, 'Civil Disobedience' (1849), he recounts the episode about his arrest by the Concord constable: 'In the morning, our [his and his fellow prisoners'] breakfasts were put through the hole in the door, in small oblong-square tin pans, made to fit, and holding a pint of chocolate, with brown bread, and an iron spoon'. Thoreau, 'Civil Disobedience', in *Walden and Civil Disobedience*, ed. M. Meyer (New York: Penguin, 1983), pp. 385–413, on p. 405.

19. L. M. Alcott, *Little Women*, Part Second (1869), ed. A. K. Phillips and G. Eiselein (New York: Norton, 2004), p. 211.

20. Ibid., p. 362.

21. Ibid.

22. L. M. Alcott, 'Silver Pitchers', in *Silver Pitchers; and Independence, A Centennial Love Story* (Boston, MA: Roberts Brothers, 1888), pp. 1–46, on p. 1.

23. Ibid., pp. 1–2.

24. S. O. Jewett, 'The Garden Tea', in *Betty Leicester: A Story for Girls* (Boston, MA: Houghton Mifflin, 1890), pp. 60–72, on p. 66. The chapter was later reprinted as a short story, 'The Tea Party'.

25. E. S. Phelps, 'The Sacrifice of Antigone', in *Fourteen to One* (Boston, MA: Houghton Mifflin, 1891), pp. 231–47, on p. 240.

26. Ibid.

27. Ibid., p. 245.

28. Jean-Étienne Liotard's 'Belle Chocolatière' can be viewed on http://commons.wikimedia.org/wiki/File%3ALiotard_Schokoladen_Maedchen.jpg [accessed 8 August 2013].

29. For the history of the Viennese chocolate girl that Baker's adopted for their logo, see Kimmerle, *Chocolate*, pp. 78–83, and A. Blaschke, 'Chocolate, Manufacturing and Marketing in Massachusetts, 1700–1920', in Grivetti and Shapiro (eds), *Chocolate*, pp. 345–58, on pp. 349–56; 'Sweet History: Dorchester and the Chocolate Factory', www.bostonhistory.org/sub/bakerschocolate [accessed 10 October 2010].

30. Fuller, *Chocolate Fads*, p. 182.

31. Abbott, *Sugar*, p. 366.

32. A. Dix and L. Piatti, '"Bonbons in Abundance": The Politics of Sweetness in Kate Chopin's Fiction', in M. Elbert and M. Drews (eds), *Culinary Aesthetics and Practices in Nineteenth-Century American Literature* (New York: Palgrave Macmillan, 2009), pp. 53–69.

33. K. Chopin, *The Awakening and Other Stories*, ed. S. M. Gilbert (New York: Penguin, 1986), pp. 43–178, on p. 91.

34. Ibid.

35. Ibid., p. 97.

36. Ibid., p. 100.

37. Ibid., p. 133.

38. F. Norris, *McTeague*, ed. J. Loving (New York: Oxford University Press, 1995), p. 25.

39. Ibid., p. 104.

40. Ibid., p. 151; emphasis added.

41. Ibid., pp. 173, 193.

42. Ibid., p. 219.

43. Ibid., p. 218.

44. E. Wharton, *The Valley of Decision* (Cirencester, England: Echo Library, 2005), p. 11. Although Wharton's depiction of French eighteenth-century aristocracy is fictional, the association of chocolate with the decadence of aristocracy is historically accurate: 'Chocolate became a reified commodity, a fetish item, an excuse for license, and a mark of privilege'. (B. Lekatsas, 'Inside the Pastilles of the Marquis de Sade', in A. Szogyi (ed.), *Chocolate: Food of the Gods* (Westport, CT: Greenwood Press, 1997), pp. 99–107, on p. 105).

45. Wharton, *Valley of Decision*, p. 14.

46. Ibid., p. 38.

47. Ibid., p. 55.

48. E. Wharton, 'The Duchess at Prayer', in *Crucial Instances* (1901; New York: Charles Scribner's Sons, 1909), pp. 1–32, on p. 9.

49. E. Wharton, *Summer*, intro. C. Waid (New York: Signet, 1993), p. 110.

50. Ibid., p. 158.

51. Ibid., pp. 166–7.

52. B. P. Gilman, [Lowney's ad], *Forerunner*, 1:1 (November 1909), p. 28.

53. B. M. Rosenberg, *America at the Fair: Chicago's 1893 World's Columbian Exposition* (Chicago, IL: Arcadia Press, 2008), pp. 108–9.

54. B. P. Gilman, *Herland* in Herland *and Selected Stories by Charlotte Perkins Gilman*, ed. B. H. Solomon (New York: Signet Classic, 1992), pp. 1–148, on p. 29.

55. H. James, *The American Scene*, ed. J. Sears (New York: Penguin, 1994), p. 147.

56. Ibid.

57. Ibid.

58. Ibid.

59. Ibid., pp. 147–8.

14 Schenkel, 'The Power of the Potion: From Gothic Horror to Health Drink, or, How the Elixir became a Commodity'

1. As written on the information board at the entrance of the monument; see http://www.anglesey.info/barclodiad-y-gawres.htm [accessed 5 February 2013].

2. W. Benjamin, 'The Work of Art in the Age of Mechanical Reproduction', in Benjamin, *Illuminations*, ed. H. Arendt (London: Fontana, 1968), pp. 214–18.

Notes to pages 168–74 223

3. E. T. A. Hoffmann, *Der Goldene Topf*, in *Fantasiestücke in Callots Manier*, ed. H. Kraft (Frankfurt: Insel, 1967), pp. 126–204.

4. As Marty Roth put it: 'At the core of intoxication's negativity lies the mystery of the self: drink introduces a division in the self'; Roth, *Drunk the Night Before: An Anatomy of Intoxication* (Minneapolis, MN: University of Minnesota Press, 2005), p. 73.

5. W. Shakespeare, *The Tempest*, IV.i.150.

6. E. T. A. Hoffmann, *Die Elixiere des Teufels*, ed. H. Kraft (Frankfurt: Insel, 1967), p. 529, my translation; German original: '*Ich* war es, der dies gesprochen, als ich mich aber von meinem toten Selbst getrennt fühlte, merkte ich wohl, daß ich der wesenlose Gedanke meines Ichs sei, und bald erkannte ich mich als das im Äther schwimmende Rot'.

7. On alchemy and literature, see E. Schenkel, *Die Elixiere der Schrift. Literatur und Alchemie* (Eggingen: edition isele, 2003); A. Lembert and E. Schenkel (eds), *The Golden Egg: Alchemy in Art and Literature* (Berlin: Galda & Wilch, 2002).

8. See L. Boia, *Forever Young: A Cultural History of Longevity* (London: Reaktion, 2004), pp. 120–1.

9. H. de Balzac, *L'Élixir de longue vie*, ed. H. Mimouni (1830; Paris: Gallimard, 2009).

10. M. Shelley, 'The Mortal Immortal', in *The Mortal Immortal, and The Evil Eye*, digital reprint (1833; Breinigsville, PA: Dodo Press, 2009), pp. 1–14, on p. 5.

11. Ibid., p. 12.

12. Ibid., pp. 12–13.

13. Ibid., p. 13.

14. W. H. Ainsworth, *Auriol or The Elixir of Life and A Night in Rome*, digital reprint (1844; Teddington: Echo Library, 2007), p. 76.

15. E. Bulwer-Lytton, *A Strange Story* (1862; London: Routledge, [*c.*1880]); E. Bulwer-Lytton, *Zanoni* (1842; London: Routledge, 1975).

16. See Bulwer-Lytton, *A Strange Story*, pp. 443–5. Compare the strange cooperation of dreams in the regeneration of the Leipzig physicist and psychologist Gustav Theodor Fechner, who apparently regained his strength after a long illness through a recipe dreamt up by a Leipzig housewife; see G. Mattenklott, *Blindgänger. Physiognomische Essays* (Frankfurt: Suhrkamp, 1986), pp. 148–56.

17. See Boia, *Forever Young*, p. 121.

18. Bulwer-Lytton, *A Strange Story*, p. 467.

19. Ibid., p. 489.

20. N. Hawthorne, 'Dr. Heidegger's Experiment', in *The Complete Novels and Selected Tales of Nathaniel Hawthorne*, ed. N. H. Pearson (New York: Modern Library, 1937), pp. 945–51.

21. See Roth, *Drunk the Night Before*, p. 65.

22. H. Godfrey [C. O'Conor Eccles], *The Rejuvenation of Miss Semaphore: A Farcical Novel* (London: Jarrold & Sons, 1897), p. 30.

23. See ibid., p. 53.

24. Ibid., p. 237.

25. See ibid., p. 238.

26. L. Carroll, *The Annotated Alice*, ed. M. Gardner (1960; London: Penguin 2001), p. 17.

27. Ibid.

28. Ibid.

29. Ibid.

30. W. Empson, '*Alice in Wonderland*: The Child as Swain', in R. Phillips (ed.), *Aspects of Alice* (Harmondsworth: Penguin, 1971), pp. 400–35, esp. p. 411. Empson mentions

Michael Faraday's chemical history of a candle told for children (1861). One could call this method an early form of 'Kinderuniversität' (university for children).

31. S. Goodacre, 'On Alice's Changes of Size in Wonderland', *Jabberwocky*, 29 (1977), pp. 20–4.

32. Carroll, *Alice*, pp. 17–18.

33. K. W. Sweeney reads this recipe with an adult's taste: 'Alice's report, I say this with a smile, sounds like a fairly accurate evaluative description of a distinctive style of white wine – a high-extract, large-format Chardonnay, probably a Grand Cru white Burgundy such as a Corton-Charlemagne'; Sweeney, 'Alice's Discriminating Palate', *Philosophy and Literature*, 23:1 (1999), pp. 17–31, on p. 17.

34. C. Rossetti, *Goblin Market* (1862; New York: Dover, 1983), p. 35.

35. See M. W. Carpenter, '"Eat me, Drink me, Love me": The Consumable Female Body in Christina Rossetti's *Goblin Market*', *Victorian Poetry*, 29:4 (1991), pp. 415–34, on p. 427.

36. N. Armstrong, 'The Occidental Alice', *Differences*, 2 (1990), pp. 3–40.

37. Carpenter, '"Eat me, Drink me, Love me"', p. 415.

38. See J. Dusinberre's chapter on 'Children's Books, Childhood and Modernism' in her *Alice to the Lighthouse: Children's Books and Radical Experiments in Art* (Basingstoke: Macmillan, 1987), pp. 1–40.

39. J. Swan, *Dr Jonathan Swan's Quack Magic: The Dubious History of Health Fads and Cures* (London: Random House, 2003), pp. 208–9.

40. Ibid., p. 211.

41. Ibid. Coca wine entered the scene with Vin Mariani in the 1860s and eventually led to Coca Cola, which lost its alcohol and was introduced as a temperance drink by John Pemberton; see D. T. Courtwright, *Forces of Habit: Drugs and the Making of the Modern World* (Cambridge, MA: Harvard University Press, 2001), pp. 25–6.

42. See R. Holmes, *The Age of Wonder: How the Romantic Generation Discovered the Beauty and Terror of Science* (London: HarperCollins, 2009), pp. 259–65.

43. See E. Schenkel, 'H. G. Wells and Speed', in V. Tinkler-Villani and C. C. Barfoot (eds), *Restoring the Mystery of the Rainbow: Literature's Refractions of Science* (Amsterdam: Rodopi, 2011), pp. 729–41, on 'The New Accelerator' esp. pp. 737–41.

44. H. de Balzac, *Histoire de la grandeur et de la décadence de César Birotteau* (1837), in *La comédie humaine*, ed. P.-G. Castex, avec la collaboration de P. Citron, R. Guise, A. Lorant et A.-M. Meiniger (Paris: Pléiade, 1977), vol. 6, pp. 37–312.

45. H. G. Wells, *Tono-Bungay*, ed. B. Cheyette (Oxford: Oxford University Press, 1997), pp. 140–1.

46. Ibid., p. 168.

47. Ibid., p. 65.

48. Ibid., p. 161.

49. Ibid., p. 136.

50. Ibid., pp. 162–3.

51. Ibid., p. 163.

52. Ibid., p. 168.

53. Ibid., p. 354.

54. Ibid., p. 355.

INDEX

Adams, John, 146
Addison, Joseph, 41, 42, 43, 51, 56
Aeschylus, 66
Ainsworth, William Harrison, 171
Al Capone, 149
Alcott, Bronson, 154
Alcott, Louisa May, 155–7
Alexander III (the Great), King of Macedon, 85
Allen, John, 149
Ames, Richard, 51
Amis, Martin, 60
Anstie, Francis, 135–6, 138
Archenholz, Johann Wilhelm von, 45, 61
Armstrong, Nancy, 175
Arnold, Matthew, 117
Arnold, William, 75

Bacardi family, 150
Bagshaw, Charles Frederick, 98
Baker, James, 157
Baker, Walter, 151, 153, 158, 160
Baker's, 152, 153, 157–60
Baltauf, Anna, 157–9
Balzac, Honoré de, 167, 170, 177
Banks, Joseph, 20
Barr, Andrew, 2
Barthes, Roland, 23
Baudelaire, Charles, 121
Beddoes, Thomas Lovell, 85
Beddoes, Thomas, 85, 86
Beecher, Catharine, 154
Benjamin, Walter, 168
Berg, Maxine, 96
Besant, Walter, 47
Bible, 27, 81, 89
Binz, Carl, 136

Blackburn, Mr, 95
Blake, William, 87
Blakiston, Peyton, 134
Boyle, T. C. (Tom Coraghessan), 143
Bradley, Richard, 4
Breen, T. H. (Timothy Hall), 12, 16
Brennan, Thomas, 2
Brewer, John, 12
Bridenbaugh, Carl, 150
Brillat-Savarin, Jean Anthelme, 153
Brontë, Anne, 126
Brown, John, 129, 130, 131, 134, 136
Brown, Tom, 47
Brühl-Cramer, Carl von, 133
Buchan, William, 129
Buckingham, Mr, 97
Bucknill, J. C. (John Charles), 137
Bukowski, Charles, 149
Bulwer-Lytton, Edward, 9, 167, 171–2
Burke, Edmund, 90
Burnett, John, 3, 5
Burney, Charles, 85
Burns, Robert, 89
Bury, James, 100
Butler, Samuel, 49

Cadbury's, 151, 159
Cailler, François-Louis, 154
Campbell, Colin, 12
Capote, Truman, 149
Carroll, Lewis, 9, 173–6
Cartwright, Anne (née Dashwood), 14, 16
Cartwright, George, 20
Cartwright, John, 6, 14–22
Cervantes Saavedra, Miguel de, 66
Chadwick, Edwin, 104
Charles II, King of England, 171

Charlotte, Queen of England, 83
Chartres, John, 61
Chaucer, Geoffrey, 60, 62
Cheyne, George, 131–2
Child, Lydia Maria, 29
Chopin, Kate, 9, 152, 161–2, 163
Clark, Peter, 60
Clouston, Thomas, 137
Cobb, James, 82
Cochrane, A. L. (Archibald Leman), 127
Coleridge, Samuel Taylor, 82
Coltelli, Francesco Procopio dei, 39
Columbus, Christopher, 141, 153
Conley, Carolyn, 79
Constantin, Marc, 41, 42
Corley, William, 74
Cornwall, Barry, 86
Cortés, Hernán, 151
Cowan, Brian, 2, 7
Cruikshank, George, 83
Cruikshank, Isaac, 83
Cullen, William, 128–30, 138
Cummins, Maria S., 24
Cundy, Simeon, 96, 99
Currie, James, 89

Dacre, Charlotte, 88
Damerell, John, 75
Darwall, John, 131
Darwin, Charles, 122, 175
Darwin, Erasmus, 81, 84, 90
Daunton, Martin, 13
De la Roque, Jean, 38–9
De Quincey, Thomas, 177
Defoe, Daniel, 3
Devine, Christine, 107
Dickens, Charles, 104, 116, 117, 122, 125, 126
Dietrichstein, Prince, 157
Diodato, Johannes, 39
Drews, Marie, 2, 29
Drummond, J. C. (Jack Cecil), 51
Dryden, John, 48, 49, 53
Dudingston, William, 148
Dukes, Richard, 74–5
Dumas, Alexandre, 170
Duncan, Andrew, 88

Earnshaw, Steven, 4, 60
Eccles, Charlotte O'Conor, *see* Godfrey, Hal
Edgar, John, 83
Edgerton, Robert, 71, 80
Edwards, Daniel, 38
Elbert, Monika, 2, 9, 29
Elderton, Ethel, 138
Ellis, George, 90
Ellis, Markman, 2
Emerson, Ralph Waldo, 24, 32, 33, 154
Engels, Friedrich, 92, 93, 97
Epstein, James, 22
Esquirol, J. E. D. (Jean-Étienne Dominique), 137

Faucher, Léon, 99
Fenwick, Simon, 95
Fergusson, Robert, 89
Fielding, Henry, 4, 7, 60, 61, 65–7, 82
Fitzgerald, Scott F., 149
Forbes-Winslow, L. (Lyttleton Stewart), 137
Foucault, Michel, 63, 82
Fox, Charles James, 14, 90
Fox, George, 53
Francis, Alan David, 51
Franklin, Benjamin, 153
Frederick II (the Great), King of Prussia, 169
Freud, Sigmund, 168

Gairdner, William T., 135
Garrett, John, 132
Gaskell, Elizabeth, 81
Gaskell, Peter, 92, 97, 99
Geertz, Clifford, 57
George III, King of Great Britain and Ireland, 14, 83, 132, 142, 149
George IV, King of Great Britain and Ireland, 171
Ghirardelli, Domenico, 153
Gillray, James, 5, 83
Gilman, Charlotte Perkins, 152, 161, 164
Gissing, George, 5, 8, 103–14
Godfrey, Hal (Eccles, Charlotte O'Conor), 172
Goethe, Johann Wolfgang von, 87, 169, 170
Gonson, John, 51
Gooch, Robert, 90
Goudeau, Émile, 41

Gounod, Charles, 170
Graves, Robert J., 134, 138
Grenville, George, 146
Grigg, David, 23, 28

Habermas, Jürgen, 4, 7, 36–7, 43, 62
Hackwood, Frederick W., 61
Haggard, Rider, 172
Hales, Stephen, 131
Hall, Percival, 95
Halperin, John, 103
Handel, George Frideric (Händel, Georg Friedrich), 85
Hanks, Tom, 165
Hardy, Thomas, 5, 8, 115–26
Harlow, Jean, 165
Harris, Benjamin, 45
Harrison, Helen ('Nell'), 103, 104
Hartley, Green & Co., 13, 15, 17, 21
Harvey, Karen, 6
Hawthorne, Elizabeth, 154
Hawthorne, Nathaniel, 24, 25, 26, 33, 152–3, 154, 172–3
Hazlitt, William, 86
Heath, William, 83
Heine, Heinrich, 89, 117
Hemingway, Ernest, 143, 149
Hemmings, Ray, 14
Henderson, Alexander Farquharson, 131
Henry, Patrick, 149
Hershey's, 164
Hilton, Matthew, 13
Hirschfelder, Gunther, 8
Hodges, Thomas Hallet, 16–17
Hoeller, Hildegard, 27, 29
Hoffmann, E. T. A. (Ernst Theodor Amadeus), 168–9
Hogarth, Richard, 40
Hogarth, William, 4, 5, 7, 40, 55, 60, 63–4, 82, 84, 91, 104
Hohenzollern, House of, 39
Horrocks, John, 98
Horsley, Victor, 138
Houghton, John, 42
Hunt, Leigh, 86–7
Huss, Magnus, 137
Huysmans, Joris-Karl, 121

Iser, Wolfgang, 104

James, Henry, 152, 165
Jameson, Fredric, 106–7
Jauss, Hans Robert, 104
Jeggle, Utz, 92
Jenyns, Soame, 19
Jewett, Sarah Orne, 156–7
Johnson, Matthew, 12
Jones, Arthur, 2
Jonson, Ben, 119
Joyce, James, 126
Judt, Tony, 35
Jung, C. G. (Carl Gustav), 169

Kaplan, Amy, 32, 33
Keating, Justice, 78
Keats, John, 86–7, 88, 89, 115–16, 117, 126
Keats, Tom, 86
Keble, John, 111
Kennedy, John L., 101
Kinsey, Alfred, 143
Kneller, Godfrey, 56·
Koselleck, Reinhart, 93
Kraepelin, Emil, 138
Kümin, Beat, 60

Lamb, Charles, 86, 87, 90
Langley, John, 75–6
Lawrence, D. H. (David Herbert), 126
Lennartz, Norbert, 8
Lessenich, Rolf, 7–8
Lettsom, John Coakley, 131
Lewis, Matthew, 168
Liotard, Jean-Étienne, 157, 159
Livesey, Joseph, 83, 88
Lonsdale, William, Earl of, 86
Lorraine, Claude, 16, 17, 18
Lowney's, 164
Lucia, Salvatore, 127

MacAndrew, Craig, 71, 80
McCrae, Niall, 133
Machen, Arthur, 172
McKendrick, Neil, 12
Macky, John, 41
Magnan, Victor, 137
Mandeville, Bernard, 57
Manet, Édouard, 118

Marteau, Dave, 77
Mather, Cotton, 153
Mather, Increase, 143
Matthiessen, F. O. (Francis Otto), 24, 31
Maudsley, Henry, 137
Maugham, Somerset, 172
Melville, Herman, 24, 26, 33, 154
Meyer, Stephenie, 173
Mill, John Stuart, 78
Miller, Daniel, 12
Mintz, Sydney, 29
Moore, F., 127
Morel, B. A. (Bénédict Augustin), 137
Müller-Wood, Anja, 8

Nash, Ogden, 141
Nayler (Naylor), James, 53
Needham, Richard, 95
Neumann, Fritz-Wilhelm, 7
Nicholson, George, 84, 85, 88
Norris, Frank, 9, 152, 161, 162
North, Frederick, second Earl of Guilford
    (Lord North), 14, 19, 149
Northeast, James, 75
Nunen, Mary Ann, 74

O'Shaughnessy, A. J. (Andrew Jackson),
    146–7
Owen, Robert, 104
Owen, Thomas, 75, 77

Paine, Thomas, 149
Paracelsus, 86
Pargeter, William, 132
Pascal, 39
Paul, Harry, 127–8
Paulson, Ronald, 64
Pearson, Karl, 138
Pemberton, John, 176
Percy, John, 137
Perfect, William, 87
Phelps, Elizabeth Stuart, 156–7
Philips, John, 1
Pierce, William Henry, 157
Pincus, Steve, 43
Pinel, Philippe, 88
Pinkham, Jennie, 176
Pinkham, Lydia, 176

Pitt, William, the Younger, 14, 86, 142
Plumb, John H., 12
Pocock, Edward, 5
Poe, Edgar Allan, 123, 149, 177
Pomroy, Abraham, 74–5
Ponce de Léon, Juan, 172
Pope, Alexander, 47, 52, 53, 56, 83
Posner, Roland, 48, 52
Pott, Hans Hinrich, 145
Pringle, John, 129

Quevedo, Francisco de, 56

Radcliffe, John, 5
Reach, Angus Bethune, 99
Reinarz, Jonathan, 8–9
Rice, John, 75
Richardson, Benjamin Ward, 138–9
Richardson, John, 96
Riches, David, 76
Risse, Guenter, 130
Ritson, Joseph, 85
Rivinus, Timothy M., 117
Robert I Bruce, King of Scotland, 31
Roe, Nicholas, 86
Roosevelt, Theodore, 153
Rosee, Pasqua, 38
Rosenthal, Caroline, 6–7
Rossetti, Christina, 9, 175
Roth, Marty, 172
Rowbotham, Titus, 99
Rowling, J. K. (Joanne Kathleen), 173
Rush, Benjamin, 131

Sade, Donatien Alphonse-François, Marquis
    de, 82
St Germain, Count of, 170
St Leger, A. S., 127
Sayers, James, 90
Schenkel, Elmar, 9
Schlegel, August Wilhelm, 87
Schmid, Susanne, 7
Scott, Sir Walter, 7, 60, 65
Shakespeare, William, 47, 107, 116, 120,
    126, 167, 169, 172
Shammas, Carole, 20
Shaw, Peter, 132
Shelley, Mary, 170

Shelley, Percy Bysshe, 87, 121
Shoemaker, Robert, 72, 76
Shore, Jay H., 80
Skae, David, 137
Sloane, Hans, 5
Smith, Henry Nash, 25
Smith, William, 145
Smollett, Tobias, 7, 59, 60, 63, 67–70
Socrates, 41
Southworth, E. D. E. N., 24
Spicer, Paul, 80
Steele, Richard, 41, 42–3, 51–2
Stevens, Thomas, 75
Stevenson, Robert Louis, 121, 169, 176
Stokes, William, 134
Stollwerck, 157, 164
Stone, Job, 76, 77
Storace, Stephen, 82
Stowe, Harriet Beecher, 154
Strang, John, 40, 44
Strickland, Sir George, 133
Sturge, Mary, 138
Swift, Jonathan, 47, 48

Tacitus, 84
Thackrah, Charles Turner, 131
Thomas, Dylan, 149
Thompson, E. P. (Edward Palmer), 92
Thompson, Hunter S., 149
Thomson, James, 84–5, 90
Thoreau, Henry David, 24, 29, 33, 154, 155
Thornton, Bonnell, 64
Thorp, William, 75–6
Todd, Robert Bentley, 128, 134–6, 138
Tolkien, J. R. R. (John Ronald Reuel), 172
Tolksdorf, Ulrich, 94
Tompkins, Jane, 25
Tooke, John Horne, 90
Toulouse-Lautrec, Henri de, 118
Toussaint-Samat, Maguelonne, 5
Trentmann, Frank, 11
Trollope, Anthony, 176
Trotter, David, 105

Trotter, Thomas, 5, 84–5, 132, 133, 137
Troyer, Howard, 47
Turner, J. Edward, 137
Turner, James, 100

Uffenbach, Zacharias Conrad von, 40

Van Houten, Coenraad, 154
Venedey, Jakob, 98
Victoria, Queen of England, 176
Virgil, 49

Walding, John, 75–6, 77
Walpole, Sir Robert, 50
Ward, Ned (Edward), 2, 4, 7, 47–57
Warner, John Harley, 134, 139
Warner, Susan, 5, 6, 23–33
Washington, George, 20, 31, 153
Watson, Mary, 72
Wedgwood, Josiah, 13
Welch, Mary Ann, 72
Wells, H. G. (Herbert George), 9, 168, 170, 176–9
Wesley, John, 132
Wharton, Edith, 9, 152, 161, 162–4
Whitelegg, Thomas, 94
Whitman, Walt, 24
Wiener, Martin, 77, 78
Wilbraham, Anne, 51
Wilde, Oscar, 118
William of Orange, King of England, 82
Williams, Gordon, 47
Williams, Ian, 144
Williams, Raymond, 57
Wilson, C. Anne, 2
Wilson, George Bailey, 92
Wood, John Carter, 7
Wordsworth, William, 86, 87
Wynter, Rebecca, 8–9

Zehelein, Eva-Sabine, 9
Zola, Émile, 81, 118
Zweig, Stefan, 42